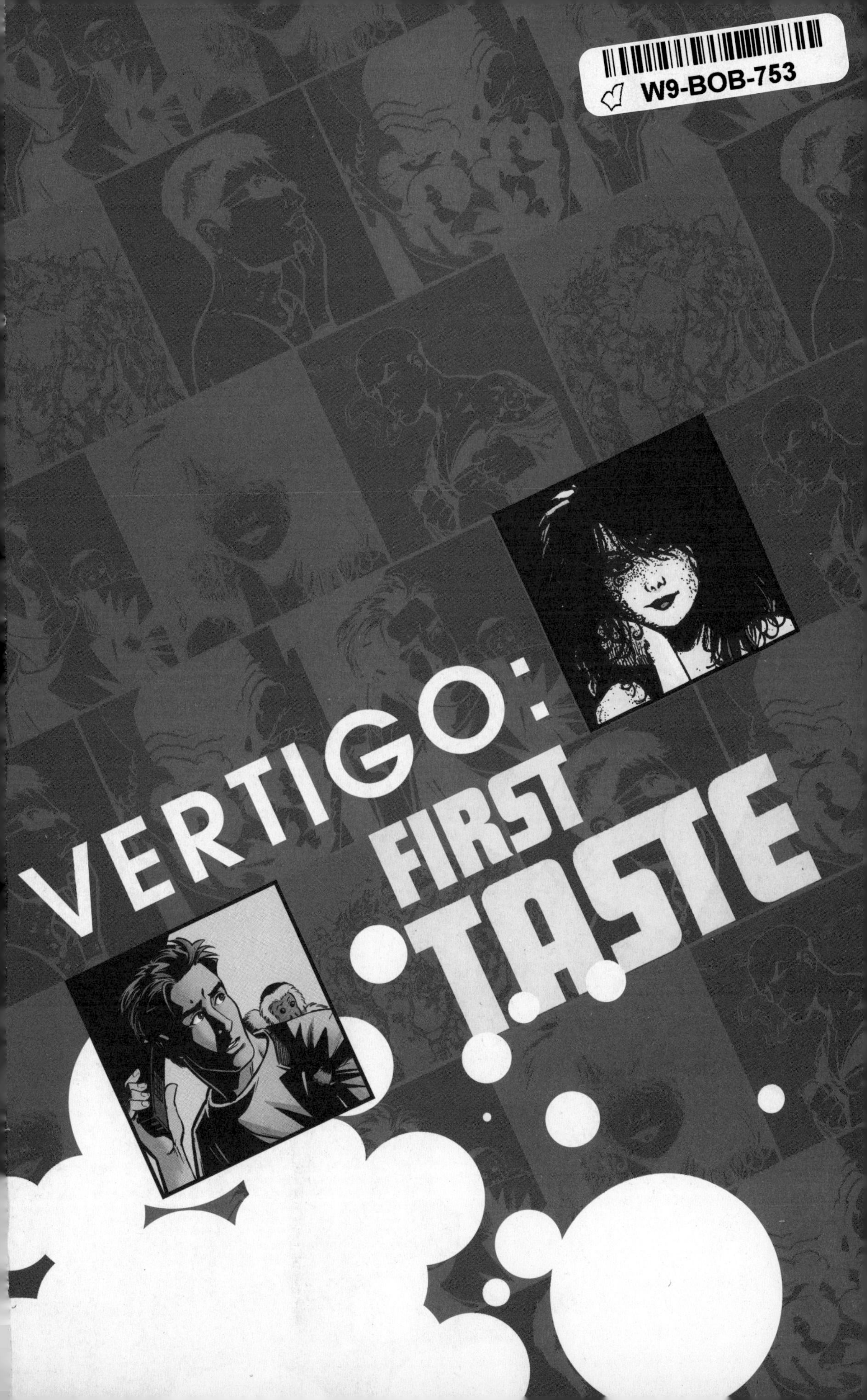
VERTIGO:
FIRST
TASTE

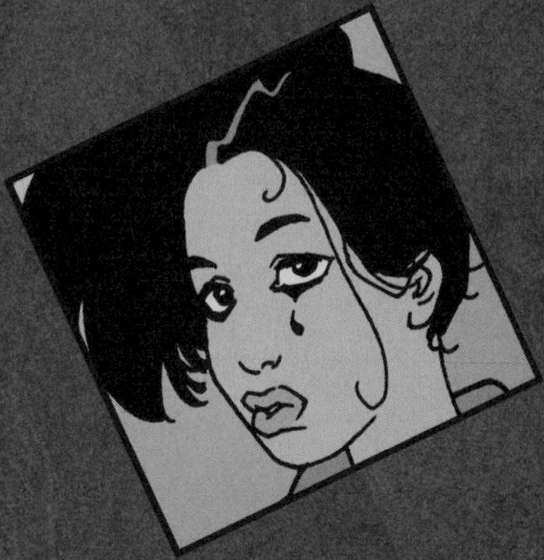

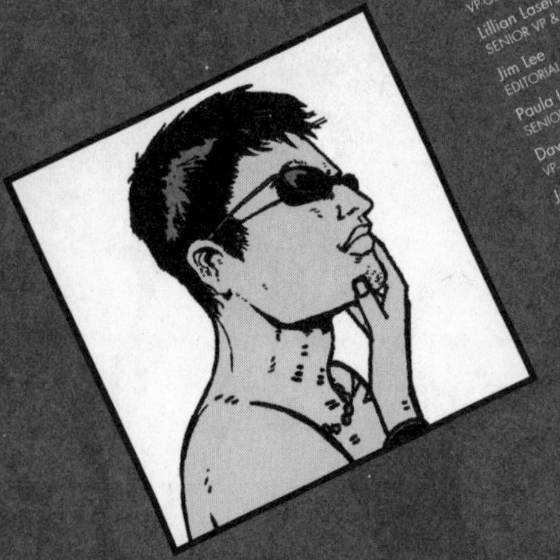

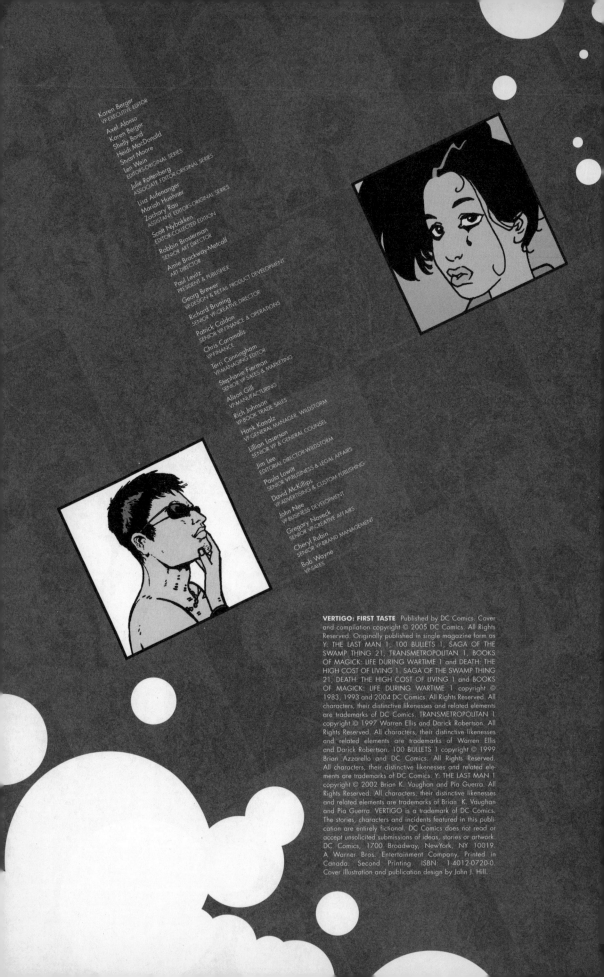

CONTENTS

4   Y: THE LAST MAN #1
WRITTEN BY BRIAN K. VAUGHAN
PENCILLED BY PIA GUERRA
INKED BY JOSÉ MARZÁN, JR.
COLORED BY PAMELA RAMBO
LETTERED BY CLEM ROBINS

38   100 BULLETS #1
WRITTEN BY BRIAN AZZARELLO
PENCILLED AND INKED BY EDUARDO RISSO
COLORED BY GRANT GOLEASH
LETTERED BY CLEM ROBINS

62   SAGA OF THE SWAMP THING #21
WRITTEN BY ALAN MOORE
PENCILLED BY STEPHEN BISSETTE
INKED BY JOHN TOTLEBEN
COLORED BY TATJANA WOOD
LETTERED BY JOHN COSTANZA

86   TRANSMETROPOLITAN #1
WRITTEN BY WARREN ELLIS
PENCILLED BY DARICK ROBERTSON
INKED BY JEROME K. MOORE
COLORED BY NATHAN EYRING
LETTERED BY CLEM ROBINS

111   BOOKS OF MAGICK: LIFE DURING WARTIME #1
WRITTEN BY SI SPENCER
FROM A STORY BY NEIL GAIMAN AND SI SPENCER
PENCILLED AND INKED BY DEAN ORMSTON
COLORED BY FIONA STEPHENSON
LETTERED BY TODD KLEIN

136   DEATH: THE HIGH COST OF LIVING #1
WRITTEN BY NEIL GAIMAN
PENCILLED BY CHRIS BACHALO
INKED BY MARK BUCKINGHAM
COLORED BY STEVE OLIFF
LETTERED BY TODD KLEIN

100 BULLETS CREATED BY BRIAN AZZARELLO AND EDUARDO RISSO
DEATH CREATED BY NEIL GAIMAN AND MIKE DRINGENBERG
SWAMP THING CREATED BY LEN WEIN AND BERNI WRIGHTSON
TIMOTHY HUNTER CREATED BY NEIL GAIMAN AND JOHN BOLTON
TRANSMETROPOLITAN CREATED BY WARREN ELLIS AND DARICK ROBERTSON
Y: THE LAST MAN CREATED BY BRIAN K. VAUGHAN AND PIA GUERRA

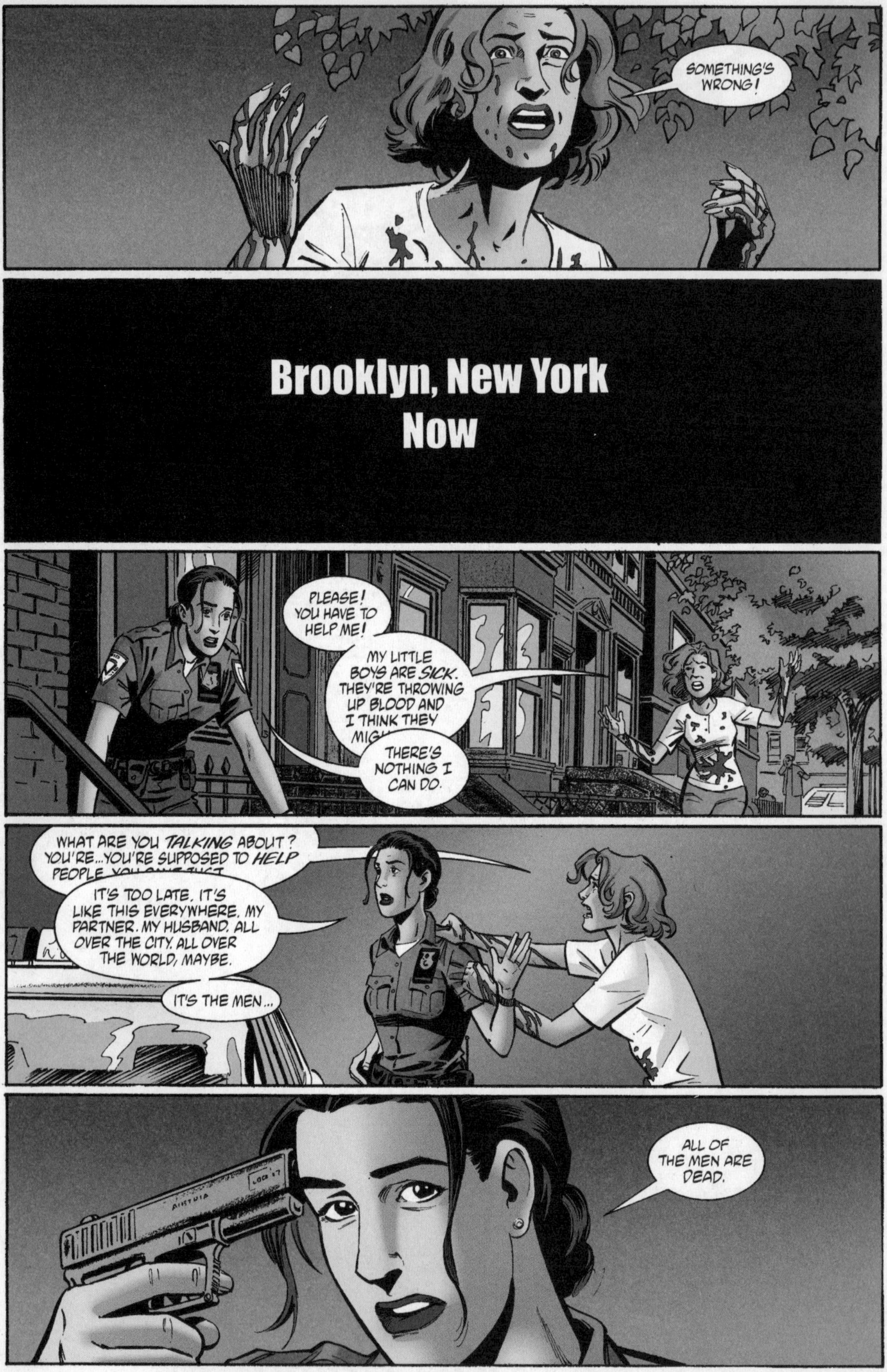
SOMETHING'S WRONG!
Brooklyn, New York
Now
PLEASE! YOU HAVE TO HELP ME!
MY LITTLE BOYS ARE *SICK*. THEY'RE THROWING UP BLOOD AND I THINK THEY
THERE'S NOTHING I CAN DO.
WHAT ARE YOU *TALKING* ABOUT? YOU'RE...YOU'RE SUPPOSED TO *HELP* PEOPLE.
IT'S TOO LATE. IT'S LIKE THIS EVERYWHERE. MY PARTNER. MY HUSBAND. ALL OVER THE CITY. ALL OVER THE WORLD, MAYBE.
IT'S THE MEN...
ALL OF THE MEN ARE DEAD.

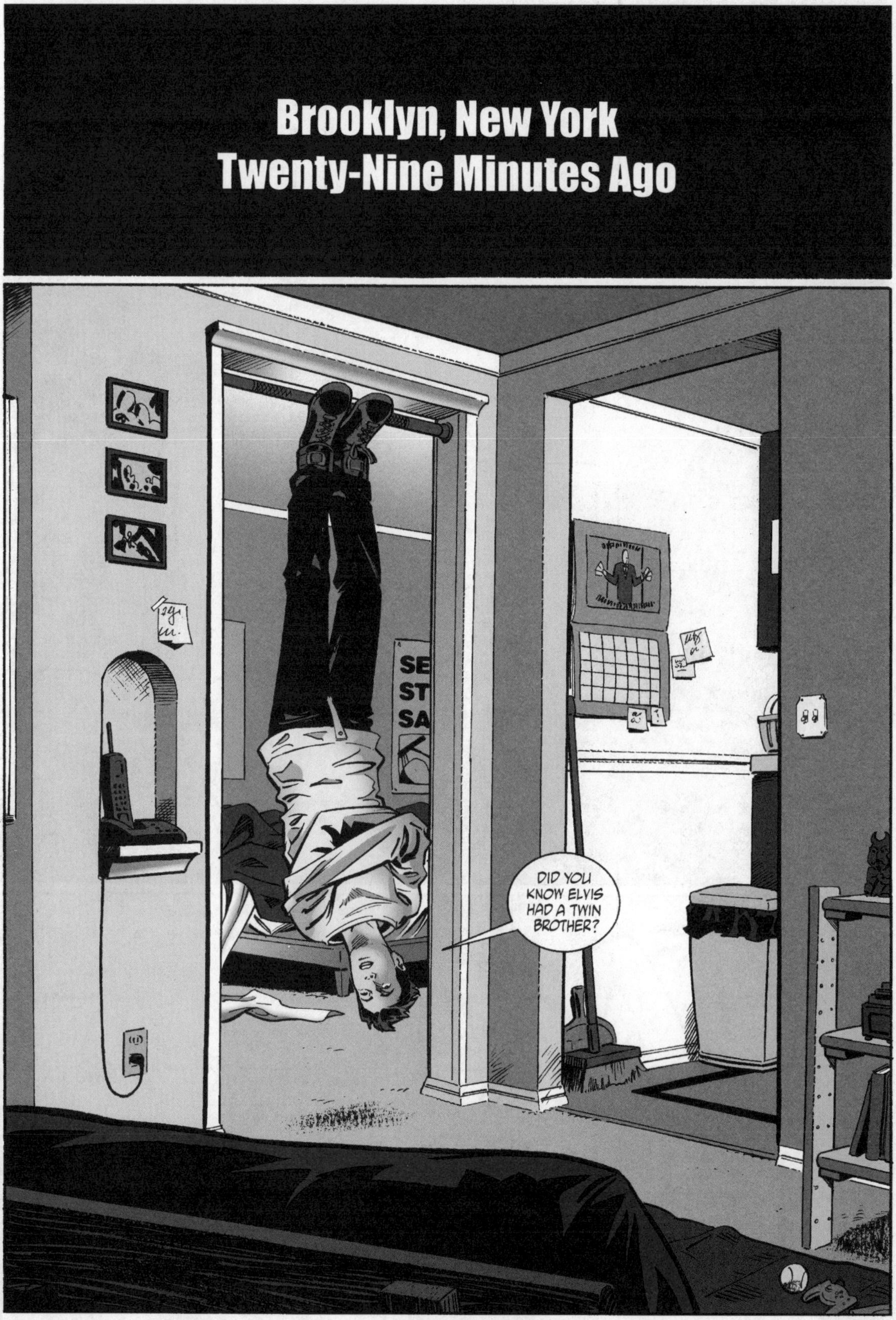
Brooklyn, New York
Twenty-Nine Minutes Ago
DID YOU KNOW ELVIS HAD A TWIN BROTHER?

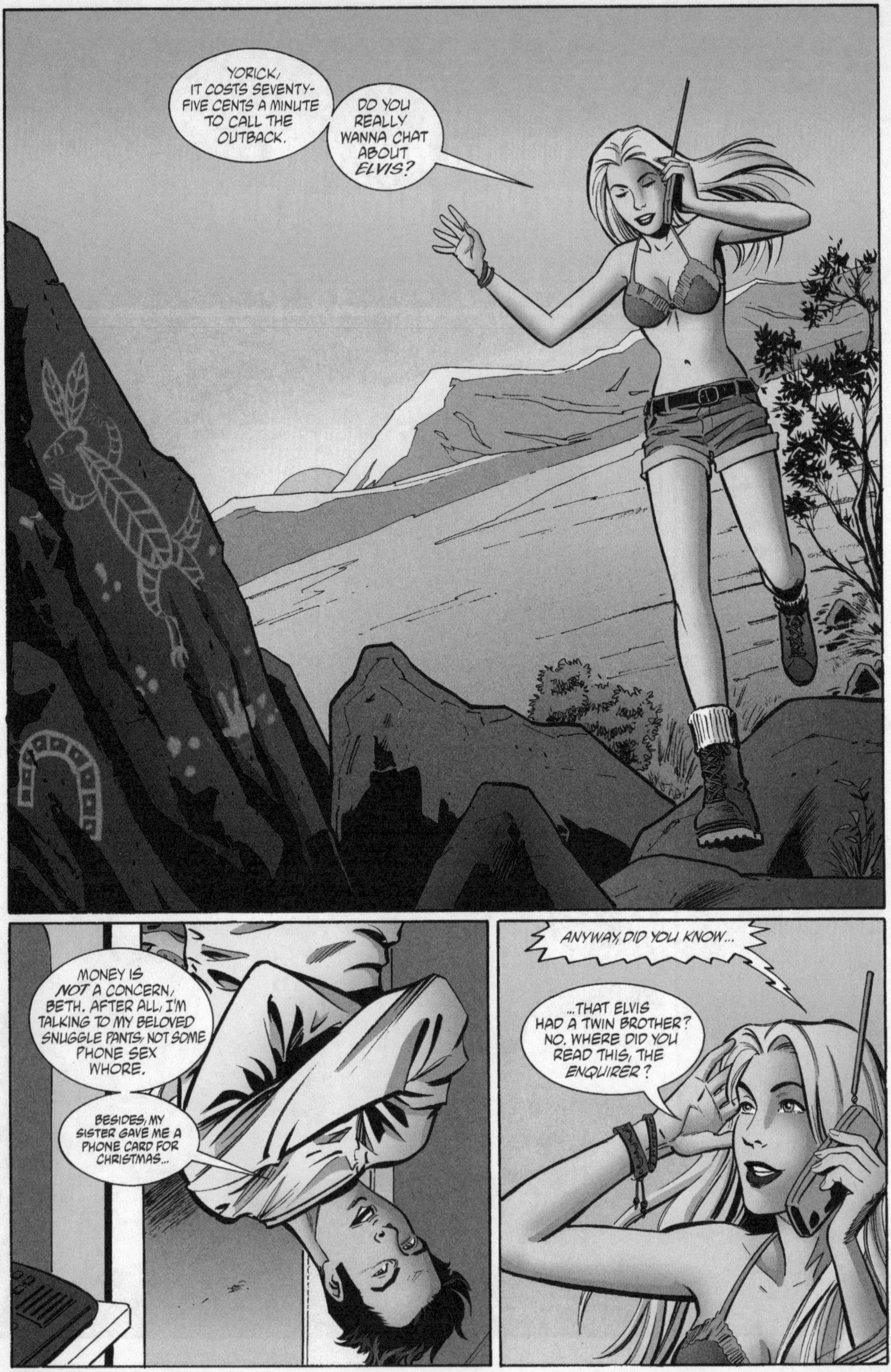
YORICK, IT COSTS SEVENTY-FIVE CENTS A MINUTE TO CALL THE OUTBACK.
DO YOU REALLY WANNA CHAT ABOUT *ELVIS?*
MONEY IS *NOT* A CONCERN, BETH. AFTER ALL, I'M TALKING TO MY BELOVED SNUGGLE PANTS, NOT SOME PHONE SEX WHORE.
BESIDES, MY SISTER GAVE ME A PHONE CARD FOR CHRISTMAS...
ANYWAY, DID YOU KNOW...
...THAT ELVIS HAD A TWIN BROTHER? NO. WHERE DID YOU READ THIS, THE *ENQUIRER?*

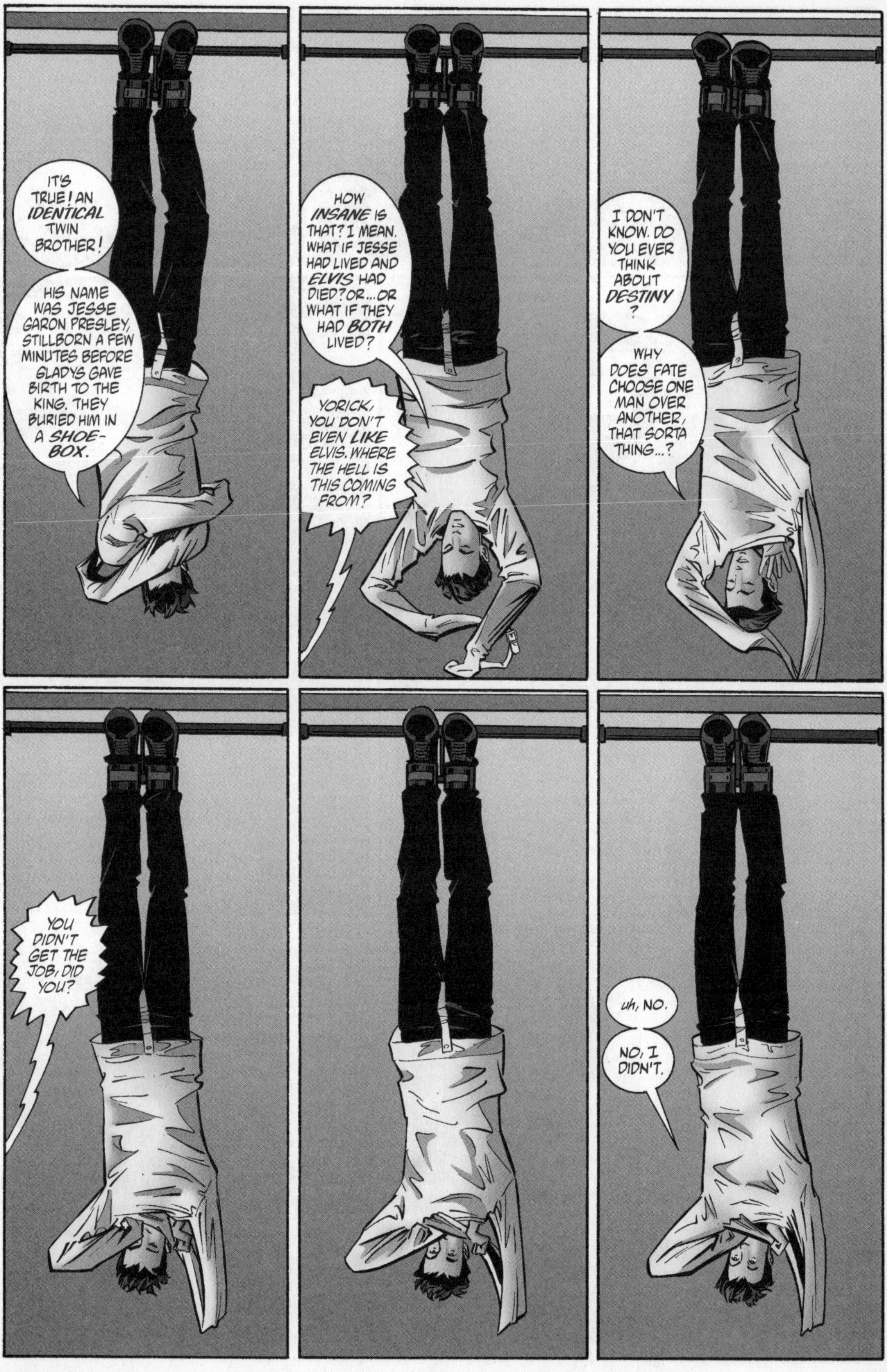

IT'S TRUE! AN IDENTICAL TWIN BROTHER!
HIS NAME WAS JESSE GARON PRESLEY, STILLBORN A FEW MINUTES BEFORE GLADYS GAVE BIRTH TO THE KING. THEY BURIED HIM IN A SHOE-BOX.
HOW INSANE IS THAT? I MEAN. WHAT IF JESSE HAD LIVED AND ELVIS HAD DIED? OR...OR WHAT IF THEY HAD BOTH LIVED?
YORICK, YOU DON'T EVEN LIKE ELVIS. WHERE THE HELL IS THIS COMING FROM?
I DON'T KNOW. DO YOU EVER THINK ABOUT DESTINY?
WHY DOES FATE CHOOSE ONE MAN OVER ANOTHER, THAT SORTA THING...?
YOU DIDN'T GET THE JOB, DID YOU?
uh, NO.
NO, I DIDN'T.

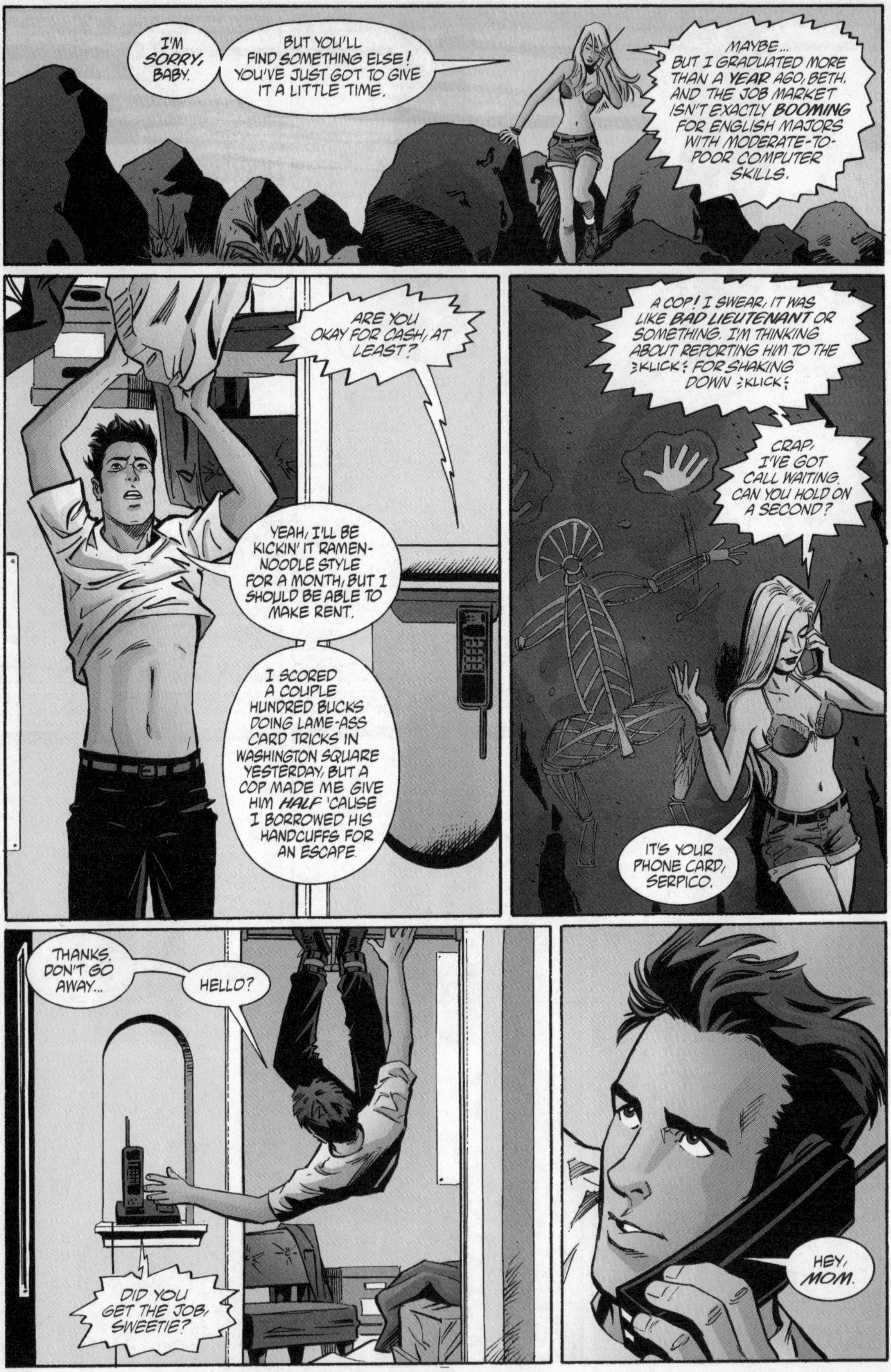

I'M SORRY, BABY.
BUT YOU'LL FIND SOMETHING ELSE! YOU'VE JUST GOT TO GIVE IT A LITTLE TIME.
MAYBE... BUT I GRADUATED MORE THAN A YEAR AGO, BETH, AND THE JOB MARKET ISN'T EXACTLY BOOMING FOR ENGLISH MAJORS WITH MODERATE-TO-POOR COMPUTER SKILLS.
ARE YOU OKAY FOR CASH, AT LEAST?
YEAH, I'LL BE KICKIN' IT RAMEN-NOODLE STYLE FOR A MONTH, BUT I SHOULD BE ABLE TO MAKE RENT.
I SCORED A COUPLE HUNDRED BUCKS DOING LAME-ASS CARD TRICKS IN WASHINGTON SQUARE YESTERDAY, BUT A COP MADE ME GIVE HIM HALF 'CAUSE I BORROWED HIS HANDCUFFS FOR AN ESCAPE.
A COP! I SWEAR, IT WAS LIKE BAD LIEUTENANT OR SOMETHING. I'M THINKING ABOUT REPORTING HIM TO THE KLICK FOR SHAKING DOWN KLICK
CRAP, I'VE GOT CALL WAITING. CAN YOU HOLD ON A SECOND?
IT'S YOUR PHONE CARD, SERPICO.
THANKS. DON'T GO AWAY...
HELLO?
DID YOU GET THE JOB, SWEETIE?
HEY, MOM.

Washington, D.C.
Twenty-Four Minutes Ago

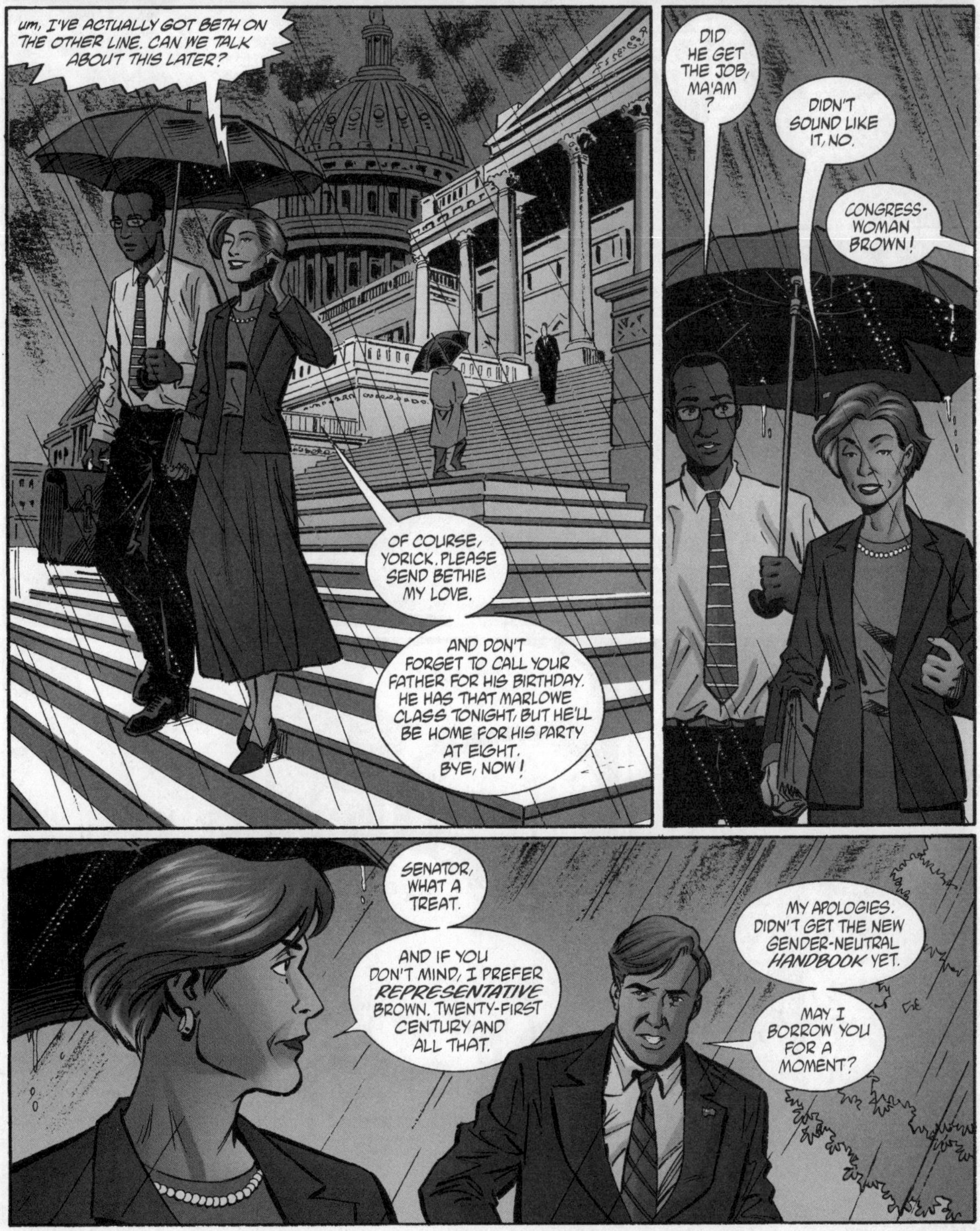
UM, I'VE ACTUALLY GOT BETH ON THE OTHER LINE. CAN WE TALK ABOUT THIS LATER?
OF COURSE, YORICK. PLEASE SEND BETHIE MY LOVE.
AND DON'T FORGET TO CALL YOUR FATHER FOR HIS BIRTHDAY. HE HAS THAT MARLOWE CLASS TONIGHT, BUT HE'LL BE HOME FOR HIS PARTY AT EIGHT. BYE, NOW!
DID HE GET THE JOB, MA'AM?
DIDN'T SOUND LIKE IT, NO.
CONGRESS-WOMAN BROWN!
SENATOR, WHAT A TREAT.
AND IF YOU DON'T MIND, I PREFER *REPRESENTATIVE* BROWN. TWENTY-FIRST CENTURY AND ALL THAT.
MY APOLOGIES. DIDN'T GET THE NEW GENDER-NEUTRAL *HANDBOOK* YET.
MAY I BORROW YOU FOR A MOMENT?

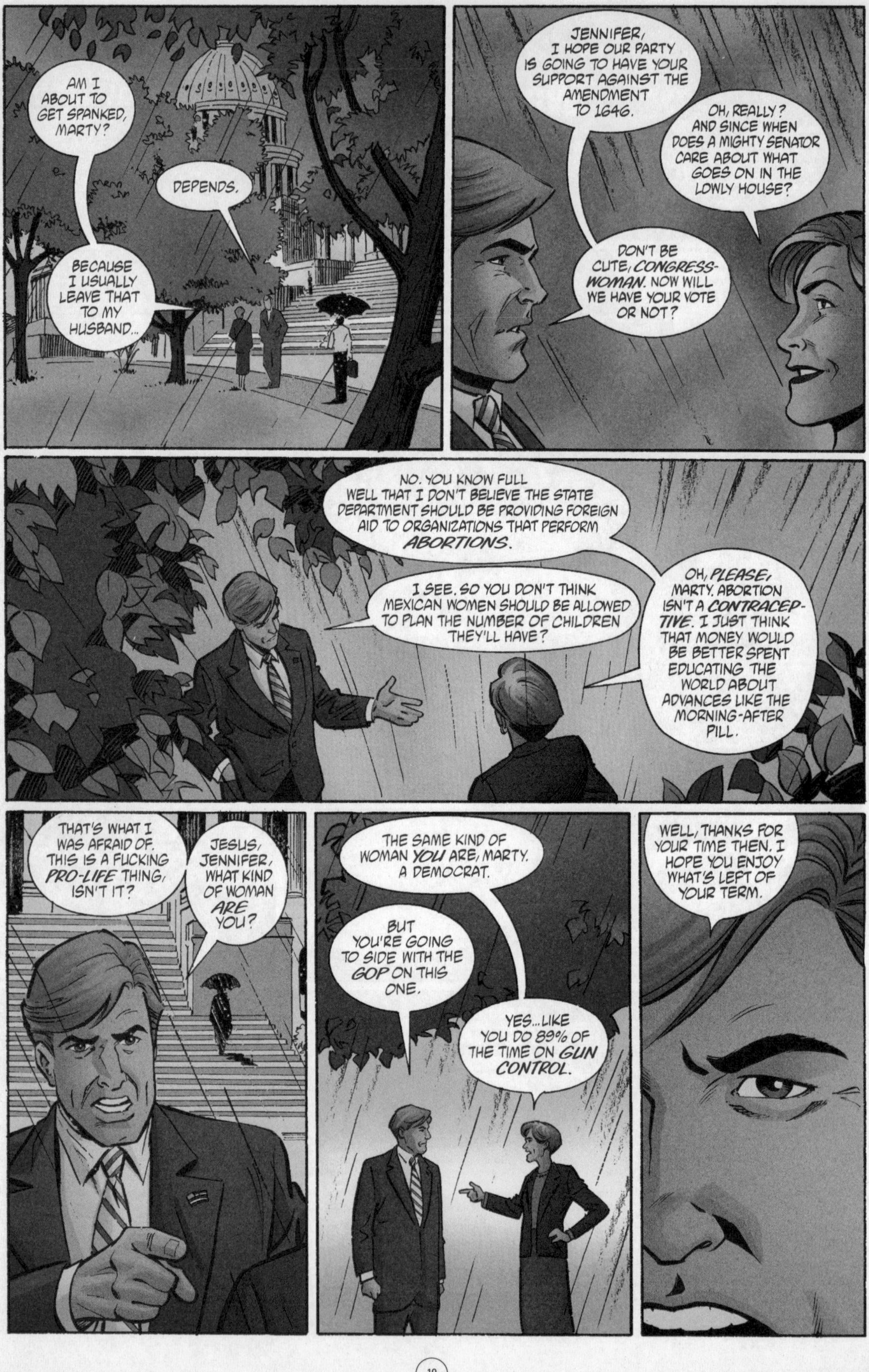
AM I ABOUT TO GET SPANKED, MARTY?
DEPENDS.
BECAUSE I USUALLY LEAVE THAT TO MY HUSBAND...
JENNIFER, I HOPE OUR PARTY IS GOING TO HAVE YOUR SUPPORT AGAINST THE AMENDMENT TO 1646.
OH, REALLY? AND SINCE WHEN DOES A MIGHTY SENATOR CARE ABOUT WHAT GOES ON IN THE LOWLY HOUSE?
DON'T BE CUTE, CONGRESS-WOMAN. NOW WILL WE HAVE YOUR VOTE OR NOT?
NO. YOU KNOW FULL WELL THAT I DON'T BELIEVE THE STATE DEPARTMENT SHOULD BE PROVIDING FOREIGN AID TO ORGANIZATIONS THAT PERFORM ABORTIONS.
I SEE. SO YOU DON'T THINK MEXICAN WOMEN SHOULD BE ALLOWED TO PLAN THE NUMBER OF CHILDREN THEY'LL HAVE?
OH, PLEASE, MARTY. ABORTION ISN'T A CONTRACEP-TIVE. I JUST THINK THAT MONEY WOULD BE BETTER SPENT EDUCATING THE WORLD ABOUT ADVANCES LIKE THE MORNING-AFTER PILL.
THAT'S WHAT I WAS AFRAID OF. THIS IS A FUCKING PRO-LIFE THING, ISN'T IT?
JESUS, JENNIFER, WHAT KIND OF WOMAN ARE YOU?
THE SAME KIND OF WOMAN YOU ARE, MARTY. A DEMOCRAT.
BUT YOU'RE GOING TO SIDE WITH THE GOP ON THIS ONE.
YES...LIKE YOU DO 89% OF THE TIME ON GUN CONTROL.
WELL, THANKS FOR YOUR TIME THEN. I HOPE YOU ENJOY WHAT'S LEFT OF YOUR TERM.

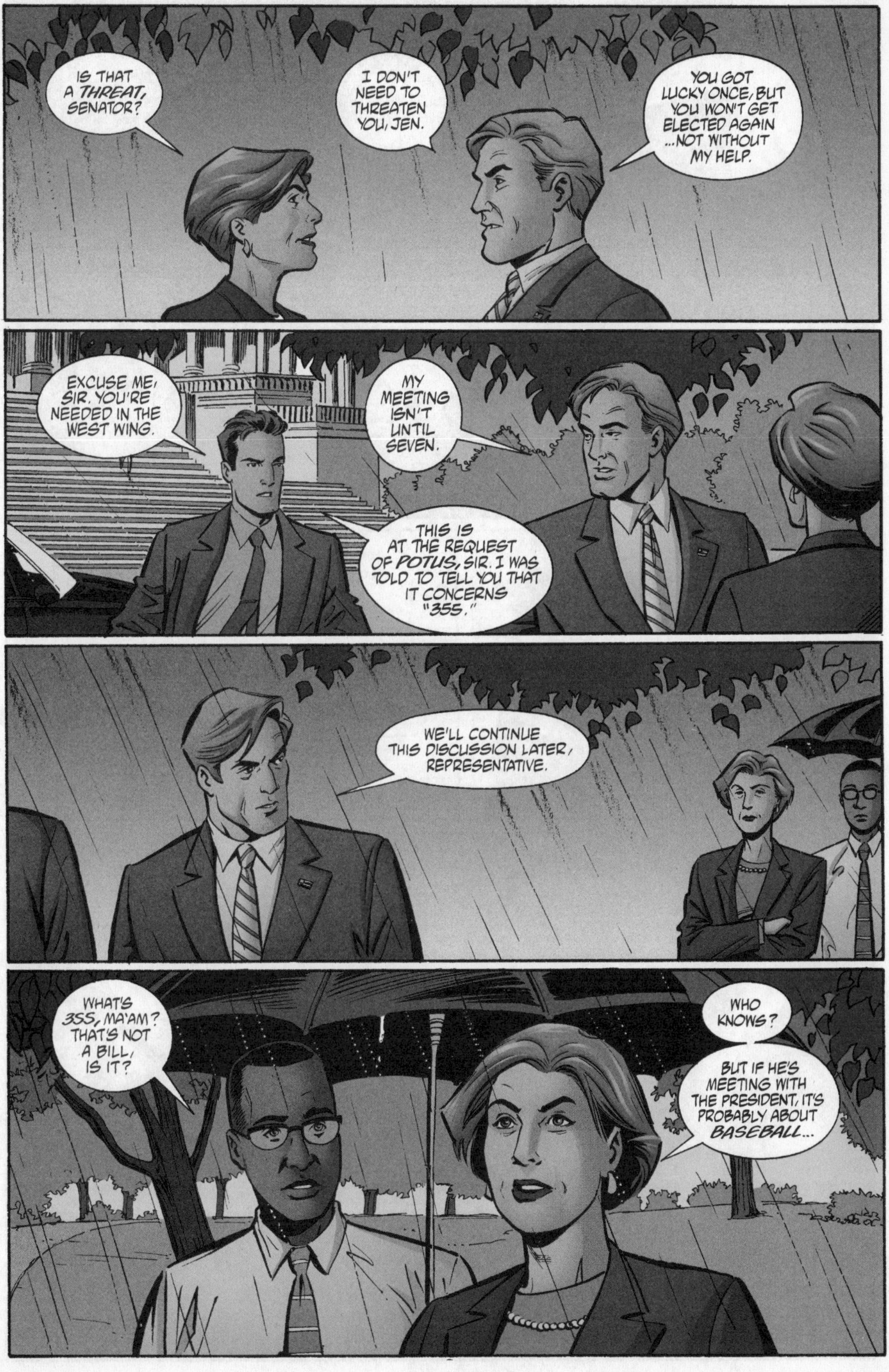
IS THAT A *THREAT,* SENATOR?
I DON'T NEED TO THREATEN YOU, JEN.
YOU GOT LUCKY ONCE, BUT YOU WON'T GET ELECTED AGAIN ...NOT WITHOUT MY HELP.
EXCUSE ME, SIR. YOU'RE NEEDED IN THE WEST WING.
MY MEETING ISN'T UNTIL SEVEN.
THIS IS AT THE REQUEST OF *POTUS,* SIR. I WAS TOLD TO TELL YOU THAT IT CONCERNS "355."
WE'LL CONTINUE THIS DISCUSSION LATER, REPRESENTATIVE.
WHAT'S *355,* MA'AM? THAT'S NOT A BILL, IS IT?
WHO KNOWS?
BUT IF HE'S MEETING WITH THE PRESIDENT, IT'S PROBABLY ABOUT *BASEBALL...*

SORRY, THAT WAS MOMMY DEAREST, BUSY BRINGING SHAME TO OHIO'S 22ND DISTRICT.

ANYWAY, HOW'S LIFE DOWN UNDER?

FUCKING *INCREDIBLE.* I WISH I COULD STAY OUT HERE ANOTHER MONTH... NO OFFENSE, OF COURSE.

YESTERDAY, THIS BIG-TIME ANTHRO-POLOGIST TOOK US ON A TOUR OF THE DHARAWAL PEOPLE'S ANCIENT ROCK DWELLINGS AND SHOWED ME—

GODDAMN IT, AMPERSAND! STOP IT!

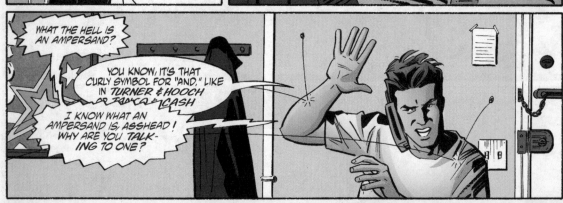

WHAT THE HELL IS AN AMPERSAND?

YOU KNOW, IT'S THAT CURLY SYMBOL FOR "AND," LIKE IN *TURNER & HOOCH* OR *JOHNNY CASH.*

I KNOW WHAT AN AMPERSAND IS, ASSHEAD! WHY ARE YOU TALK-ING TO ONE?

BECAUSE HE'S THROWING HIS OWN SHIT AT ME!

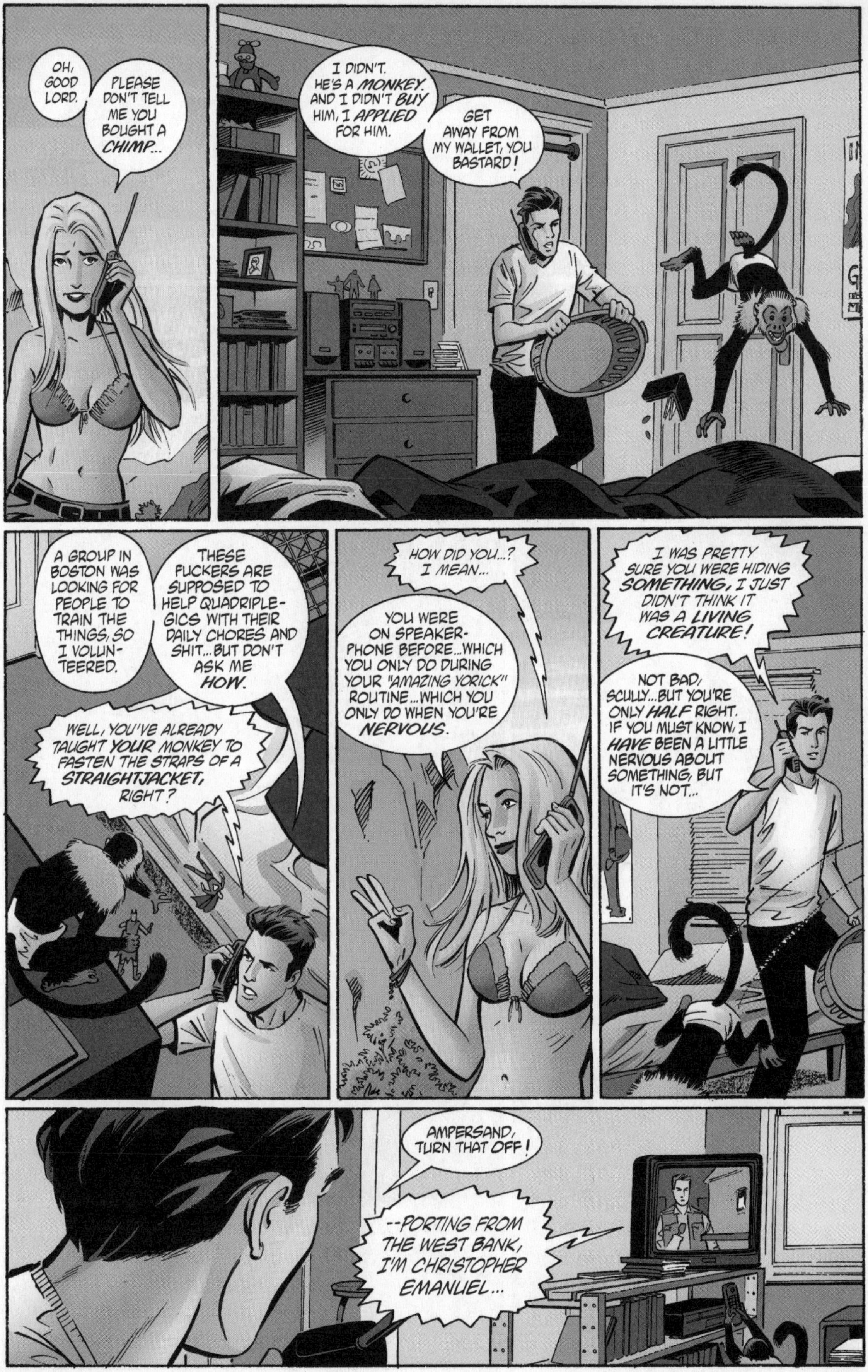
OH, GOOD LORD.
PLEASE DON'T TELL ME YOU BOUGHT A CHIMP...
I DIDN'T. HE'S A MONKEY. AND I DIDN'T BUY HIM, I APPLIED FOR HIM.
GET AWAY FROM MY WALLET, YOU BASTARD!
A GROUP IN BOSTON WAS LOOKING FOR PEOPLE TO TRAIN THE THINGS, SO I VOLUNTEERED.
THESE FUCKERS ARE SUPPOSED TO HELP QUADRIPLEGICS WITH THEIR DAILY CHORES AND SHIT...BUT DON'T ASK ME HOW.
WELL, YOU'VE ALREADY TAUGHT YOUR MONKEY TO FASTEN THE STRAPS OF A STRAIGHTJACKET, RIGHT?
HOW DID YOU...? I MEAN...
YOU WERE ON SPEAKERPHONE BEFORE...WHICH YOU ONLY DO DURING YOUR "AMAZING YORICK" ROUTINE...WHICH YOU ONLY DO WHEN YOU'RE NERVOUS.
I WAS PRETTY SURE YOU WERE HIDING SOMETHING, I JUST DIDN'T THINK IT WAS A LIVING CREATURE!
NOT BAD, SCULLY...BUT YOU'RE ONLY HALF RIGHT. IF YOU MUST KNOW, I HAVE BEEN A LITTLE NERVOUS ABOUT SOMETHING, BUT IT'S NOT...
AMPERSAND, TURN THAT OFF!
--PORTING FROM THE WEST BANK, I'M CHRISTOPHER EMANUEL...

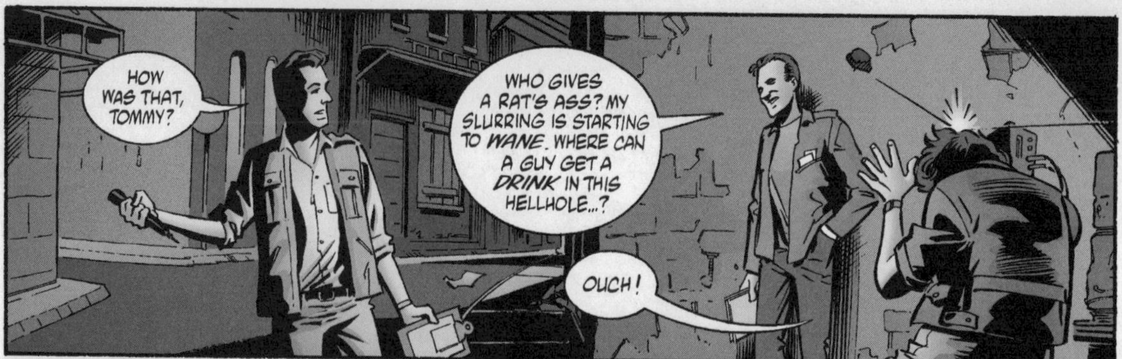
HOW WAS THAT, TOMMY?
WHO GIVES A RAT'S ASS? MY SLURRING IS STARTING TO WANE. WHERE CAN A GUY GET A DRINK IN THIS HELLHOLE...?
OUCH!

Nablus, West Bank
Eighteen Minutes Ago

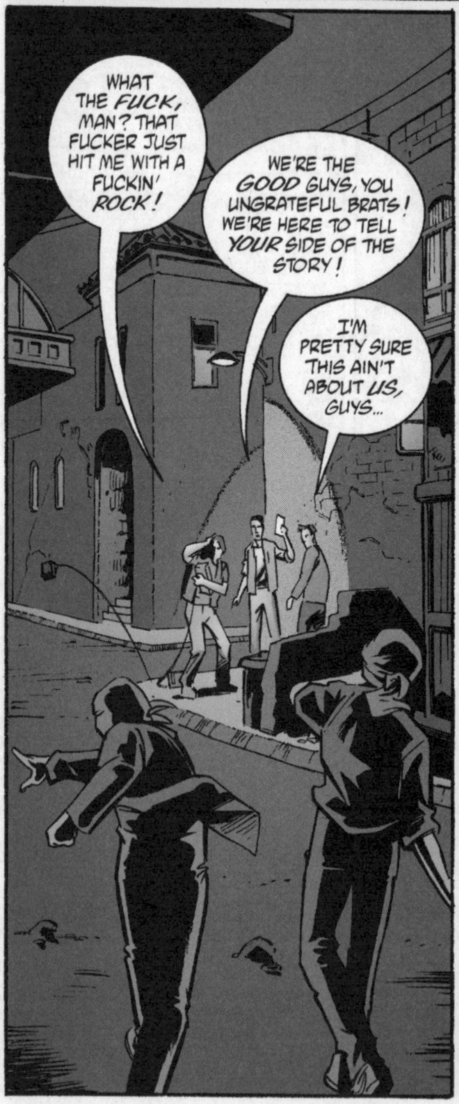
WHAT THE FUCK, MAN? THAT FUCKER JUST HIT ME WITH A FUCKIN' ROCK!
WE'RE THE GOOD GUYS, YOU UNGRATEFUL BRATS! WE'RE HERE TO TELL YOUR SIDE OF THE STORY!
I'M PRETTY SURE THIS AIN'T ABOUT US, GUYS...

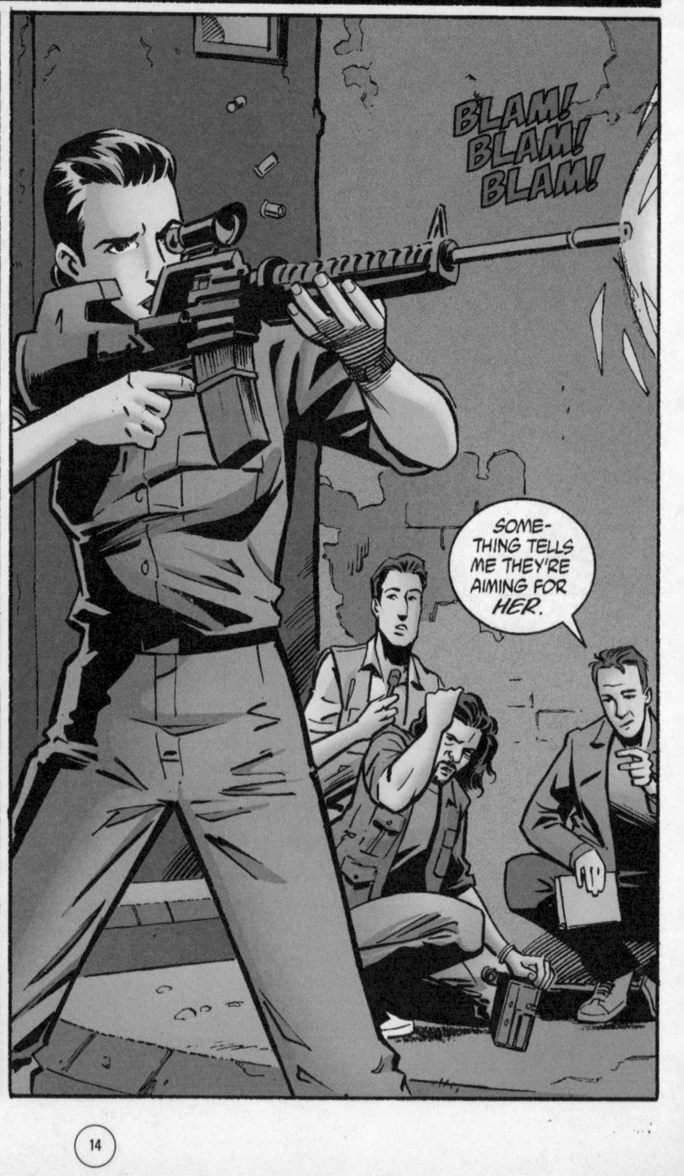
BLAM! BLAM! BLAM!
SOME-THING TELLS ME THEY'RE AIMING FOR HER.

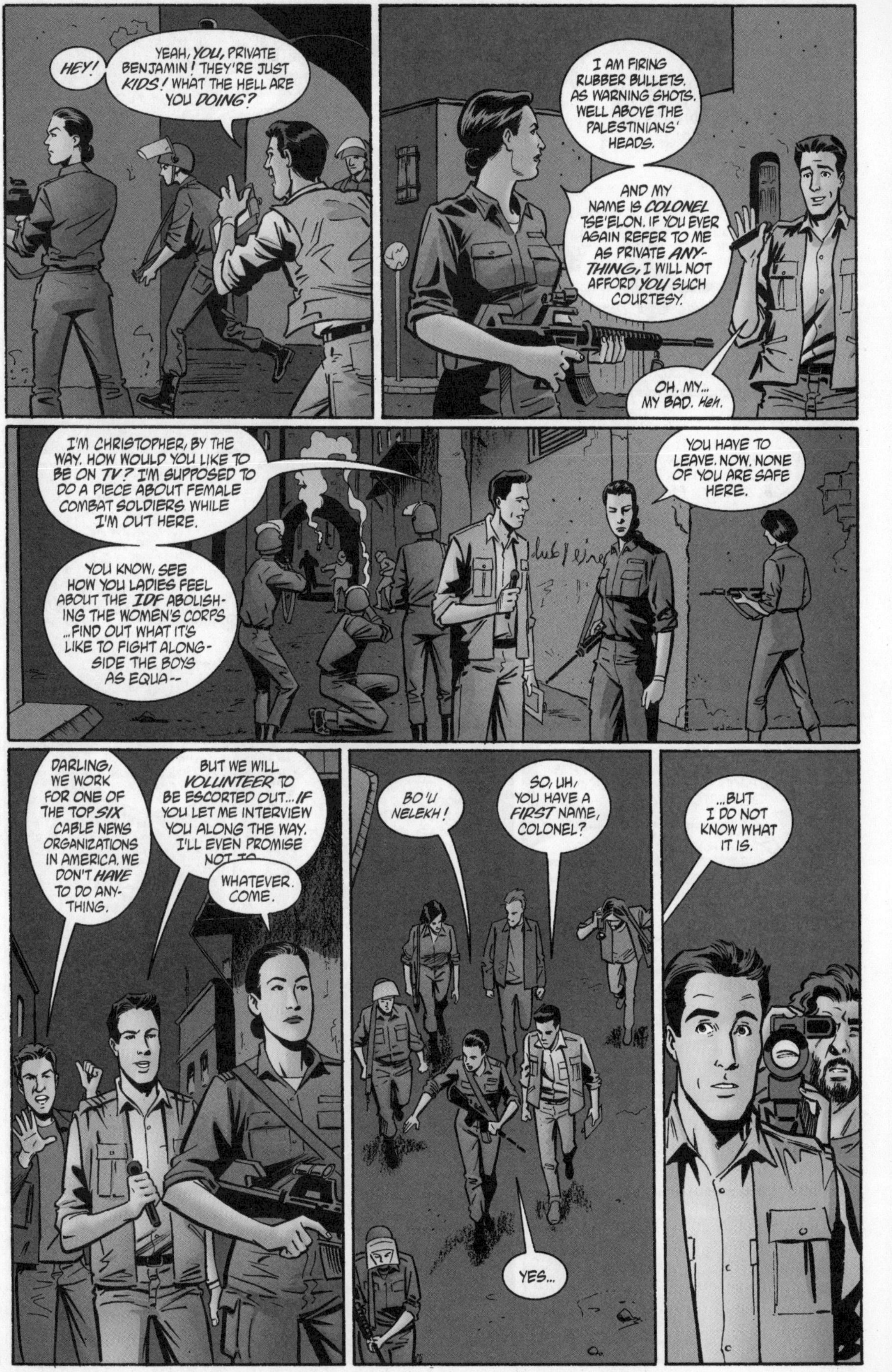
HEY!
YEAH, YOU, PRIVATE BENJAMIN! THEY'RE JUST KIDS! WHAT THE HELL ARE YOU DOING?
I AM FIRING RUBBER BULLETS. AS WARNING SHOTS. WELL ABOVE THE PALESTINIANS' HEADS.
AND MY NAME IS COLONEL TSE'ELON. IF YOU EVER AGAIN REFER TO ME AS PRIVATE ANY-THING, I WILL NOT AFFORD YOU SUCH COURTESY.
OH. MY... MY BAD. Heh.
I'M CHRISTOPHER, BY THE WAY. HOW WOULD YOU LIKE TO BE ON TV? I'M SUPPOSED TO DO A PIECE ABOUT FEMALE COMBAT SOLDIERS WHILE I'M OUT HERE.
YOU KNOW, SEE HOW YOU LADIES FEEL ABOUT THE IDF ABOLISH-ING THE WOMEN'S CORPS ...FIND OUT WHAT IT'S LIKE TO FIGHT ALONG-SIDE THE BOYS AS EQUA--
YOU HAVE TO LEAVE. NOW. NONE OF YOU ARE SAFE HERE.
DARLING, WE WORK FOR ONE OF THE TOP SIX CABLE NEWS ORGANIZATIONS IN AMERICA. WE DON'T HAVE TO DO ANY-THING.
BUT WE WILL VOLUNTEER TO BE ESCORTED OUT... IF YOU LET ME INTERVIEW YOU ALONG THE WAY. I'LL EVEN PROMISE NOT TO
WHATEVER. COME.
BO'U NELEKH!
SO, UH, YOU HAVE A FIRST NAME, COLONEL?
YES...
...BUT I DO NOT KNOW WHAT IT IS.

KEEP YOUR HEADS DOWN...

TWO OF MY SIBLINGS DIED AT BIRTH, SO WHEN MY PARENTS HAD ME, THEY DECIDED NOT TO SPEAK MY NAME OUT LOUD.

IT IS A STUPID OLD TRADITION, DONE TO "DECEIVE THE ANGEL OF DEATH," CONFUSE HIM SO THAT HE WILL NOT KNOW WHERE TO FIND ME.

BUT... WHAT DO YOUR FRIENDS CALL YOU?

ALTER.

A NICKNAME. MEANS "OLD ONE." IT IS A...LONG STORY.

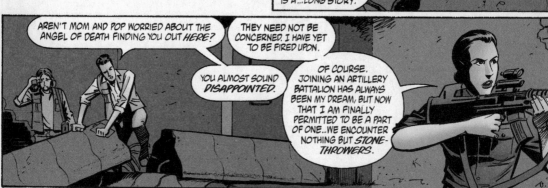

AREN'T MOM AND POP WORRIED ABOUT THE ANGEL OF DEATH FINDING YOU OUT HERE?

THEY NEED NOT BE CONCERNED. I HAVE YET TO BE FIRED UPON.

YOU ALMOST SOUND DISAPPOINTED.

OF COURSE. JOINING AN ARTILLERY BATTALION HAS ALWAYS BEEN MY DREAM, BUT NOW THAT I AM FINALLY PERMITTED TO BE A PART OF ONE...WE ENCOUNTER NOTHING BUT STONE-THROWERS.

MAN, YOU ARE HARDCORE. EVERY OTHER DAUGHTER OF ISRAEL I TALK TO OUT HERE IS JUST HAPPY THAT IT'S ALL QUIET ON THE WESTERN FRONT.

THOSE GIRLS COULD BE PARATROOPERS OR NAVAL COMMANDERS...BUT MEN HAVE TAUGHT THEM TO BE CONTENT BEHIND A TYPEWRITER OR RADAR SCREEN. NOT ME.

MY GRANDMOTHER CROSSED INTO ENEMY LINES DURING OUR WAR OF INDEPENDENCE, AND HER GRANDMOTHER WAS PART OF THE ALL-FEMALE BATTALION OF DEATH DURING THE RUSSIAN REVOLUTION.

THIS IS WHO I AM...

I DON'T GET IT. I MEAN, OFF THE RECORD, I UNDERSTAND FIGHTING FOR EQUAL PAY AND ALL THAT GARBAGE...BUT I THOUGHT YOU FEMINISTS WERE PACIFISTS, TOO.

WHO WANTS PEACE...

...WHEN WE HAVE NOT YET BEGUN TO FIGHT?

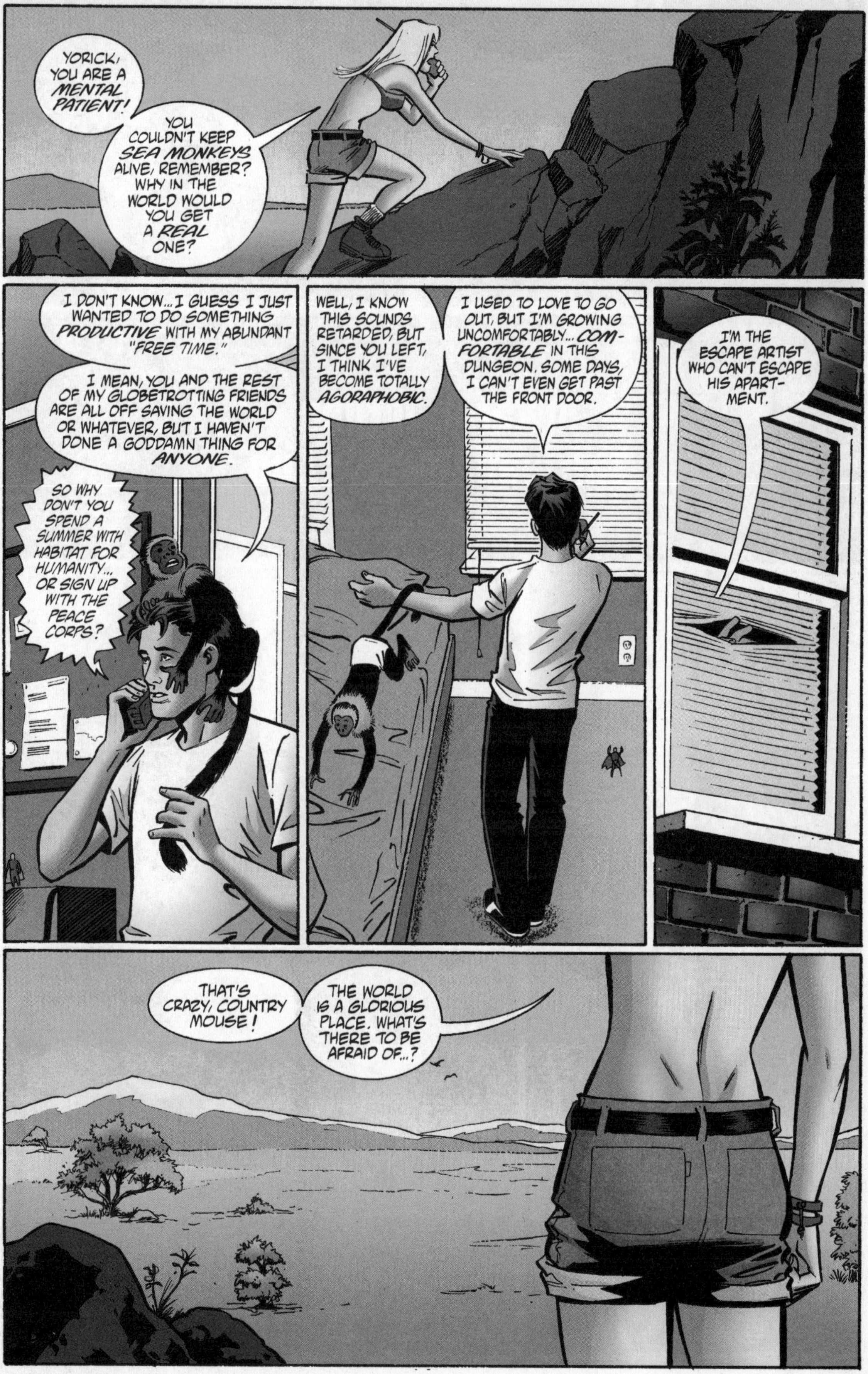
YORICK, YOU ARE A *MENTAL PATIENT!*
YOU COULDN'T KEEP *SEA MONKEYS* ALIVE, REMEMBER? WHY IN THE WORLD WOULD YOU GET A *REAL* ONE?
I DON'T KNOW... I GUESS I JUST WANTED TO DO SOMETHING *PRODUCTIVE* WITH MY ABUNDANT *"FREE TIME."*
I MEAN, YOU AND THE REST OF MY GLOBETROTTING FRIENDS ARE ALL OFF SAVING THE WORLD OR WHATEVER, BUT I HAVEN'T DONE A GODDAMN THING FOR *ANYONE*.
SO WHY DON'T YOU SPEND A SUMMER WITH HABITAT FOR HUMANITY... OR SIGN UP WITH THE PEACE CORPS?
WELL, I KNOW THIS SOUNDS RETARDED, BUT SINCE YOU LEFT, I THINK I'VE BECOME TOTALLY *AGORAPHOBIC*.
I USED TO LOVE TO GO OUT, BUT I'M GROWING UNCOMFORTABLY... *COMFORTABLE* IN THIS DUNGEON. SOME DAYS, I CAN'T EVEN GET PAST THE FRONT DOOR.
I'M THE ESCAPE ARTIST WHO CAN'T ESCAPE HIS APARTMENT.
THAT'S CRAZY, COUNTRY MOUSE!
THE WORLD IS A GLORIOUS PLACE. WHAT'S THERE TO BE AFRAID OF...?

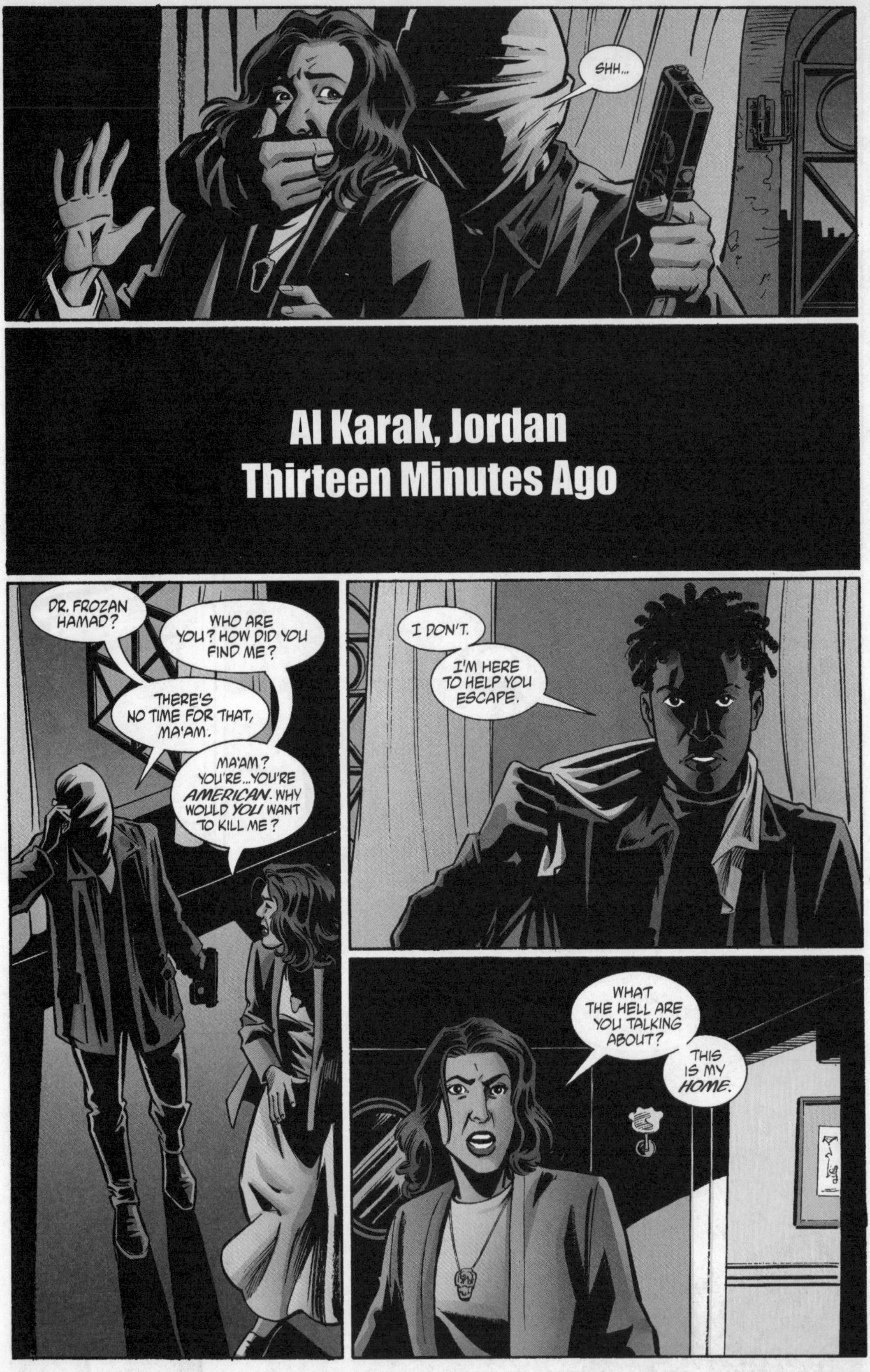
SHH...
Al Karak, Jordan
Thirteen Minutes Ago
DR. FROZAN HAMAD?
WHO ARE YOU? HOW DID YOU FIND ME?
THERE'S NO TIME FOR THAT, MA'AM.
MA'AM? YOU'RE...YOU'RE AMERICAN. WHY WOULD YOU WANT TO KILL ME?
I DON'T.
I'M HERE TO HELP YOU ESCAPE.
WHAT THE HELL ARE YOU TALKING ABOUT?
THIS IS MY HOME.

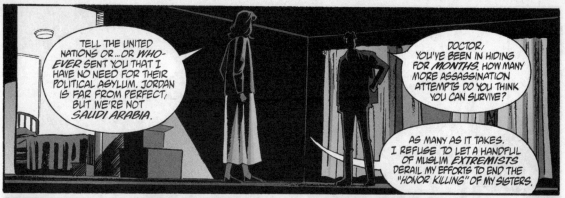

TELL THE UNITED NATIONS OR...OR *WHO- EVER* SENT YOU THAT I HAVE NO NEED FOR THEIR POLITICAL ASYLUM. JORDAN IS FAR FROM PERFECT, BUT WE'RE NOT *SAUDI ARABIA.*

DOCTOR, YOU'VE BEEN IN HIDING FOR *MONTHS.* HOW MANY MORE ASSASSINATION ATTEMPTS DO YOU THINK YOU CAN SURVIVE?

AS MANY AS IT TAKES. I REFUSE TO LET A HANDFUL OF MUSLIM *EXTREMISTS* DERAIL MY EFFORTS TO END THE "HONOR KILLING" OF MY SISTERS.

THAT'S NOT WHAT THIS IS ABOUT.

OH, NO?

ONE FOURTH OF THE MURDERS COMMITTED IN MY COUNTRY ARE WOMEN KILLED BY MALE RELATIVES WHO SIMPLY *ACCUSE* THEM OF ADULTERY OR...OR "FORNICATION".

OUR PENAL CODE *SANCTIONS* THOSE CRIMES BY GRANTING LESSER SENTENCES, IF *ANY* SENTENCES, TO THE MON- STERS WH...

YOU DON'T UNDERSTAND, FROZAN.

THE MEN WHO'VE MADE ATTEMPTS ON YOUR LIFE AREN'T INTERESTED IN YOUR POLITICS.

THEY'RE INTERESTED IN WHAT'S AROUND YOUR NECK.

I...I DON'T FOLLOW.

THEY'RE AFTER THE AMULET OF HELENE, DOCTOR.

AMULET?

IT'S A WORTHLESS NECKLACE, A... A CRUDE STONE IDOL!

THEN YOU'LL PART WITH IT? BEFORE SOMEONE GETS HURT?

NEVER.

MY FATHER TOLD ME THAT A CATASTROPHE COMPARABLE TO THE *TROJAN WAR* WOULD TAKE PLACE IF IT WERE EVER REMOVED FROM THIS LAND.

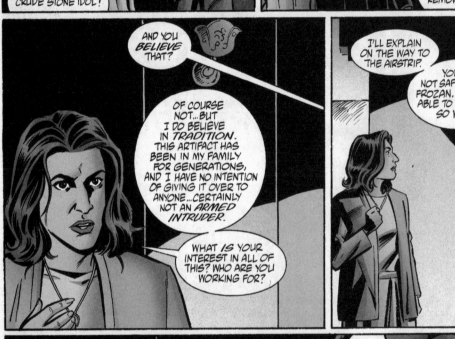

AND YOU *BELIEVE* THAT?

OF COURSE NOT... BUT I DO BELIEVE IN *TRADITION*. THIS ARTIFACT HAS BEEN IN MY FAMILY FOR GENERATIONS, AND I HAVE NO INTENTION OF GIVING IT OVER TO ANYONE... CERTAINLY NOT AN *ARMED INTRUDER*.

WHAT *IS* YOUR INTEREST IN ALL OF THIS? WHO ARE YOU WORKING FOR?

I'LL EXPLAIN ON THE WAY TO THE AIRSTRIP.

YOU'RE NOT SAFE HERE, FROZAN. IF *I* WAS ABLE TO FIND YOU, SO WILL...

BLAM! BLAM! BLAM!

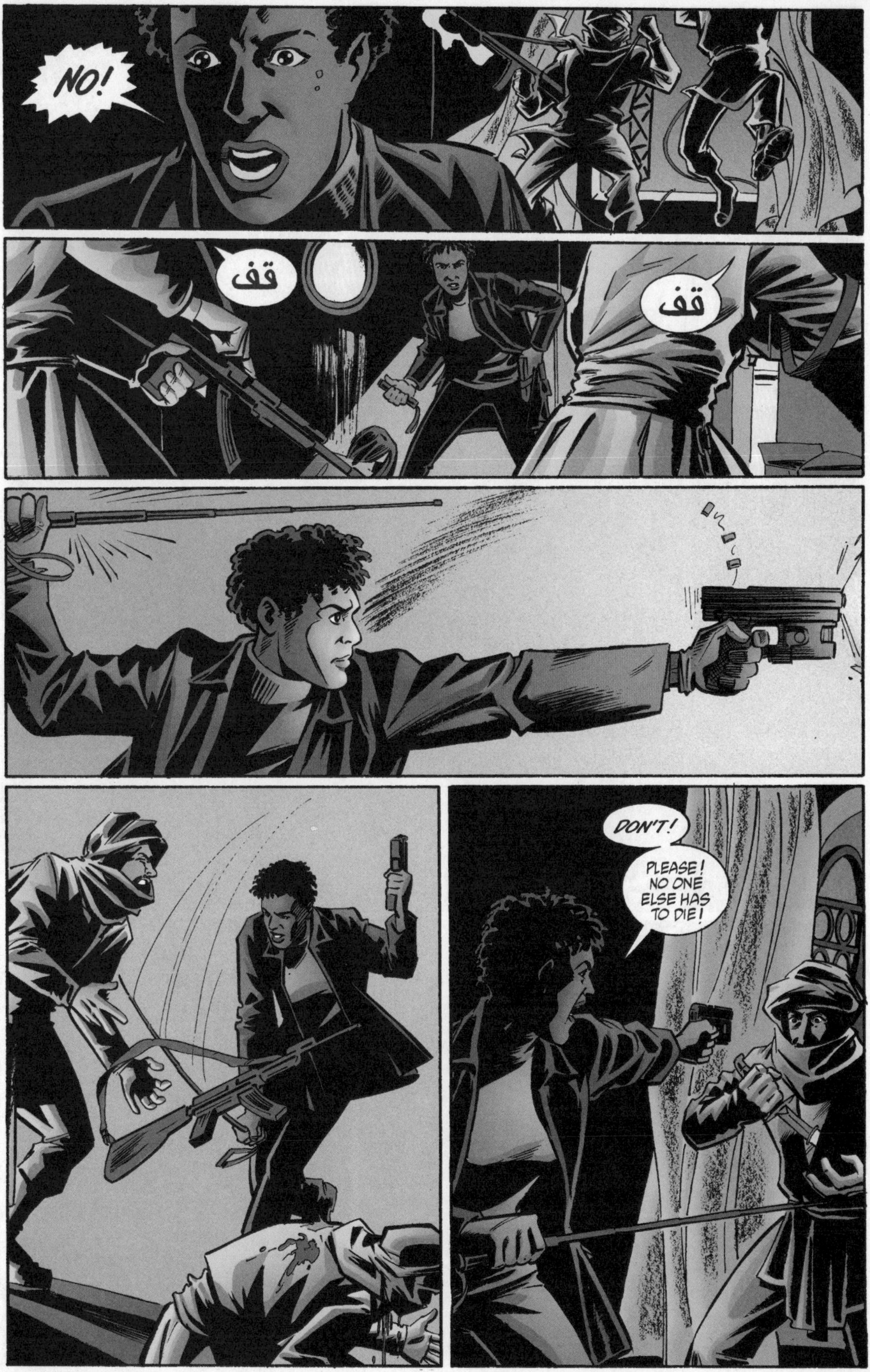
NO!
قف
قف
DON'T!
PLEASE! NO ONE ELSE HAS TO DIE!

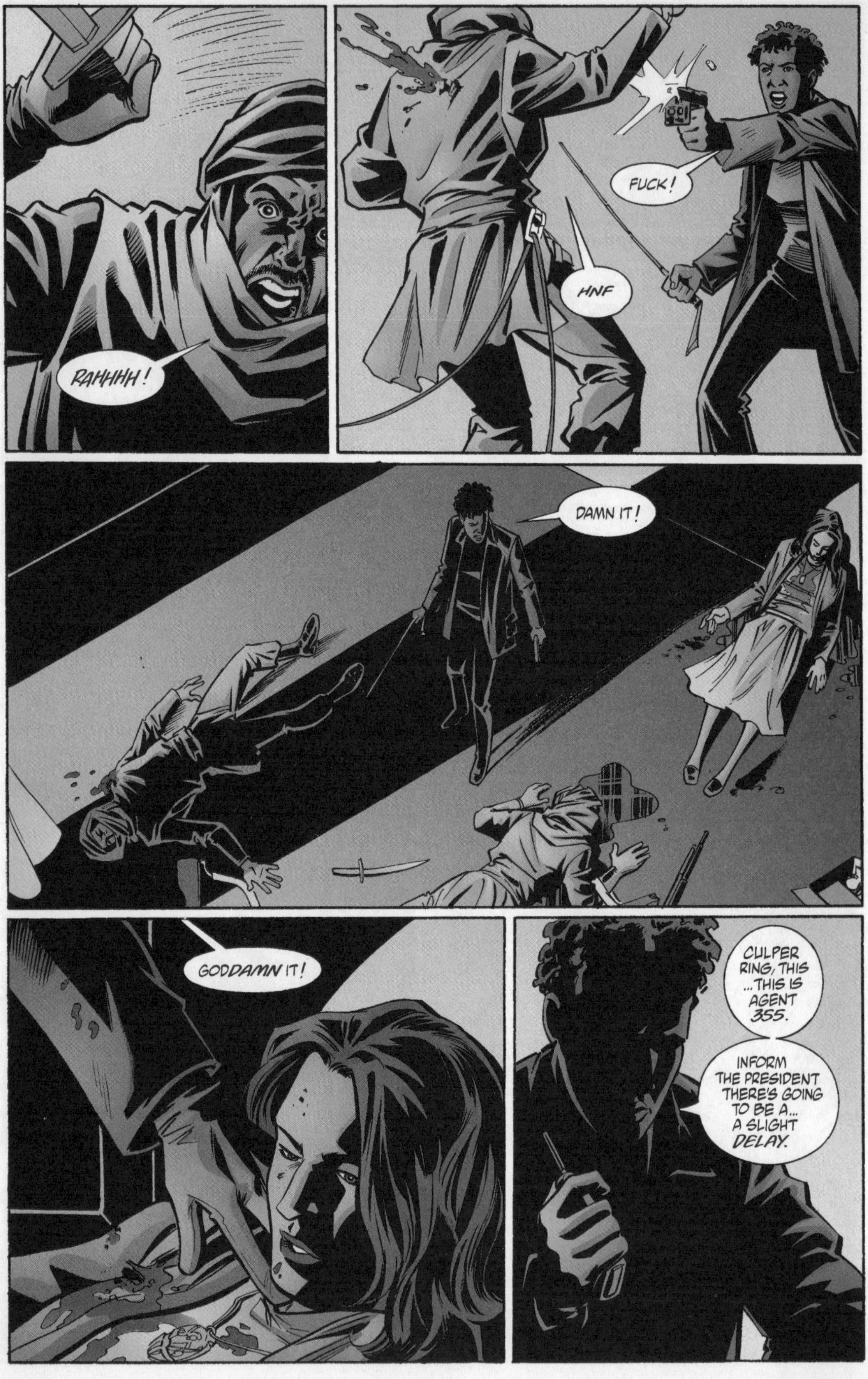
RAHHHH!
HNF
FUCK!
DAMN IT!
GODDAMN IT!
CULPER RING, THIS ...THIS IS AGENT 355.
INFORM THE PRESIDENT THERE'S GOING TO BE A... A SLIGHT DELAY.

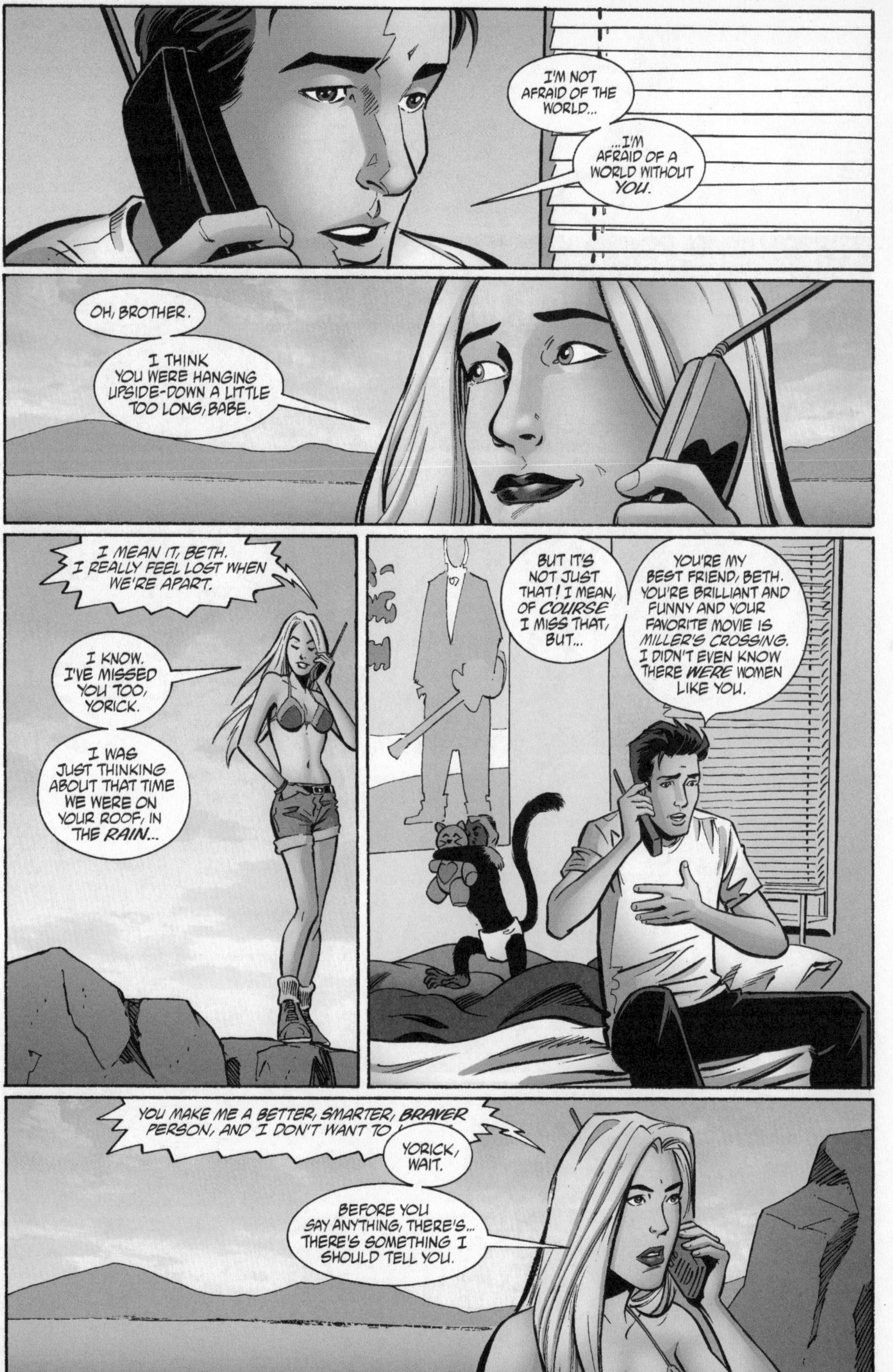
I'M NOT AFRAID OF THE WORLD...
...I'M AFRAID OF A WORLD WITHOUT YOU.
OH, BROTHER.
I THINK YOU WERE HANGING UPSIDE-DOWN A LITTLE TOO LONG, BABE.
I MEAN IT, BETH. I REALLY FEEL LOST WHEN WE'RE APART.
I KNOW. I'VE MISSED YOU TOO, YORICK.
I WAS JUST THINKING ABOUT THAT TIME WE WERE ON YOUR ROOF, IN THE RAIN...
BUT IT'S NOT JUST THAT! I MEAN, OF COURSE I MISS THAT, BUT...
YOU'RE MY BEST FRIEND, BETH. YOU'RE BRILLIANT AND FUNNY AND YOUR FAVORITE MOVIE IS MILLER'S CROSSING. I DIDN'T EVEN KNOW THERE WERE WOMEN LIKE YOU.
YOU MAKE ME A BETTER, SMARTER, BRAVER PERSON, AND I DON'T WANT TO
YORICK, WAIT.
BEFORE YOU SAY ANYTHING, THERE'S... THERE'S SOMETHING I SHOULD TELL YOU.

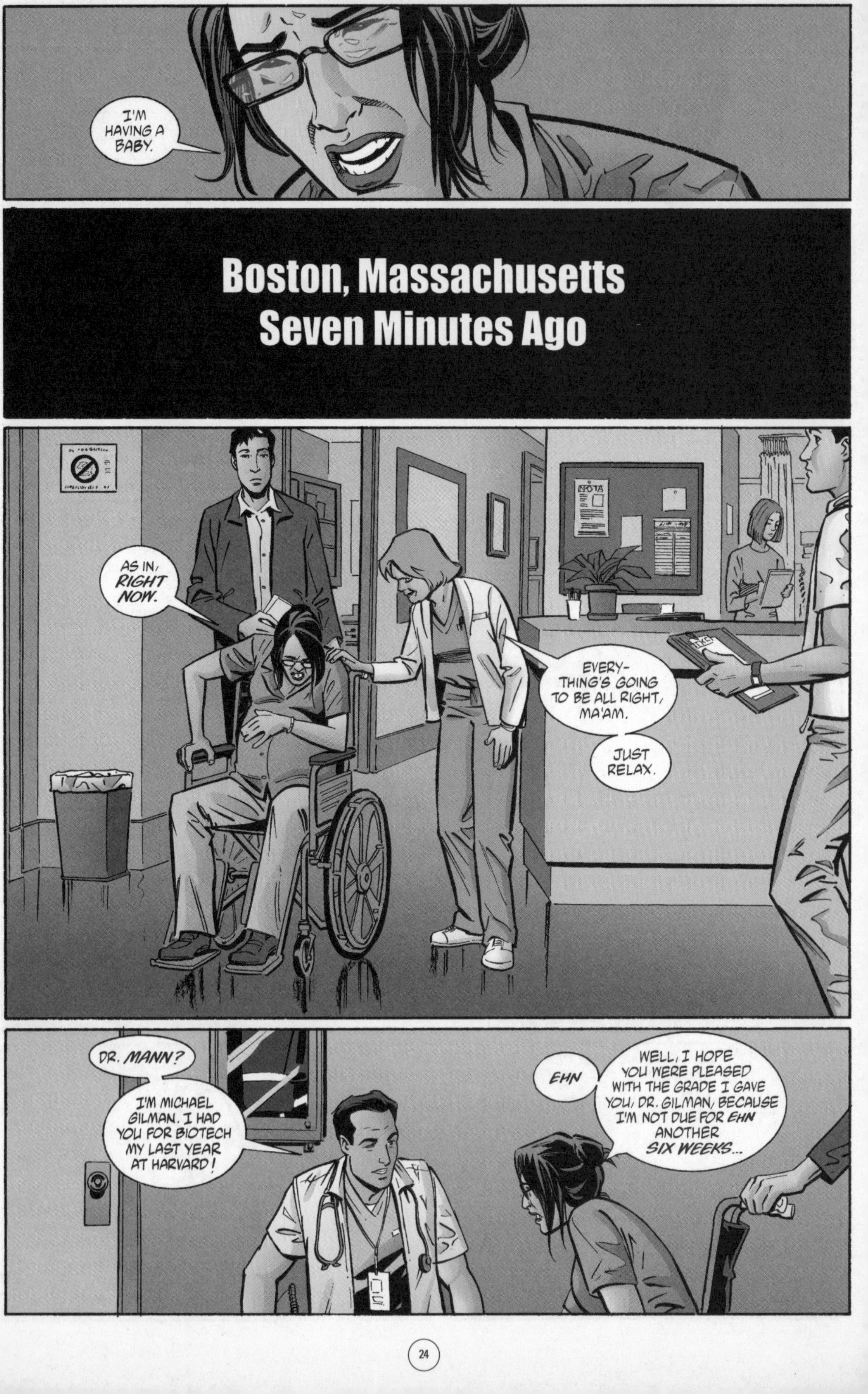
I'M HAVING A BABY.
Boston, Massachusetts
Seven Minutes Ago
AS IN, RIGHT NOW.
EVERY-THING'S GOING TO BE ALL RIGHT, MA'AM.
JUST RELAX.
DR. MANN?
I'M MICHAEL GILMAN. I HAD YOU FOR BIOTECH MY LAST YEAR AT HARVARD!
EHN
WELL, I HOPE YOU WERE PLEASED WITH THE GRADE I GAVE YOU, DR. GILMAN, BECAUSE I'M NOT DUE FOR EHN ANOTHER SIX WEEKS...

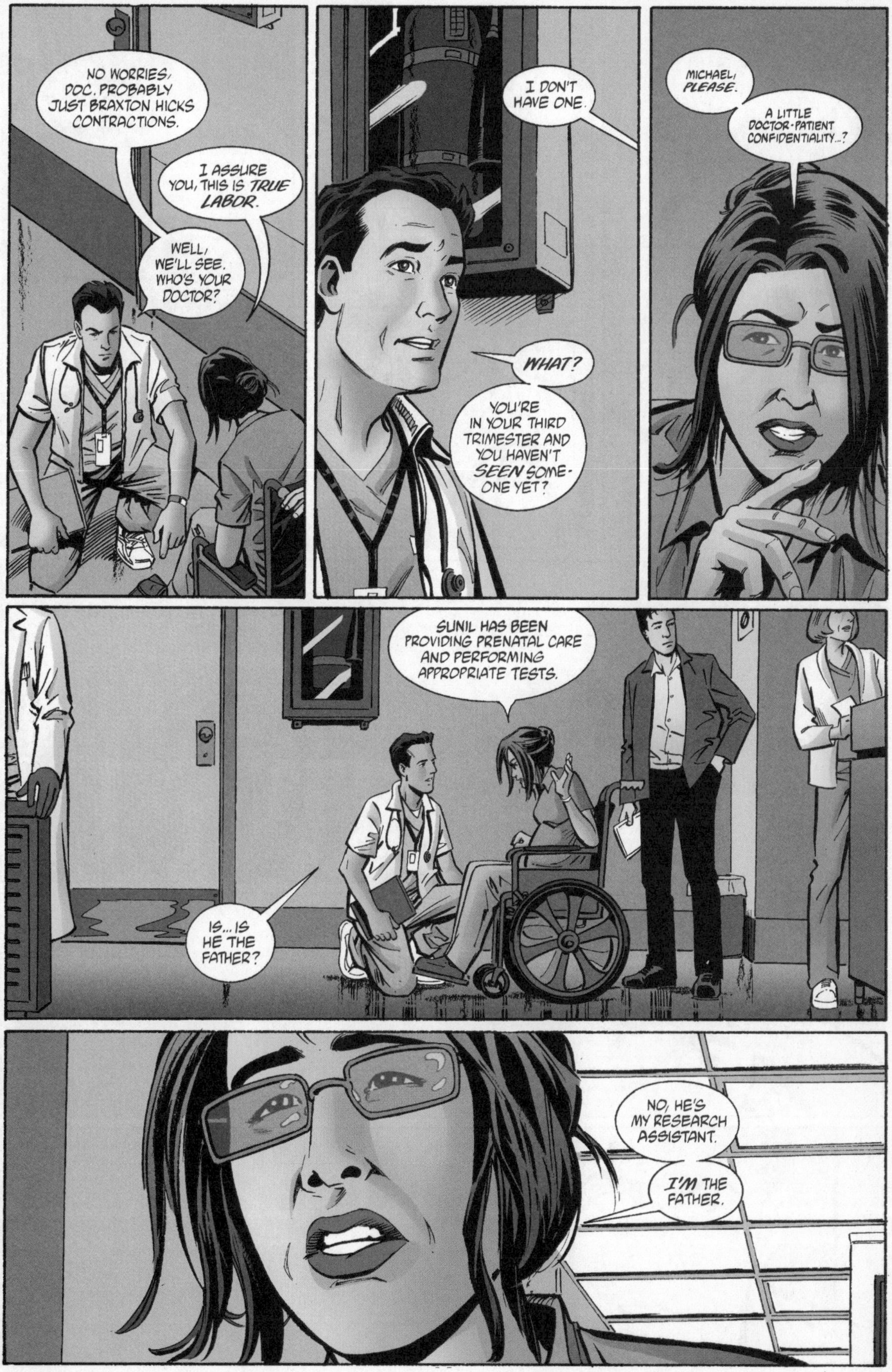
NO WORRIES, DOC. PROBABLY JUST BRAXTON HICKS CONTRACTIONS.
I ASSURE YOU, THIS IS TRUE LABOR.
WELL, WE'LL SEE. WHO'S YOUR DOCTOR?
I DON'T HAVE ONE.
WHAT?
YOU'RE IN YOUR THIRD TRIMESTER AND YOU HAVEN'T SEEN SOME-ONE YET?
MICHAEL, PLEASE.
A LITTLE DOCTOR-PATIENT CONFIDENTIALITY...?
SUNIL HAS BEEN PROVIDING PRENATAL CARE AND PERFORMING APPROPRIATE TESTS.
IS... IS HE THE FATHER?
NO, HE'S MY RESEARCH ASSISTANT.
I'M THE FATHER.

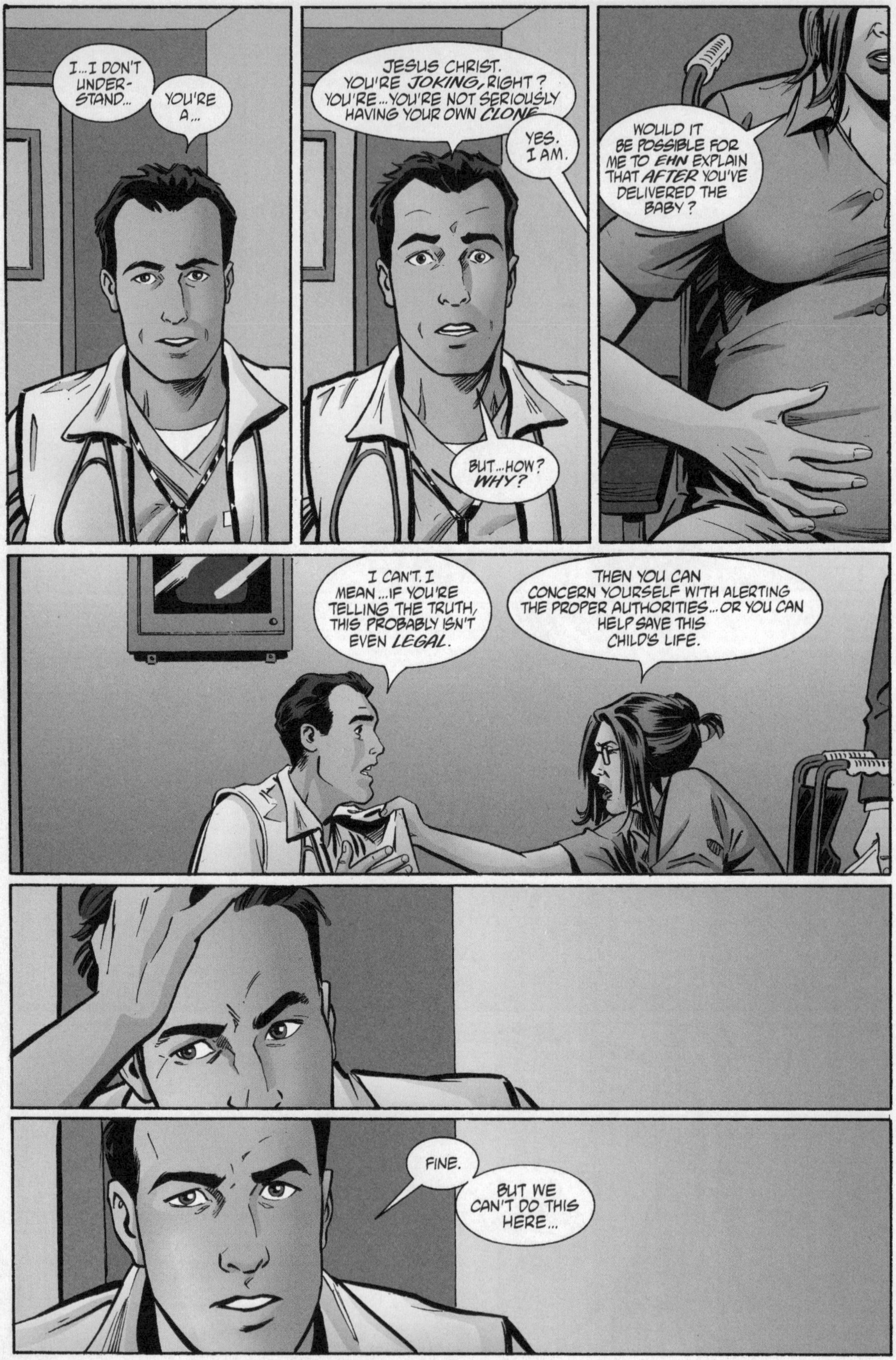
I...I DON'T UNDER-STAND...
YOU'RE A...
JESUS CHRIST. YOU'RE JOKING, RIGHT? YOU'RE...YOU'RE NOT SERIOUSLY HAVING YOUR OWN CLONE
YES. I AM.
BUT...HOW? WHY?
WOULD IT BE POSSIBLE FOR ME TO EHN EXPLAIN THAT AFTER YOU'VE DELIVERED THE BABY?
I CAN'T. I MEAN...IF YOU'RE TELLING THE TRUTH, THIS PROBABLY ISN'T EVEN LEGAL.
THEN YOU CAN CONCERN YOURSELF WITH ALERTING THE PROPER AUTHORITIES...OR YOU CAN HELP SAVE THIS CHILD'S LIFE.
FINE.
BUT WE CAN'T DO THIS HERE...

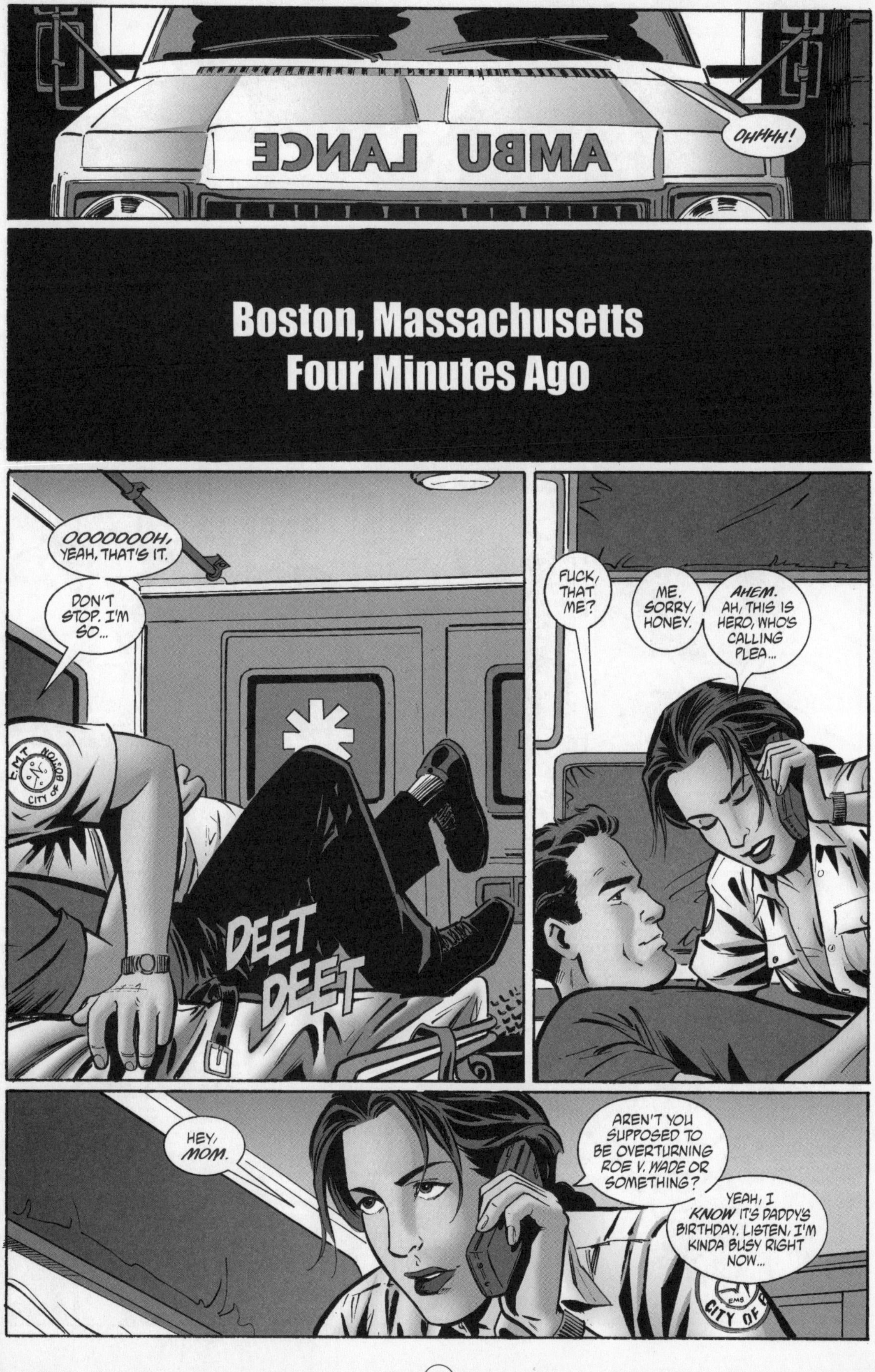
AMBU LANCE
OHHHH!
Boston, Massachusetts
Four Minutes Ago
OOOOOOOH, YEAH, THAT'S IT.
DON'T STOP. I'M SO...
DEET DEET
FUCK, THAT ME?
ME. SORRY, HONEY.
AHEM. AH, THIS IS HERO, WHO'S CALLING PLEA...
HEY, MOM.
AREN'T YOU SUPPOSED TO BE OVERTURNING ROE V. WADE OR SOMETHING?
YEAH, I KNOW IT'S DADDY'S BIRTHDAY. LISTEN, I'M KINDA BUSY RIGHT NOW...

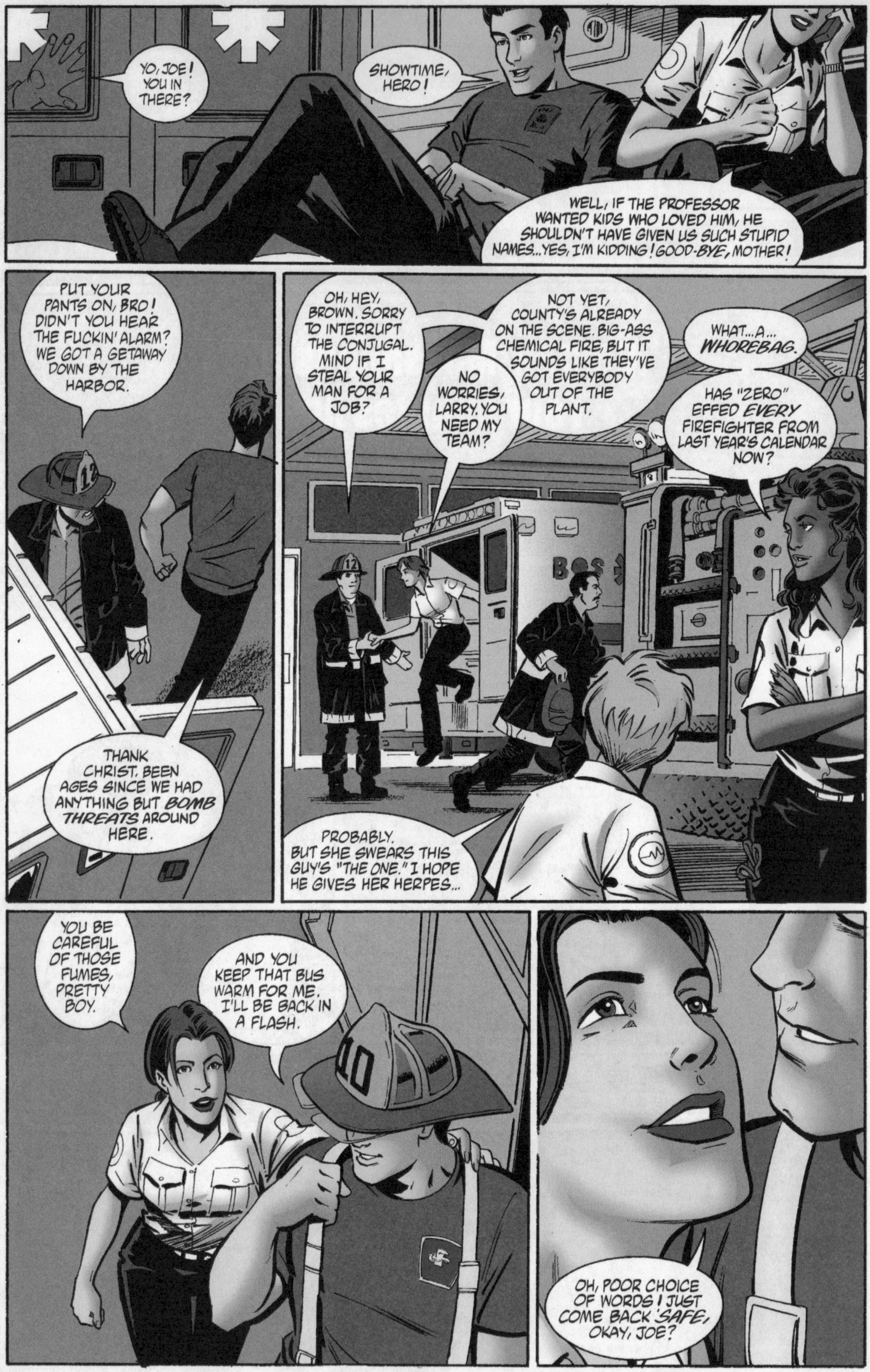
YO, JOE! YOU IN THERE?
SHOWTIME, HERO!
WELL, IF THE PROFESSOR WANTED KIDS WHO LOVED HIM, HE SHOULDN'T HAVE GIVEN US SUCH STUPID NAMES...YES, I'M KIDDING! GOOD-BYE, MOTHER!
PUT YOUR PANTS ON, BRO! DIDN'T YOU HEAR THE FUCKIN' ALARM? WE GOT A GETAWAY DOWN BY THE HARBOR.
THANK CHRIST. BEEN AGES SINCE WE HAD ANYTHING BUT BOMB THREATS AROUND HERE.
OH, HEY, BROWN. SORRY TO INTERRUPT THE CONJUGAL. MIND IF I STEAL YOUR MAN FOR A JOB?
NO WORRIES, LARRY. YOU NEED MY TEAM?
NOT YET, COUNTY'S ALREADY ON THE SCENE. BIG-ASS CHEMICAL FIRE, BUT IT SOUNDS LIKE THEY'VE GOT EVERYBODY OUT OF THE PLANT.
WHAT... A... WHOREBAG.
HAS "ZERO" EFFED EVERY FIREFIGHTER FROM LAST YEAR'S CALENDAR NOW?
PROBABLY. BUT SHE SWEARS THIS GUY'S "THE ONE." I HOPE HE GIVES HER HERPES...
YOU BE CAREFUL OF THOSE FUMES, PRETTY BOY.
AND YOU KEEP THAT BUS WARM FOR ME. I'LL BE BACK IN A FLASH.
OH, POOR CHOICE OF WORDS! JUST COME BACK 'SAFE, OKAY, JOE?

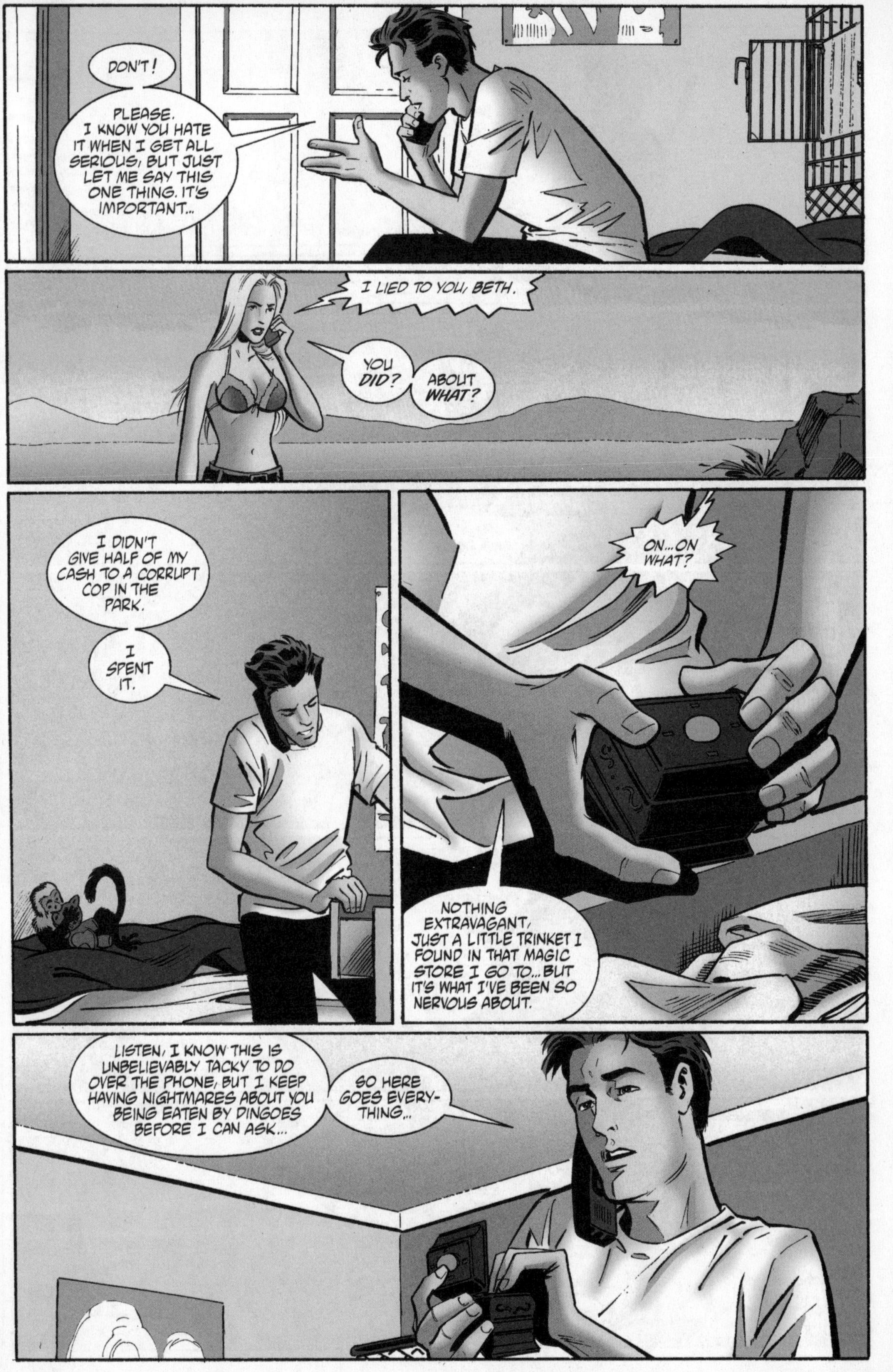
DON'T!
PLEASE. I KNOW YOU HATE IT WHEN I GET ALL SERIOUS, BUT JUST LET ME SAY THIS ONE THING. IT'S IMPORTANT...
I LIED TO YOU, BETH.
YOU DID?
ABOUT WHAT?
I DIDN'T GIVE HALF OF MY CASH TO A CORRUPT COP IN THE PARK.
I SPENT IT.
ON...ON WHAT?
NOTHING EXTRAVAGANT, JUST A LITTLE TRINKET I FOUND IN THAT MAGIC STORE I GO TO...BUT IT'S WHAT I'VE BEEN SO NERVOUS ABOUT.
LISTEN, I KNOW THIS IS UNBELIEVABLY TACKY TO DO OVER THE PHONE, BUT I KEEP HAVING NIGHTMARES ABOUT YOU BEING EATEN BY DINGOES BEFORE I CAN ASK...
SO HERE GOES EVERY-THING...

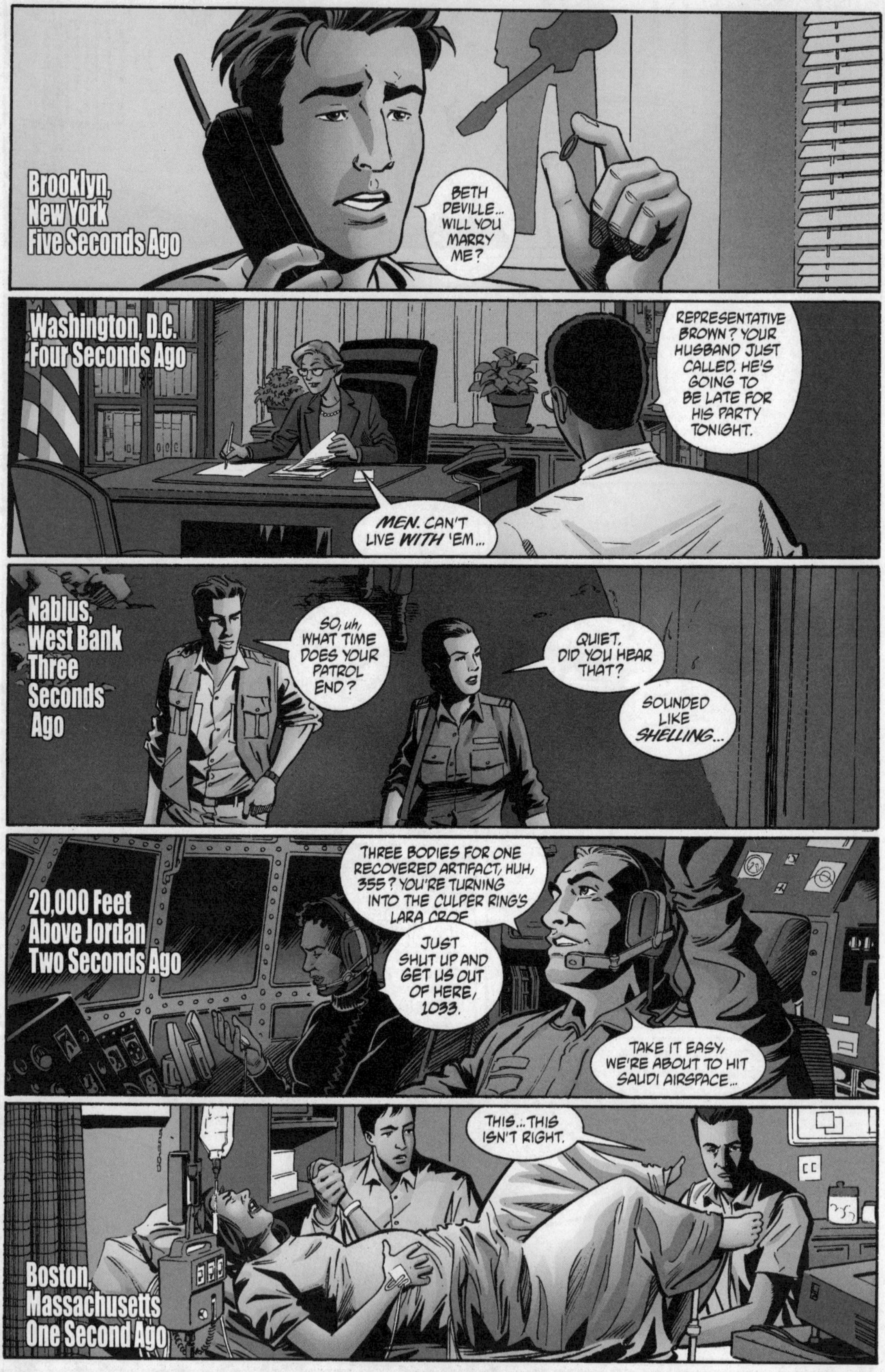

Brooklyn, New York Five Seconds Ago
BETH DEVILLE... WILL YOU MARRY ME?
Washington, D.C. Four Seconds Ago
REPRESENTATIVE BROWN? YOUR HUSBAND JUST CALLED. HE'S GOING TO BE LATE FOR HIS PARTY TONIGHT.
MEN. CAN'T LIVE WITH 'EM...
Nablus, West Bank Three Seconds Ago
SO, uh, WHAT TIME DOES YOUR PATROL END?
QUIET. DID YOU HEAR THAT?
SOUNDED LIKE SHELLING...
20,000 Feet Above Jordan Two Seconds Ago
THREE BODIES FOR ONE RECOVERED ARTIFACT, HUH, 355? YOU'RE TURNING INTO THE CULPER RING'S LARA CROF
JUST SHUT UP AND GET US OUT OF HERE, 1033.
TAKE IT EASY, WE'RE ABOUT TO HIT SAUDI AIRSPACE...
Boston, Massachusetts One Second Ago
THIS... THIS ISN'T RIGHT.

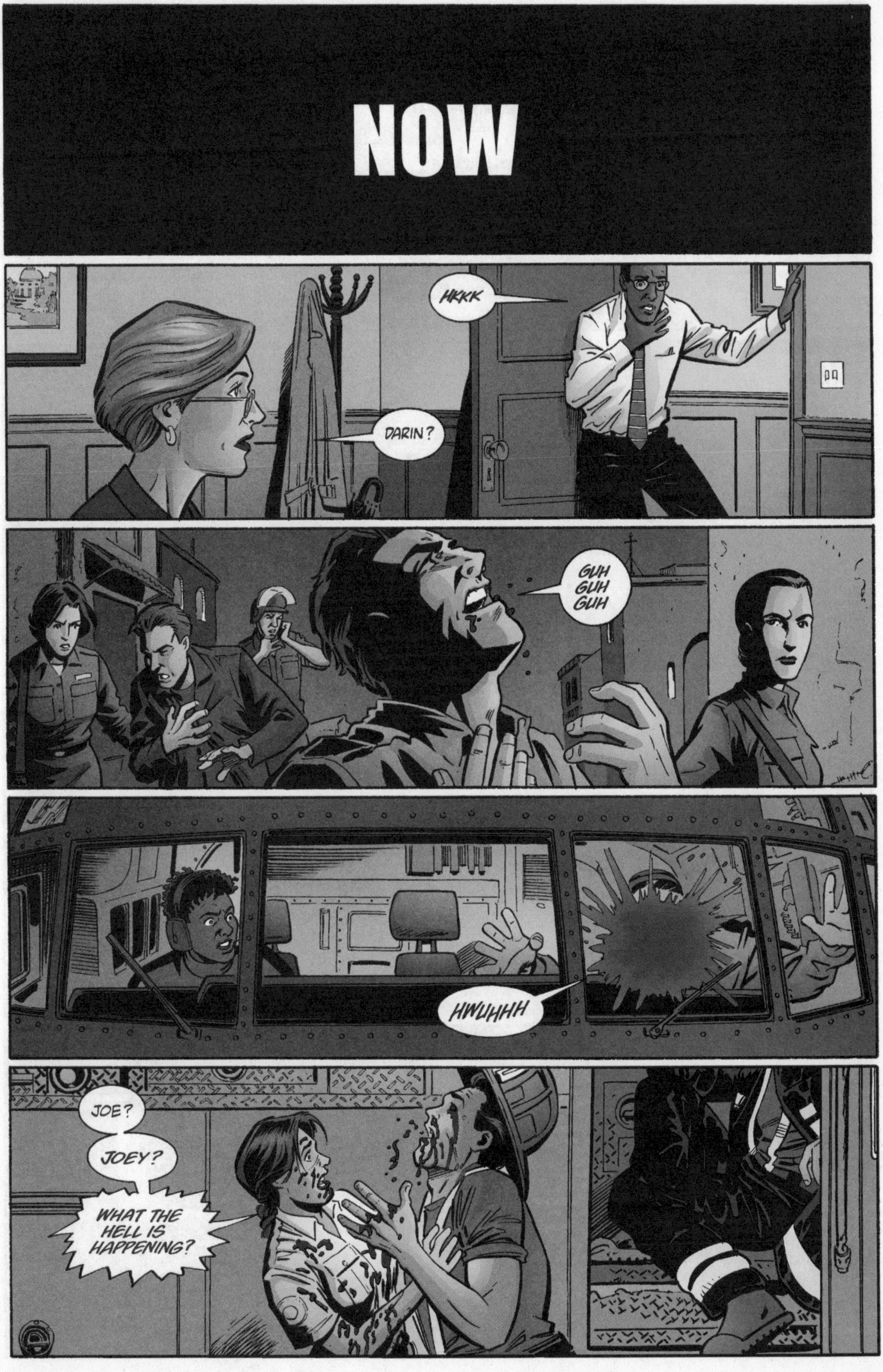
NOW
HRKK
DARIN?
GUH GUH GUH
HWUHHH
JOE?
JOEY?
WHAT THE HELL IS HAPPENING?

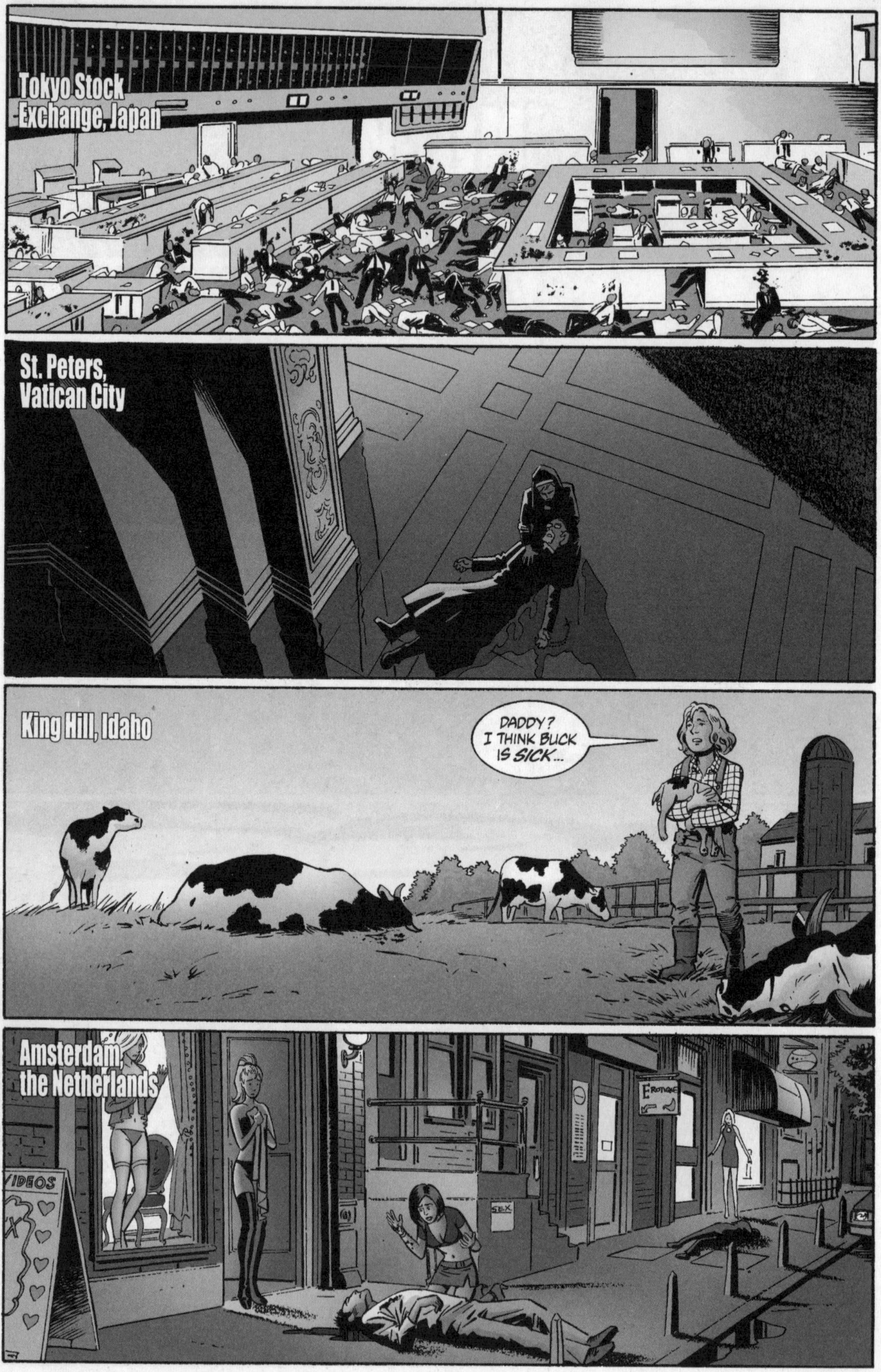
Tokyo Stock Exchange, Japan
St. Peters, Vatican City
King Hill, Idaho
DADDY? I THINK BUCK IS SICK...
Amsterdam, the Netherlands
VIDEOS
SEX

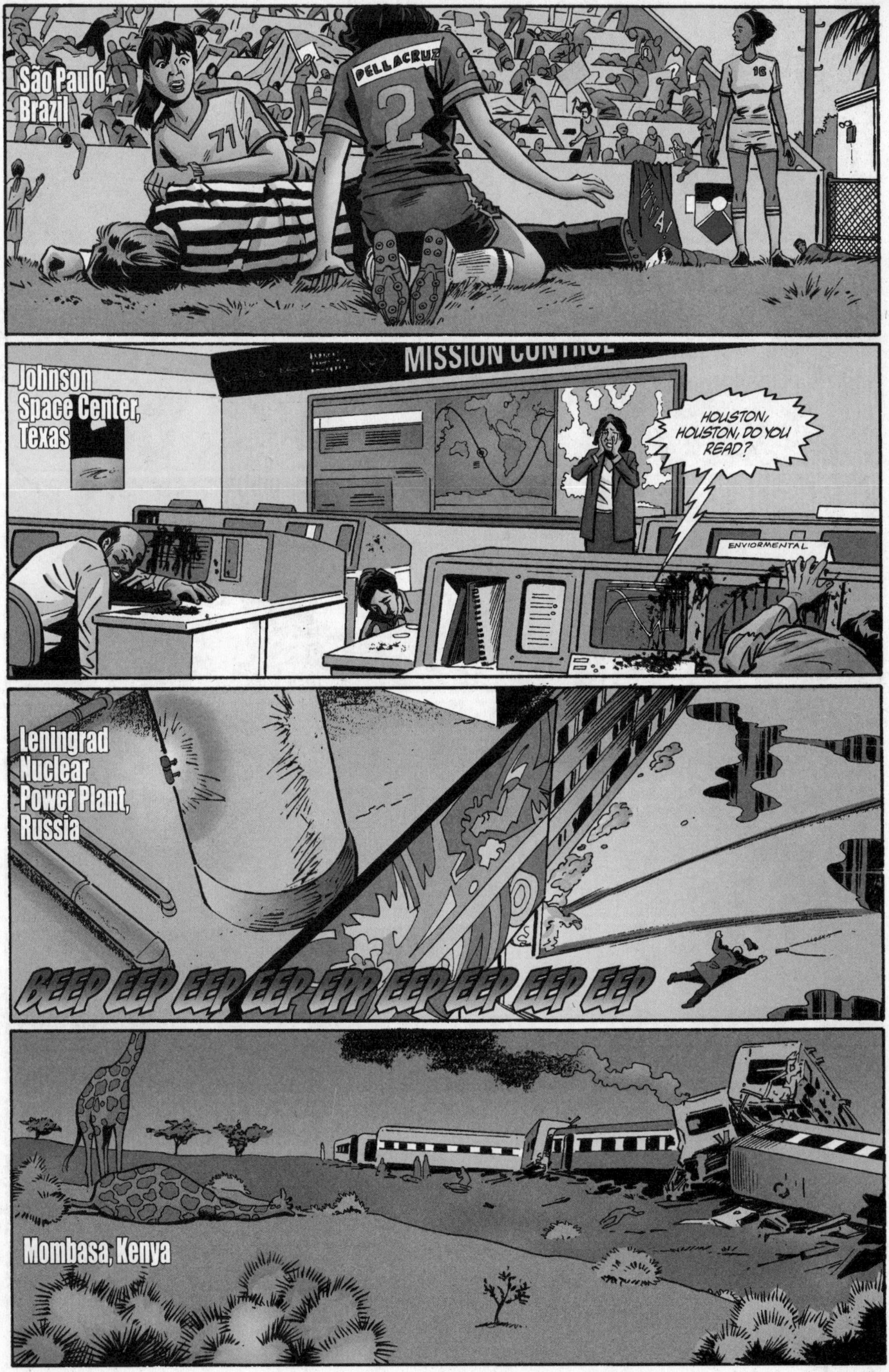
São Paulo, Brazil
DELLACRUZ
2
71
16
VIVA!
MISSION CONTROL
Johnson Space Center, Texas
HOUSTON, HOUSTON, DO YOU READ?
ENVIORMENTAL
Leningrad Nuclear Power Plant, Russia
BEEP EEP EEP EEP EPP EEP EEP EEP EEP
Mombasa, Kenya

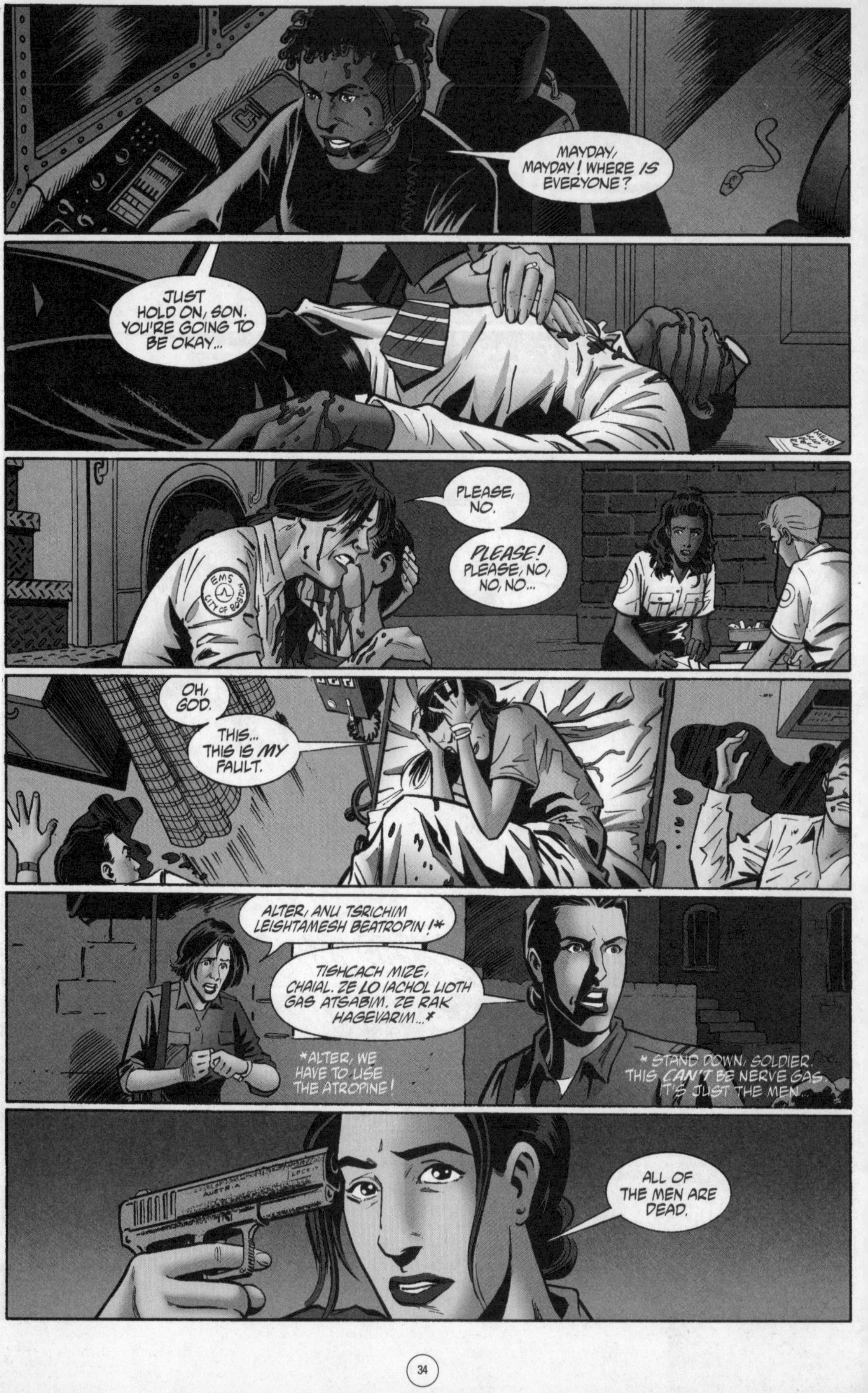
MAYDAY, MAYDAY! WHERE IS EVERYONE?
JUST HOLD ON, SON. YOU'RE GOING TO BE OKAY...
EMS CITY OF BOSTON
PLEASE, NO.
PLEASE! PLEASE, NO, NO, NO...
OH, GOD.
THIS... THIS IS MY FAULT.
ALTER, ANU TSRICHIM LEISHTAMESH BEATROPIN!*
TISHCACH MIZE, CHAIAL. ZE LO IACHOL LIOTH GAS ATSABIM. ZE RAK HAGEVARIM...*
*ALTER, WE HAVE TO USE THE ATROPINE!
* STAND DOWN, SOLDIER. THIS CAN'T BE NERVE GAS. IT'S JUST THE MEN...
AUSTRIA
ALL OF THE MEN ARE DEAD.

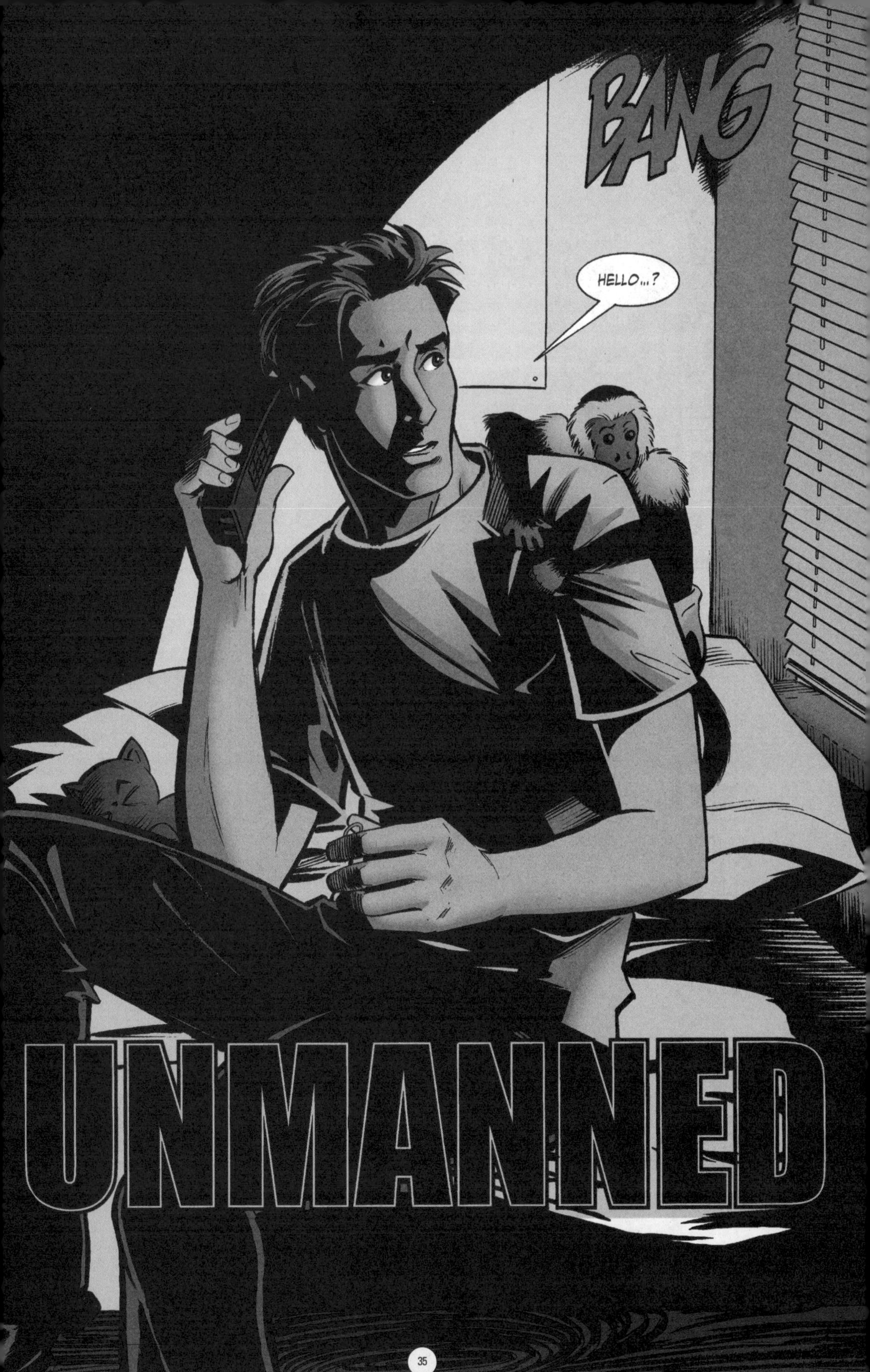
BANG
HELLO...?
UNMANNED

WELCOME TO THE UNMANNED WORLD

Y THE LAST MAN

In the summer of 2002, a plague of unknown origin destroyed every last sperm, fetus, and fully developed mammal with a Y chromosome (with the apparent exception of one young man and his male pet).

This "gendercide" instantaneously exterminated 48% of the global population, or approximately 2.9 billion men. 495 of the Fortune 500 CEOs are now dead, as are 99% of the world's landowners.

In the United States alone, more than 95% of all commercial pilots, truck drivers, and ship captains died... as did 92% of violent felons.

Internationally, 99% of all mechanics, electricians, and construction workers are now deceased...though 51% of the planet's *agricultural* labor force is still alive.

14 nations, including Spain and Germany, have women soldiers who have served in ground combat units. *None* of the United States' nearly 200,000 female troops have ever participated in ground combat. Australia, Norway and Sweden are the only countries that have women serving on board submarines.

In Israel, all women between the ages of 18 and 26 have performed compulsory military service in the IDF for at least one year and nine months. Before the Plague, at least three Palestinian suicide bombers had been women.

Worldwide, 85% of all government representatives are now dead... as are 100% of Catholic priests, Muslim imams and Orthodox Jewish rabbis.

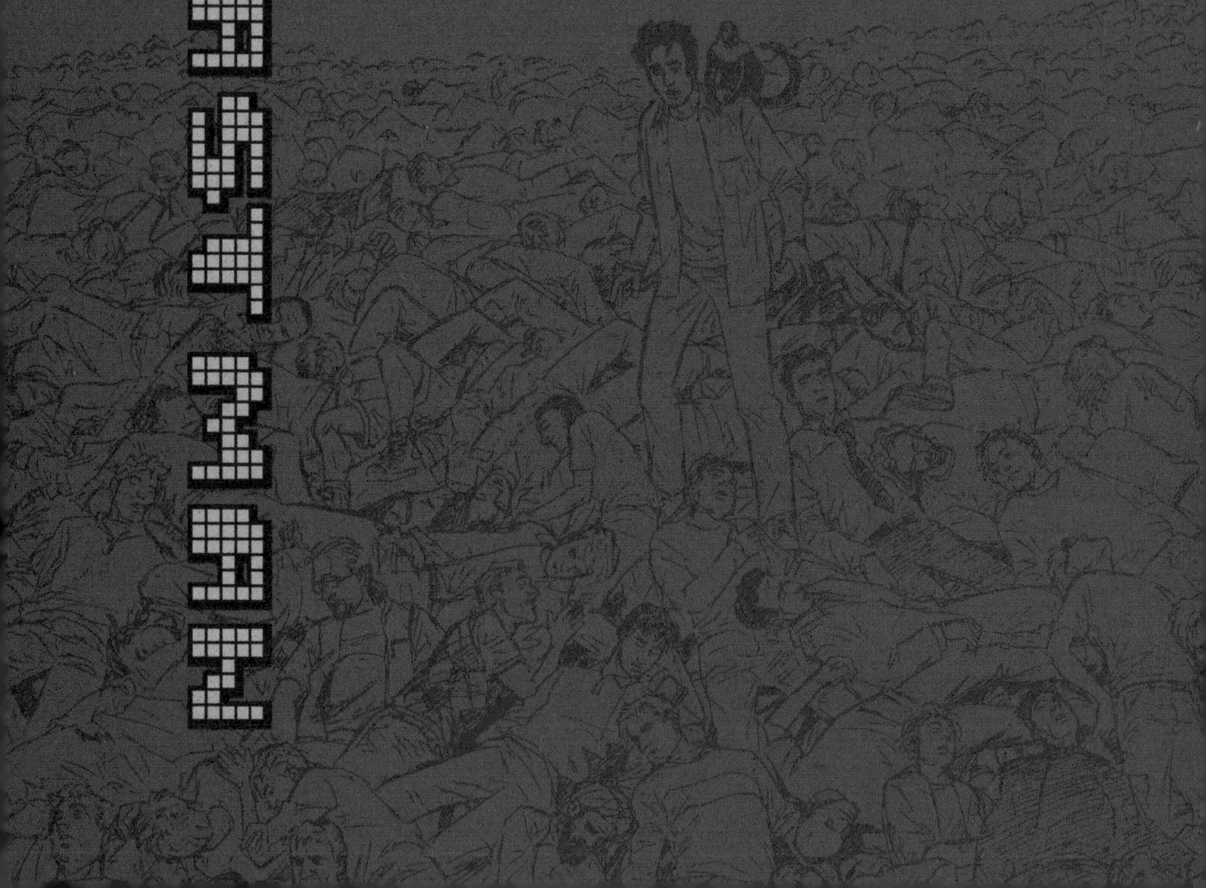

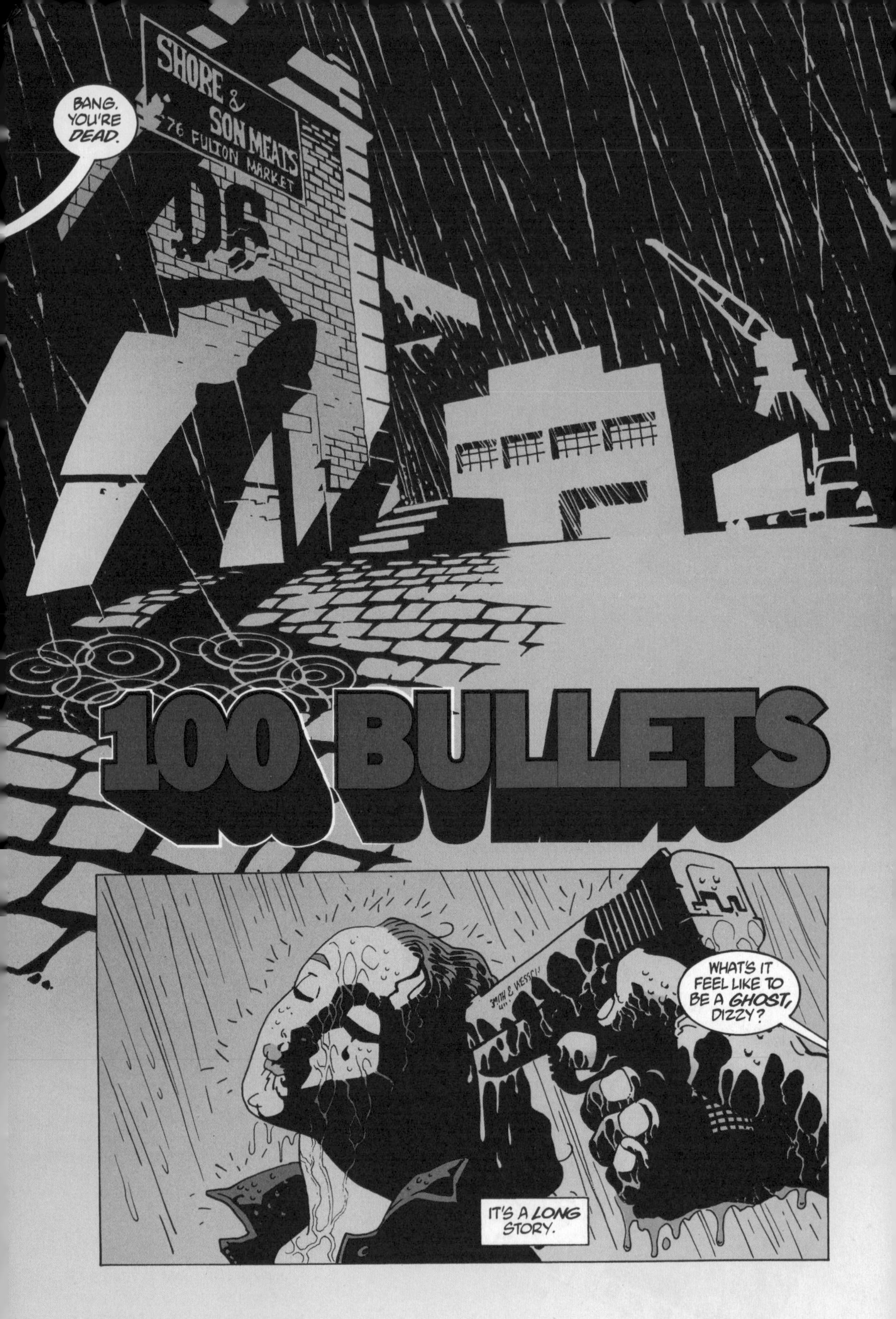
SHORE & SON MEATS
76 FULTON MARKET
BANG, YOU'RE *DEAD.*
100 BULLETS
WHAT'S IT FEEL LIKE TO BE A *GHOST,* DIZZY?
IT'S A *LONG* STORY.

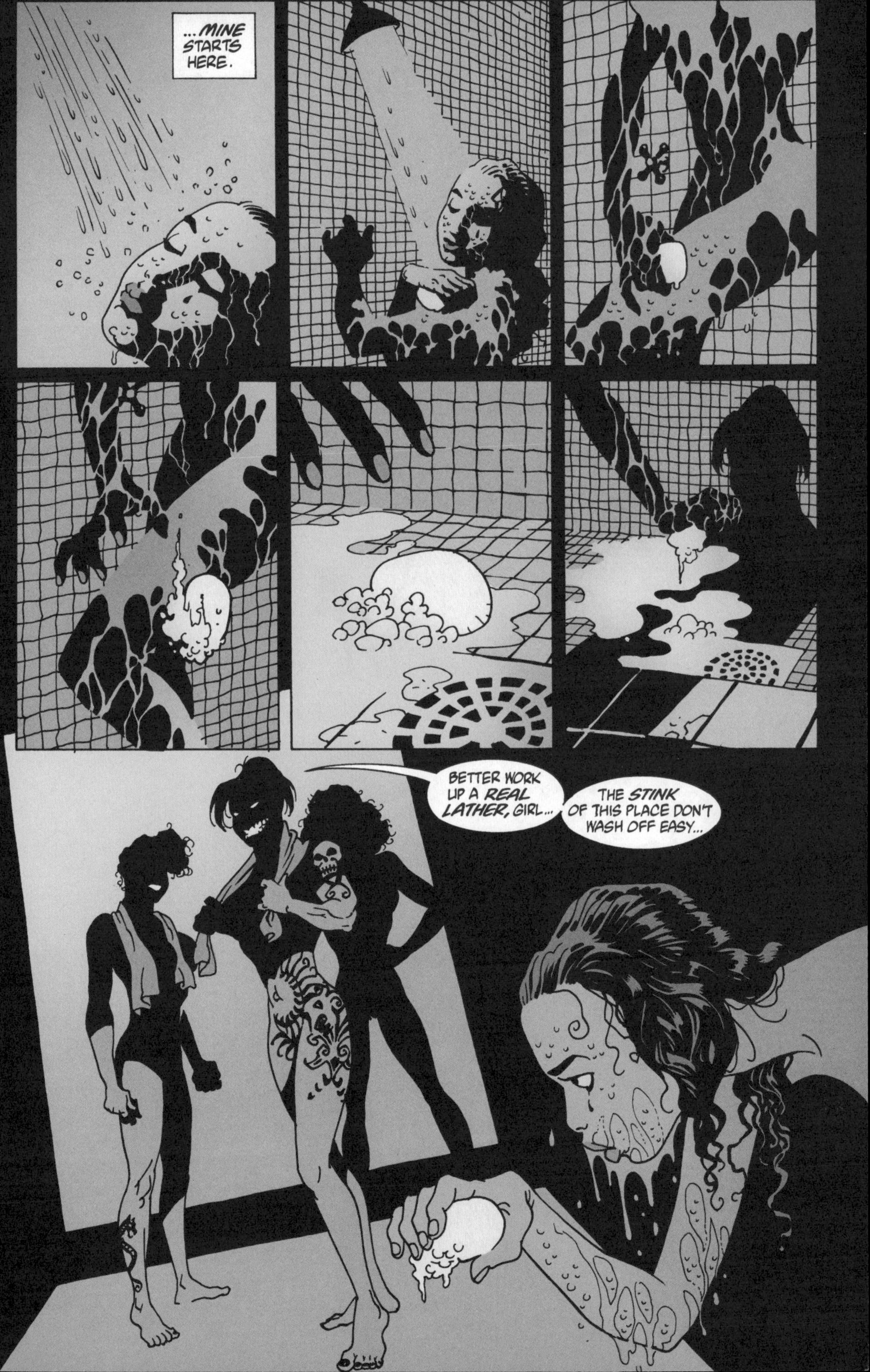
...MINE STARTS HERE.
BETTER WORK UP A REAL LATHER, GIRL...
THE STINK OF THIS PLACE DON'T WASH OFF EASY...

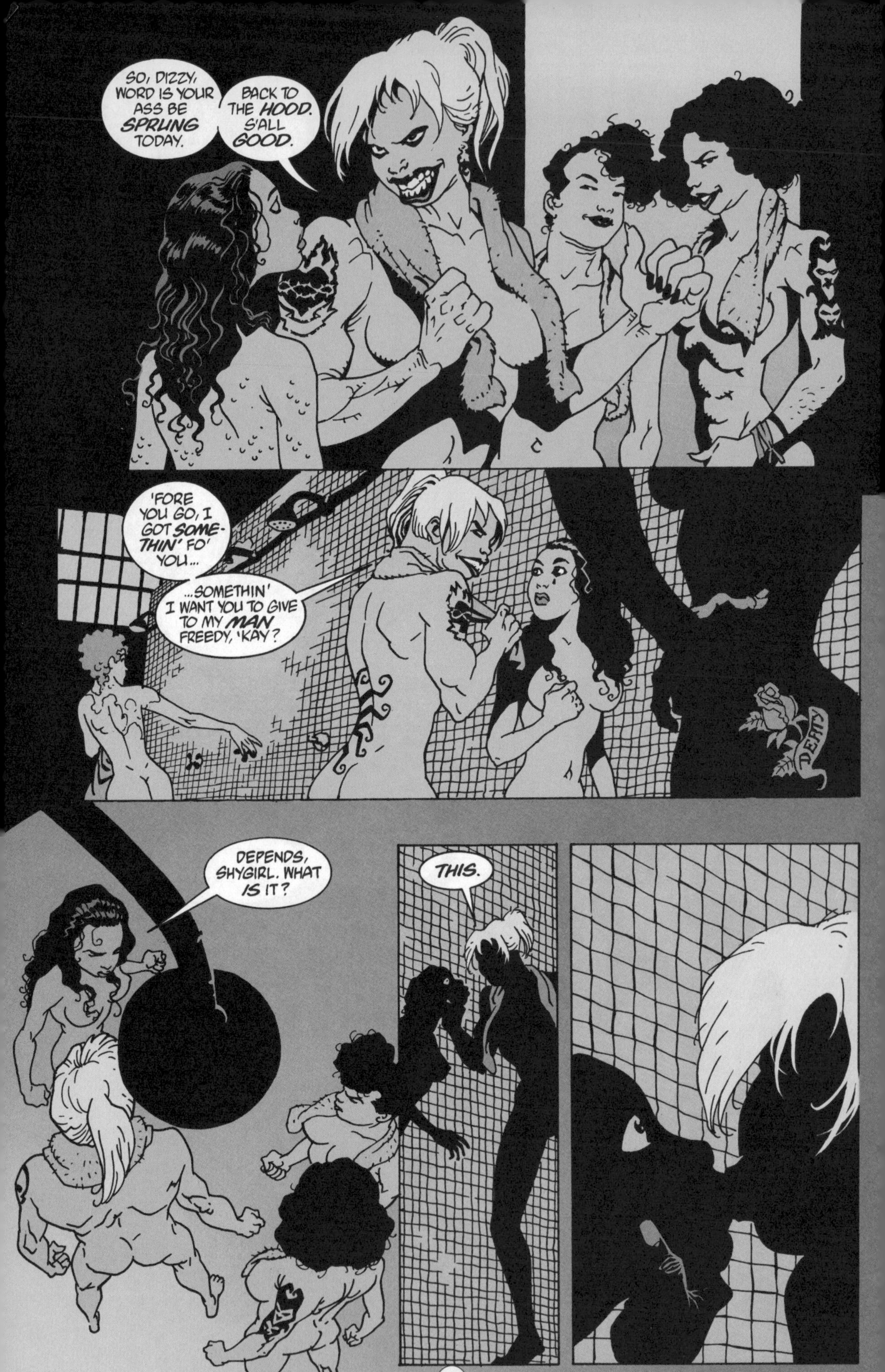
SO, DIZZY, WORD IS YOUR ASS BE SPRUNG TODAY.
BACK TO THE HOOD. S'ALL GOOD.
'FORE YOU GO, I GOT SOME-THIN' FO' YOU...
...SOMETHIN' I WANT YOU TO GIVE TO MY MAN FREEDY, 'KAY?
DEPENDS, SHYGIRL. WHAT IS IT?
THIS.

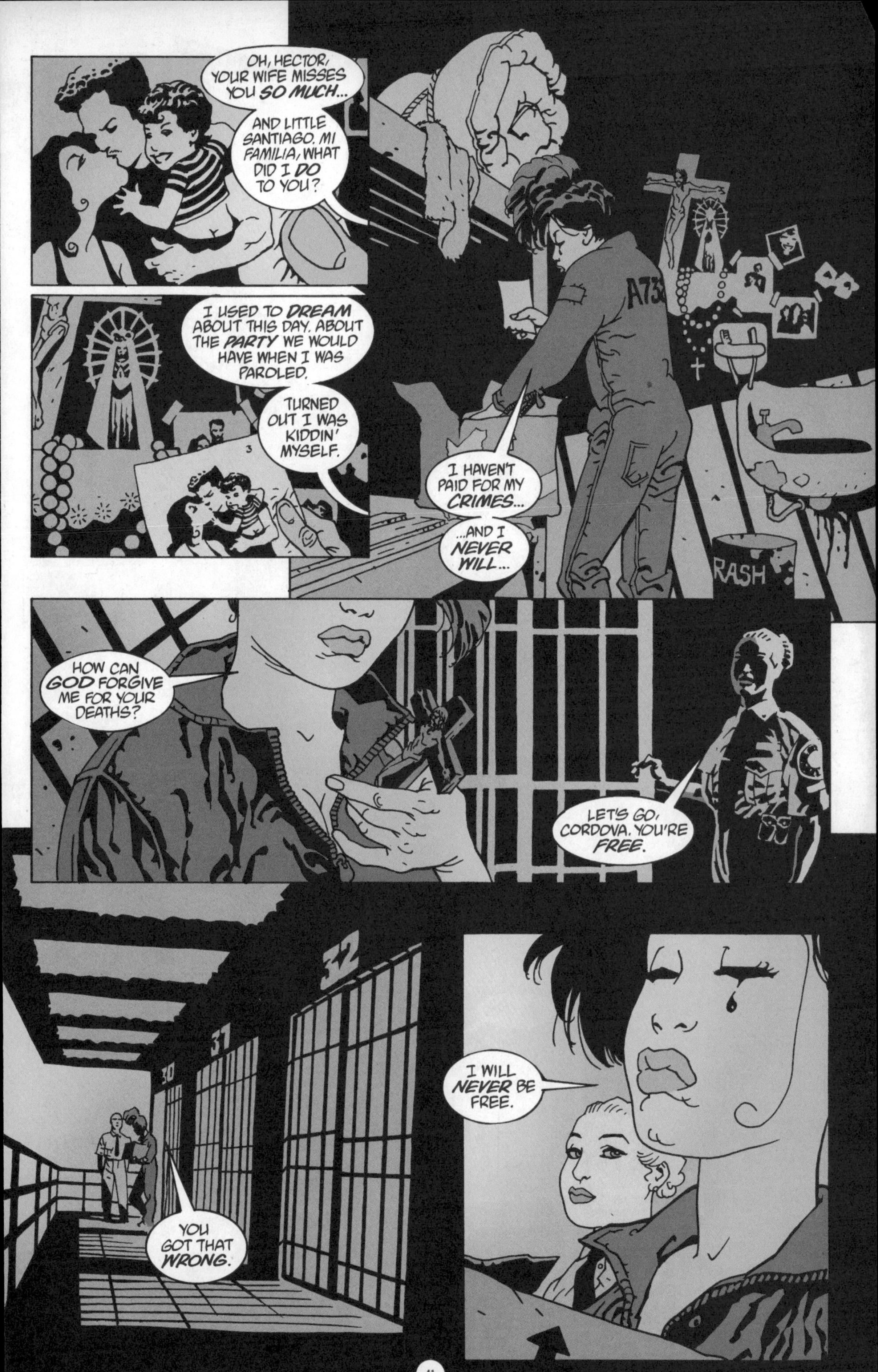
OH, HECTOR, YOUR WIFE MISSES YOU SO MUCH...
AND LITTLE SANTIAGO. MI FAMILIA, WHAT DID I DO TO YOU?
I USED TO DREAM ABOUT THIS DAY. ABOUT THE PARTY WE WOULD HAVE WHEN I WAS PAROLED.
TURNED OUT I WAS KIDDIN' MYSELF.
I HAVEN'T PAID FOR MY CRIMES...
...AND I NEVER WILL...
RASH
HOW CAN GOD FORGIVE ME FOR YOUR DEATHS?
LET'S GO, CORDOVA. YOU'RE FREE.
32
31
30
YOU GOT THAT WRONG.
I WILL NEVER BE FREE.

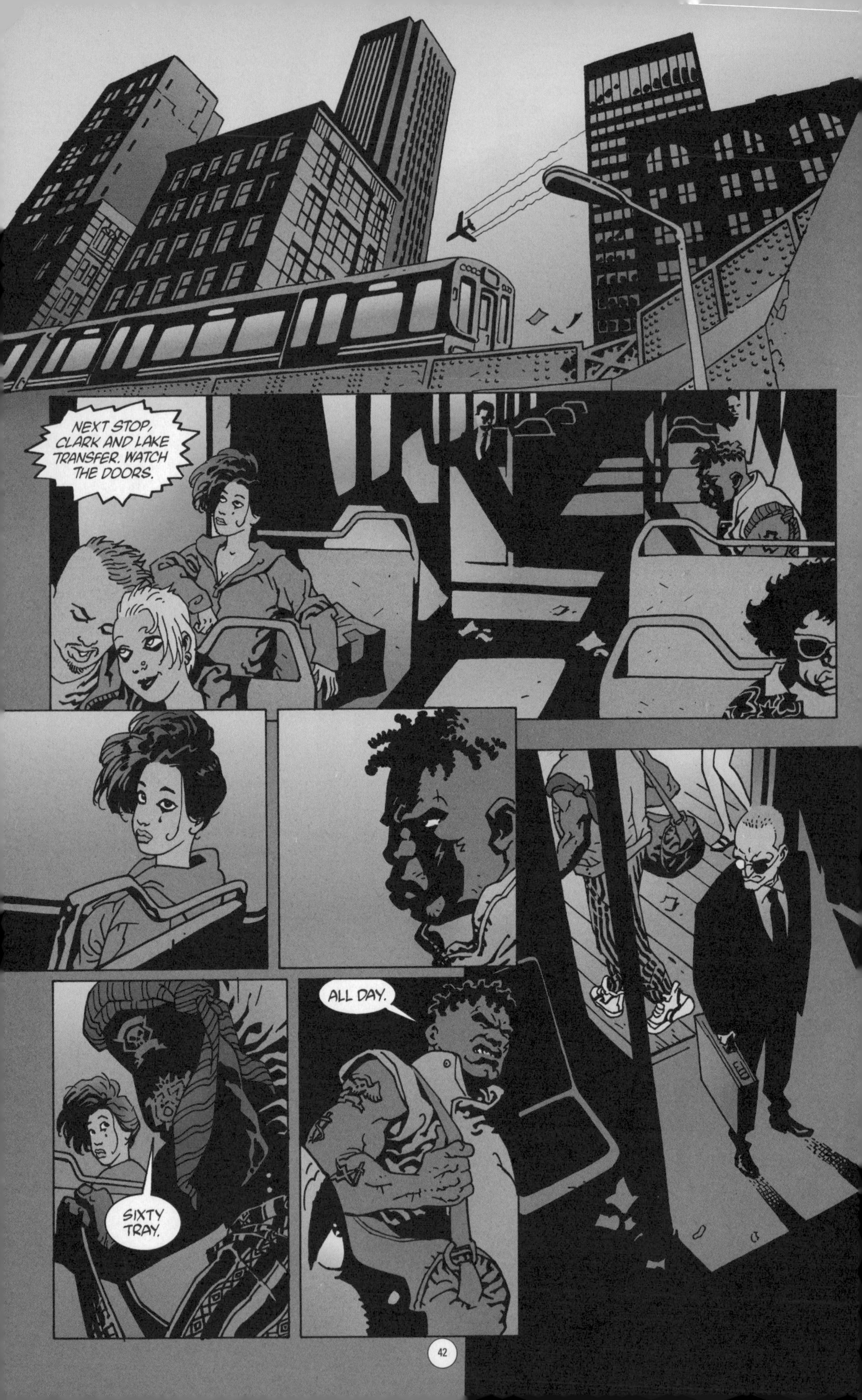
NEXT STOP, CLARK AND LAKE TRANSFER. WATCH THE DOORS.
ALL DAY.
SIXTY TRAY.

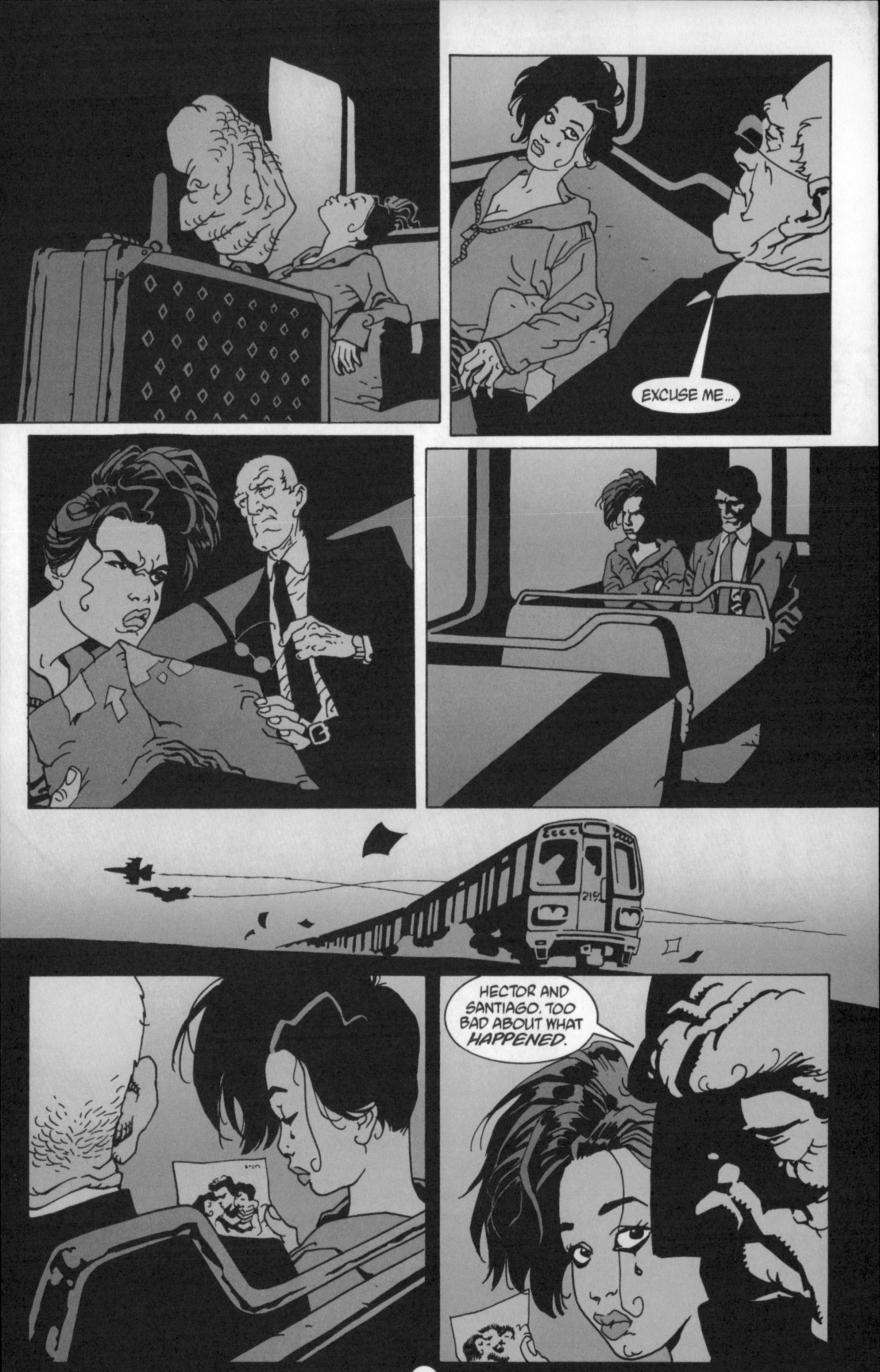
EXCUSE ME...
HECTOR AND SANTIAGO. TOO BAD ABOUT WHAT *HAPPENED*.

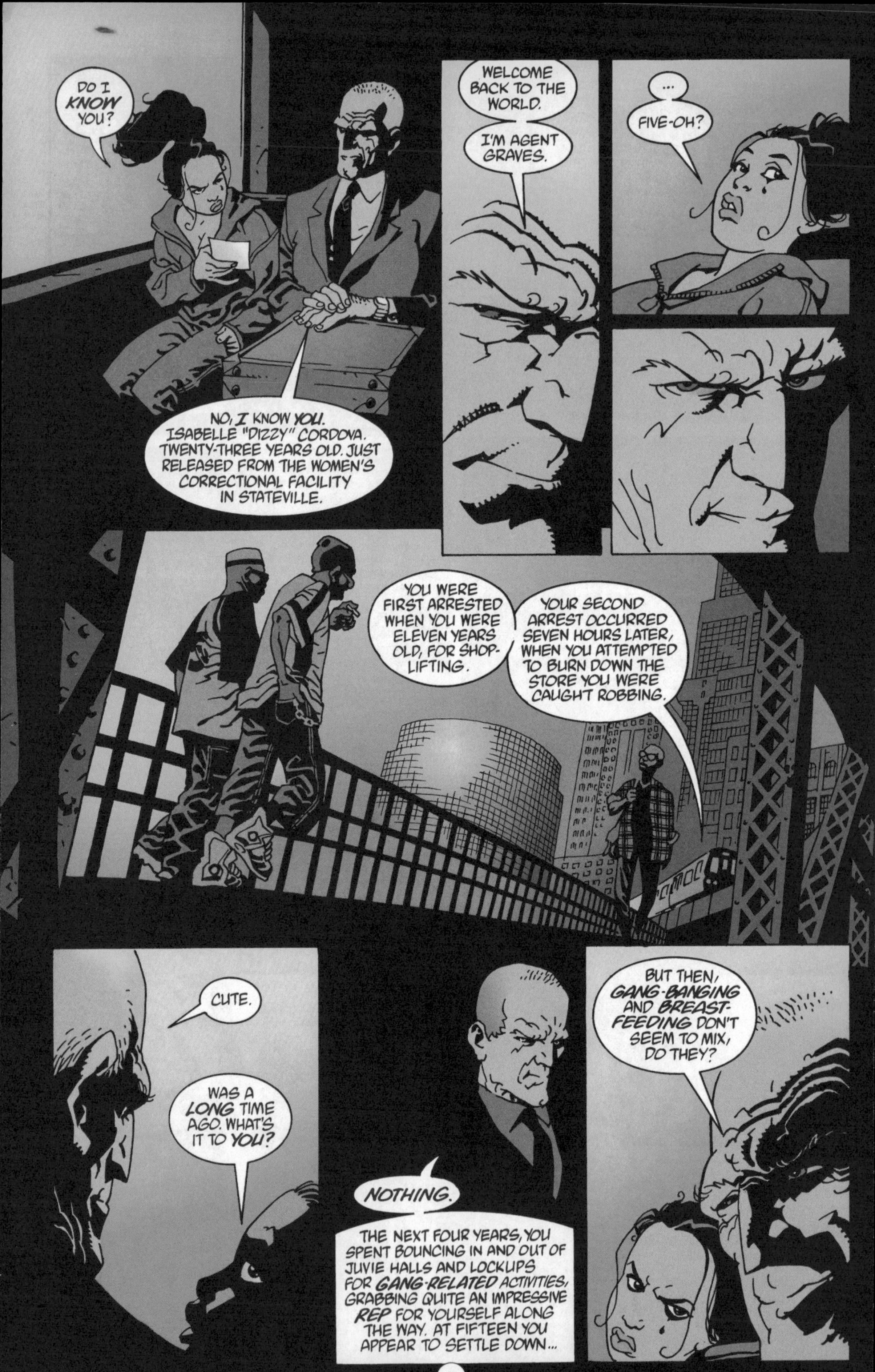
DO I KNOW YOU?
NO, I KNOW YOU. ISABELLE "DIZZY" CORDOVA. TWENTY-THREE YEARS OLD. JUST RELEASED FROM THE WOMEN'S CORRECTIONAL FACILITY IN STATEVILLE.
WELCOME BACK TO THE WORLD.
I'M AGENT GRAVES.
...
FIVE-OH?
YOU WERE FIRST ARRESTED WHEN YOU WERE ELEVEN YEARS OLD, FOR SHOP-LIFTING.
YOUR SECOND ARREST OCCURRED SEVEN HOURS LATER, WHEN YOU ATTEMPTED TO BURN DOWN THE STORE YOU WERE CAUGHT ROBBING.
CUTE.
WAS A LONG TIME AGO. WHAT'S IT TO YOU?
NOTHING.
THE NEXT FOUR YEARS, YOU SPENT BOUNCING IN AND OUT OF JUVIE HALLS AND LOCKUPS FOR GANG-RELATED ACTIVITIES, GRABBING QUITE AN IMPRESSIVE REP FOR YOURSELF ALONG THE WAY. AT FIFTEEN YOU APPEAR TO SETTLE DOWN...
BUT THEN, GANG-BANGING AND BREAST-FEEDING DON'T SEEM TO MIX, DO THEY?

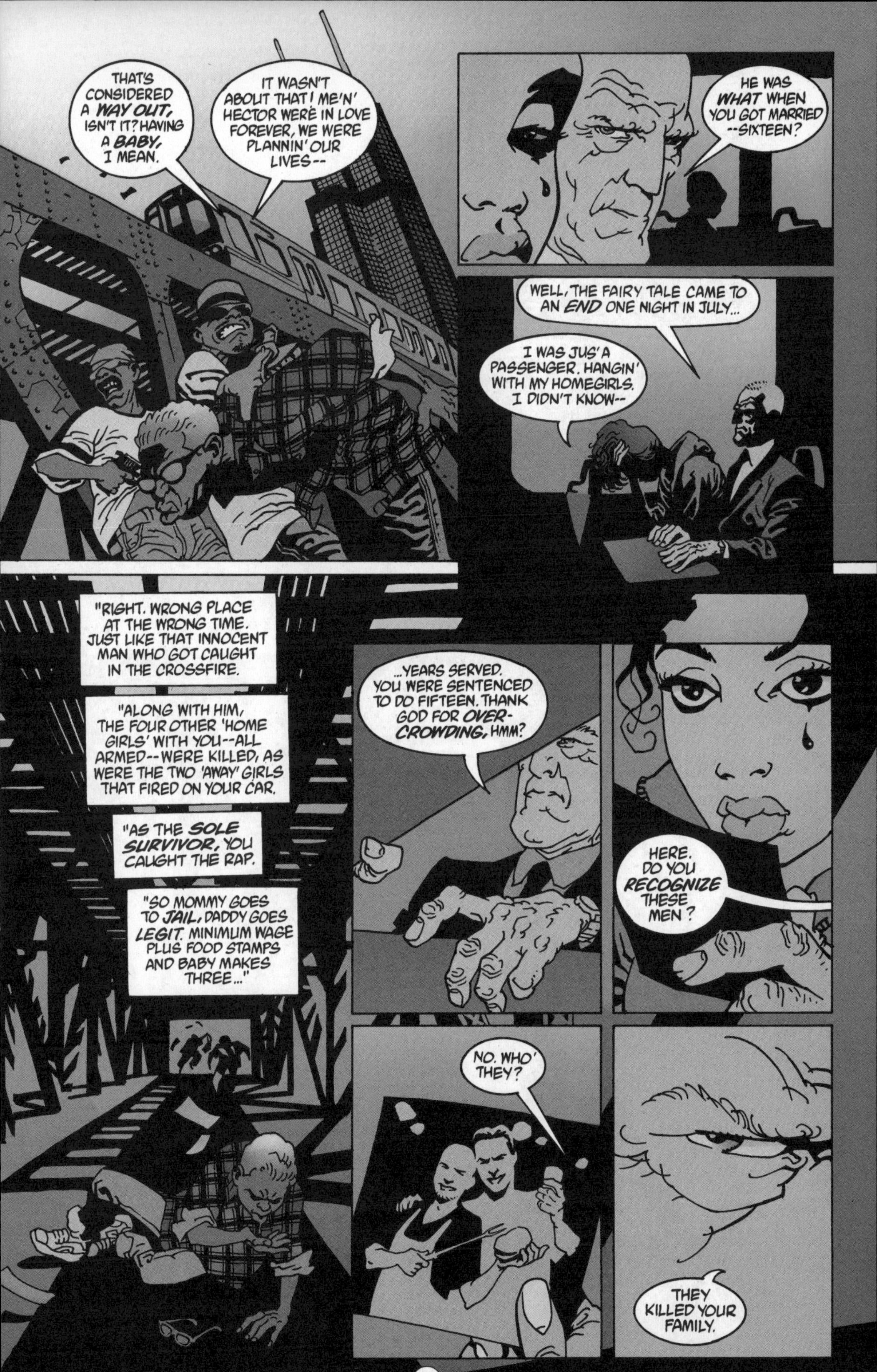
THAT'S CONSIDERED A WAY OUT, ISN'T IT? HAVING A BABY, I MEAN.
IT WASN'T ABOUT THAT! ME'N' HECTOR WERE IN LOVE FOREVER, WE WERE PLANNIN' OUR LIVES--
HE WAS WHAT WHEN YOU GOT MARRIED --SIXTEEN?
WELL, THE FAIRY TALE CAME TO AN END ONE NIGHT IN JULY...
I WAS JUS' A PASSENGER. HANGIN' WITH MY HOMEGIRLS. I DIDN'T KNOW--
"RIGHT. WRONG PLACE AT THE WRONG TIME. JUST LIKE THAT INNOCENT MAN WHO GOT CAUGHT IN THE CROSSFIRE.
"ALONG WITH HIM, THE FOUR OTHER 'HOME GIRLS' WITH YOU--ALL ARMED--WERE KILLED, AS WERE THE TWO 'AWAY' GIRLS THAT FIRED ON YOUR CAR.
"AS THE SOLE SURVIVOR, YOU CAUGHT THE RAP.
"SO MOMMY GOES TO JAIL, DADDY GOES LEGIT. MINIMUM WAGE PLUS FOOD STAMPS AND BABY MAKES THREE..."
...YEARS SERVED. YOU WERE SENTENCED TO DO FIFTEEN. THANK GOD FOR OVER-CROWDING, HMM?
HERE. DO YOU RECOGNIZE THESE MEN?
NO. WHO' THEY?
THEY KILLED YOUR FAMILY.

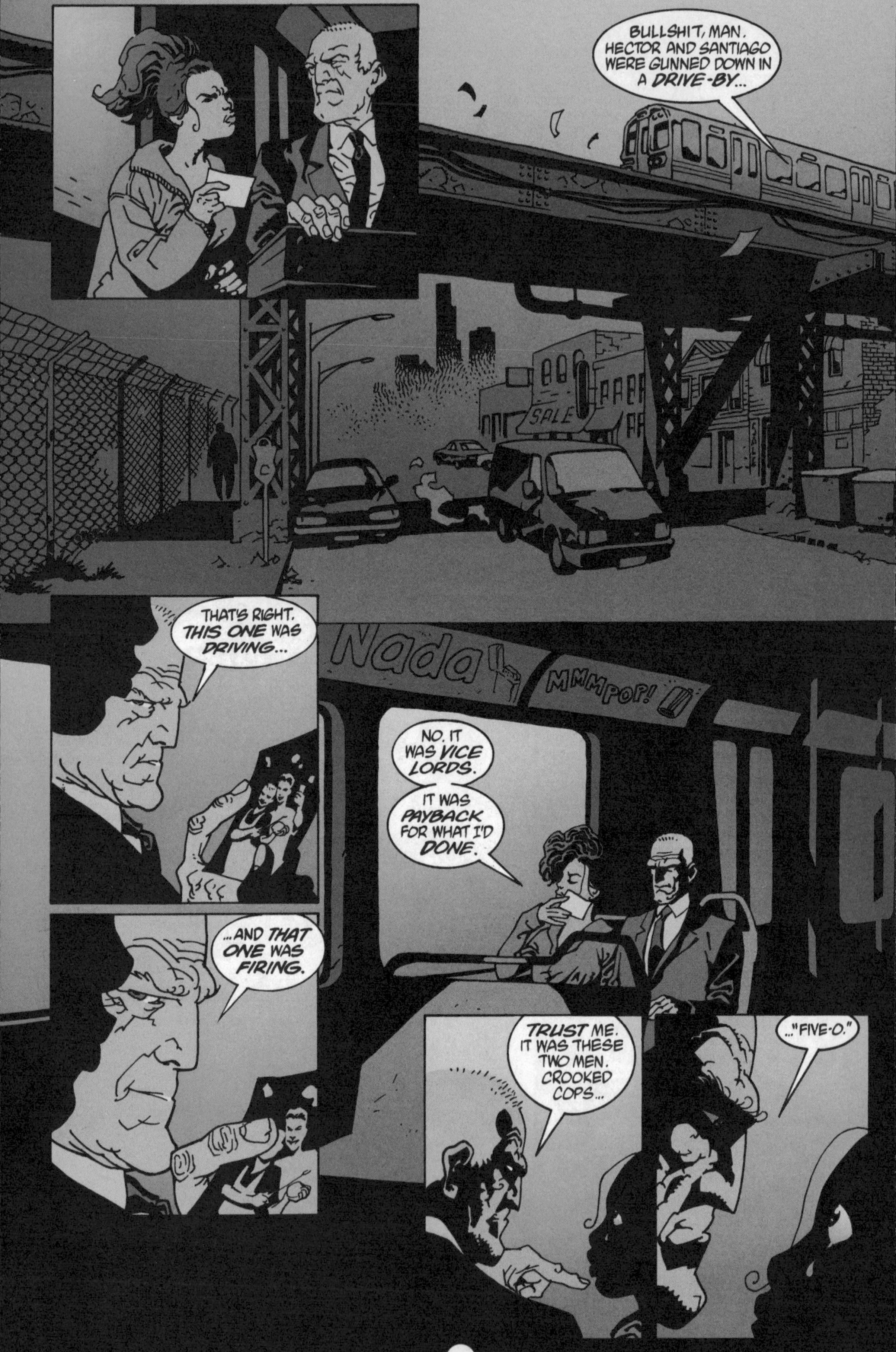
BULLSHIT, MAN. HECTOR AND SANTIAGO WERE GUNNED DOWN IN A DRIVE-BY...
SALE
SALE
THAT'S RIGHT. THIS ONE WAS DRIVING...
Nada
MMMPOP!
NO. IT WAS VICE LORDS.
IT WAS PAYBACK FOR WHAT I'D DONE.
...AND THAT ONE WAS FIRING.
TRUST ME. IT WAS THESE TWO MEN. CROOKED COPS...
..."FIVE-O."

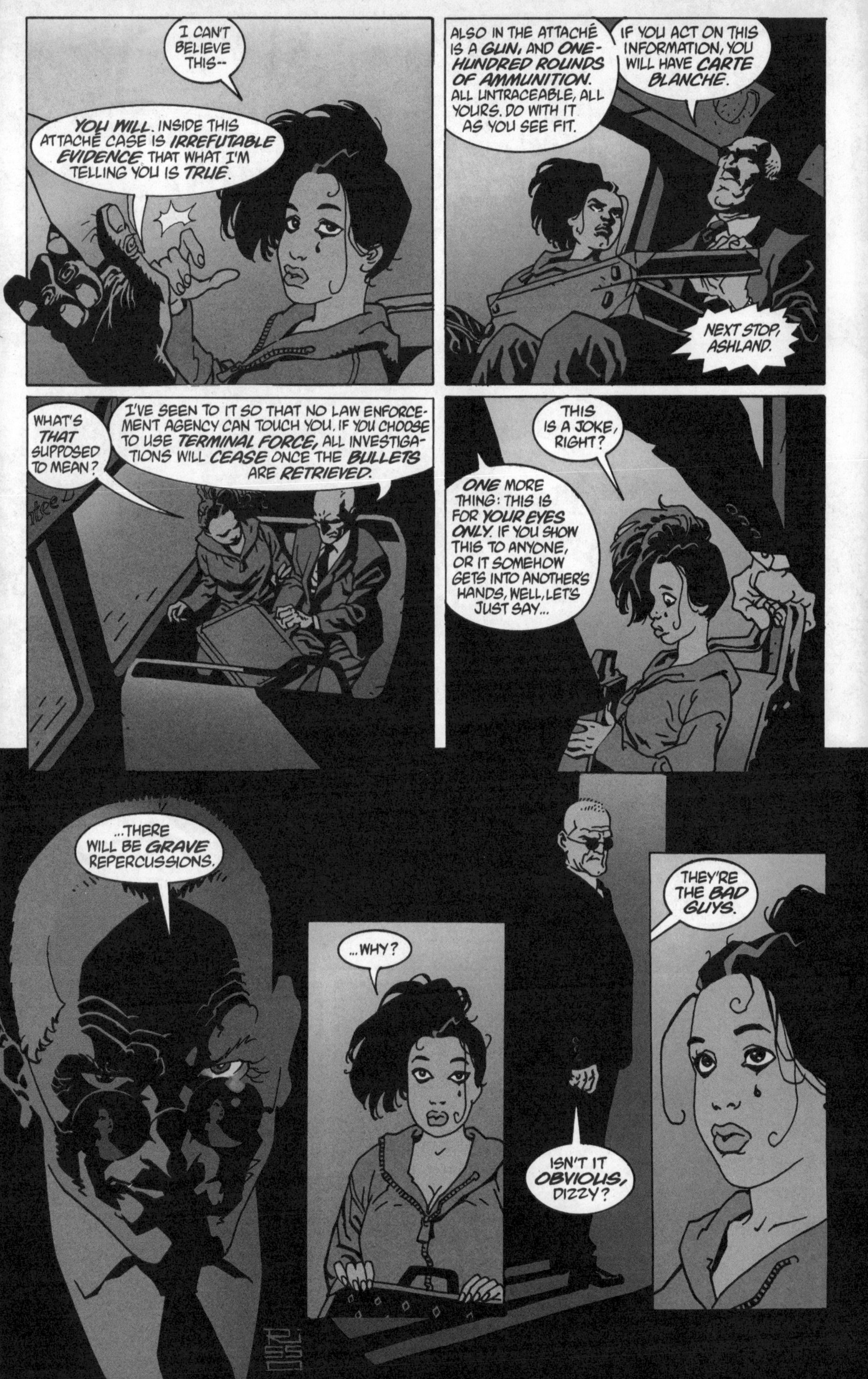

I CAN'T BELIEVE THIS--
YOU WILL. INSIDE THIS ATTACHÉ CASE IS IRREFUTABLE EVIDENCE THAT WHAT I'M TELLING YOU IS TRUE.
ALSO IN THE ATTACHÉ IS A GUN, AND ONE-HUNDRED ROUNDS OF AMMUNITION. ALL UNTRACEABLE, ALL YOURS. DO WITH IT AS YOU SEE FIT.
IF YOU ACT ON THIS INFORMATION, YOU WILL HAVE CARTE BLANCHE.
NEXT STOP, ASHLAND.
WHAT'S THAT SUPPOSED TO MEAN?
I'VE SEEN TO IT SO THAT NO LAW ENFORCEMENT AGENCY CAN TOUCH YOU. IF YOU CHOOSE TO USE TERMINAL FORCE, ALL INVESTIGATIONS WILL CEASE ONCE THE BULLETS ARE RETRIEVED.
THIS IS A JOKE, RIGHT?
ONE MORE THING: THIS IS FOR YOUR EYES ONLY. IF YOU SHOW THIS TO ANYONE, OR IT SOMEHOW GETS INTO ANOTHER'S HANDS, WELL, LET'S JUST SAY...
...THERE WILL BE GRAVE REPERCUSSIONS.
...WHY?
ISN'T IT OBVIOUS, DIZZY?
THEY'RE THE BAD GUYS.

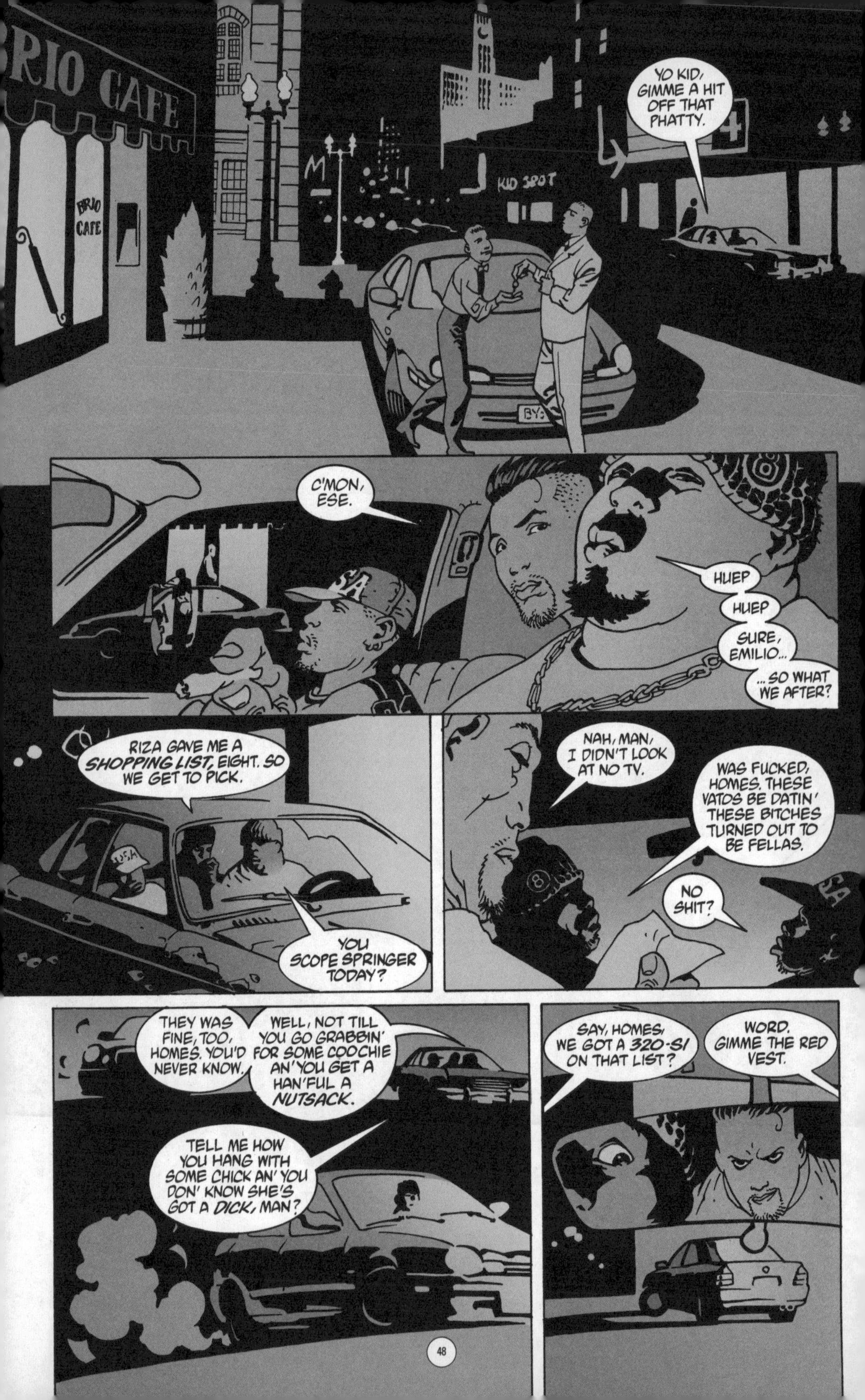
BRIO CAFE
BRIO CAFE
KID SPOT
YO KID, GIMME A HIT OFF THAT PHATTY.
C'MON, ESE.
HUEP
HUEP
SURE, EMILIO...
...SO WHAT WE AFTER?
RIZA GAVE ME A SHOPPING LIST, EIGHT. SO WE GET TO PICK.
YOU SCOPE SPRINGER TODAY?
NAH, MAN, I DIDN'T LOOK AT NO TV.
WAS FUCKED, HOMES. THESE VATOS BE DATIN' THESE BITCHES TURNED OUT TO BE FELLAS.
NO SHIT?
THEY WAS FINE, TOO, HOMES. YOU'D NEVER KNOW.
WELL, NOT TILL YOU GO GRABBIN' FOR SOME COOCHIE AN' YOU GET A HAN'FUL A NUTSACK.
TELL ME HOW YOU HANG WITH SOME CHICK AN' YOU DON' KNOW SHE'S GOT A DICK, MAN?
SAY, HOMES, WE GOT A 320-SI ON THAT LIST?
WORD. GIMME THE RED VEST.

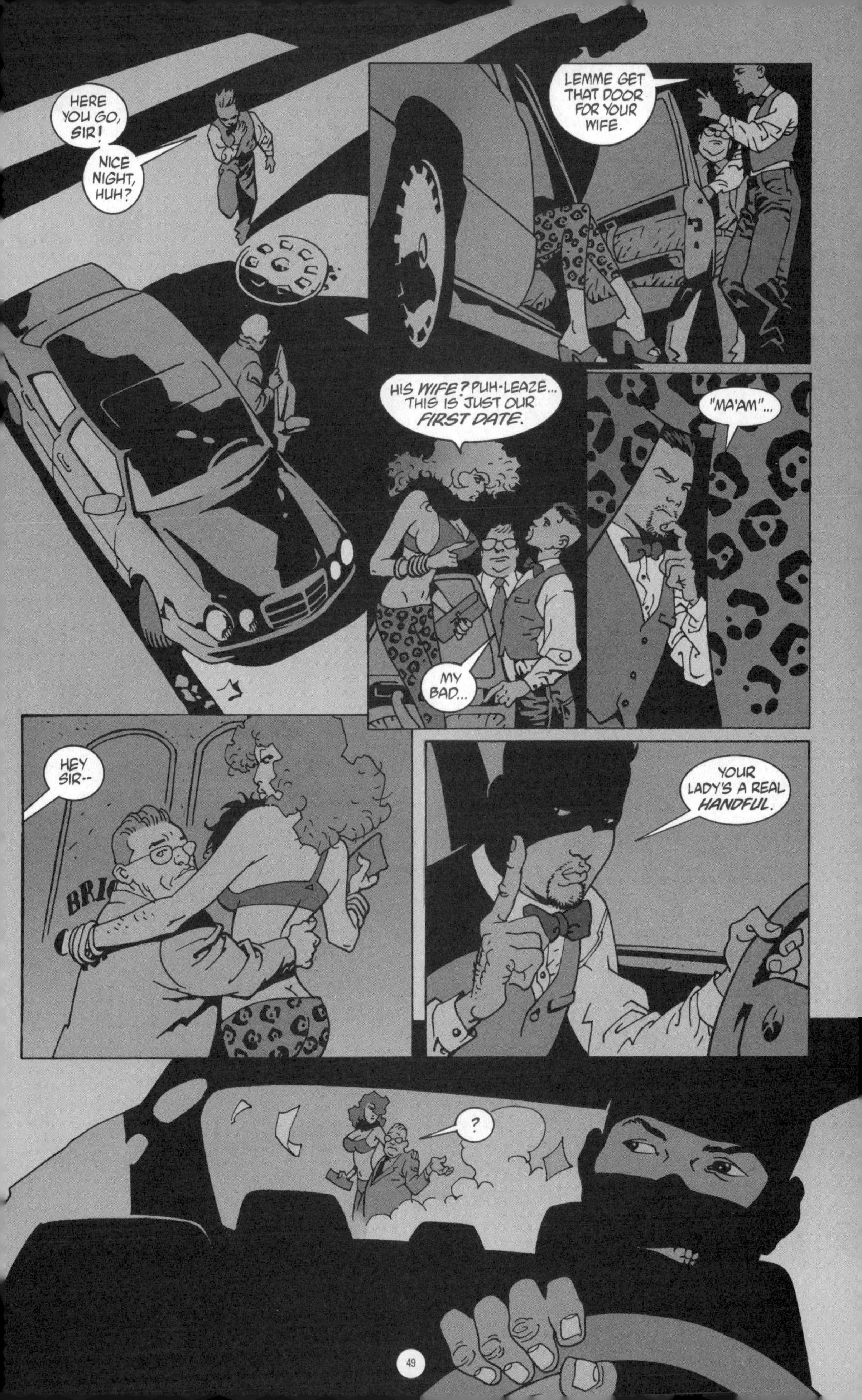
HERE YOU GO, SIR!
NICE NIGHT, HUH?
LEMME GET THAT DOOR FOR YOUR WIFE.
HIS WIFE? PUH-LEAZE... THIS IS JUST OUR FIRST DATE.
MY BAD...
"MA'AM"...
HEY SIR--
YOUR LADY'S A REAL HANDFUL.
?

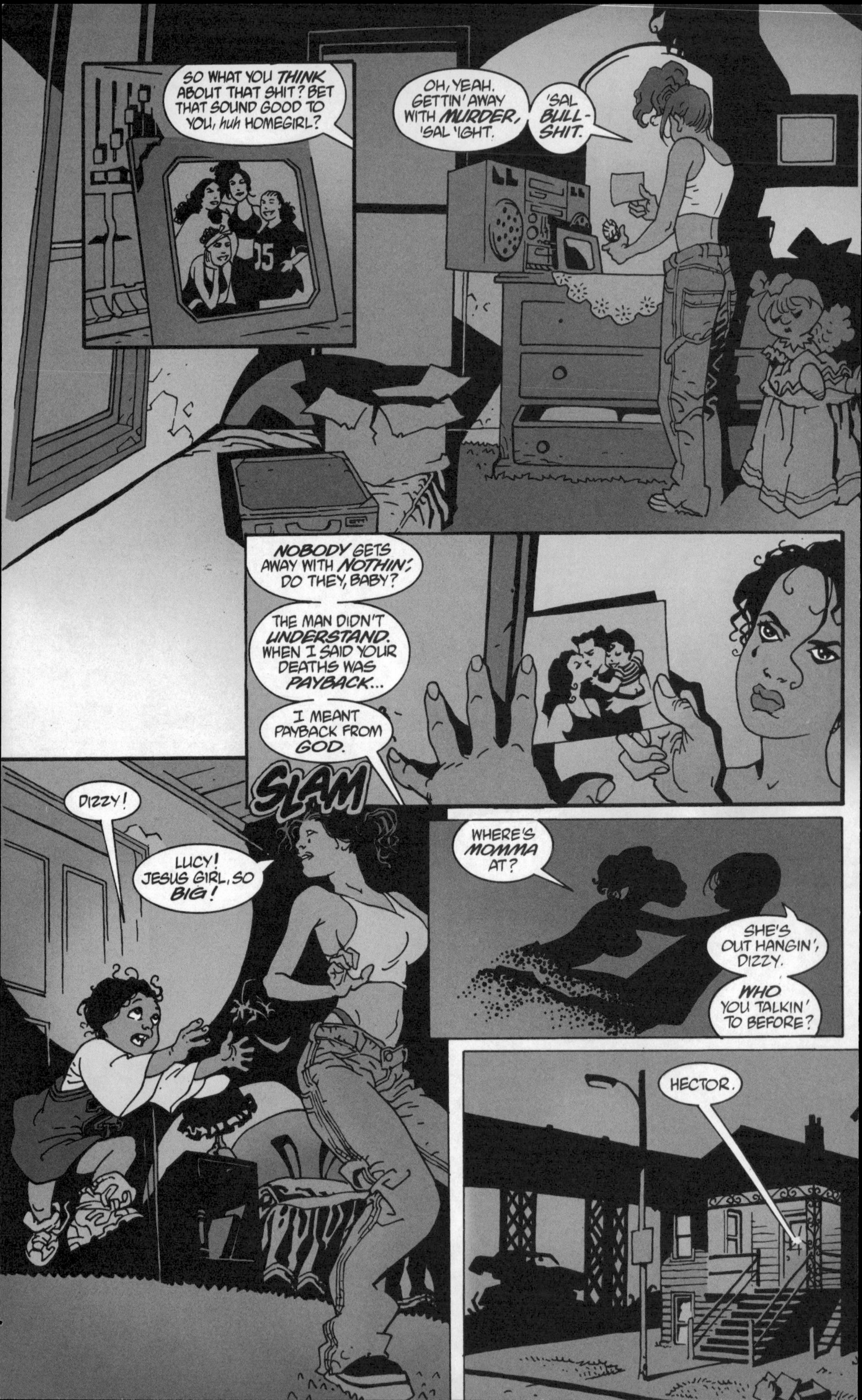
SO WHAT YOU THINK ABOUT THAT SHIT? BET THAT SOUND GOOD TO YOU, huh HOMEGIRL?
OH, YEAH. GETTIN' AWAY WITH MURDER, 'SAL 'IGHT.
'SAL BULL-SHIT.
NOBODY GETS AWAY WITH NOTHIN', DO THEY, BABY?
THE MAN DIDN'T UNDERSTAND. WHEN I SAID YOUR DEATHS WAS PAYBACK...
I MEANT PAYBACK FROM GOD.
SLAM
DIZZY!
LUCY! JESUS GIRL, SO BIG!
WHERE'S MOMMA AT?
SHE'S OUT HANGIN', DIZZY.
WHO YOU TALKIN' TO BEFORE?
HECTOR.

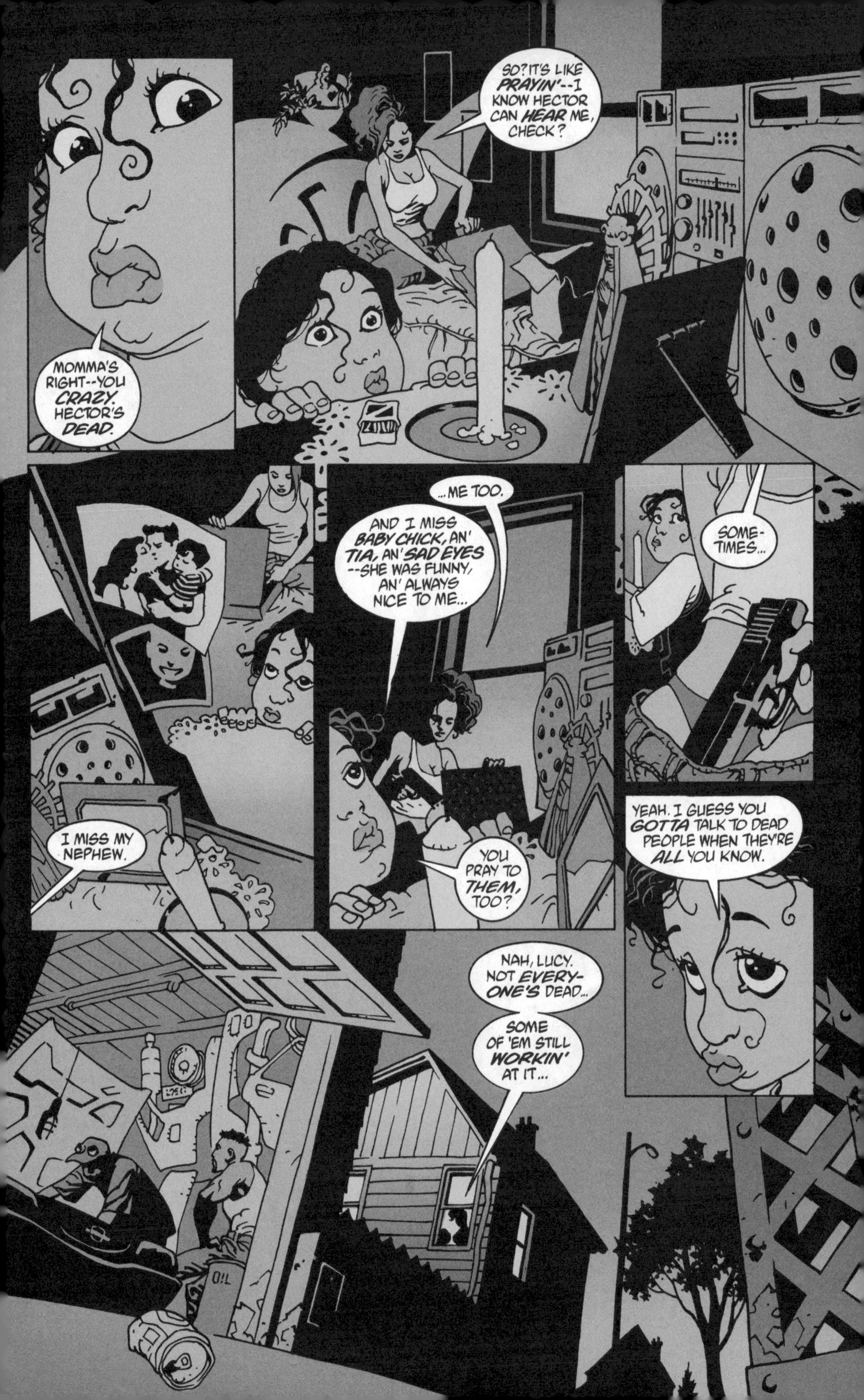
SO? IT'S LIKE PRAYIN'--I KNOW HECTOR CAN HEAR ME, CHECK?
MOMMA'S RIGHT--YOU CRAZY. HECTOR'S DEAD.
I MISS MY NEPHEW.
...ME TOO.
AND I MISS BABY CHICK, AN' TIA, AN' SAD EYES --SHE WAS FUNNY, AN' ALWAYS NICE TO ME...
YOU PRAY TO THEM, TOO?
SOME- TIMES...
YEAH. I GUESS YOU GOTTA TALK TO DEAD PEOPLE WHEN THEY'RE ALL YOU KNOW.
NAH, LUCY. NOT EVERY- ONE'S DEAD...
SOME OF 'EM STILL WORKIN' AT IT...
OIL

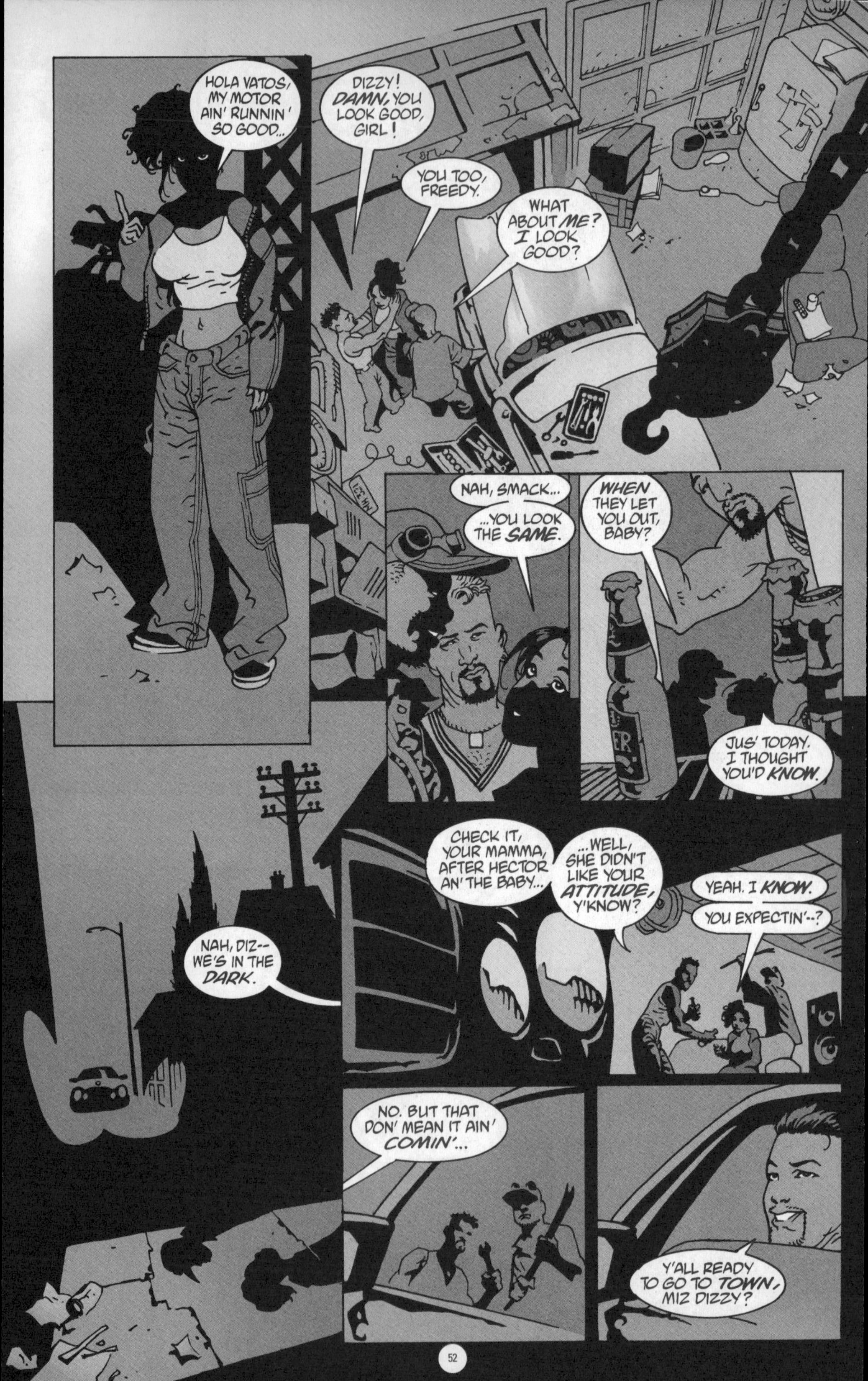
HOLA VATOS, MY MOTOR AIN' RUNNIN' SO GOOD...
DIZZY! DAMN, YOU LOOK GOOD, GIRL!
YOU TOO, FREEDY.
WHAT ABOUT ME? I LOOK GOOD?
NAH, SMACK...
...YOU LOOK THE SAME.
WHEN THEY LET YOU OUT, BABY?
JUS' TODAY. I THOUGHT YOU'D KNOW.
CHECK IT, YOUR MAMMA, AFTER HECTOR AN' THE BABY...
...WELL, SHE DIDN'T LIKE YOUR ATTITUDE, Y'KNOW?
YEAH. I KNOW.
YOU EXPECTIN'--?
NAH, DIZ-- WE'S IN THE DARK.
NO. BUT THAT DON' MEAN IT AIN' COMIN'...
Y'ALL READY TO GO TO TOWN, MIZ DIZZY?

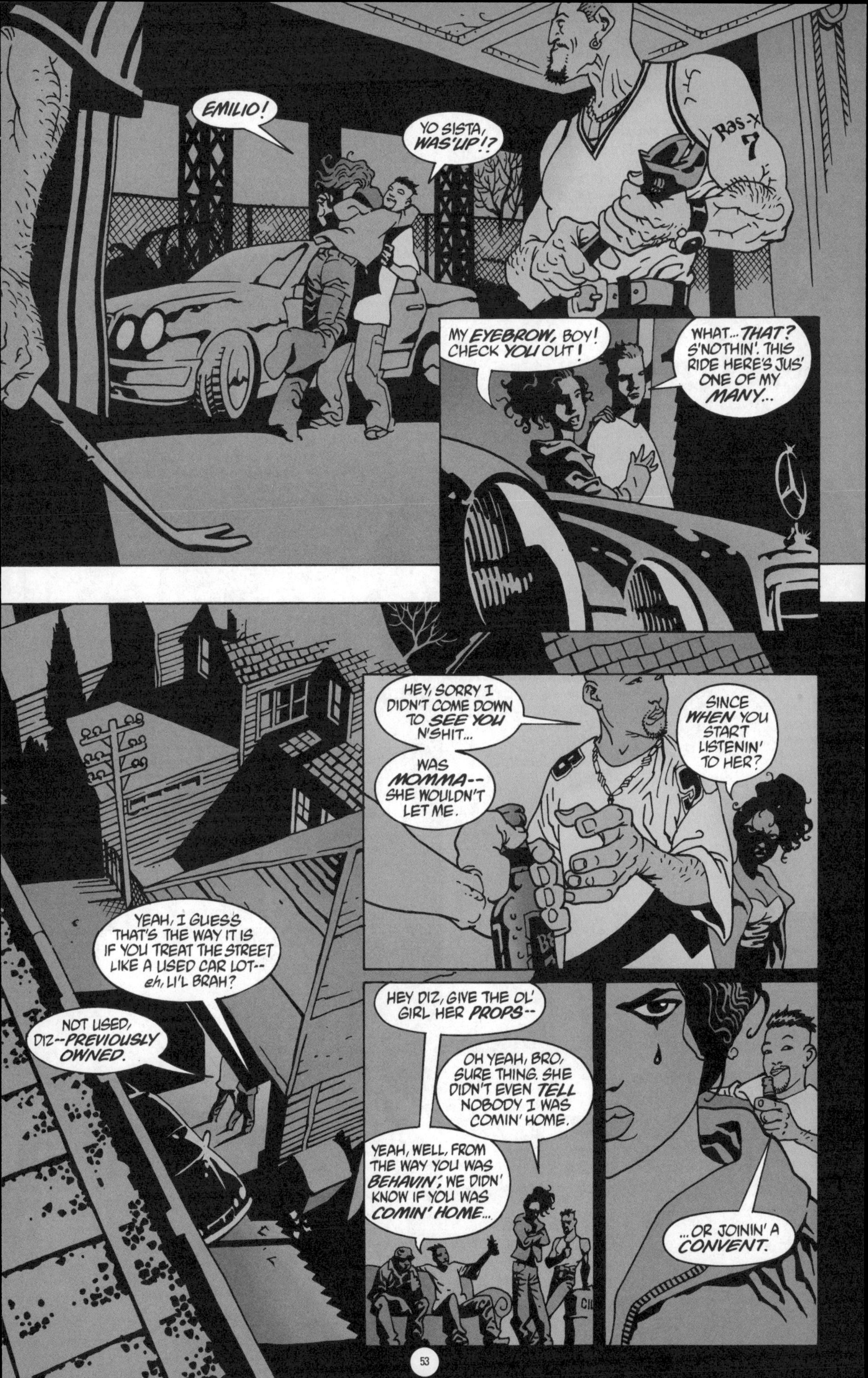

EMILIO!
YO SISTA, WAS'UP!?
MY EYEBROW, BOY! CHECK YOU OUT!
WHAT... THAT? S'NOTHIN'. THIS RIDE HERE'S JUS' ONE OF MY MANY...
Ras-X 7
HEY, SORRY I DIDN'T COME DOWN TO SEE YOU N'SHIT...
WAS MOMMA-- SHE WOULDN'T LET ME.
SINCE WHEN YOU START LISTENIN' TO HER?
YEAH, I GUESS THAT'S THE WAY IT IS IF YOU TREAT THE STREET LIKE A USED CAR LOT-- eh, LI'L BRAH?
NOT USED, DIZ--PREVIOUSLY OWNED.
HEY DIZ, GIVE THE OL' GIRL HER PROPS--
OH YEAH, BRO, SURE THING. SHE DIDN'T EVEN TELL NOBODY I WAS COMIN' HOME.
YEAH, WELL, FROM THE WAY YOU WAS BEHAVIN', WE DIDN' KNOW IF YOU WAS COMIN' HOME...
...OR JOININ' A CONVENT.

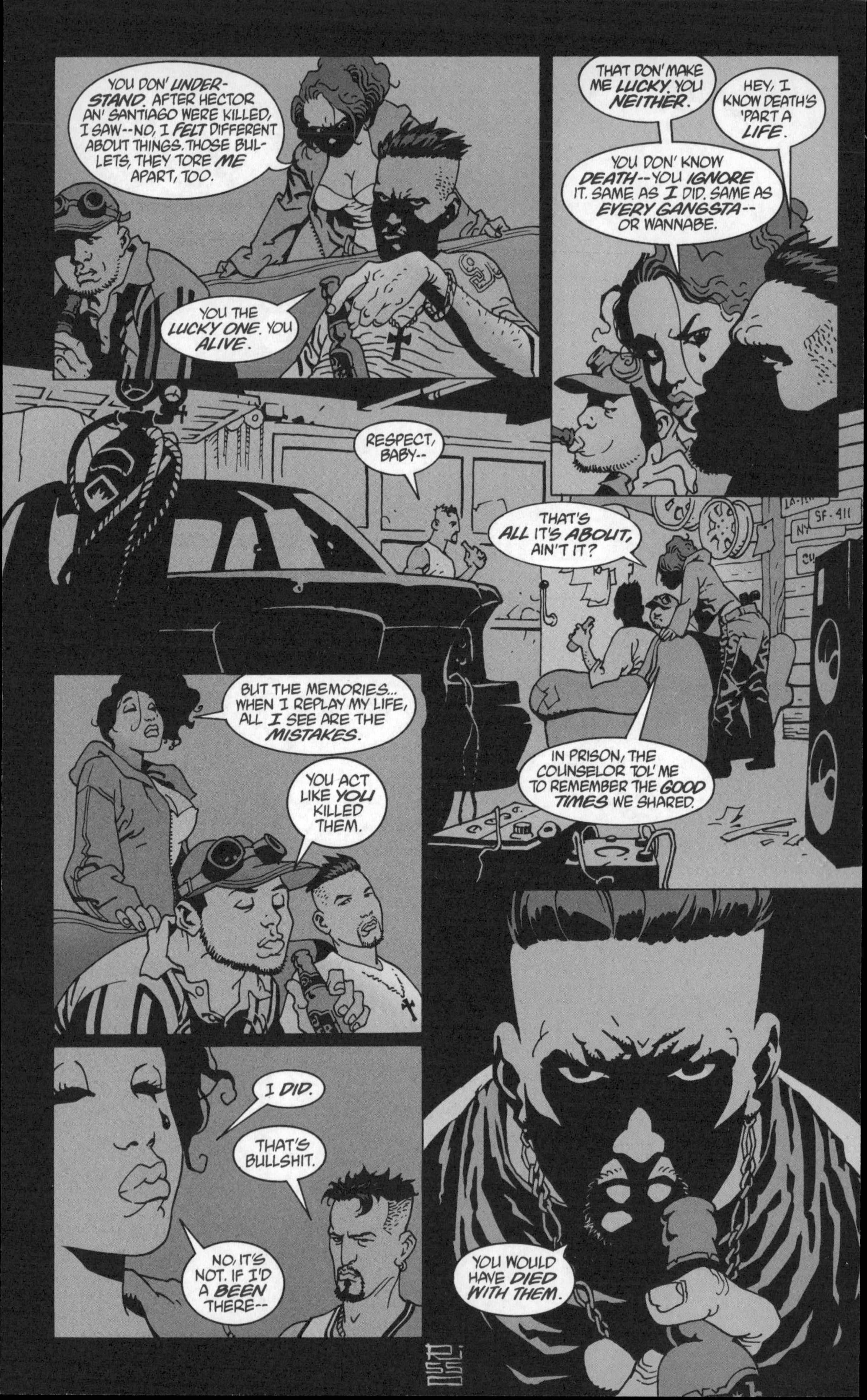
YOU DON' UNDER-STAND. AFTER HECTOR AN' SANTIAGO WERE KILLED, I SAW--NO, I FELT DIFFERENT ABOUT THINGS. THOSE BUL-LETS, THEY TORE ME APART, TOO.
YOU THE LUCKY ONE. YOU ALIVE.
THAT DON' MAKE ME LUCKY. YOU NEITHER.
HEY, I KNOW DEATH'S 'PART A LIFE.
YOU DON' KNOW DEATH--YOU IGNORE IT. SAME AS I DID. SAME AS EVERY GANGSTA--OR WANNABE.
RESPECT, BABY--
THAT'S ALL IT'S ABOUT, AIN'T IT?
SF-411
IN PRISON, THE COUNSELOR TOL' ME TO REMEMBER THE GOOD TIMES WE SHARED.
BUT THE MEMORIES... WHEN I REPLAY MY LIFE, ALL I SEE ARE THE MISTAKES.
YOU ACT LIKE YOU KILLED THEM.
I DID.
THAT'S BULLSHIT.
NO, IT'S NOT. IF I'D A BEEN THERE--
YOU WOULD HAVE DIED WITH THEM.

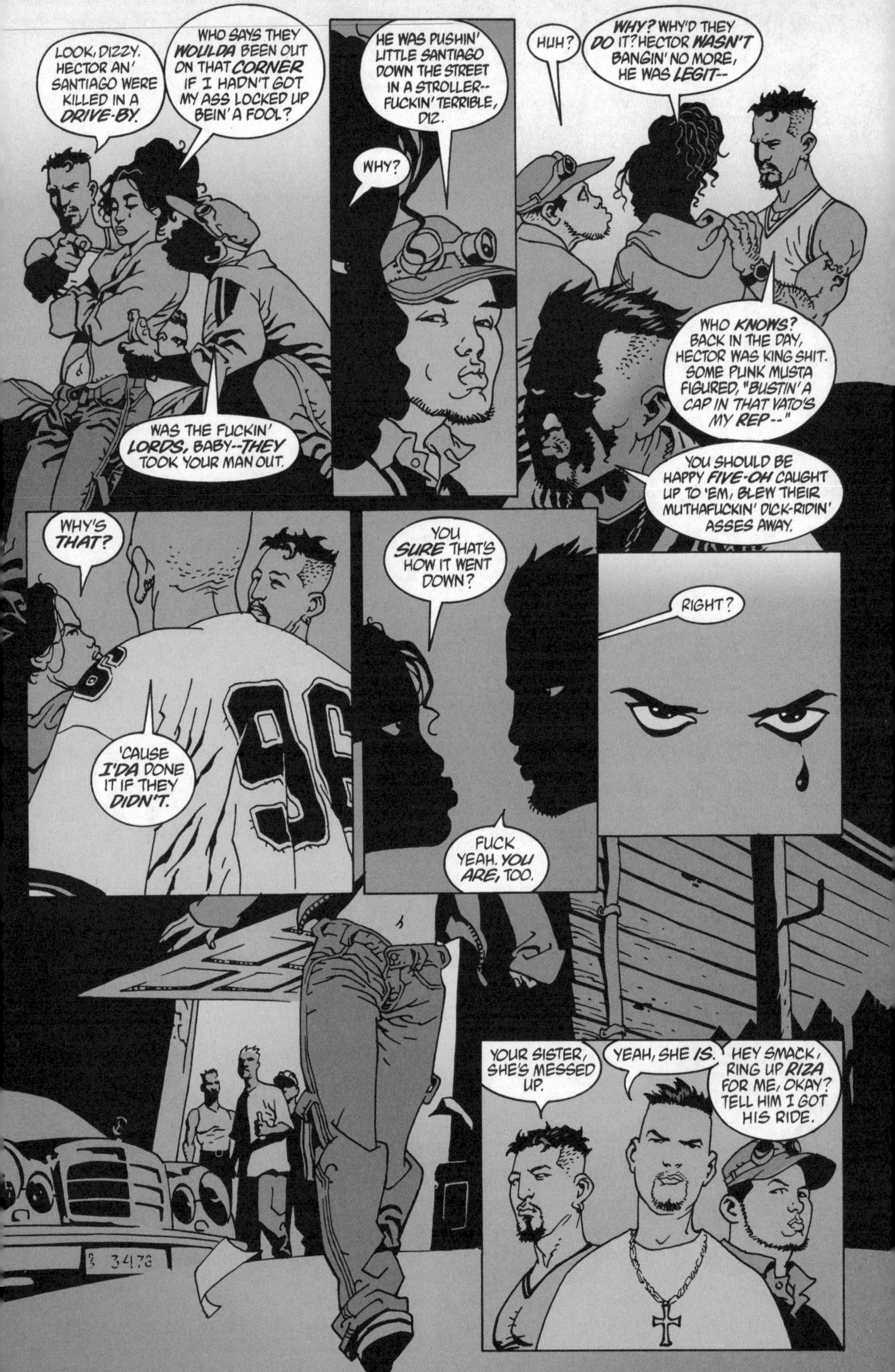
LOOK, DIZZY. HECTOR AN' SANTIAGO WERE KILLED IN A DRIVE-BY.
WHO SAYS THEY WOULDA BEEN OUT ON THAT CORNER IF I HADN'T GOT MY ASS LOCKED UP BEIN' A FOOL?
WAS THE FUCKIN' LORDS, BABY--THEY TOOK YOUR MAN OUT.
HE WAS PUSHIN' LITTLE SANTIAGO DOWN THE STREET IN A STROLLER-- FUCKIN' TERRIBLE, DIZ.
WHY?
HUH?
WHY? WHY'D THEY DO IT? HECTOR WASN'T BANGIN' NO MORE, HE WAS LEGIT--
WHO KNOWS? BACK IN THE DAY, HECTOR WAS KING SHIT. SOME PUNK MUSTA FIGURED, "BUSTIN' A CAP IN THAT VATO'S MY REP--"
YOU SHOULD BE HAPPY FIVE-OH CAUGHT UP TO 'EM, BLEW THEIR MUTHAFUCKIN' DICK-RIDIN' ASSES AWAY.
WHY'S THAT?
'CAUSE I'DA DONE IT IF THEY DIDN'T.
YOU SURE THAT'S HOW IT WENT DOWN?
FUCK YEAH. YOU ARE, TOO.
RIGHT?
YOUR SISTER, SHE'S MESSED UP.
YEAH, SHE IS.
HEY SMACK, RING UP RIZA FOR ME, OKAY? TELL HIM I GOT HIS RIDE.

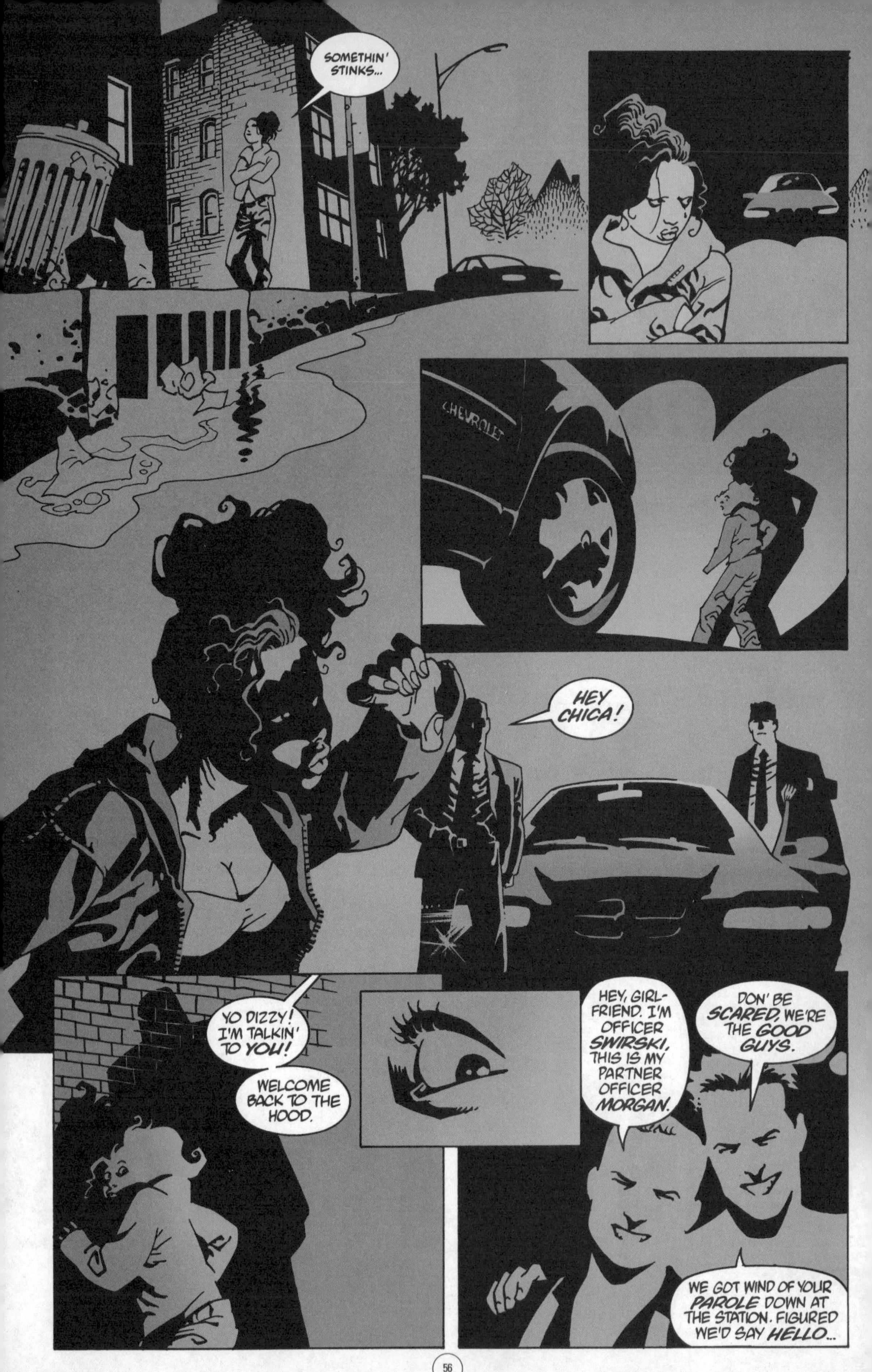
SOMETHIN' STINKS...
HEY CHICA!
YO DIZZY! I'M TALKIN' TO YOU!
WELCOME BACK TO THE HOOD.
HEY, GIRL-FRIEND. I'M OFFICER SWIRSKI, THIS IS MY PARTNER OFFICER MORGAN.
DON' BE SCARED, WE'RE THE GOOD GUYS.
WE GOT WIND OF YOUR PAROLE DOWN AT THE STATION. FIGURED WE'D SAY HELLO...

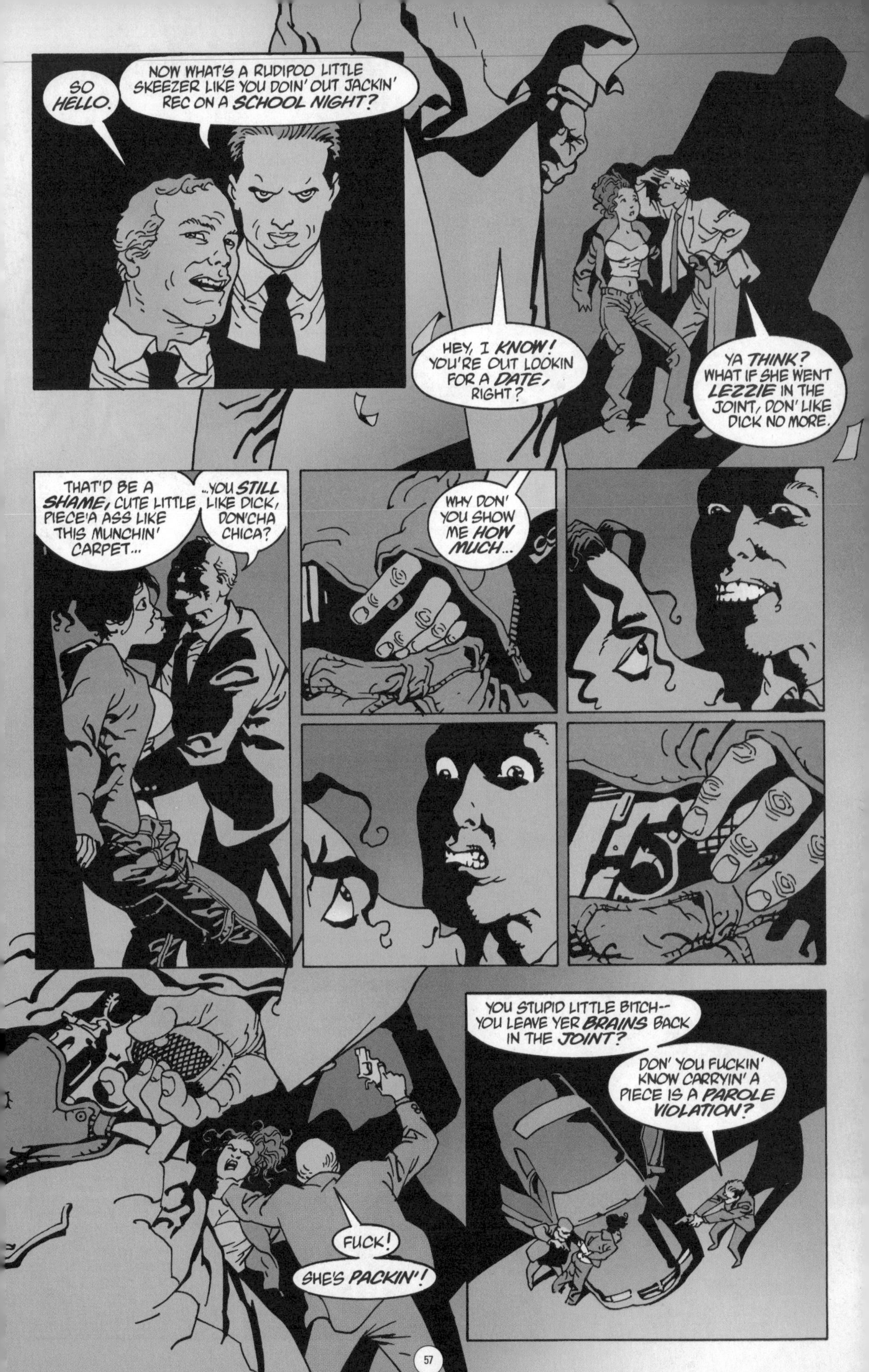
SO HELLO.
NOW WHAT'S A RUDIPOO LITTLE SKEEZER LIKE YOU DOIN' OUT JACKIN' REC ON A SCHOOL NIGHT?
HEY, I KNOW! YOU'RE OUT LOOKIN FOR A DATE, RIGHT?
YA THINK? WHAT IF SHE WENT LEZZIE IN THE JOINT, DON' LIKE DICK NO MORE.
THAT'D BE A SHAME, CUTE LITTLE PIECE'A ASS LIKE THIS MUNCHIN' CARPET...
...YOU STILL LIKE DICK, DON'CHA CHICA?
WHY DON' YOU SHOW ME HOW MUCH...
FUCK!
SHE'S PACKIN'!
YOU STUPID LITTLE BITCH-- YOU LEAVE YER BRAINS BACK IN THE JOINT?
DON' YOU FUCKIN' KNOW CARRYIN' A PIECE IS A PAROLE VIOLATION?

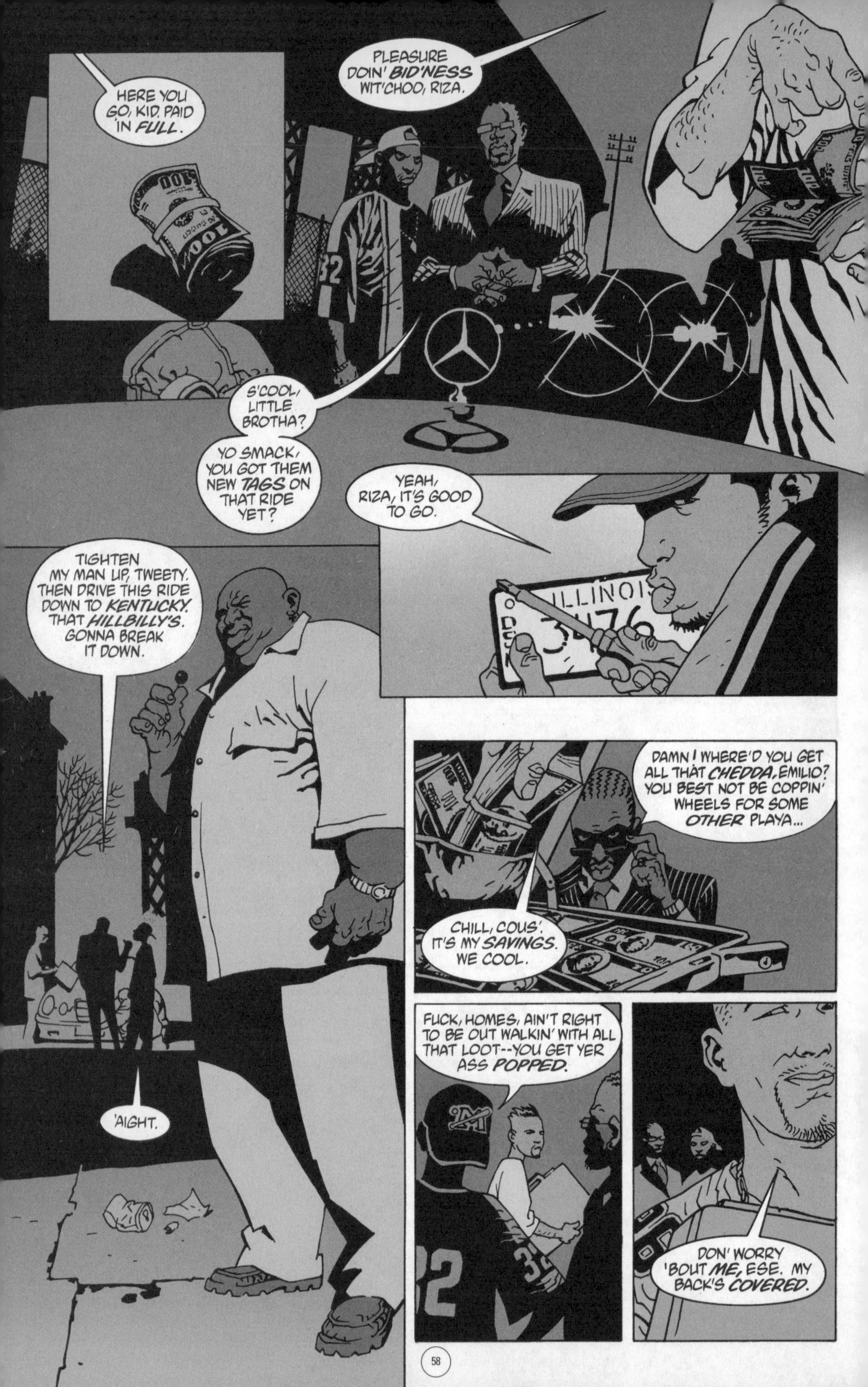
HERE YOU GO, KID. PAID IN FULL.
PLEASURE DOIN' BID'NESS WIT'CHOO, RIZA.
S'COOL, LITTLE BROTHA?
YO SMACK, YOU GOT THEM NEW TAGS ON THAT RIDE YET?
YEAH, RIZA, IT'S GOOD TO GO.
ILLINOIS
TIGHTEN MY MAN UP, TWEETY. THEN DRIVE THIS RIDE DOWN TO KENTUCKY. THAT HILLBILLY'S GONNA BREAK IT DOWN.
'AIGHT.
DAMN! WHERE'D YOU GET ALL THAT CHEDDA, EMILIO? YOU BEST NOT BE COPPIN' WHEELS FOR SOME OTHER PLAYA...
CHILL, COUS'. IT'S MY SAVINGS. WE COOL.
FUCK, HOMES, AIN'T RIGHT TO BE OUT WALKIN' WITH ALL THAT LOOT--YOU GET YER ASS POPPED.
DON' WORRY 'BOUT ME, ESE. MY BACK'S COVERED.

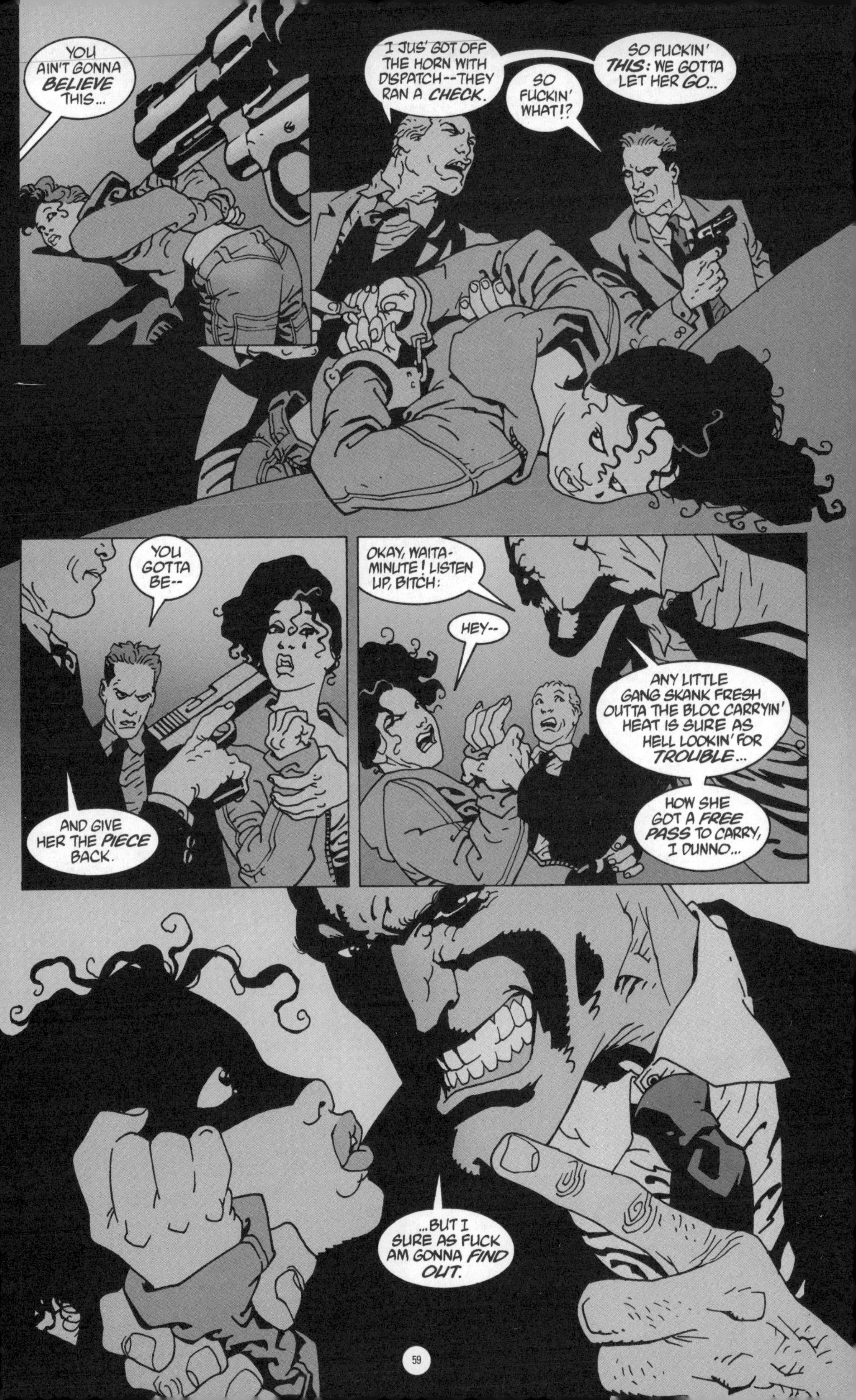

YOU AIN'T GONNA BELIEVE THIS...
I JUS' GOT OFF THE HORN WITH DISPATCH--THEY RAN A CHECK.
SO FUCKIN' WHAT!?
SO FUCKIN' THIS: WE GOTTA LET HER GO...
YOU GOTTA BE--
AND GIVE HER THE PIECE BACK.
OKAY, WAITA-MINUTE! LISTEN UP, BITCH:
HEY--
ANY LITTLE GANG SKANK FRESH OUTTA THE BLOC CARRYIN' HEAT IS SURE AS HELL LOOKIN' FOR TROUBLE...
HOW SHE GOT A FREE PASS TO CARRY, I DUNNO...
...BUT I SURE AS FUCK AM GONNA FIND OUT.

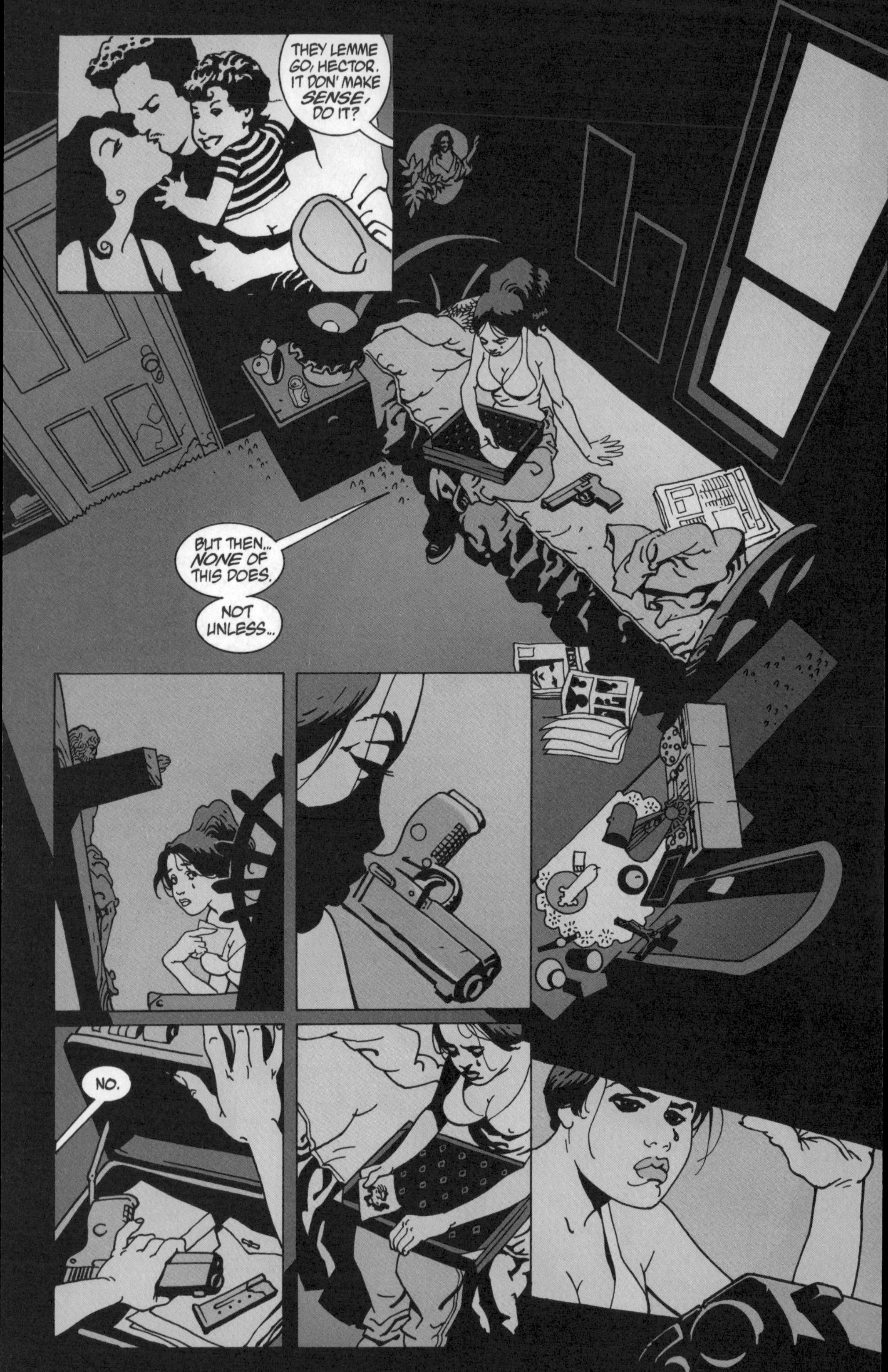
THEY LEMME GO, HECTOR. IT DON' MAKE SENSE, DO IT?
BUT THEN... NONE OF THIS DOES.
NOT UNLESS...
NO.

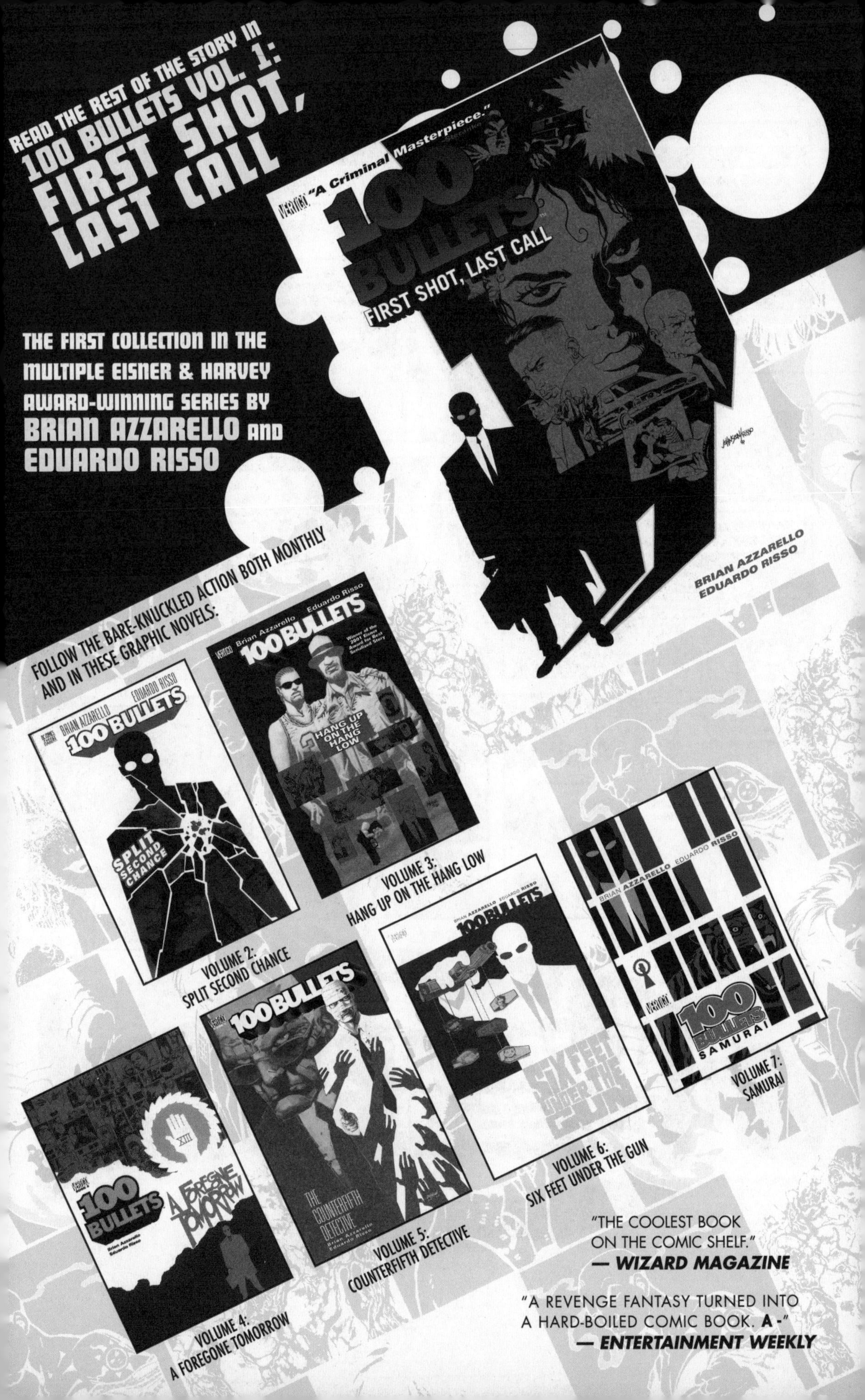
READ THE REST OF THE STORY IN
100 BULLETS VOL. 1:
FIRST SHOT, LAST CALL
THE FIRST COLLECTION IN THE MULTIPLE EISNER & HARVEY AWARD-WINNING SERIES BY BRIAN AZZARELLO AND EDUARDO RISSO
"A Criminal Masterpiece."
100 BULLETS
FIRST SHOT, LAST CALL
BRIAN AZZARELLO
EDUARDO RISSO
FOLLOW THE BARE-KNUCKLED ACTION BOTH MONTHLY AND IN THESE GRAPHIC NOVELS:
VOLUME 2: SPLIT SECOND CHANCE
VOLUME 3: HANG UP ON THE HANG LOW
VOLUME 4: A FOREGONE TOMORROW
VOLUME 5: COUNTERFIFTH DETECTIVE
VOLUME 6: SIX FEET UNDER THE GUN
VOLUME 7: SAMURAI
"THE COOLEST BOOK ON THE COMIC SHELF."
— WIZARD MAGAZINE
"A REVENGE FANTASY TURNED INTO A HARD-BOILED COMIC BOOK. A-"
— ENTERTAINMENT WEEKLY

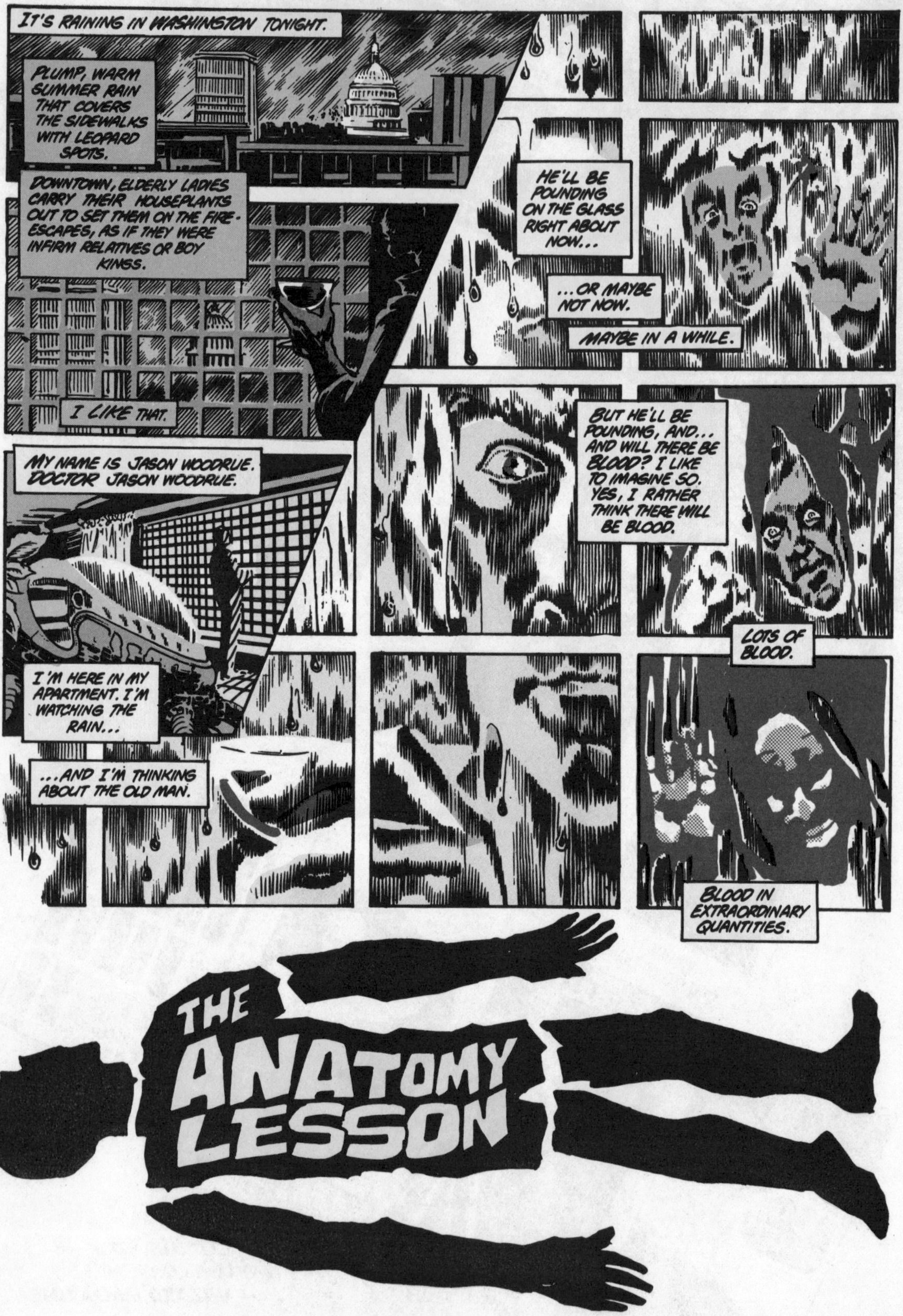

IT'S RAINING IN WASHINGTON TONIGHT.
PLUMP, WARM SUMMER RAIN THAT COVERS THE SIDEWALKS WITH LEOPARD SPOTS.
DOWNTOWN, ELDERLY LADIES CARRY THEIR HOUSEPLANTS OUT TO SET THEM ON THE FIRE-ESCAPES, AS IF THEY WERE INFIRM RELATIVES OR BOY KINGS.
I LIKE THAT.
HE'LL BE POUNDING ON THE GLASS RIGHT ABOUT NOW...
...OR MAYBE NOT NOW.
MAYBE IN A WHILE.
MY NAME IS JASON WOODRUE. DOCTOR JASON WOODRUE.
I'M HERE IN MY APARTMENT. I'M WATCHING THE RAIN...
...AND I'M THINKING ABOUT THE OLD MAN.
BUT HE'LL BE POUNDING, AND... AND WILL THERE BE BLOOD? I LIKE TO IMAGINE SO. YES, I RATHER THINK THERE WILL BE BLOOD.
LOTS OF BLOOD.
BLOOD IN EXTRAORDINARY QUANTITIES.
THE ANATOMY LESSON

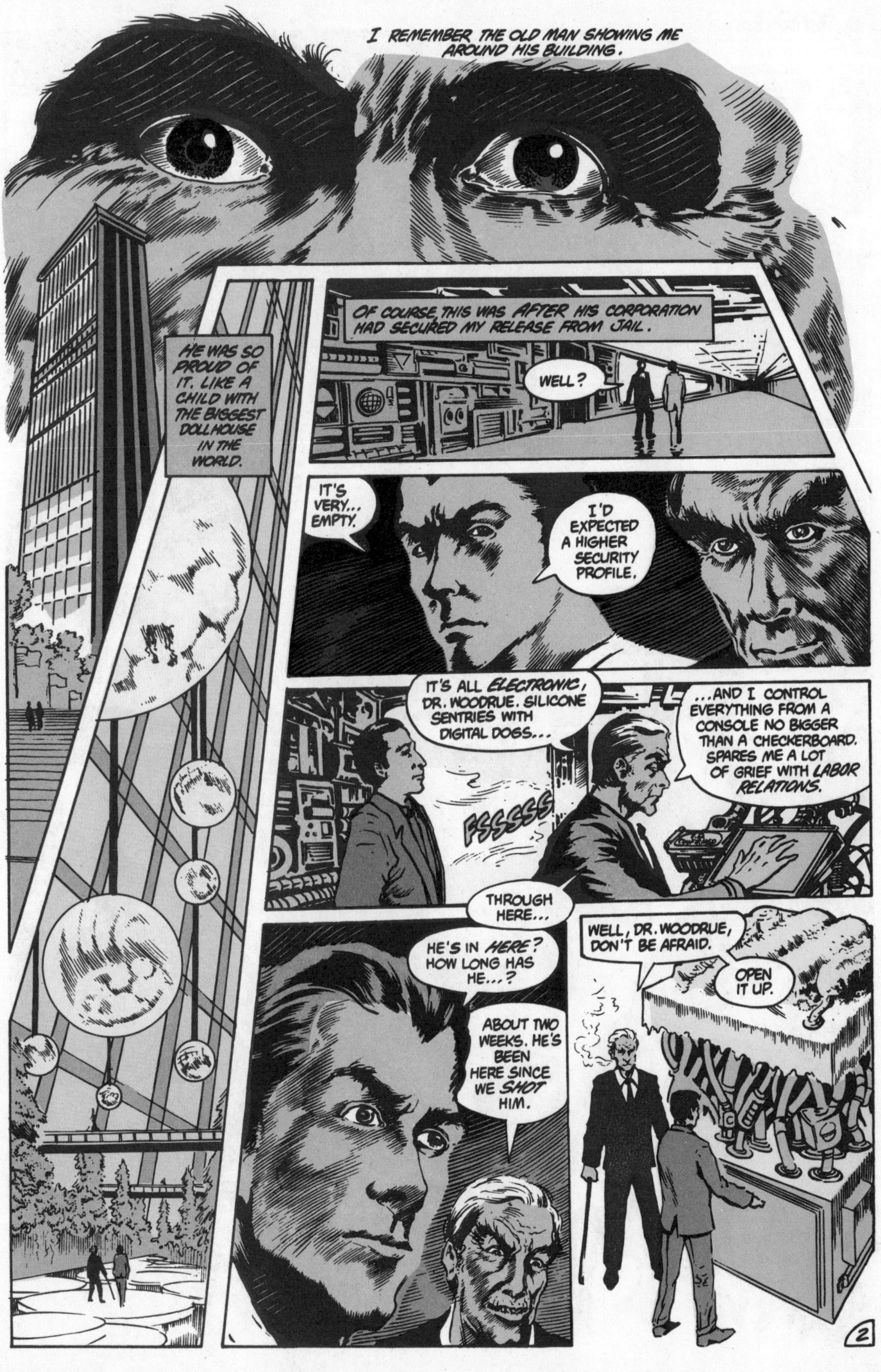
I REMEMBER THE OLD MAN SHOWING ME AROUND HIS BUILDING.
HE WAS SO PROUD OF IT. LIKE A CHILD WITH THE BIGGEST DOLLHOUSE IN THE WORLD.
OF COURSE, THIS WAS AFTER HIS CORPORATION HAD SECURED MY RELEASE FROM JAIL.
WELL?
IT'S VERY... EMPTY.
I'D EXPECTED A HIGHER SECURITY PROFILE.
IT'S ALL ELECTRONIC, DR. WOODRUE. SILICONE SENTRIES WITH DIGITAL DOGS...
...AND I CONTROL EVERYTHING FROM A CONSOLE NO BIGGER THAN A CHECKERBOARD. SPARES ME A LOT OF GRIEF WITH LABOR RELATIONS.
FSSSSS
THROUGH HERE...
HE'S IN HERE? HOW LONG HAS HE...?
ABOUT TWO WEEKS. HE'S BEEN HERE SINCE WE SHOT HIM.
WELL, DR. WOODRUE, DON'T BE AFRAID.
OPEN IT UP.
2

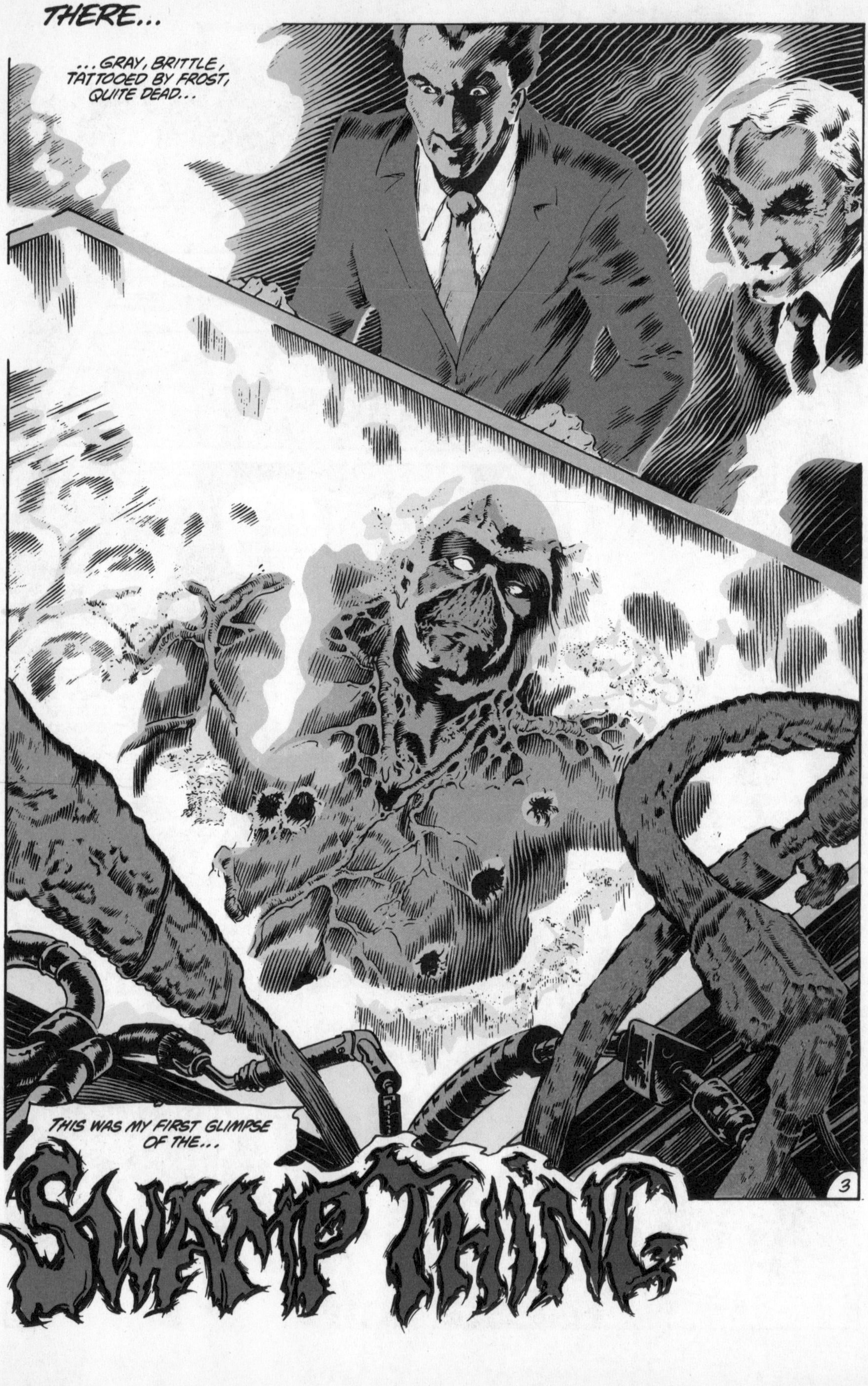
THERE...
...GRAY, BRITTLE, TATTOOED BY FROST, QUITE DEAD...
THIS WAS MY FIRST GLIMPSE OF THE...
SWAMP THING
3

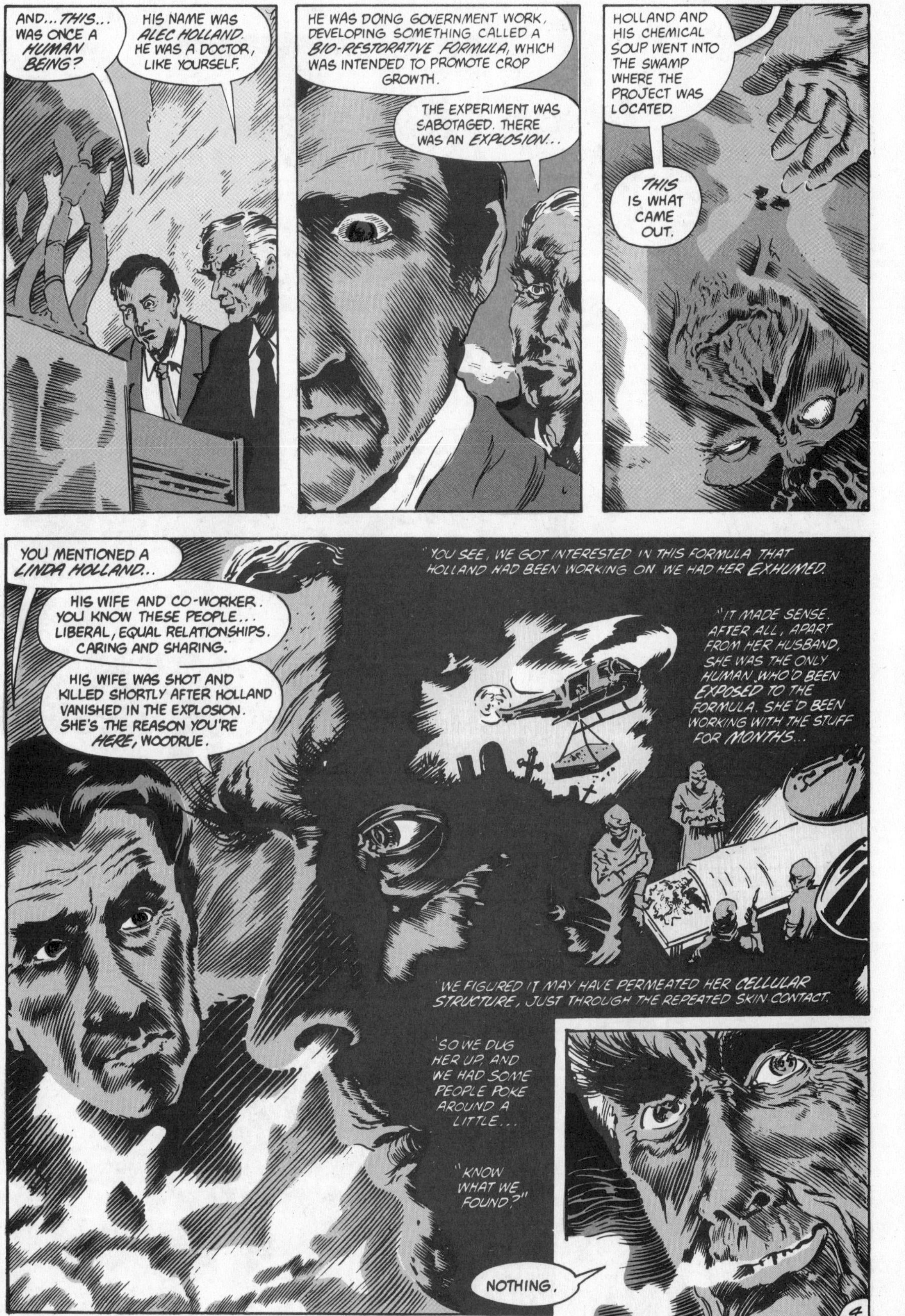
AND... THIS... WAS ONCE A HUMAN BEING?
HIS NAME WAS ALEC HOLLAND. HE WAS A DOCTOR, LIKE YOURSELF.
HE WAS DOING GOVERNMENT WORK, DEVELOPING SOMETHING CALLED A BIO-RESTORATIVE FORMULA, WHICH WAS INTENDED TO PROMOTE CROP GROWTH.
THE EXPERIMENT WAS SABOTAGED. THERE WAS AN EXPLOSION...
HOLLAND AND HIS CHEMICAL SOUP WENT INTO THE SWAMP WHERE THE PROJECT WAS LOCATED.
THIS IS WHAT CAME OUT.
YOU MENTIONED A LINDA HOLLAND...
HIS WIFE AND CO-WORKER. YOU KNOW THESE PEOPLE... LIBERAL, EQUAL RELATIONSHIPS. CARING AND SHARING.
HIS WIFE WAS SHOT AND KILLED SHORTLY AFTER HOLLAND VANISHED IN THE EXPLOSION. SHE'S THE REASON YOU'RE HERE, WOODRUE.
"YOU SEE, WE GOT INTERESTED IN THIS FORMULA THAT HOLLAND HAD BEEN WORKING ON. WE HAD HER EXHUMED.
"IT MADE SENSE. AFTER ALL, APART FROM HER HUSBAND, SHE WAS THE ONLY HUMAN WHO'D BEEN EXPOSED TO THE FORMULA. SHE'D BEEN WORKING WITH THE STUFF FOR MONTHS...
"WE FIGURED IT MAY HAVE PERMEATED HER CELLULAR STRUCTURE, JUST THROUGH THE REPEATED SKIN-CONTACT.
"SO WE DUG HER UP, AND WE HAD SOME PEOPLE POKE AROUND A LITTLE...
"KNOW WHAT WE FOUND?"
NOTHING.
4

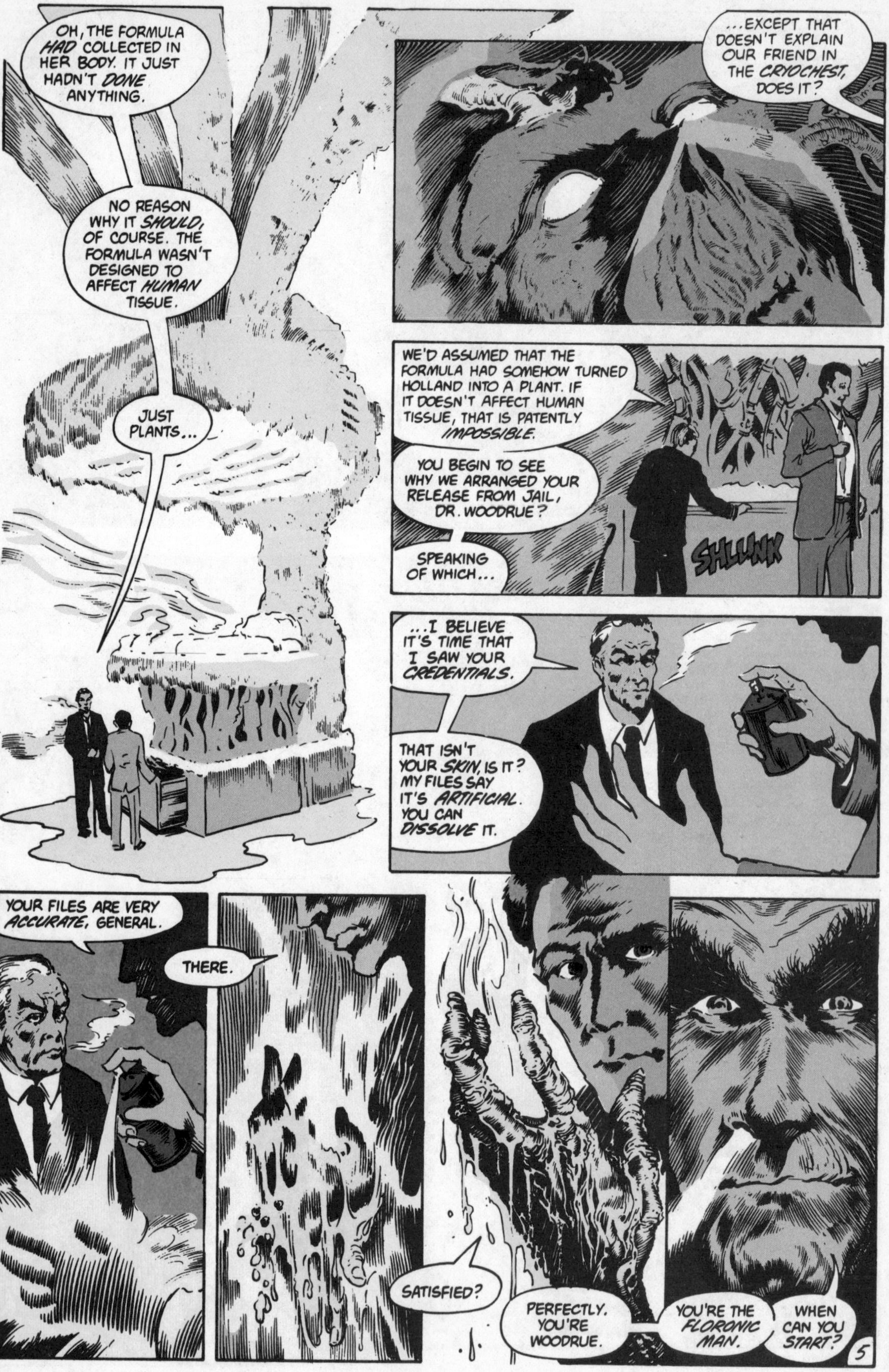
OH, THE FORMULA HAD COLLECTED IN HER BODY. IT JUST HADN'T DONE ANYTHING.
NO REASON WHY IT SHOULD, OF COURSE. THE FORMULA WASN'T DESIGNED TO AFFECT HUMAN TISSUE.
JUST PLANTS...
...EXCEPT THAT DOESN'T EXPLAIN OUR FRIEND IN THE CRYOCHEST, DOES IT?
WE'D ASSUMED THAT THE FORMULA HAD SOMEHOW TURNED HOLLAND INTO A PLANT. IF IT DOESN'T AFFECT HUMAN TISSUE, THAT IS PATENTLY IMPOSSIBLE.
YOU BEGIN TO SEE WHY WE ARRANGED YOUR RELEASE FROM JAIL, DR. WOODRUE?
SPEAKING OF WHICH...
SHLUNK
...I BELIEVE IT'S TIME THAT I SAW YOUR CREDENTIALS.
THAT ISN'T YOUR SKIN, IS IT? MY FILES SAY IT'S ARTIFICIAL. YOU CAN DISSOLVE IT.
YOUR FILES ARE VERY ACCURATE, GENERAL.
THERE.
SATISFIED?
PERFECTLY. YOU'RE WOODRUE.
YOU'RE THE FLORONIC MAN.
WHEN CAN YOU START?
5

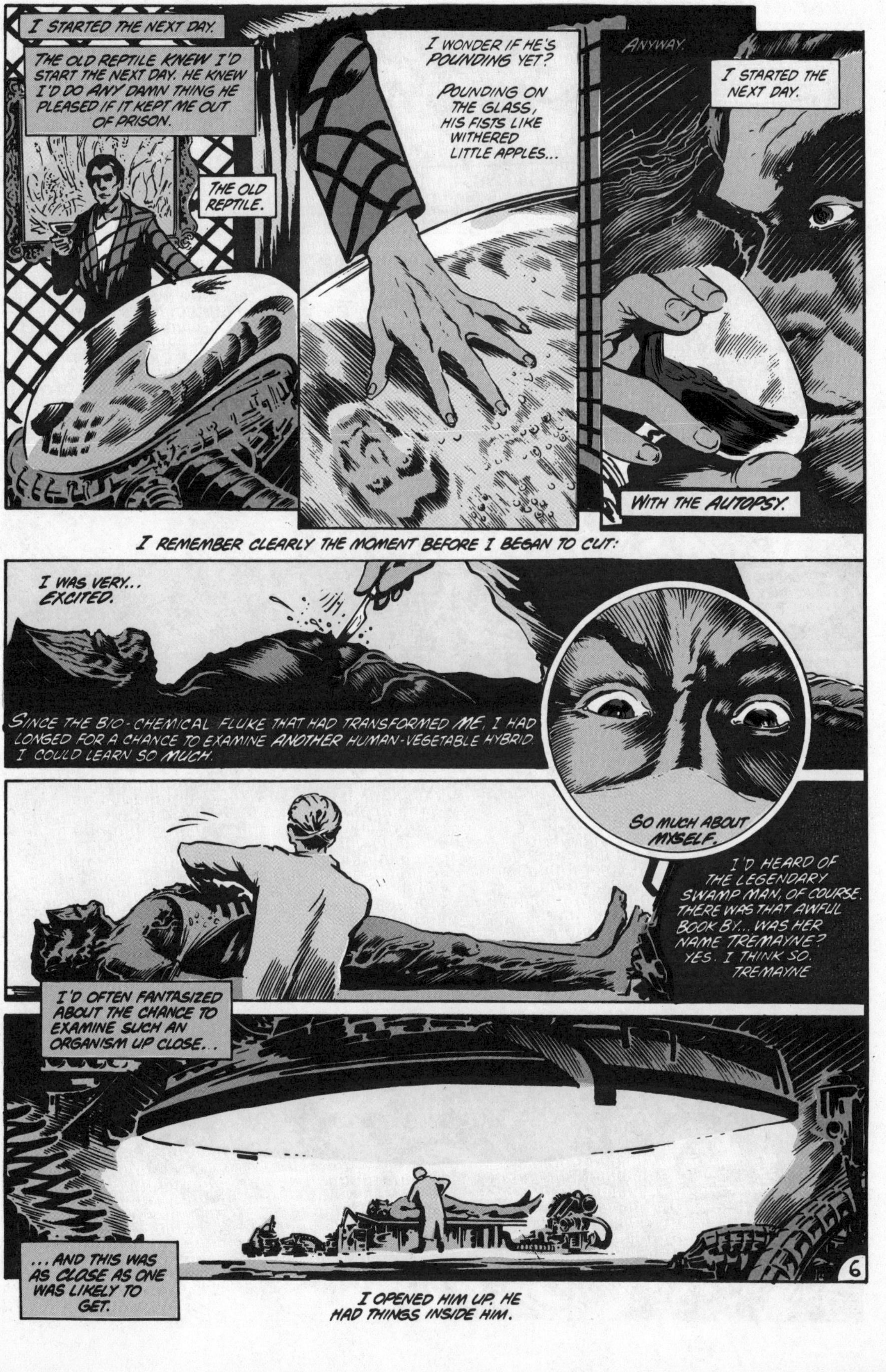

I STARTED THE NEXT DAY.
THE OLD REPTILE KNEW I'D START THE NEXT DAY. HE KNEW I'D DO ANY DAMN THING HE PLEASED IF IT KEPT ME OUT OF PRISON.
THE OLD REPTILE.
I WONDER IF HE'S POUNDING YET?
POUNDING ON THE GLASS, HIS FISTS LIKE WITHERED LITTLE APPLES...
ANYWAY.
I STARTED THE NEXT DAY.
WITH THE AUTOPSY.
I REMEMBER CLEARLY THE MOMENT BEFORE I BEGAN TO CUT:
I WAS VERY... EXCITED.
SINCE THE BIO-CHEMICAL FLUKE THAT HAD TRANSFORMED ME, I HAD LONGED FOR A CHANCE TO EXAMINE ANOTHER HUMAN-VEGETABLE HYBRID. I COULD LEARN SO MUCH.
SO MUCH ABOUT MYSELF.
I'D HEARD OF THE LEGENDARY SWAMP MAN, OF COURSE. THERE WAS THAT AWFUL BOOK BY... WAS HER NAME TREMAYNE? YES. I THINK SO. TREMAYNE
I'D OFTEN FANTASIZED ABOUT THE CHANCE TO EXAMINE SUCH AN ORGANISM UP CLOSE...
...AND THIS WAS AS CLOSE AS ONE WAS LIKELY TO GET.
6
I OPENED HIM UP. HE HAD THINGS INSIDE HIM.

THERE WERE TWO LARGE, POD-LIKE STRUCTURES WITHIN THE CHEST CAVITY...

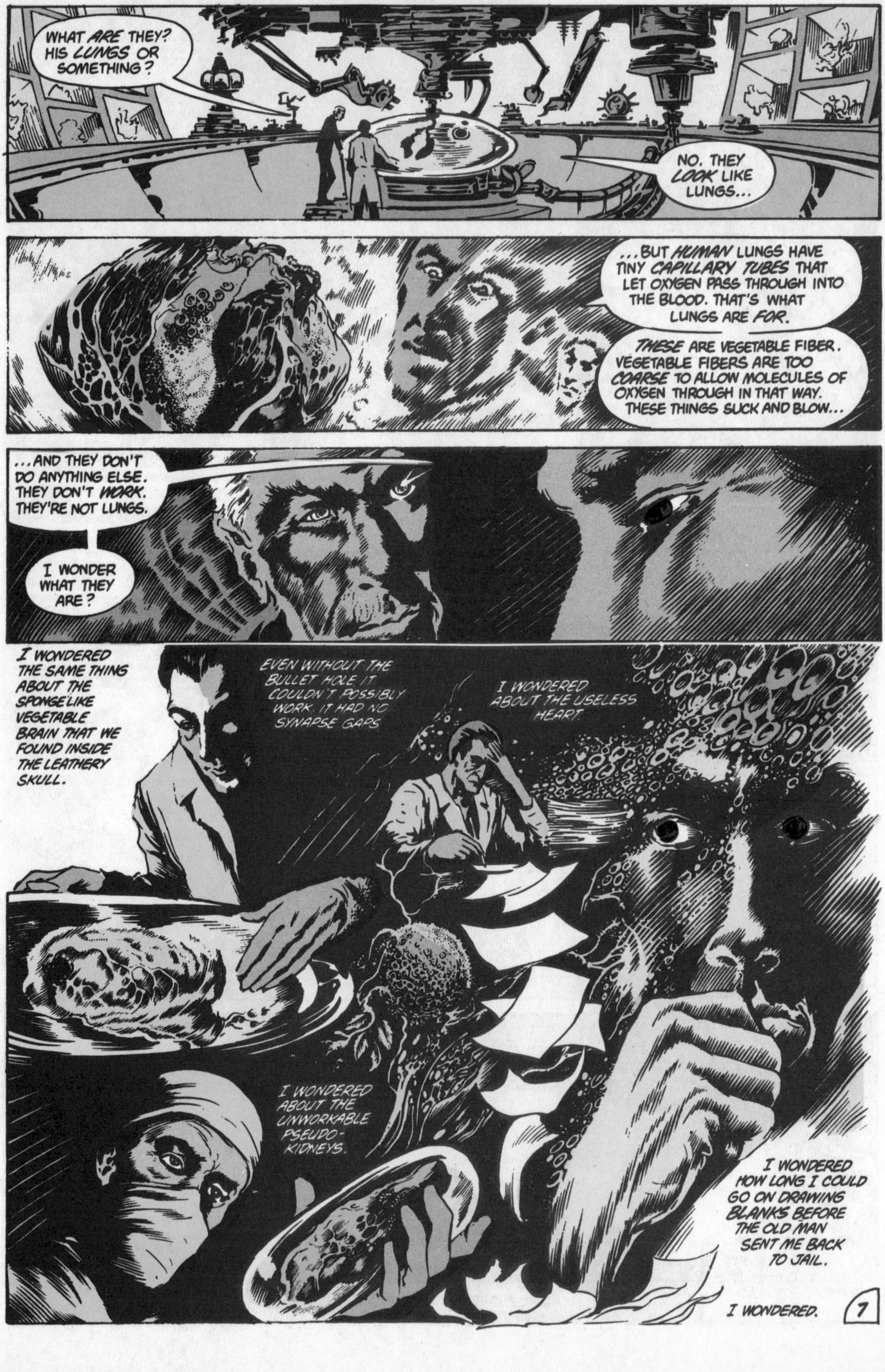
WHAT ARE THEY? HIS LUNGS OR SOMETHING?
NO. THEY LOOK LIKE LUNGS...
...BUT HUMAN LUNGS HAVE TINY CAPILLARY TUBES THAT LET OXYGEN PASS THROUGH INTO THE BLOOD. THAT'S WHAT LUNGS ARE FOR.
THESE ARE VEGETABLE FIBER. VEGETABLE FIBERS ARE TOO COARSE TO ALLOW MOLECULES OF OXYGEN THROUGH IN THAT WAY. THESE THINGS SUCK AND BLOW...
...AND THEY DON'T DO ANYTHING ELSE. THEY DON'T WORK. THEY'RE NOT LUNGS.
I WONDER WHAT THEY ARE?
I WONDERED THE SAME THING ABOUT THE SPONGE-LIKE VEGETABLE BRAIN THAT WE FOUND INSIDE THE LEATHERY SKULL.
EVEN WITHOUT THE BULLET HOLE IT COULDN'T POSSIBLY WORK. IT HAD NO SYNAPSE GAPS.
I WONDERED ABOUT THE USELESS HEART.
I WONDERED ABOUT THE UNWORKABLE PSEUDO-KIDNEYS.
I WONDERED HOW LONG I COULD GO ON DRAWING BLANKS BEFORE THE OLD MAN SENT ME BACK TO JAIL.
I WONDERED.

THOSE WERE LONG WEEKS. LONG AND FRUITLESS.

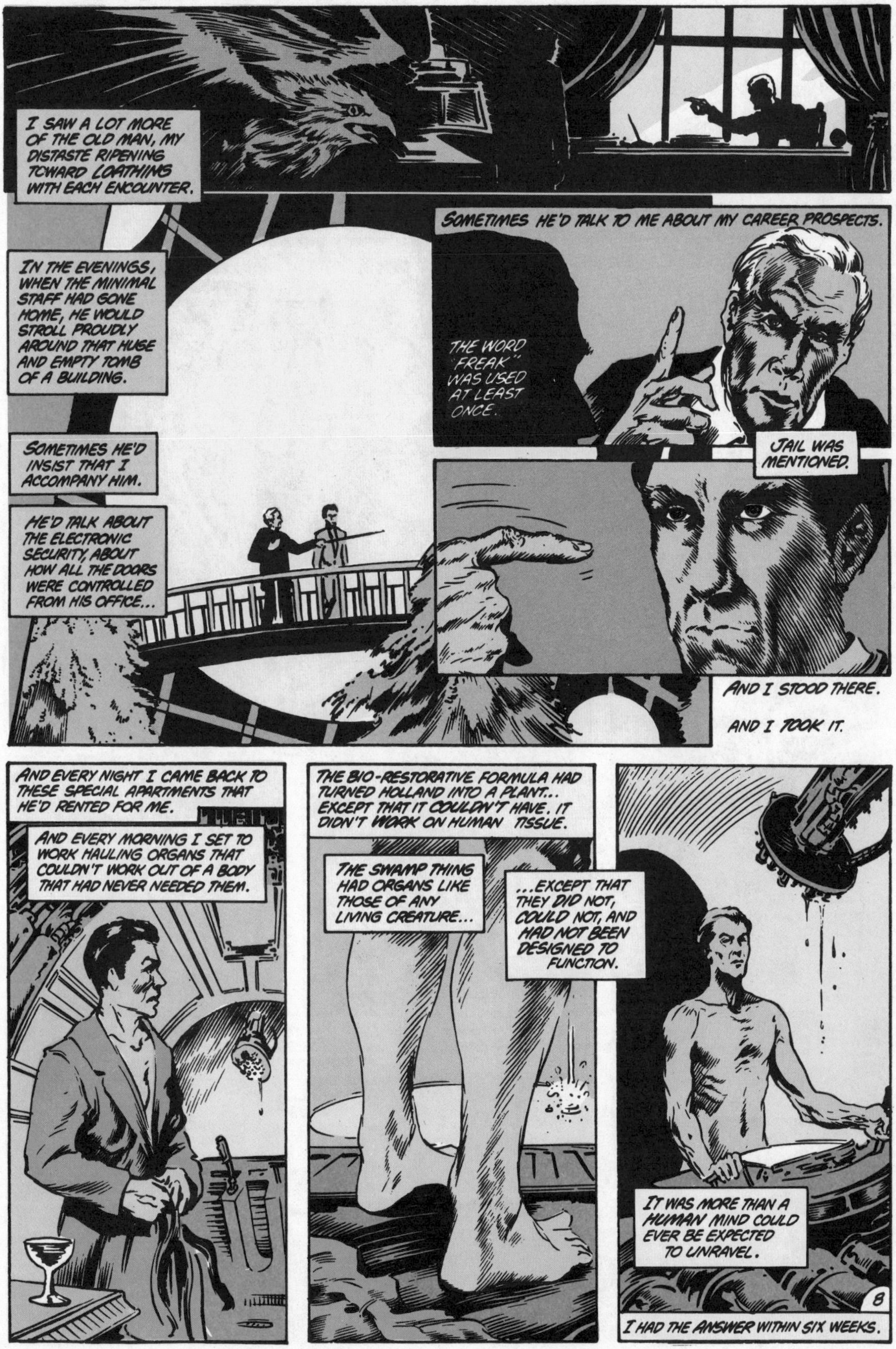

I SAW A LOT MORE OF THE OLD MAN, MY DISTASTE RIPENING TOWARD LOATHING WITH EACH ENCOUNTER.
IN THE EVENINGS, WHEN THE MINIMAL STAFF HAD GONE HOME, HE WOULD STROLL PROUDLY AROUND THAT HUGE AND EMPTY TOMB OF A BUILDING.
SOMETIMES HE'D INSIST THAT I ACCOMPANY HIM.
HE'D TALK ABOUT THE ELECTRONIC SECURITY, ABOUT HOW ALL THE DOORS WERE CONTROLLED FROM HIS OFFICE...
SOMETIMES HE'D TALK TO ME ABOUT MY CAREER PROSPECTS.
THE WORD "FREAK" WAS USED AT LEAST ONCE.
JAIL WAS MENTIONED.
AND I STOOD THERE.
AND I TOOK IT.
AND EVERY NIGHT I CAME BACK TO THESE SPECIAL APARTMENTS THAT HE'D RENTED FOR ME.
AND EVERY MORNING I SET TO WORK HAULING ORGANS THAT COULDN'T WORK OUT OF A BODY THAT HAD NEVER NEEDED THEM.
THE BIO-RESTORATIVE FORMULA HAD TURNED HOLLAND INTO A PLANT... EXCEPT THAT IT COULDN'T HAVE. IT DIDN'T WORK ON HUMAN TISSUE.
THE SWAMP THING HAD ORGANS LIKE THOSE OF ANY LIVING CREATURE...
...EXCEPT THAT THEY DID NOT, COULD NOT, AND HAD NOT BEEN DESIGNED TO FUNCTION.
IT WAS MORE THAN A HUMAN MIND COULD EVER BE EXPECTED TO UNRAVEL.
8
I HAD THE ANSWER WITHIN SIX WEEKS.

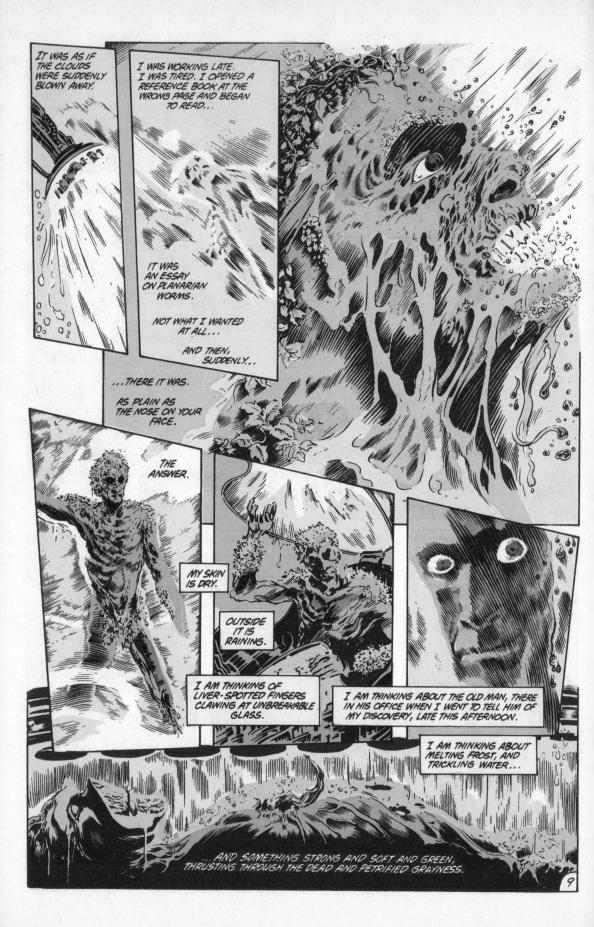

IT WAS AS IF THE CLOUDS WERE SUDDENLY BLOWN AWAY.

I WAS WORKING LATE. I WAS TIRED. I OPENED A REFERENCE BOOK AT THE WRONG PAGE AND BEGAN TO READ...

IT WAS AN ESSAY ON PLANARIAN WORMS.

NOT WHAT I WANTED AT ALL...

AND THEN, SUDDENLY...

...THERE IT WAS.

AS PLAIN AS THE NOSE ON YOUR FACE.

THE ANSWER.

MY SKIN IS DRY.

OUTSIDE IT IS RAINING.

I AM THINKING OF LIVER-SPOTTED FINGERS CLAWING AT UNBREAKABLE GLASS.

I AM THINKING ABOUT THE OLD MAN, THERE IN HIS OFFICE WHEN I WENT TO TELL HIM OF MY DISCOVERY, LATE THIS AFTERNOON.

I AM THINKING ABOUT MELTING FROST, AND TRICKLING WATER...

...AND SOMETHING STRONG AND SOFT AND GREEN, THRUSTING THROUGH THE DEAD AND PETRIFIED GRAYNESS.

9

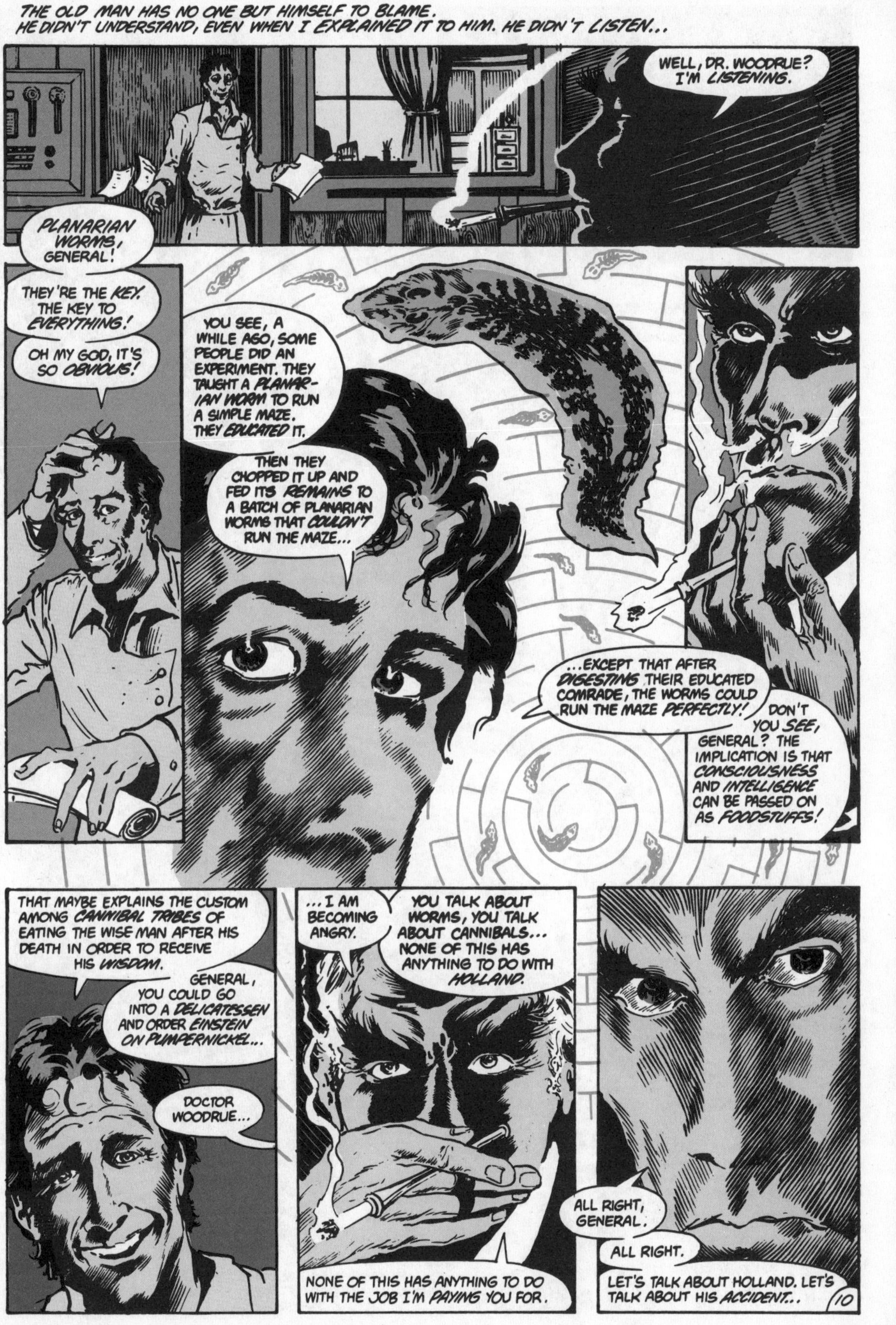

THE OLD MAN HAS NO ONE BUT HIMSELF TO BLAME.
HE DIDN'T UNDERSTAND, EVEN WHEN I EXPLAINED IT TO HIM. HE DIDN'T LISTEN...
WELL, DR. WOODRUE? I'M LISTENING.
PLANARIAN WORMS, GENERAL!
THEY'RE THE KEY. THE KEY TO EVERYTHING!
OH MY GOD, IT'S SO OBVIOUS!
YOU SEE, A WHILE AGO, SOME PEOPLE DID AN EXPERIMENT. THEY TAUGHT A PLANARIAN WORM TO RUN A SIMPLE MAZE. THEY EDUCATED IT.
THEN THEY CHOPPED IT UP AND FED ITS REMAINS TO A BATCH OF PLANARIAN WORMS THAT COULDN'T RUN THE MAZE...
...EXCEPT THAT AFTER DIGESTING THEIR EDUCATED COMRADE, THE WORMS COULD RUN THE MAZE PERFECTLY!
DON'T YOU SEE, GENERAL? THE IMPLICATION IS THAT CONSCIOUSNESS AND INTELLIGENCE CAN BE PASSED ON AS FOODSTUFFS!
THAT MAYBE EXPLAINS THE CUSTOM AMONG CANNIBAL TRIBES OF EATING THE WISE MAN AFTER HIS DEATH IN ORDER TO RECEIVE HIS WISDOM.
GENERAL, YOU COULD GO INTO A DELICATESSEN AND ORDER EINSTEIN ON PUMPERNICKEL...
DOCTOR WOODRUE...
...I AM BECOMING ANGRY.
YOU TALK ABOUT WORMS, YOU TALK ABOUT CANNIBALS... NONE OF THIS HAS ANYTHING TO DO WITH HOLLAND.
NONE OF THIS HAS ANYTHING TO DO WITH THE JOB I'M PAYING YOU FOR.
ALL RIGHT, GENERAL.
ALL RIGHT.
LET'S TALK ABOUT HOLLAND. LET'S TALK ABOUT HIS ACCIDENT...
10

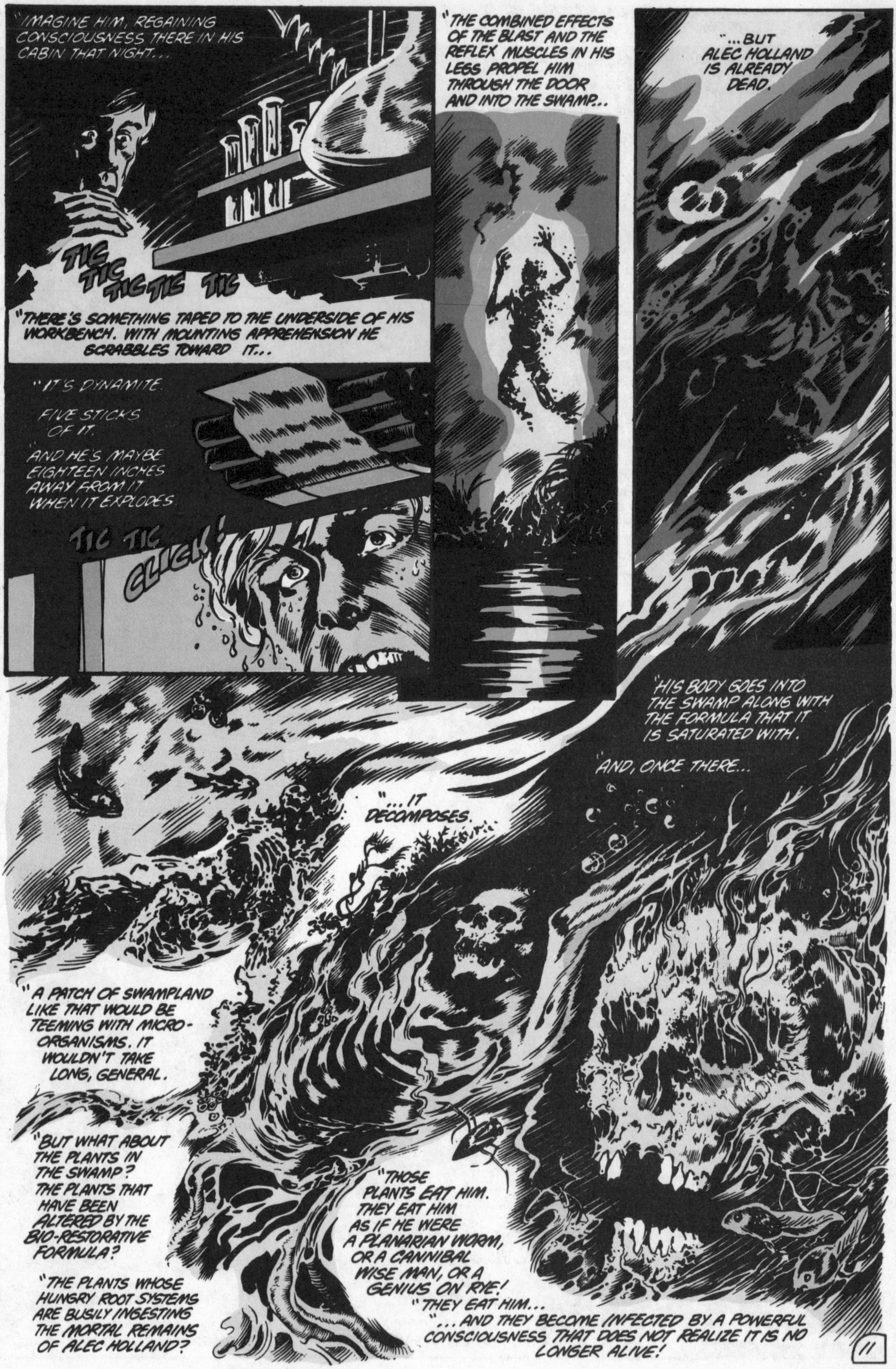
"IMAGINE HIM, REGAINING CONSCIOUSNESS THERE IN HIS CABIN THAT NIGHT...
TIC TIC TIC TIC TIC
"THERE'S SOMETHING TAPED TO THE UNDERSIDE OF HIS WORKBENCH. WITH MOUNTING APPREHENSION HE SCRABBLES TOWARD IT...
"IT'S DYNAMITE.
FIVE STICKS OF IT.
"AND HE'S MAYBE EIGHTEEN INCHES AWAY FROM IT WHEN IT EXPLODES.
TIC TIC
CLICK!
"THE COMBINED EFFECTS OF THE BLAST AND THE REFLEX MUSCLES IN HIS LEGS PROPEL HIM THROUGH THE DOOR AND INTO THE SWAMP...
"...BUT ALEC HOLLAND IS ALREADY DEAD.
"HIS BODY GOES INTO THE SWAMP ALONG WITH THE FORMULA THAT IT IS SATURATED WITH.
"AND, ONCE THERE...
"...IT DECOMPOSES.
"A PATCH OF SWAMPLAND LIKE THAT WOULD BE TEEMING WITH MICRO-ORGANISMS. IT WOULDN'T TAKE LONG, GENERAL.
"BUT WHAT ABOUT THE PLANTS IN THE SWAMP? THE PLANTS THAT HAVE BEEN ALTERED BY THE BIO-RESTORATIVE FORMULA?
"THE PLANTS WHOSE HUNGRY ROOT SYSTEMS ARE BUSILY INGESTING THE MORTAL REMAINS OF ALEC HOLLAND?
"THOSE PLANTS EAT HIM. THEY EAT HIM AS IF HE WERE A PLANARIAN WORM, OR A CANNIBAL WISE MAN, OR A GENIUS ON RYE!
"THEY EAT HIM...
"...AND THEY BECOME INFECTED BY A POWERFUL CONSCIOUSNESS THAT DOES NOT REALIZE IT IS NO LONGER ALIVE!

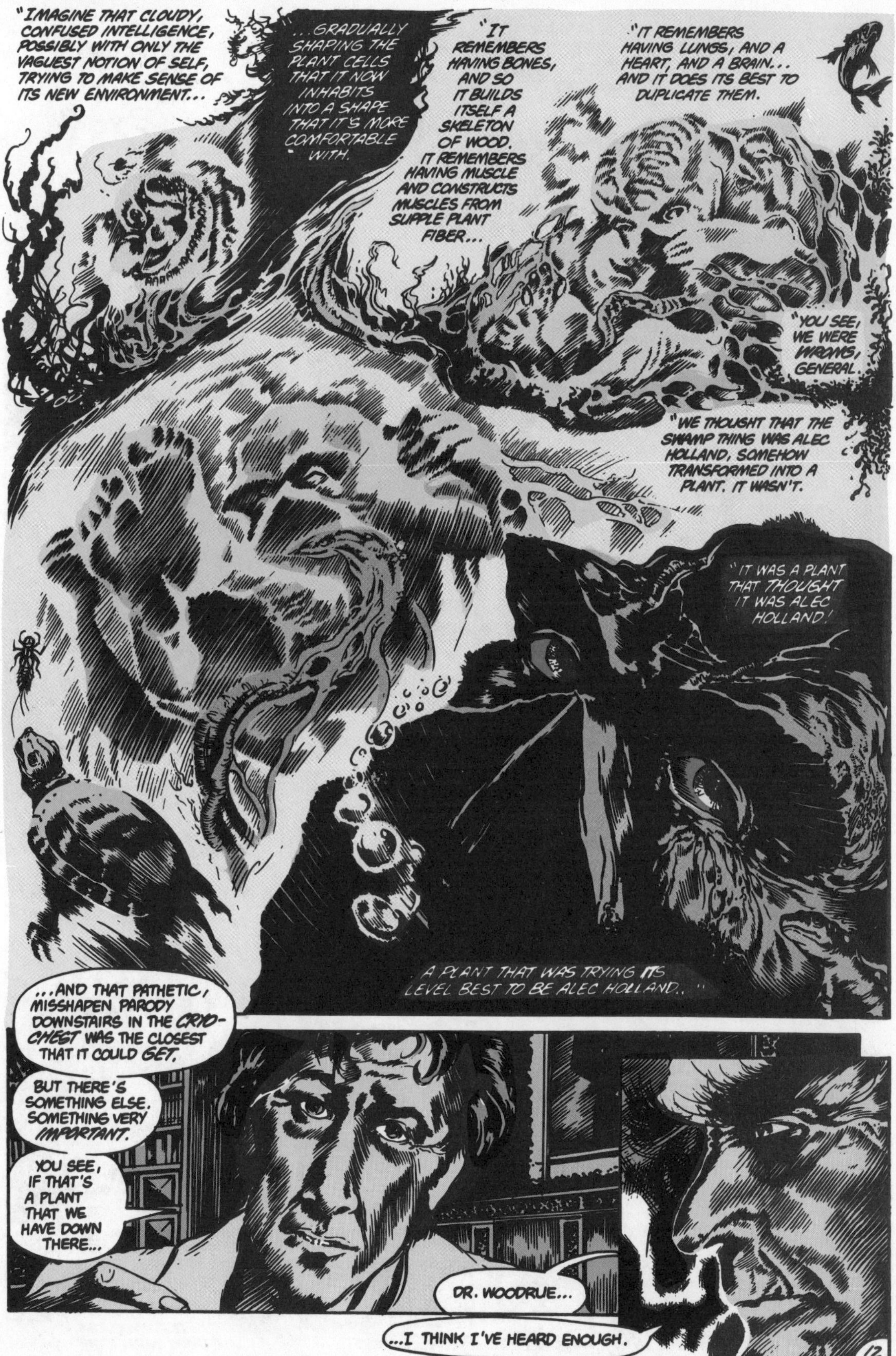
"IMAGINE THAT CLOUDY, CONFUSED INTELLIGENCE, POSSIBLY WITH ONLY THE VAGUEST NOTION OF SELF, TRYING TO MAKE SENSE OF ITS NEW ENVIRONMENT...
...GRADUALLY SHAPING THE PLANT CELLS THAT IT NOW INHABITS INTO A SHAPE THAT IT'S MORE COMFORTABLE WITH.
"IT REMEMBERS HAVING BONES, AND SO IT BUILDS ITSELF A SKELETON OF WOOD. IT REMEMBERS HAVING MUSCLE AND CONSTRUCTS MUSCLES FROM SUPPLE PLANT FIBER...
"IT REMEMBERS HAVING LUNGS, AND A HEART, AND A BRAIN... AND IT DOES ITS BEST TO DUPLICATE THEM.
"YOU SEE, WE WERE WRONG, GENERAL.
"WE THOUGHT THAT THE SWAMP THING WAS ALEC HOLLAND, SOMEHOW TRANSFORMED INTO A PLANT. IT WASN'T.
"IT WAS A PLANT THAT THOUGHT IT WAS ALEC HOLLAND!
A PLANT THAT WAS TRYING ITS LEVEL BEST TO BE ALEC HOLLAND..."
...AND THAT PATHETIC, MISSHAPEN PARODY DOWNSTAIRS IN THE CRYO-CHEST WAS THE CLOSEST THAT IT COULD GET.
BUT THERE'S SOMETHING ELSE. SOMETHING VERY IMPORTANT.
YOU SEE, IF THAT'S A PLANT THAT WE HAVE DOWN THERE...
DR. WOODRUE...
...I THINK I'VE HEARD ENOUGH.
12

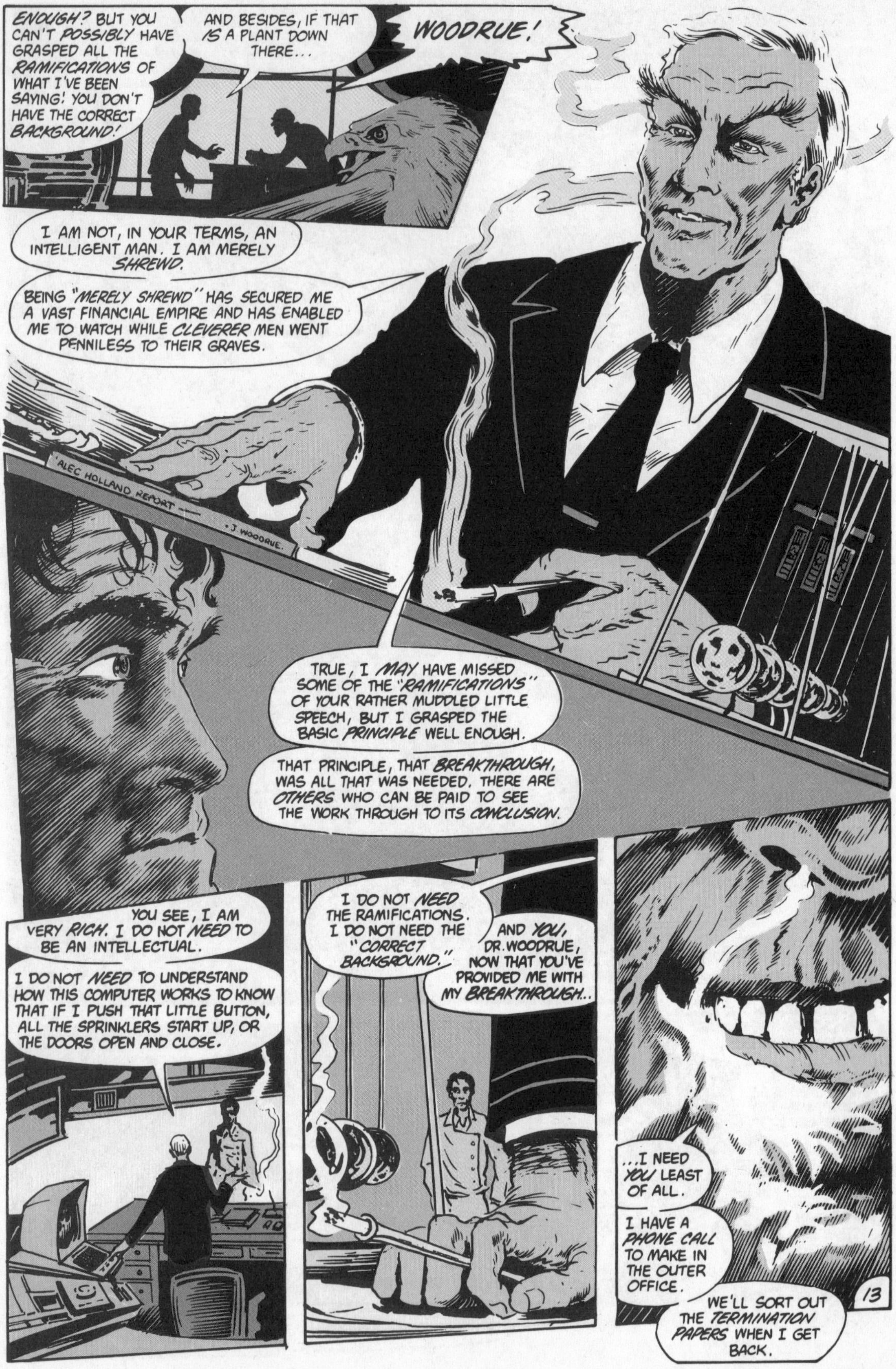
ENOUGH? BUT YOU CAN'T POSSIBLY HAVE GRASPED ALL THE RAMIFICATIONS OF WHAT I'VE BEEN SAYING! YOU DON'T HAVE THE CORRECT BACKGROUND!
AND BESIDES, IF THAT IS A PLANT DOWN THERE...
WOODRUE!
I AM NOT, IN YOUR TERMS, AN INTELLIGENT MAN. I AM MERELY SHREWD.
BEING "MERELY SHREWD" HAS SECURED ME A VAST FINANCIAL EMPIRE AND HAS ENABLED ME TO WATCH WHILE CLEVERER MEN WENT PENNILESS TO THEIR GRAVES.
'ALEC HOLLAND REPORT' — J. WOODRUE.
TRUE, I MAY HAVE MISSED SOME OF THE "RAMIFICATIONS" OF YOUR RATHER MUDDLED LITTLE SPEECH, BUT I GRASPED THE BASIC PRINCIPLE WELL ENOUGH.
THAT PRINCIPLE, THAT BREAKTHROUGH, WAS ALL THAT WAS NEEDED. THERE ARE OTHERS WHO CAN BE PAID TO SEE THE WORK THROUGH TO ITS CONCLUSION.
YOU SEE, I AM VERY RICH. I DO NOT NEED TO BE AN INTELLECTUAL.
I DO NOT NEED TO UNDERSTAND HOW THIS COMPUTER WORKS TO KNOW THAT IF I PUSH THAT LITTLE BUTTON, ALL THE SPRINKLERS START UP, OR THE DOORS OPEN AND CLOSE.
I DO NOT NEED THE RAMIFICATIONS. I DO NOT NEED THE "CORRECT BACKGROUND."
AND YOU, DR. WOODRUE, NOW THAT YOU'VE PROVIDED ME WITH MY BREAKTHROUGH...
...I NEED YOU LEAST OF ALL.
I HAVE A PHONE CALL TO MAKE IN THE OUTER OFFICE.
WE'LL SORT OUT THE TERMINATION PAPERS WHEN I GET BACK.

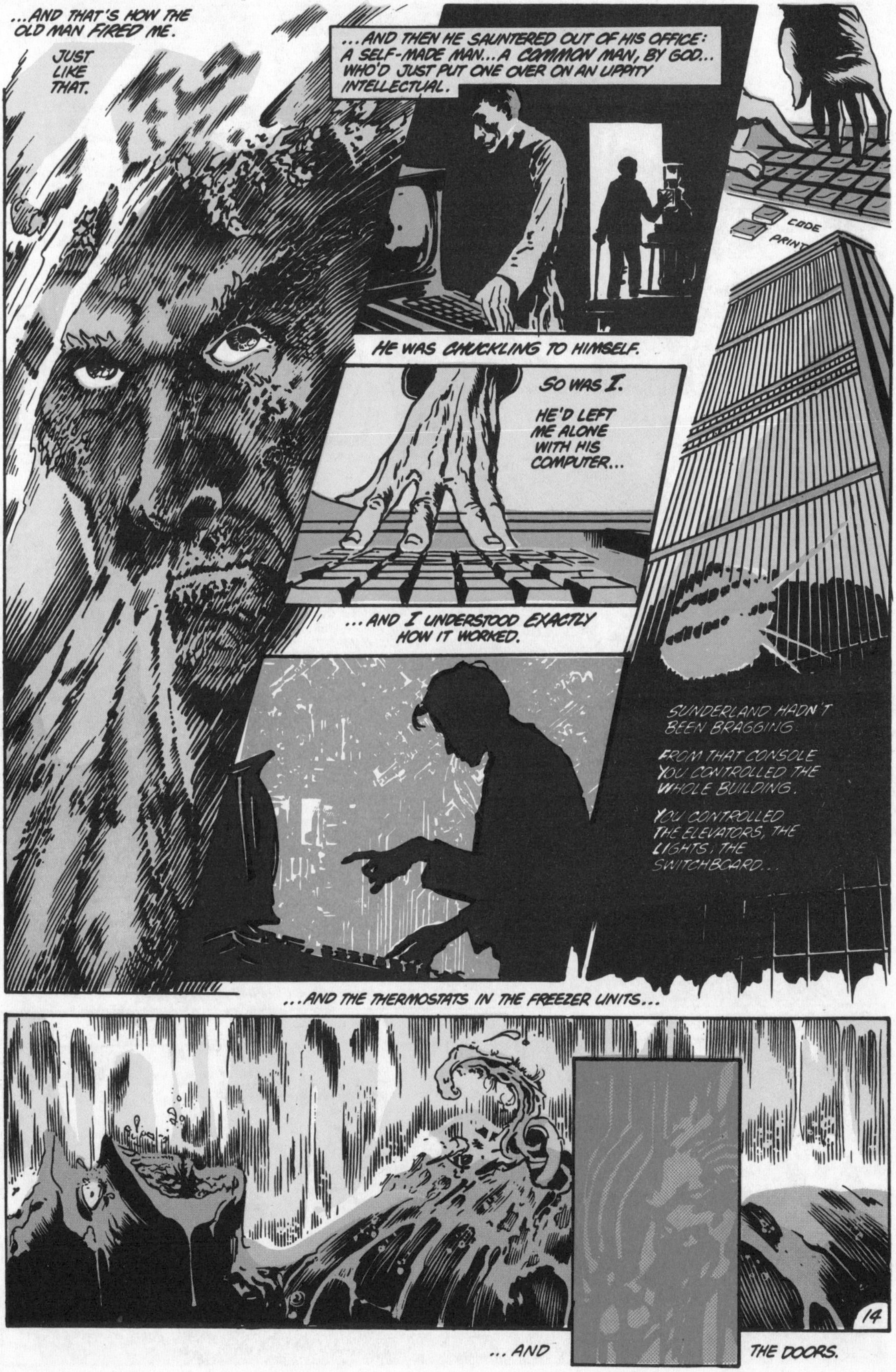
...AND THAT'S HOW THE OLD MAN FIRED ME.
JUST LIKE THAT.
...AND THEN HE SAUNTERED OUT OF HIS OFFICE: A SELF-MADE MAN...A COMMON MAN, BY GOD... WHO'D JUST PUT ONE OVER ON AN UPPITY INTELLECTUAL.
CODE
PRINT
HE WAS CHUCKLING TO HIMSELF.
SO WAS I.
HE'D LEFT ME ALONE WITH HIS COMPUTER...
...AND I UNDERSTOOD EXACTLY HOW IT WORKED.
SUNDERLAND HADN'T BEEN BRAGGING.
FROM THAT CONSOLE YOU CONTROLLED THE WHOLE BUILDING.
YOU CONTROLLED THE ELEVATORS, THE LIGHTS, THE SWITCHBOARD...
...AND THE THERMOSTATS IN THE FREEZER UNITS...
14
...AND
THE DOORS.

I AM SITTING IN MY APARTMENT. OUTSIDE, IT IS RAINING.

I AM LAUGHING. LAUGHING VERY LOUDLY.

FRIENDS HAVE TOLD ME IT IS NOT A SOUND CONDUCIVE TO TRANQUILLITY.

I AM THINKING ABOUT THE OLD MAN.

HE'LL STAY LATE, WHEN EVERYONE HAS GONE. PERHAPS HE'LL READ THROUGH THE NOTES HE WOULDN'T PERMIT ME TO KEEP...

...SKIPPING THE BIG WORDS...

ALEC HOLLAND REPORT 2034

GUMBASIA

PHOTOSYNTHESIS STRUCTURES.

VISION

EYE

RED MUCUS

...AND THEN MAYBE HE'LL WANT TO TAKE A STROLL, LIKE EVERY OTHER NIGHT. A STROLL AROUND THE BIGGEST DOLL HOUSE IN THE WORLD.

HE'LL PUNCH ONE OF HIS LITTLE BUTTONS TO SWITCH THE DOOR MECHANISMS TO MANUAL, SO THAT HE CAN CONTROL THEM WHILE HE'S AWAY FROM HIS CHECKERBOARD.

EXIT

AND THEN HE'LL STRUT PROUDLY DOWN THE HALL AND THINK HOW LUCKY HE IS TO HAVE ALL THIS.

IDENTITY CONFIR

HE SHOULD HAVE LET ME FINISH. HE SHOULD HAVE LISTENED.

THEN I'D HAVE BEEN ABLE TO EXPLAIN THE MOST IMPORTANT THING OF ALL TO HIM.

I'D HAVE BEEN ABLE TO EXPLAIN THAT YOU CAN'T KILL A VEGETABLE BY SHOOTING IT THROUGH THE HEAD.

15

OH, YOU COULD GIVE IT SUCH A SHOCK THAT IT WOULD PLUNGE INTO A *CELLULAR COMA.* YOU COULD KEEP IT IN THAT STATE BY PLACING IT IN A *FREEZER UNIT...*

...BUT YOU COULDN'T *KILL* IT.

REALLY, THE OLD MAN COULD HAVE WORKED THAT OUT FOR HIMSELF.

CRYOGE
WARNING—D

HE JUST DIDN'T HAVE THE CORRECT *BACKGROUND.*

I WONDER WHAT HE'S DOING *NOW?*

I WONDER HOW LONG HE'LL BE ABLE TO RESIST GOING DOWN THERE AND TAKING A *LOOK?*

HOLLAND

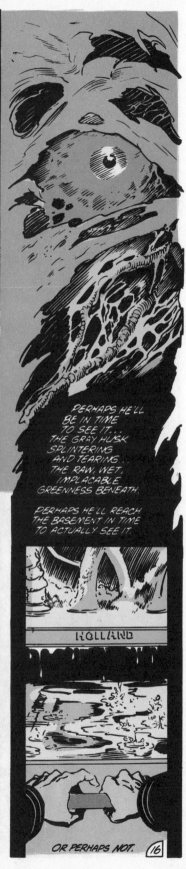

PERHAPS HE'LL BE IN TIME TO *SEE* IT... THE *GRAY HUSK* SPLINTERING AND *TEARING...* THE RAW, WET, IMPLACABLE *GREENNESS* BENEATH.

PERHAPS HE'LL REACH THE BASEMENT IN TIME TO ACTUALLY *SEE* IT.

HOLLAND

OR PERHAPS *NOT.* 16

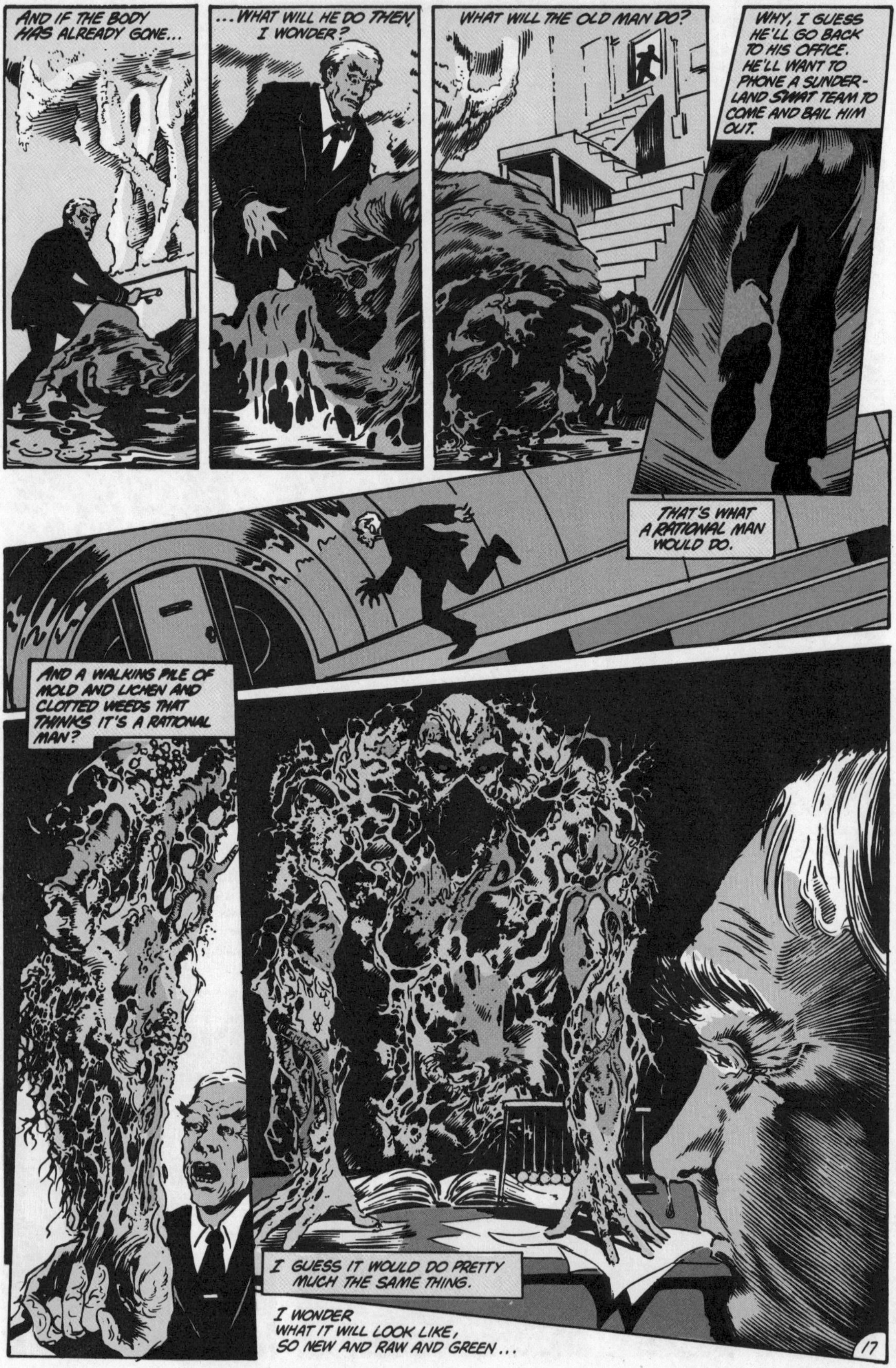
AND IF THE BODY HAS ALREADY GONE...
...WHAT WILL HE DO THEN, I WONDER?
WHAT WILL THE OLD MAN DO?
WHY, I GUESS HE'LL GO BACK TO HIS OFFICE. HE'LL WANT TO PHONE A SUNDERLAND SWAT TEAM TO COME AND BAIL HIM OUT.
THAT'S WHAT A RATIONAL MAN WOULD DO.
AND A WALKING PILE OF MOLD AND LICHEN AND CLOTTED WEEDS THAT THINKS IT'S A RATIONAL MAN?
I GUESS IT WOULD DO PRETTY MUCH THE SAME THING.
I WONDER WHAT IT WILL LOOK LIKE, SO NEW AND RAW AND GREEN...

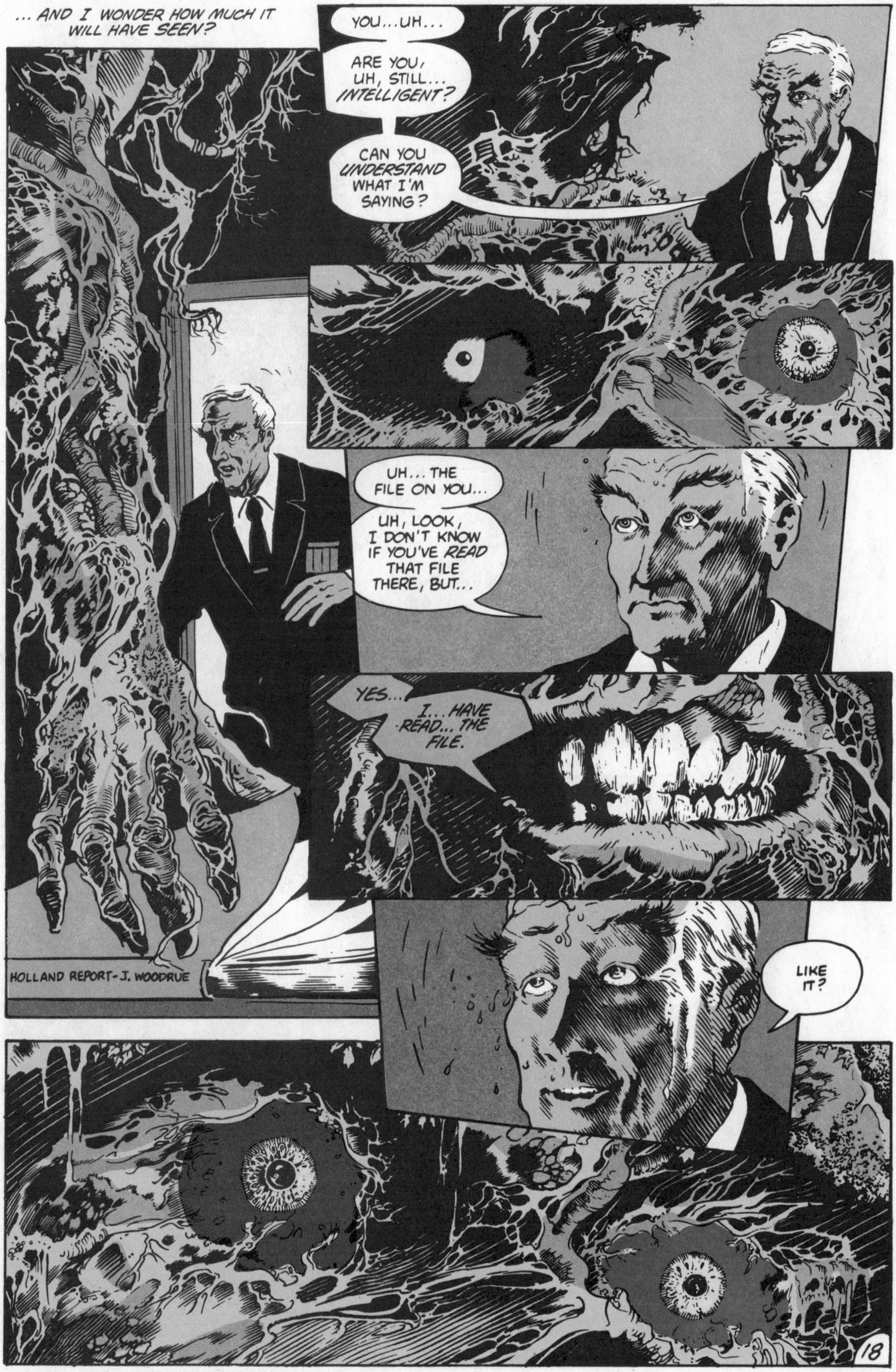
... AND I WONDER HOW MUCH IT WILL HAVE SEEN?
YOU...UH...
ARE YOU, UH, STILL... INTELLIGENT?
CAN YOU UNDERSTAND WHAT I'M SAYING?
UH... THE FILE ON YOU...
UH, LOOK, I DON'T KNOW IF YOU'VE READ THAT FILE THERE, BUT...
YES...
I...HAVE READ... THE FILE.
HOLLAND REPORT - J. WOODRUE
LIKE IT?

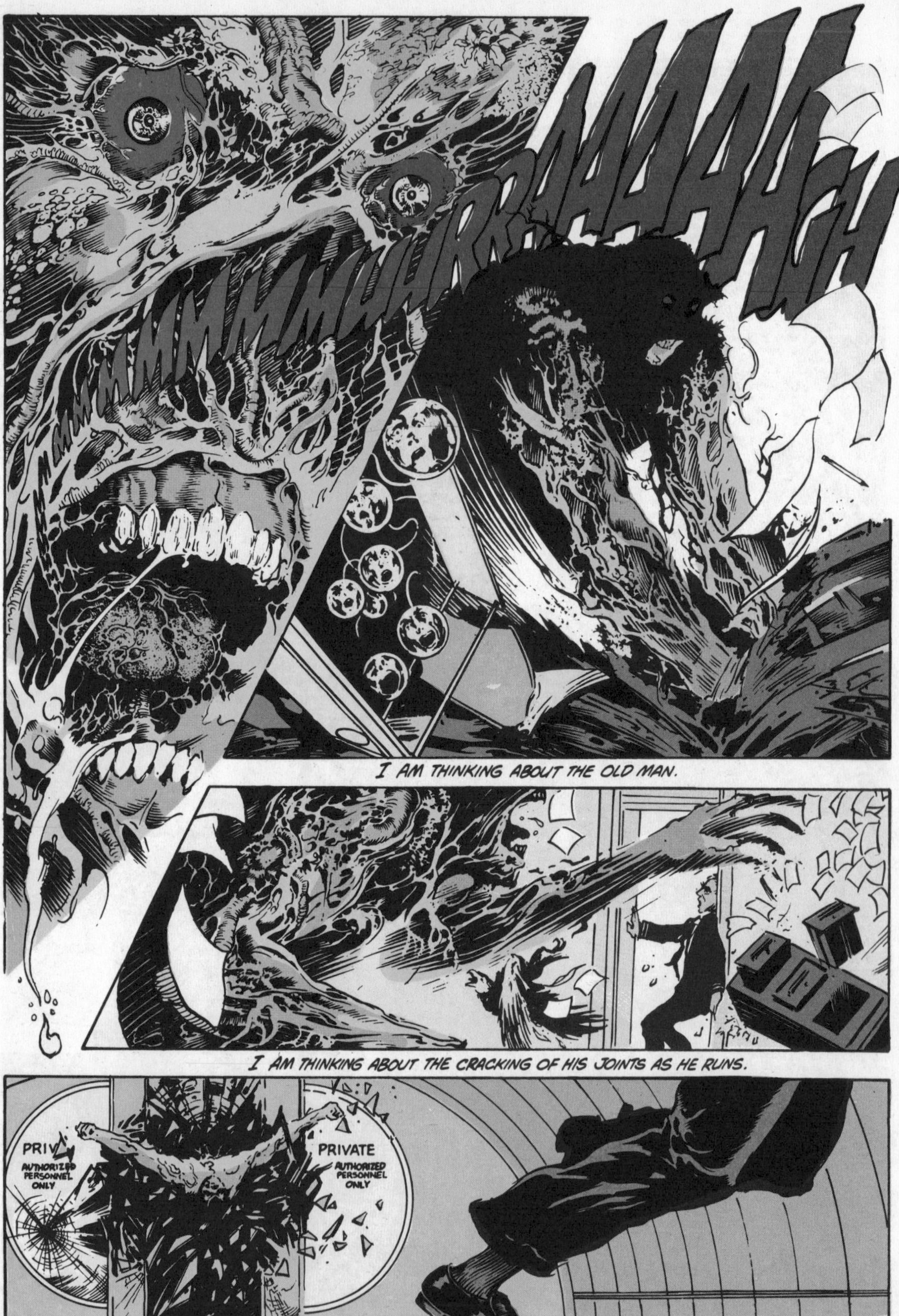
MMMMMMMMMMUHRRAAAAAAAAGH
I AM THINKING ABOUT THE OLD MAN.
I AM THINKING ABOUT THE CRACKING OF HIS JOINTS AS HE RUNS.
PRIV
AUTHORIZED PERSONNEL ONLY
PRIVATE
AUTHORIZED PERSONNEL ONLY
19
I AM THINKING OF THE TERROR IN HIS ANCIENT, ATROPHIED HEART.

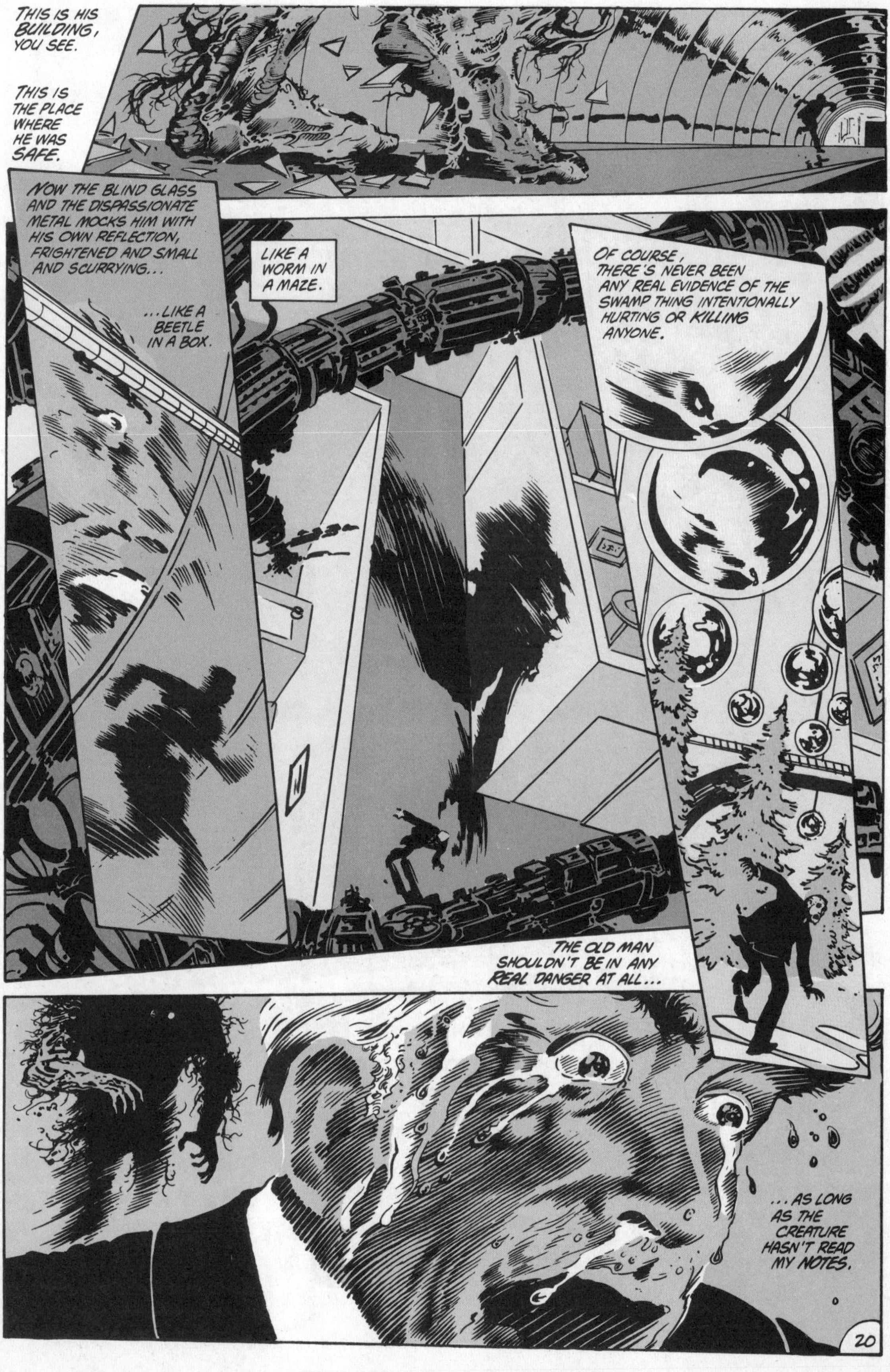

THIS IS HIS BUILDING, YOU SEE.
THIS IS THE PLACE WHERE HE WAS SAFE.
NOW THE BLIND GLASS AND THE DISPASSIONATE METAL MOCKS HIM WITH HIS OWN REFLECTION, FRIGHTENED AND SMALL AND SCURRYING...
...LIKE A BEETLE IN A BOX.
LIKE A WORM IN A MAZE.
OF COURSE, THERE'S NEVER BEEN ANY REAL EVIDENCE OF THE SWAMP THING INTENTIONALLY HURTING OR KILLING ANYONE.
THE OLD MAN SHOULDN'T BE IN ANY REAL DANGER AT ALL...
...AS LONG AS THE CREATURE HASN'T READ MY NOTES.

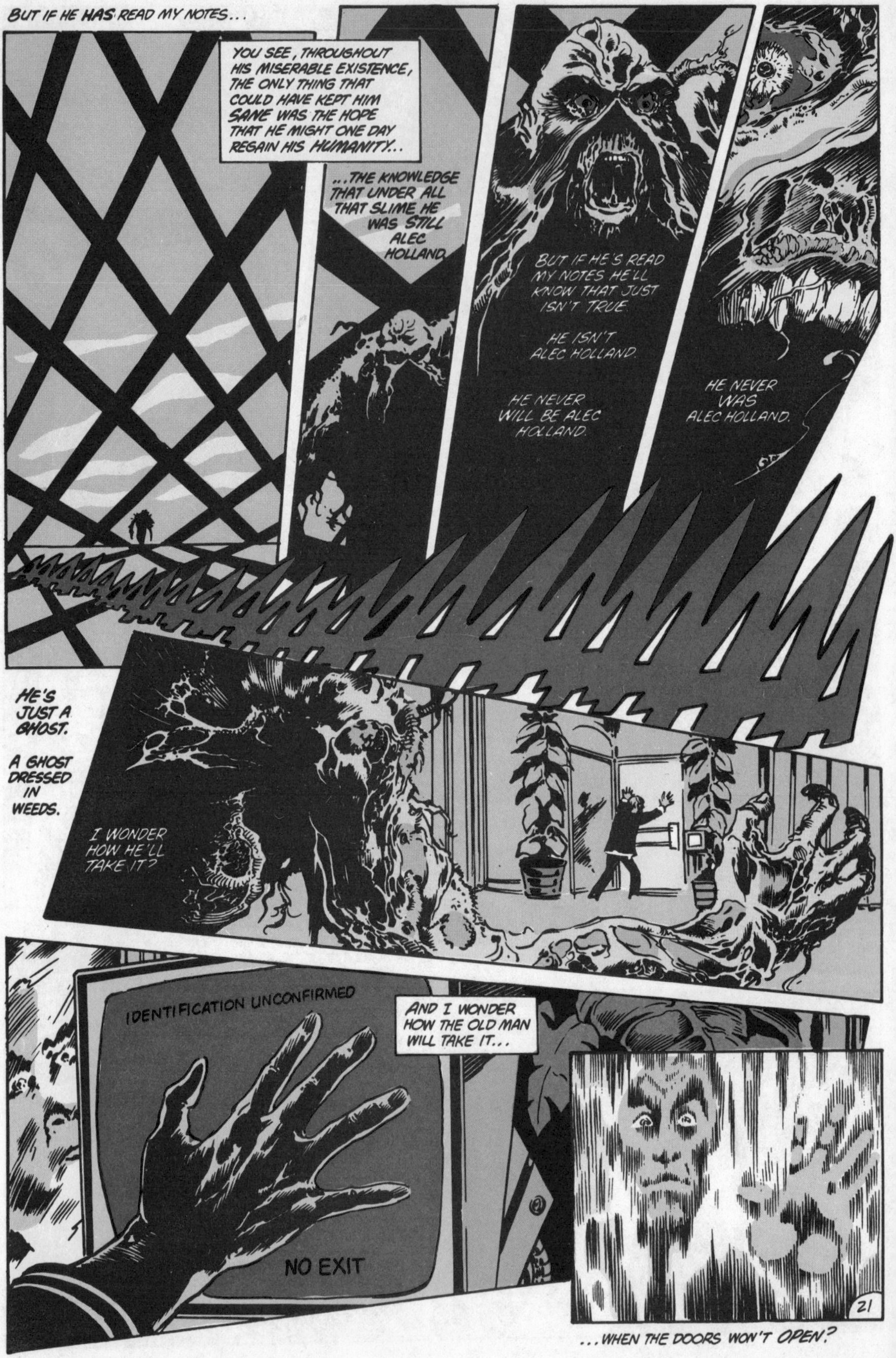
BUT IF HE HAS READ MY NOTES...
YOU SEE, THROUGHOUT HIS MISERABLE EXISTENCE, THE ONLY THING THAT COULD HAVE KEPT HIM SANE WAS THE HOPE THAT HE MIGHT ONE DAY REGAIN HIS HUMANITY...
...THE KNOWLEDGE THAT UNDER ALL THAT SLIME HE WAS STILL ALEC HOLLAND.
BUT IF HE'S READ MY NOTES HE'LL KNOW THAT JUST ISN'T TRUE.
HE ISN'T ALEC HOLLAND.
HE NEVER WILL BE ALEC HOLLAND.
HE NEVER WAS ALEC HOLLAND.
HE'S JUST A GHOST.
A GHOST DRESSED IN WEEDS.
I WONDER HOW HE'LL TAKE IT?
IDENTIFICATION UNCONFIRMED
NO EXIT
AND I WONDER HOW THE OLD MAN WILL TAKE IT...
...WHEN THE DOORS WON'T OPEN?

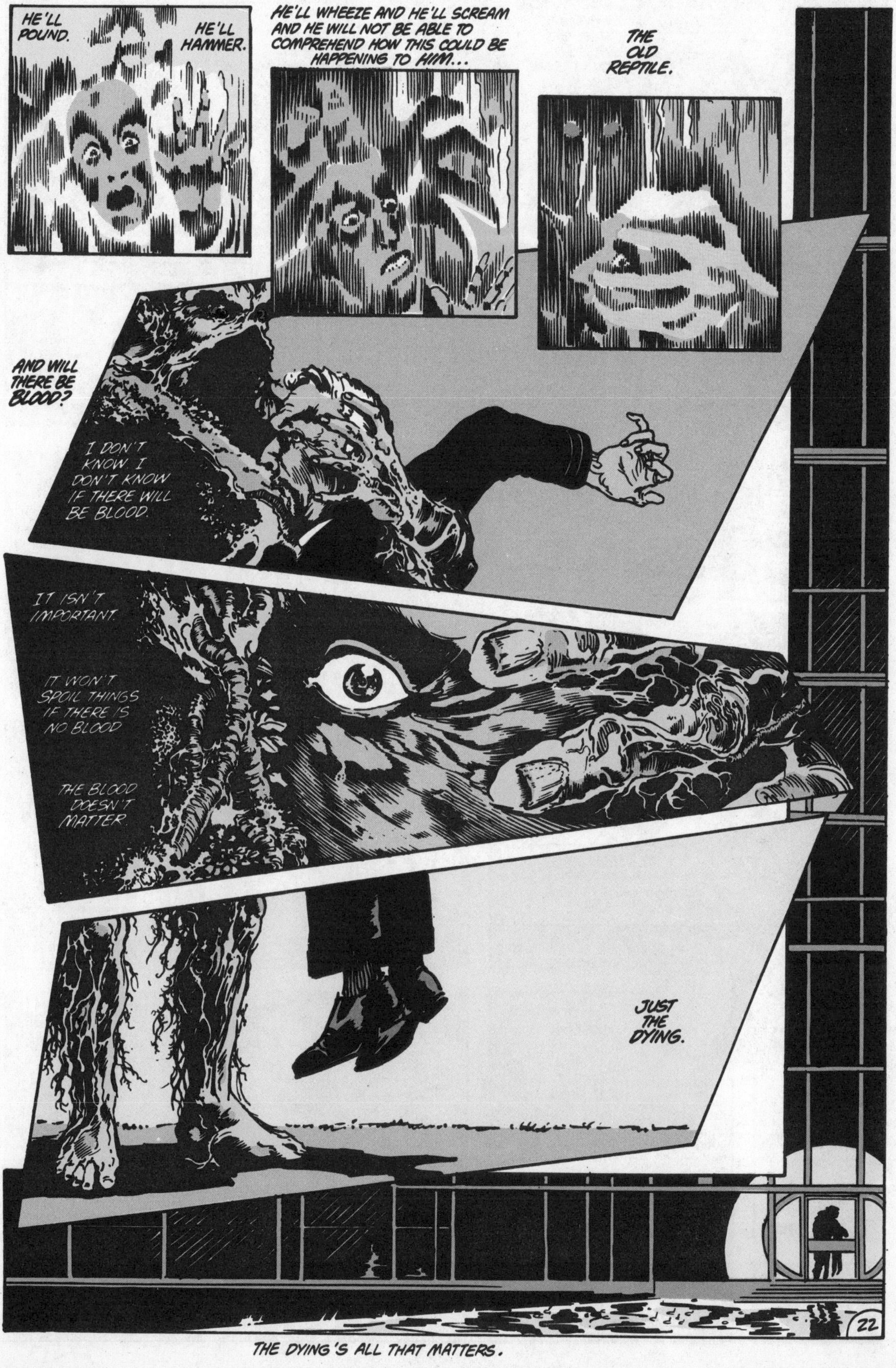
HE'LL POUND.
HE'LL HAMMER.
HE'LL WHEEZE AND HE'LL SCREAM AND HE WILL NOT BE ABLE TO COMPREHEND HOW THIS COULD BE HAPPENING TO HIM...
THE OLD REPTILE.
AND WILL THERE BE BLOOD?
I DON'T KNOW. I DON'T KNOW IF THERE WILL BE BLOOD.
IT ISN'T IMPORTANT.
IT WON'T SPOIL THINGS IF THERE IS NO BLOOD
THE BLOOD DOESN'T MATTER.
JUST THE DYING.
THE DYING'S ALL THAT MATTERS.

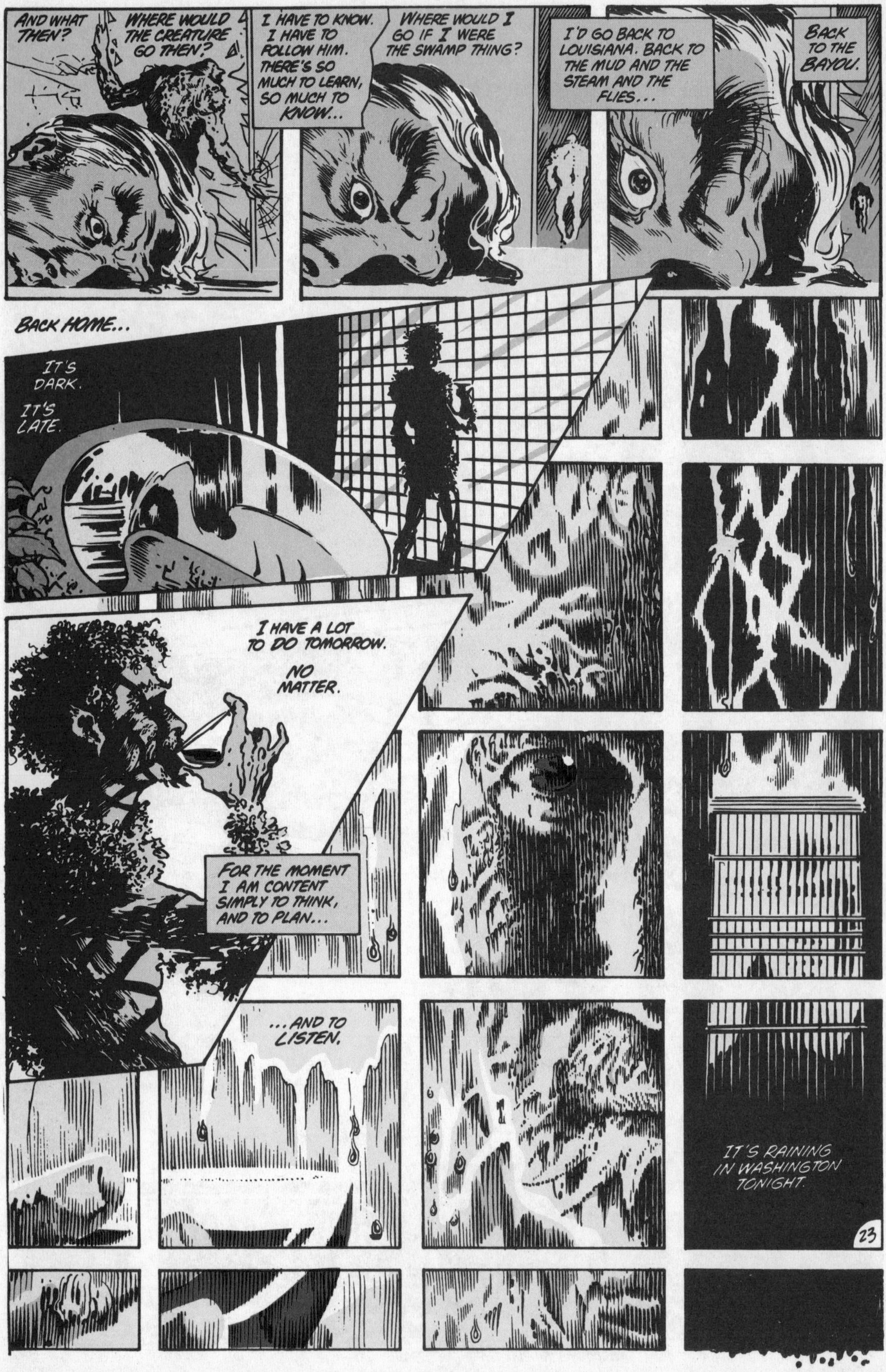
AND WHAT THEN?
WHERE WOULD THE CREATURE GO THEN?
I HAVE TO KNOW. I HAVE TO FOLLOW HIM. THERE'S SO MUCH TO LEARN, SO MUCH TO KNOW...
WHERE WOULD I GO IF I WERE THE SWAMP THING?
I'D GO BACK TO LOUISIANA. BACK TO THE MUD AND THE STEAM AND THE FLIES...
BACK TO THE BAYOU.
BACK HOME...
IT'S DARK.
IT'S LATE.
I HAVE A LOT TO DO TOMORROW.
NO MATTER.
FOR THE MOMENT I AM CONTENT SIMPLY TO THINK, AND TO PLAN...
...AND TO LISTEN.
IT'S RAINING IN WASHINGTON TONIGHT.
23

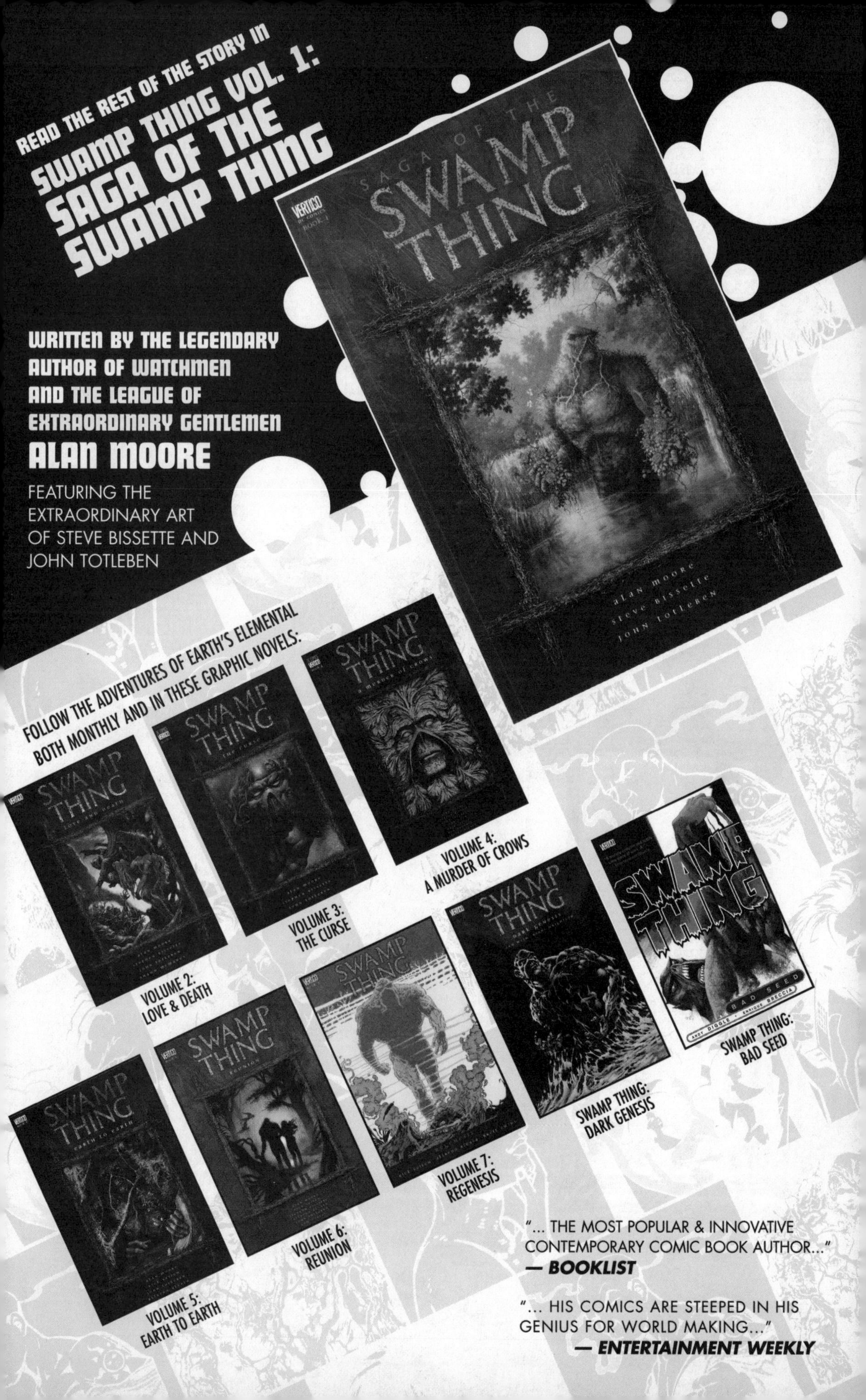
READ THE REST OF THE STORY IN
SWAMP THING VOL. 1:
SAGA OF THE
SWAMP THING
WRITTEN BY THE LEGENDARY
AUTHOR OF WATCHMEN
AND THE LEAGUE OF
EXTRAORDINARY GENTLEMEN
ALAN MOORE
FEATURING THE
EXTRAORDINARY ART
OF STEVE BISSETTE AND
JOHN TOTLEBEN
VERTIGO
DC COMICS
BOOK 1
SAGA OF THE
SWAMP
THING
alan moore
steve bissette
john totleben
FOLLOW THE ADVENTURES OF EARTH'S ELEMENTAL
BOTH MONTHLY AND IN THESE GRAPHIC NOVELS:
VOLUME 2:
LOVE & DEATH
VOLUME 3:
THE CURSE
VOLUME 4:
A MURDER OF CROWS
VOLUME 5:
EARTH TO EARTH
VOLUME 6:
REUNION
VOLUME 7:
REGENESIS
SWAMP THING:
DARK GENESIS
SWAMP THING:
BAD SEED
"... THE MOST POPULAR & INNOVATIVE
CONTEMPORARY COMIC BOOK AUTHOR..."
— BOOKLIST
"... HIS COMICS ARE STEEPED IN HIS
GENIUS FOR WORLD MAKING..."
— ENTERTAINMENT WEEKLY

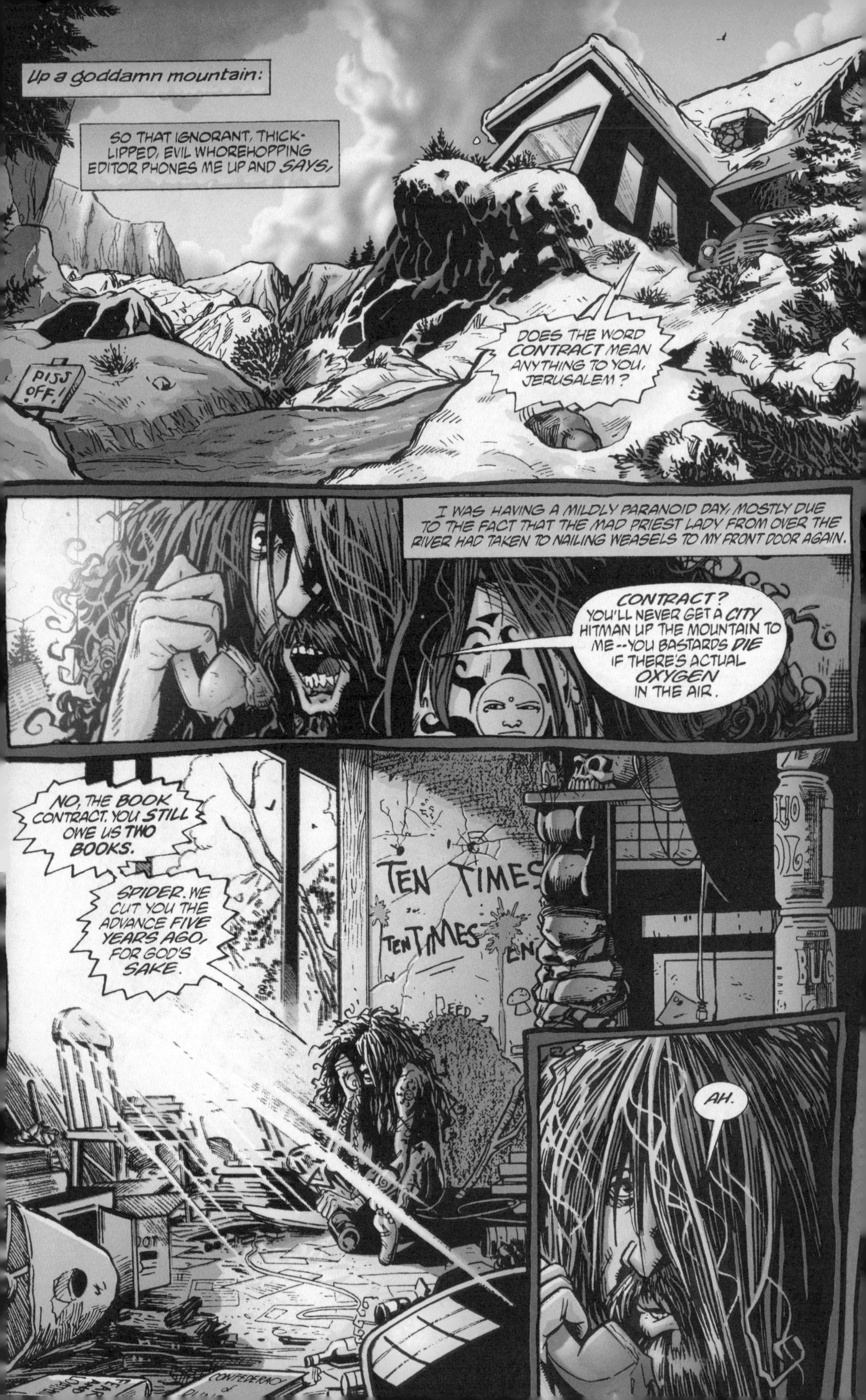
Up a goddamn mountain:
SO THAT IGNORANT, THICK-LIPPED, EVIL WHOREHOPPING EDITOR PHONES ME UP AND SAYS,
PISS OFF!
DOES THE WORD CONTRACT MEAN ANYTHING TO YOU, JERUSALEM?
I WAS HAVING A MILDLY PARANOID DAY, MOSTLY DUE TO THE FACT THAT THE MAD PRIEST LADY FROM OVER THE RIVER HAD TAKEN TO NAILING WEASELS TO MY FRONT DOOR AGAIN.
CONTRACT? YOU'LL NEVER GET A CITY HITMAN UP THE MOUNTAIN TO ME--YOU BASTARDS DIE IF THERE'S ACTUAL OXYGEN IN THE AIR.
NO, THE BOOK CONTRACT. YOU STILL OWE US TWO BOOKS.
SPIDER. WE CUT YOU THE ADVANCE FIVE YEARS AGO, FOR GOD'S SAKE.
TEN TIMES
TEN TIMES
AH.

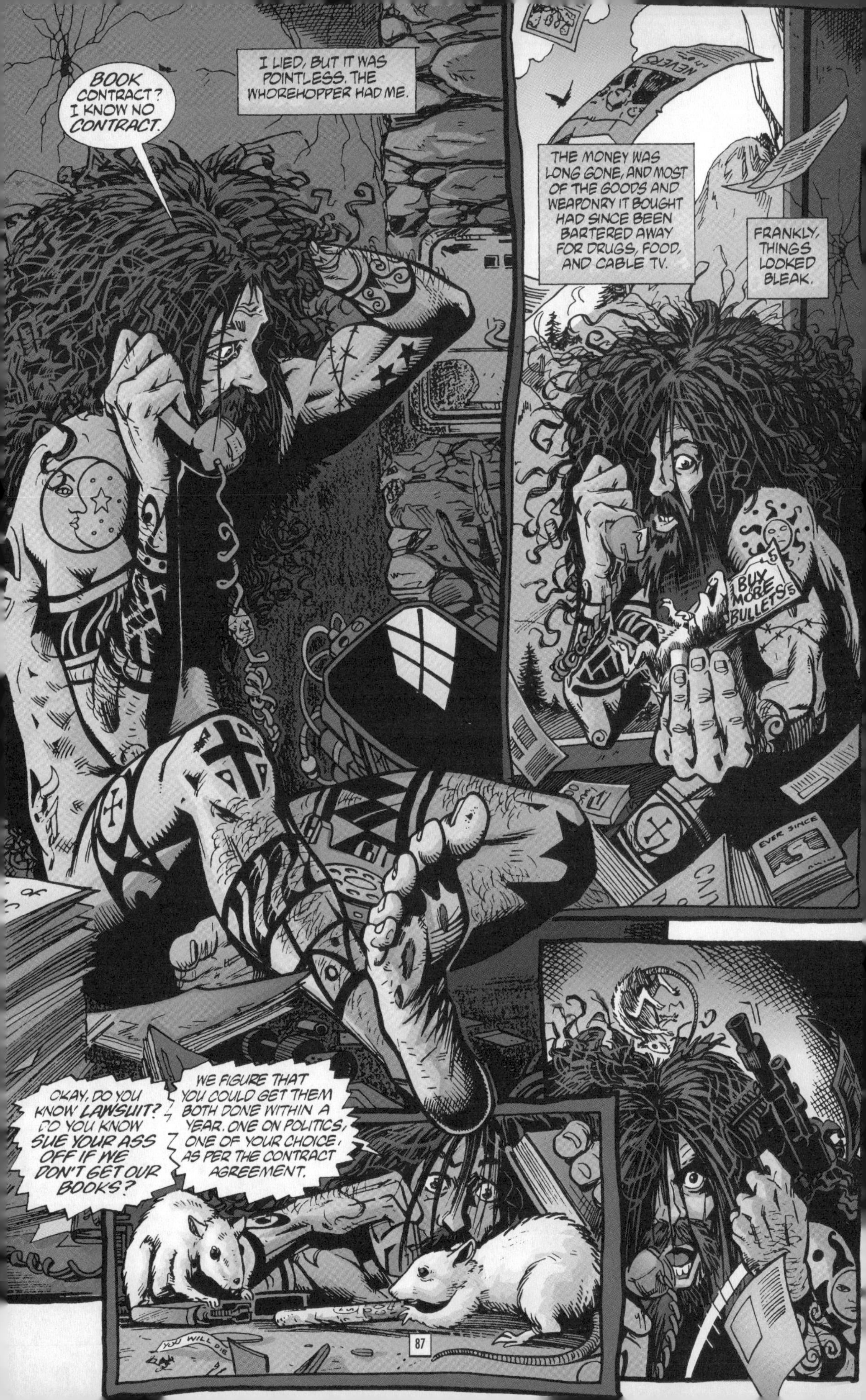
BOOK CONTRACT? I KNOW NO CONTRACT.
I LIED, BUT IT WAS POINTLESS. THE WHOREHOPPER HAD ME.
NEVERS
THE MONEY WAS LONG GONE, AND MOST OF THE GOODS AND WEAPONRY IT BOUGHT HAD SINCE BEEN BARTERED AWAY FOR DRUGS, FOOD, AND CABLE TV.
FRANKLY, THINGS LOOKED BLEAK.
BUY MORE BULLETS
EVER SINCE
OKAY, DO YOU KNOW LAWSUIT? DO YOU KNOW SUE YOUR ASS OFF IF WE DON'T GET OUR BOOKS?
WE FIGURE THAT YOU COULD GET THEM BOTH DONE WITHIN A YEAR. ONE ON POLITICS, ONE OF YOUR CHOICE, AS PER THE CONTRACT AGREEMENT.
YOU WILL DIE

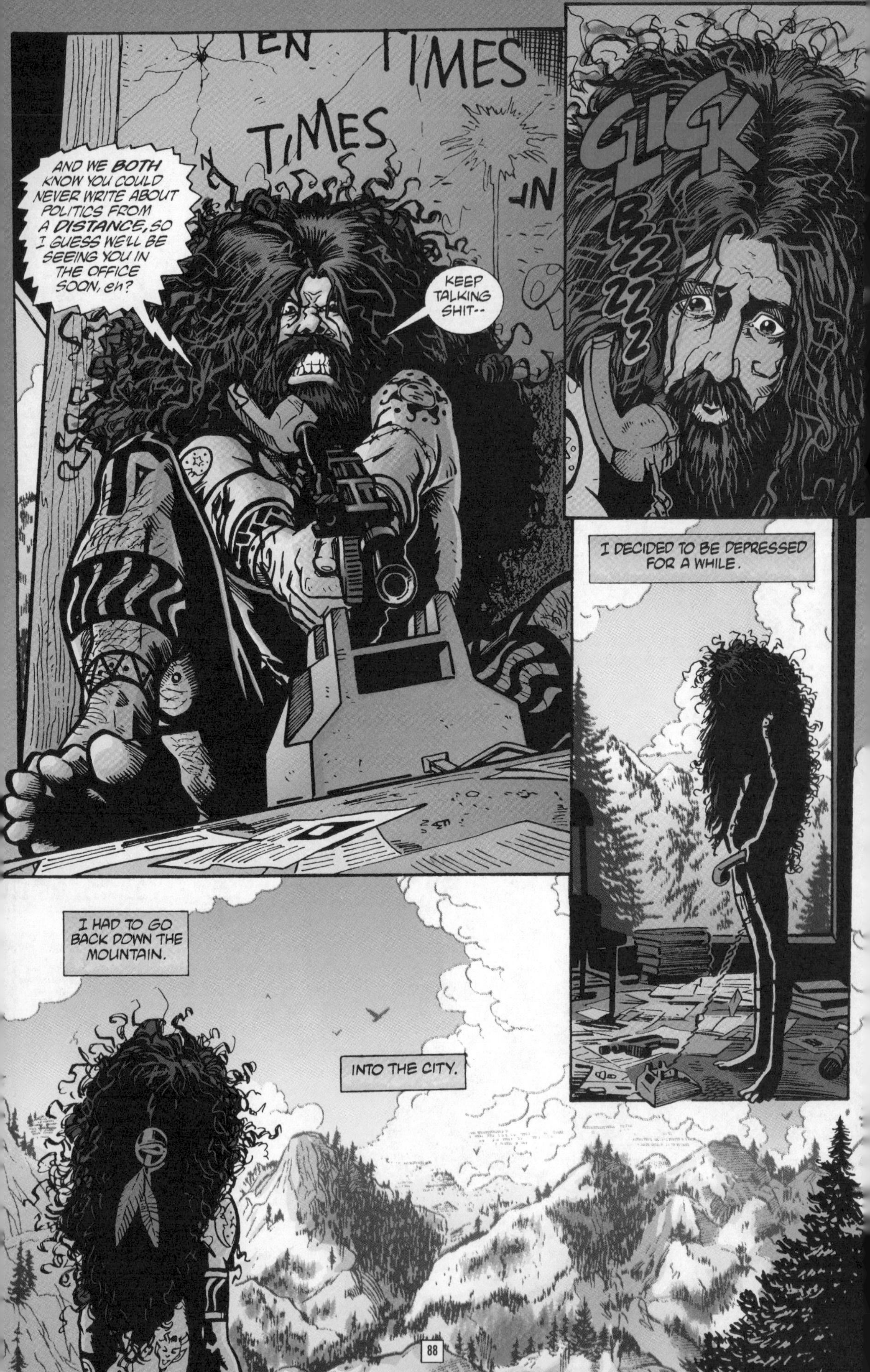

TEN TIMES
TIMES
AND WE BOTH KNOW YOU COULD NEVER WRITE ABOUT POLITICS FROM A DISTANCE, SO I GUESS WE'LL BE SEEING YOU IN THE OFFICE SOON, eh?
KEEP TALKING SHIT--
CLICK
BZZZZZ
I DECIDED TO BE DEPRESSED FOR A WHILE.
I HAD TO GO BACK DOWN THE MOUNTAIN.
INTO THE CITY.

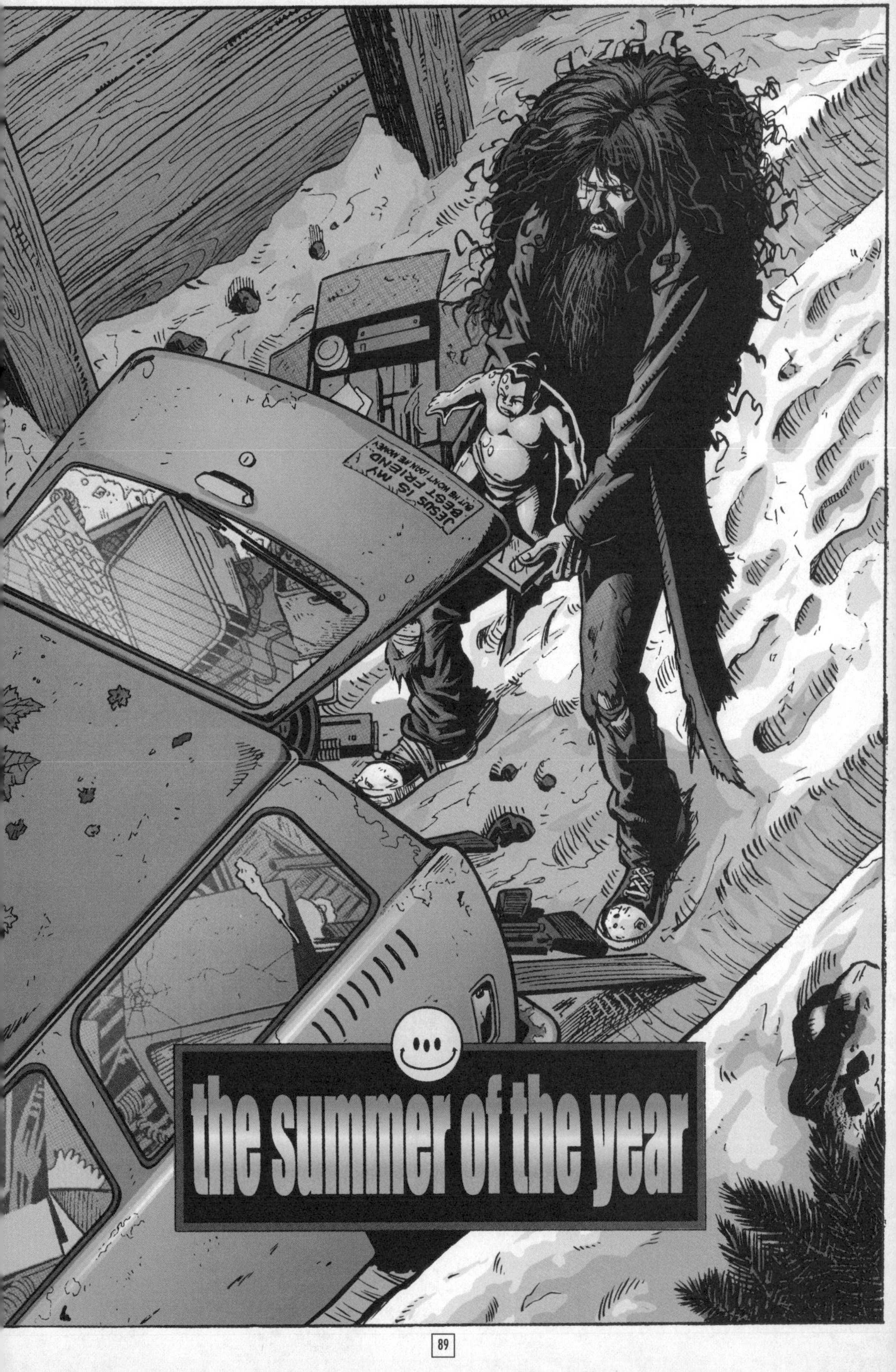
JESUS IS MY BEST FRIEND.
BUT HE WONT LOAN ME MONEY.
the summer of the year

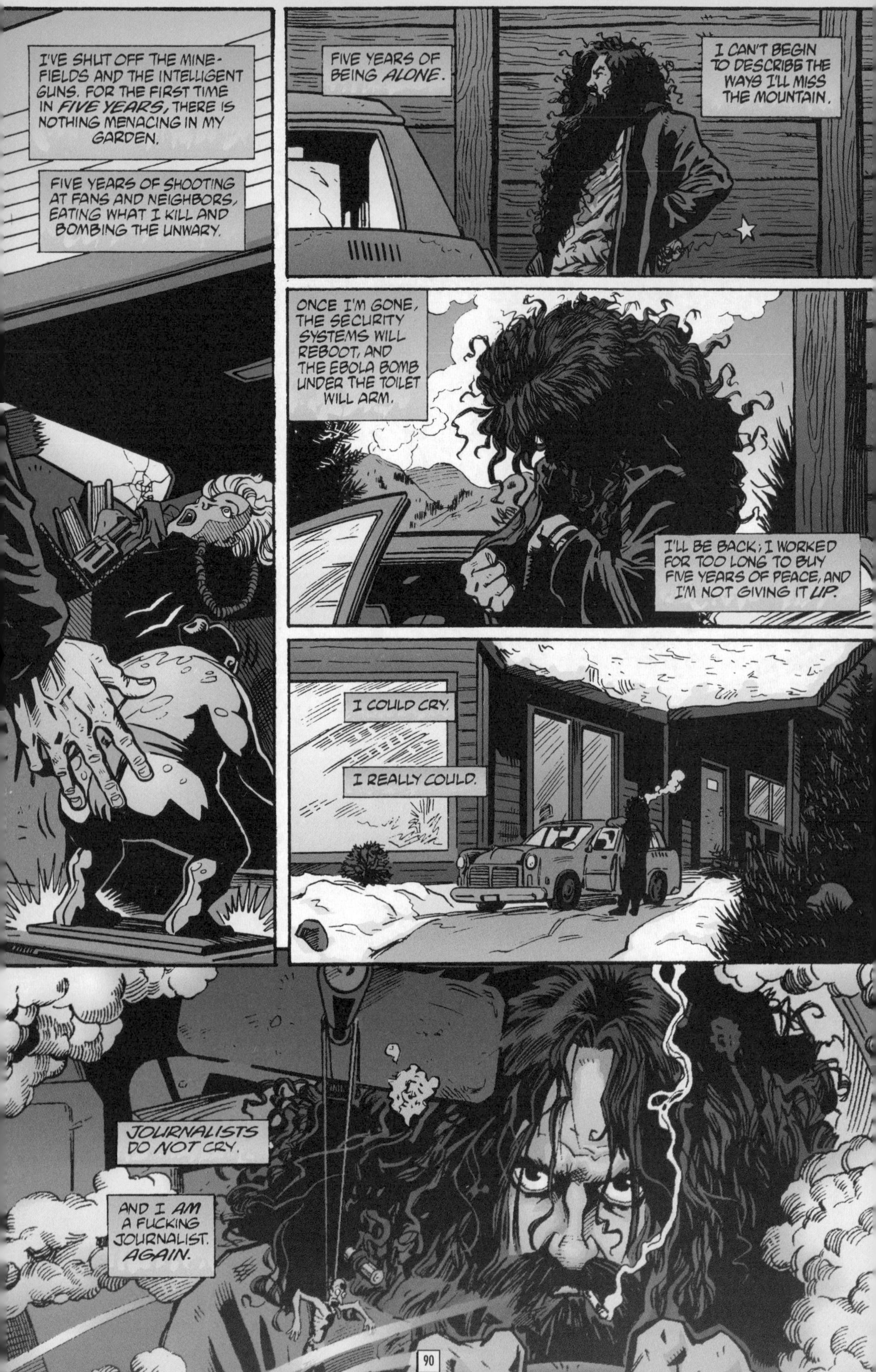
I'VE SHUT OFF THE MINE-FIELDS AND THE INTELLIGENT GUNS. FOR THE FIRST TIME IN FIVE YEARS, THERE IS NOTHING MENACING IN MY GARDEN.
FIVE YEARS OF SHOOTING AT FANS AND NEIGHBORS, EATING WHAT I KILL AND BOMBING THE UNWARY.
FIVE YEARS OF BEING ALONE.
I CAN'T BEGIN TO DESCRIBE THE WAYS I'LL MISS THE MOUNTAIN.
ONCE I'M GONE, THE SECURITY SYSTEMS WILL REBOOT, AND THE EBOLA BOMB UNDER THE TOILET WILL ARM.
I'LL BE BACK; I WORKED FOR TOO LONG TO BUY FIVE YEARS OF PEACE, AND I'M NOT GIVING IT UP.
I COULD CRY.
I REALLY COULD.
JOURNALISTS DO NOT CRY.
AND I AM A FUCKING JOURNALIST. AGAIN.

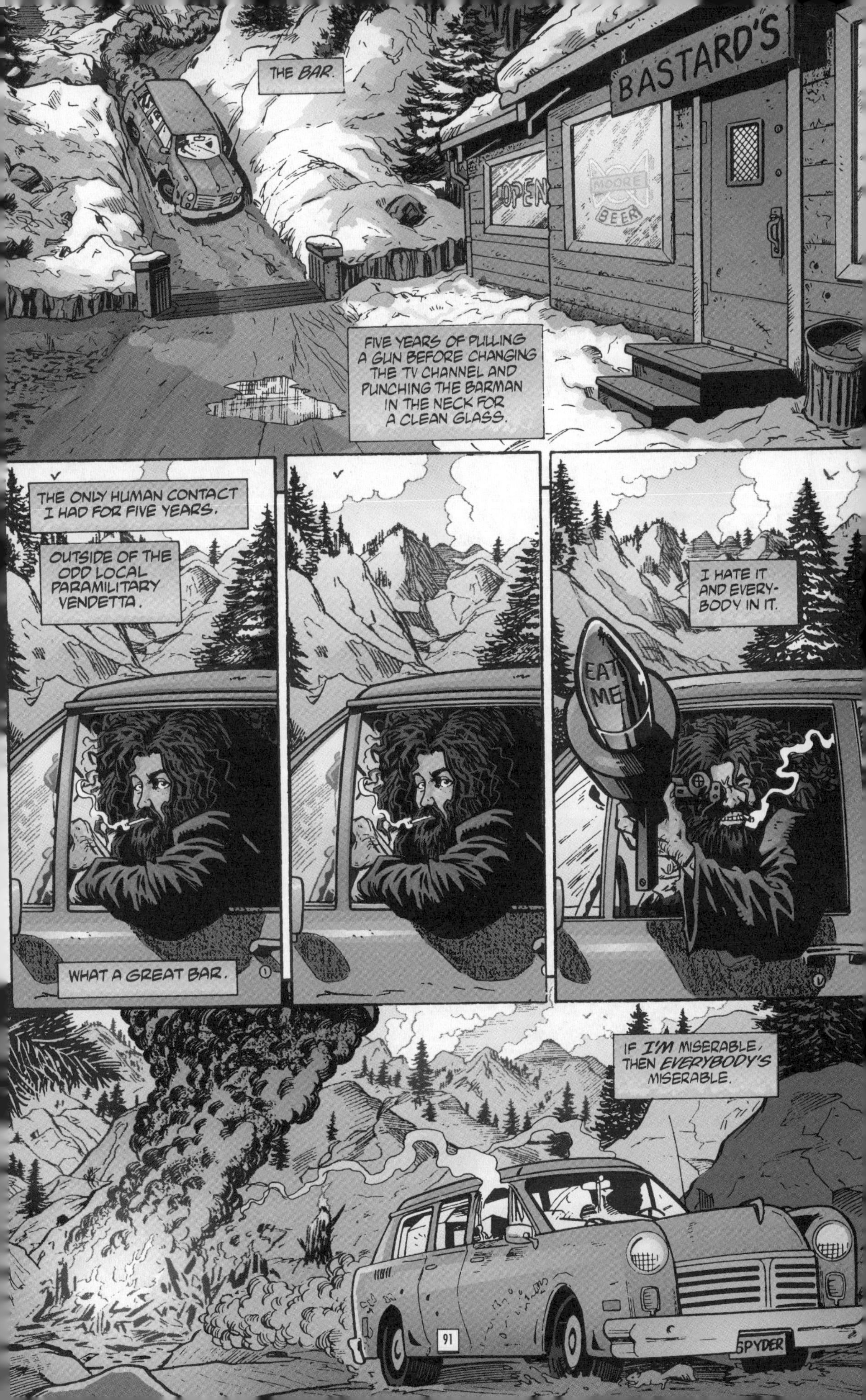
THE BAR.
BASTARD'S
OPEN
MOORE BEER
FIVE YEARS OF PULLING A GUN BEFORE CHANGING THE TV CHANNEL AND PUNCHING THE BARMAN IN THE NECK FOR A CLEAN GLASS.
THE ONLY HUMAN CONTACT I HAD FOR FIVE YEARS.
OUTSIDE OF THE ODD LOCAL PARAMILITARY VENDETTA.
WHAT A GREAT BAR.
I HATE IT AND EVERYBODY IN IT.
EAT ME
IF I'M MISERABLE, THEN EVERYBODY'S MISERABLE.
SPYDER

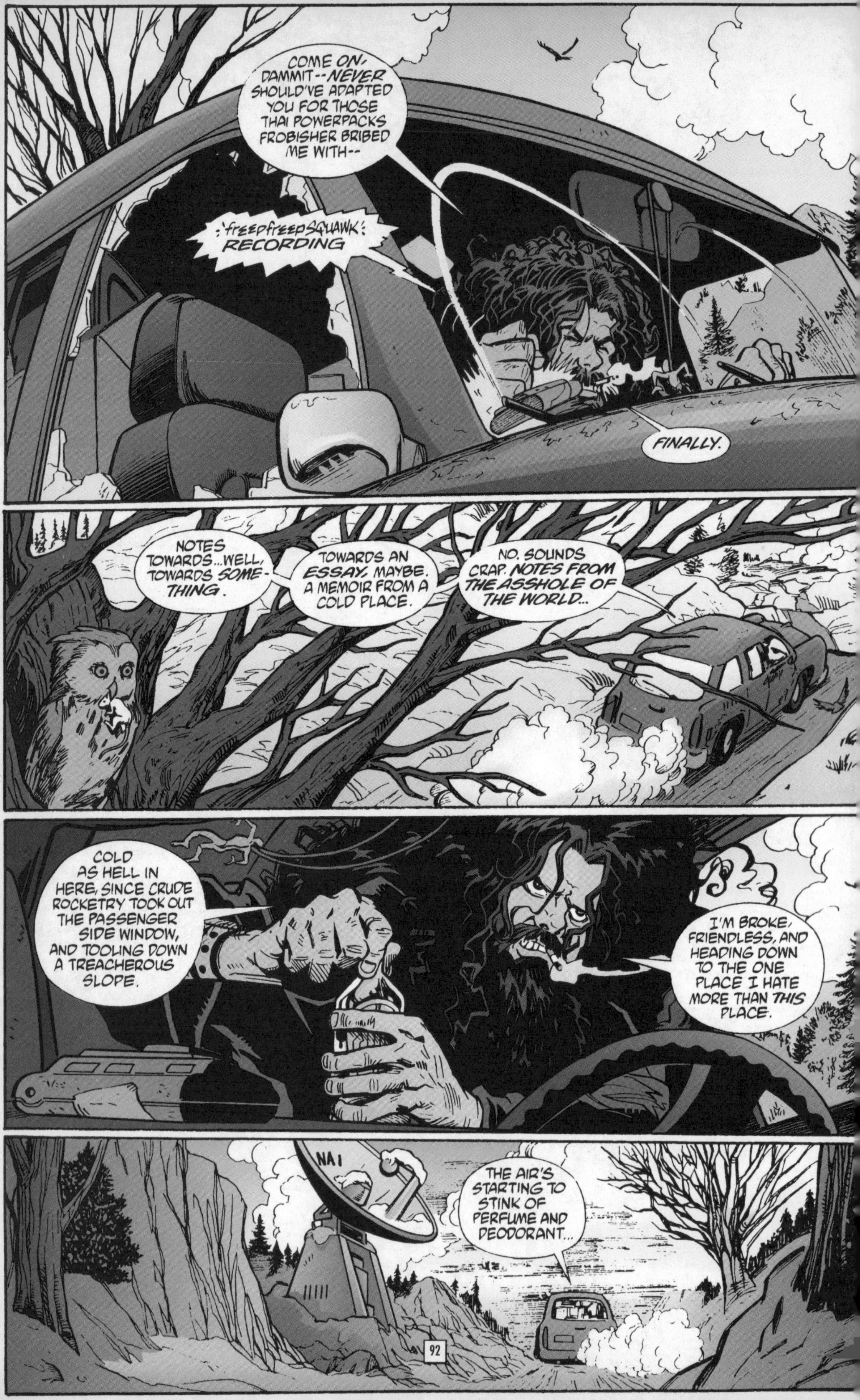
COME ON, DAMMIT--NEVER SHOULD'VE ADAPTED YOU FOR THOSE THAI POWERPACKS FROBISHER BRIBED ME WITH--
:freepfreepSQUAWK: RECORDING
FINALLY.
NOTES TOWARDS...WELL, TOWARDS SOME-THING.
TOWARDS AN ESSAY, MAYBE. A MEMOIR FROM A COLD PLACE.
NO. SOUNDS CRAP. NOTES FROM THE ASSHOLE OF THE WORLD...
COLD AS HELL IN HERE, SINCE CRUDE ROCKETRY TOOK OUT THE PASSENGER SIDE WINDOW, AND TOOLING DOWN A TREACHEROUS SLOPE.
I'M BROKE, FRIENDLESS, AND HEADING DOWN TO THE ONE PLACE I HATE MORE THAN THIS PLACE.
NAI
THE AIR'S STARTING TO STINK OF PERFUME AND DEODORANT...

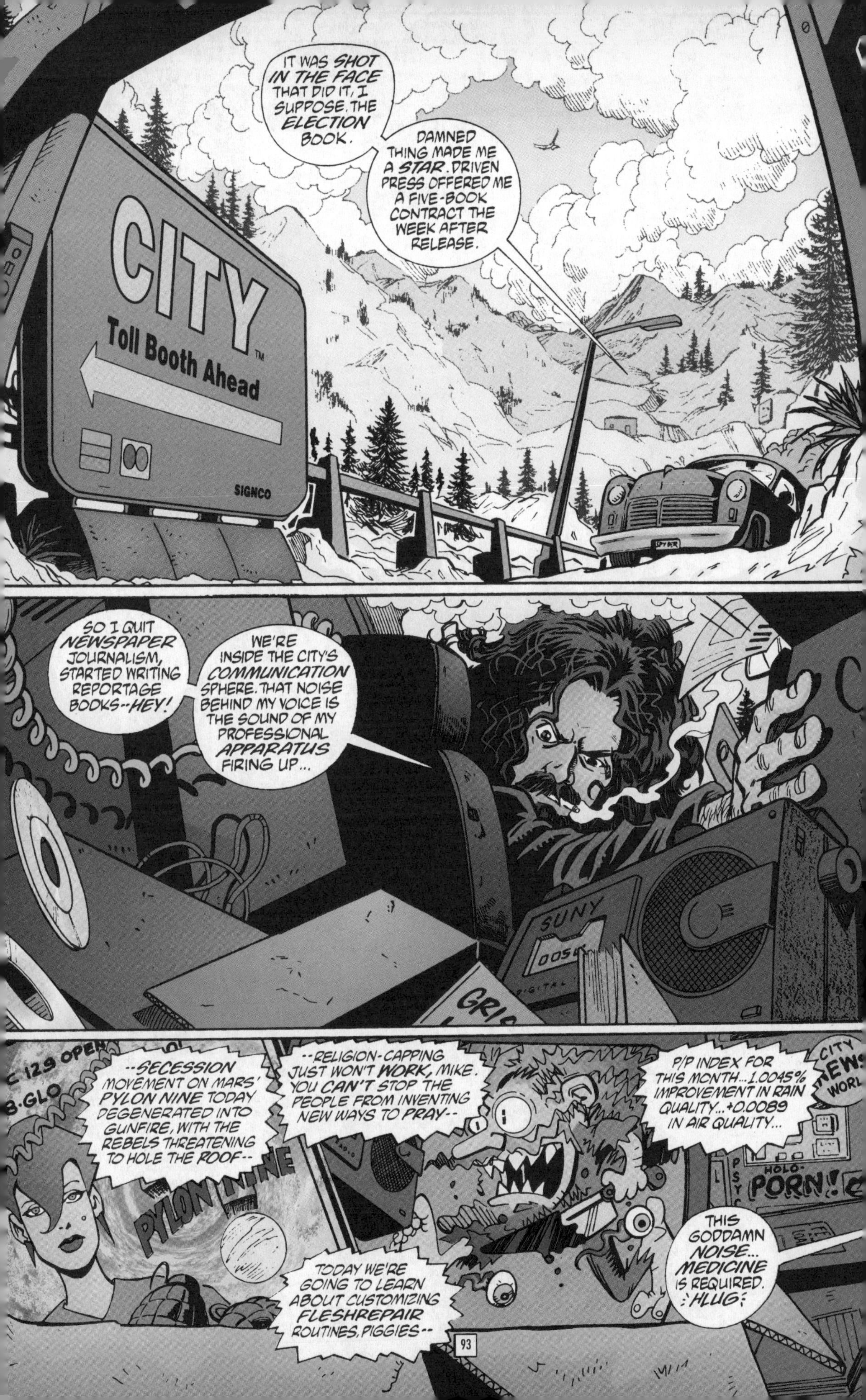
IT WAS SHOT IN THE FACE THAT DID IT, I SUPPOSE. THE ELECTION BOOK.
DAMNED THING MADE ME A STAR. DRIVEN PRESS OFFERED ME A FIVE-BOOK CONTRACT THE WEEK AFTER RELEASE.
CITY
Toll Booth Ahead
SIGNCO
SO I QUIT NEWSPAPER JOURNALISM, STARTED WRITING REPORTAGE BOOKS--HEY!
WE'RE INSIDE THE CITY'S COMMUNICATION SPHERE. THAT NOISE BEHIND MY VOICE IS THE SOUND OF MY PROFESSIONAL APPARATUS FIRING UP...
SUNY
--SECESSION MOVEMENT ON MARS' PYLON NINE TODAY DEGENERATED INTO GUNFIRE, WITH THE REBELS THREATENING TO HOLE THE ROOF--
--RELIGION-CAPPING JUST WON'T WORK, MIKE. YOU CAN'T STOP THE PEOPLE FROM INVENTING NEW WAYS TO PRAY--
P/P INDEX FOR THIS MONTH...1.0045% IMPROVEMENT IN RAIN QUALITY...+0.0089 IN AIR QUALITY...
PYLON NINE
HOLO-PORN!
TODAY WE'RE GOING TO LEARN ABOUT CUSTOMIZING FLESHREPAIR ROUTINES, PIGGIES--
THIS GODDAMN NOISE... MEDICINE IS REQUIRED. :HLUG:

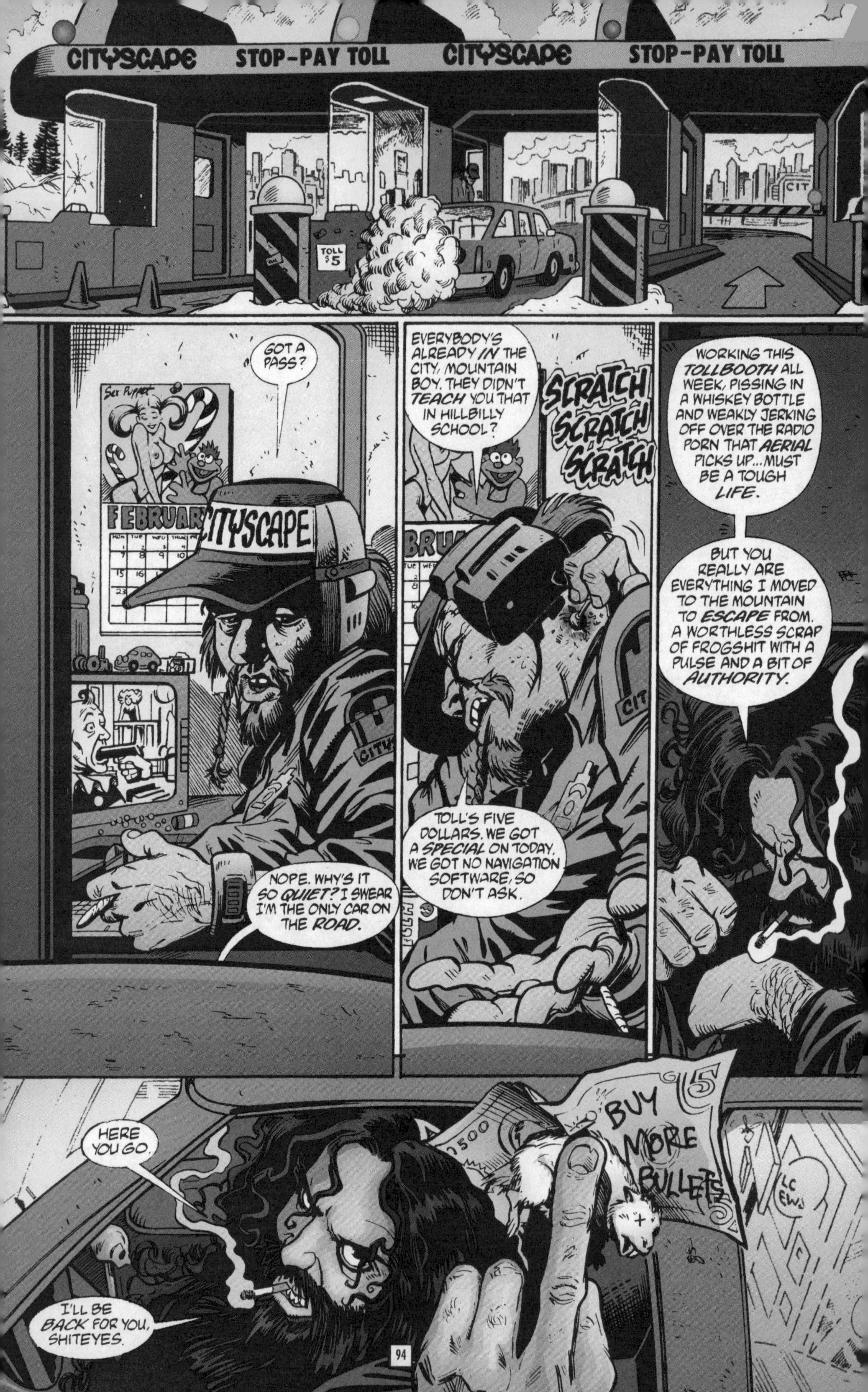
CITYSCAPE
STOP-PAY TOLL
CITYSCAPE
STOP-PAY TOLL
TOLL $5
GOT A PASS?
Sex Puppet
FEBRUARY
CITYSCAPE
NOPE. WHY'S IT SO QUIET? I SWEAR I'M THE ONLY CAR ON THE ROAD.
EVERYBODY'S ALREADY IN THE CITY, MOUNTAIN BOY. THEY DIDN'T TEACH YOU THAT IN HILLBILLY SCHOOL?
SCRATCH SCRATCH SCRATCH
TOLL'S FIVE DOLLARS. WE GOT A SPECIAL ON TODAY. WE GOT NO NAVIGATION SOFTWARE, SO DON'T ASK.
WORKING THIS TOLLBOOTH ALL WEEK, PISSING IN A WHISKEY BOTTLE AND WEAKLY JERKING OFF OVER THE RADIO PORN THAT AERIAL PICKS UP...MUST BE A TOUGH LIFE.
BUT YOU REALLY ARE EVERYTHING I MOVED TO THE MOUNTAIN TO ESCAPE FROM. A WORTHLESS SCRAP OF FROGSHIT WITH A PULSE AND A BIT OF AUTHORITY.
HERE YOU GO.
BUY MORE BULLETS
I'LL BE BACK FOR YOU, SHITEYES.

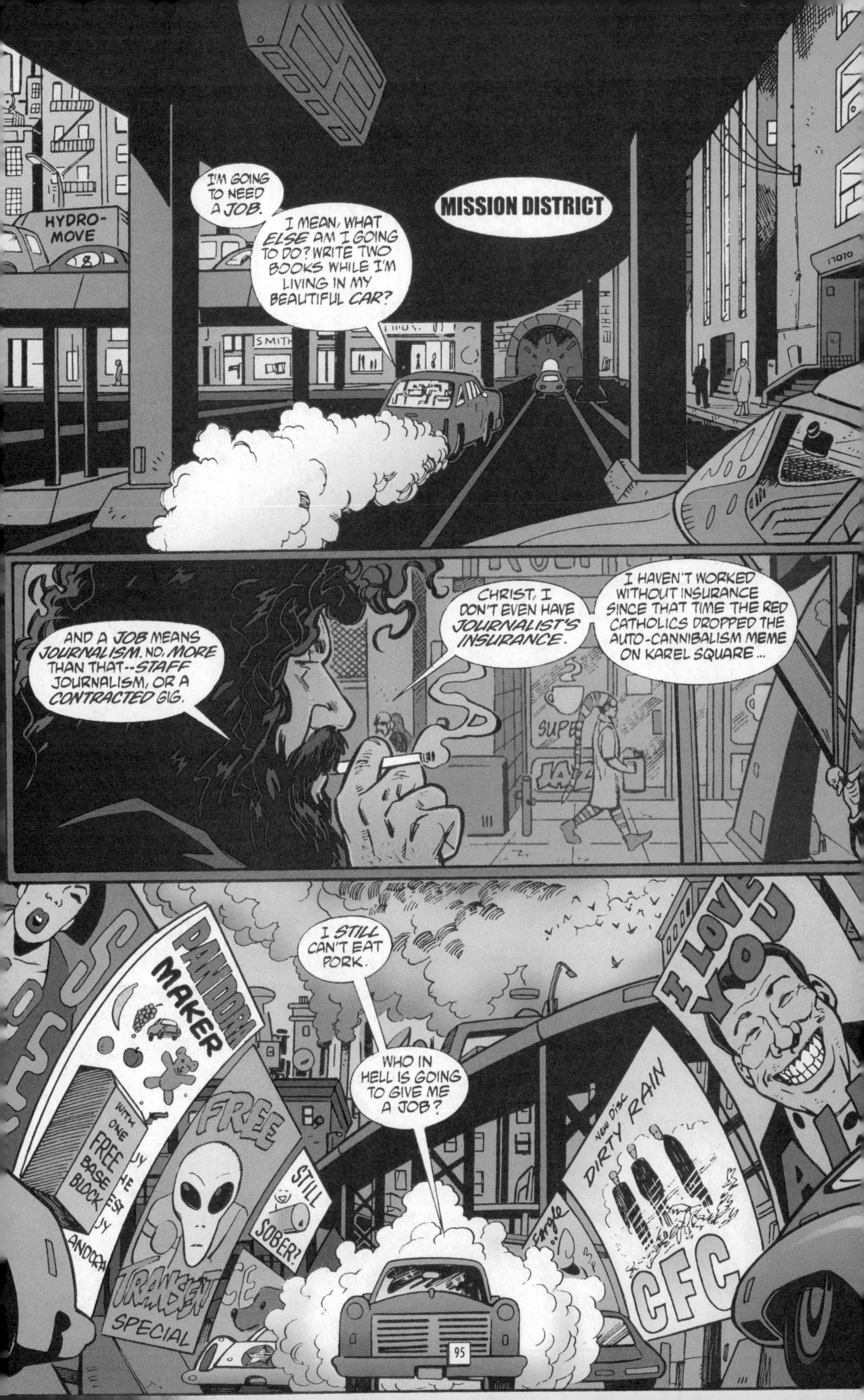
HYDRO-MOVE
I'M GOING TO NEED A *JOB*.
MISSION DISTRICT
I MEAN, WHAT *ELSE* AM I GOING TO DO? WRITE TWO BOOKS WHILE I'M LIVING IN MY BEAUTIFUL *CAR*?
SMITH
AND A *JOB* MEANS *JOURNALISM*. NO, *MORE* THAN THAT--*STAFF* JOURNALISM, OR A *CONTRACTED* GIG.
CHRIST, I DON'T EVEN HAVE *JOURNALIST'S INSURANCE*.
I HAVEN'T WORKED WITHOUT INSURANCE SINCE THAT TIME THE RED CATHOLICS DROPPED THE AUTO-CANNIBALISM MEME ON KAREL SQUARE...
I *STILL* CAN'T EAT PORK.
WHO IN HELL IS GOING TO GIVE ME A JOB?
PANDORA MAKER
WITH ONE FREE BASE BLOCK
FREE
TRANSIENT
SPECIAL
STILL SOBER?
I LOVE YOU
New Disc
DIRTY RAIN
CFC

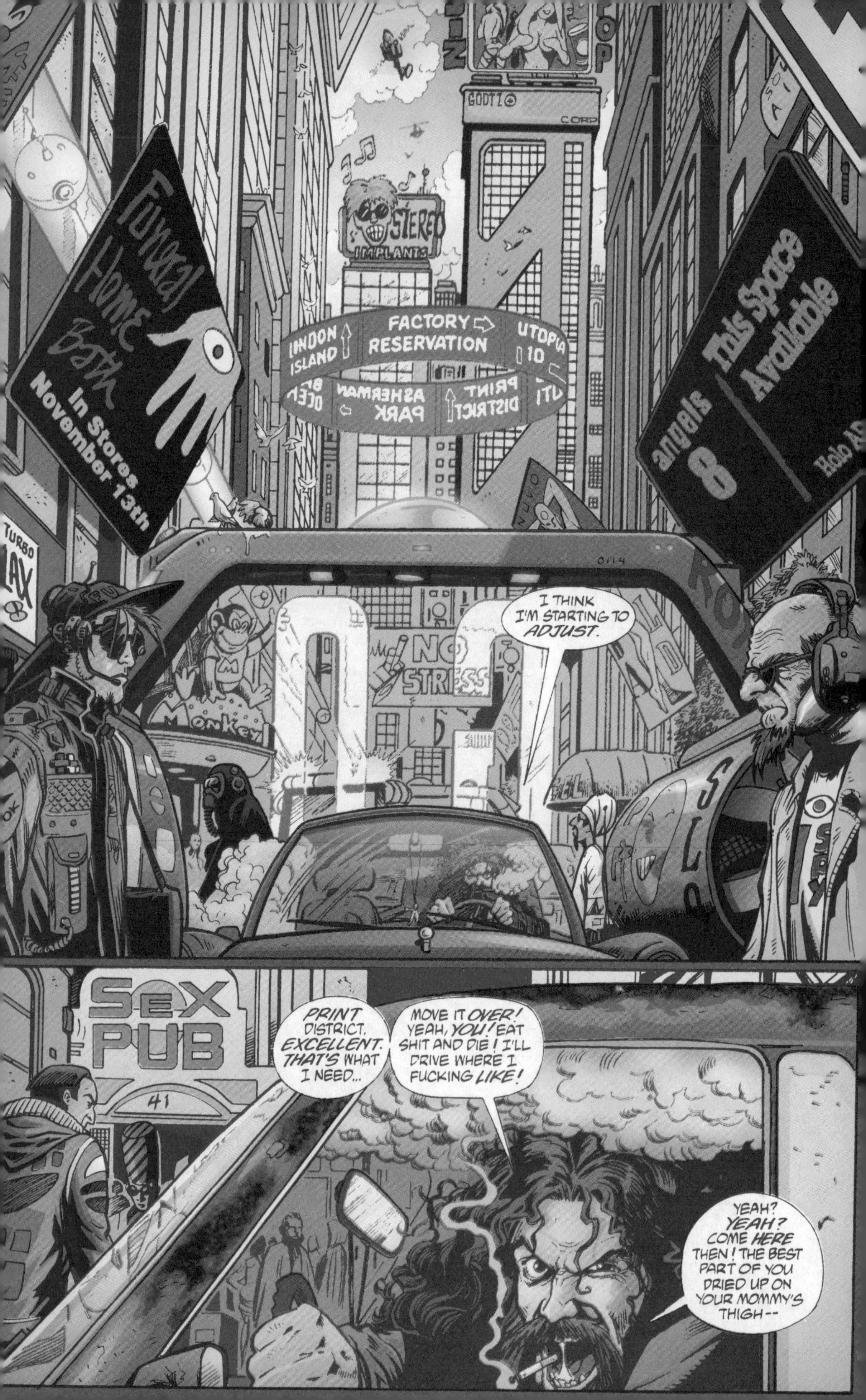

GODTI
CORP
STEREO
IMPLANTS
LONDON ISLAND
FACTORY RESERVATION
UTOPIA 10
In Stores November 13th
This Space Available
angels 8
TURBO
LAX
MONKEY
NO STRESS
I THINK I'M STARTING TO ADJUST.
SEX PUB
41
PRINT DISTRICT. EXCELLENT. THAT'S WHAT I NEED...
MOVE IT OVER! YEAH, YOU! EAT SHIT AND DIE! I'LL DRIVE WHERE I FUCKING LIKE!
YEAH? YEAH? COME HERE THEN! THE BEST PART OF YOU DRIED UP ON YOUR MOMMY'S THIGH--

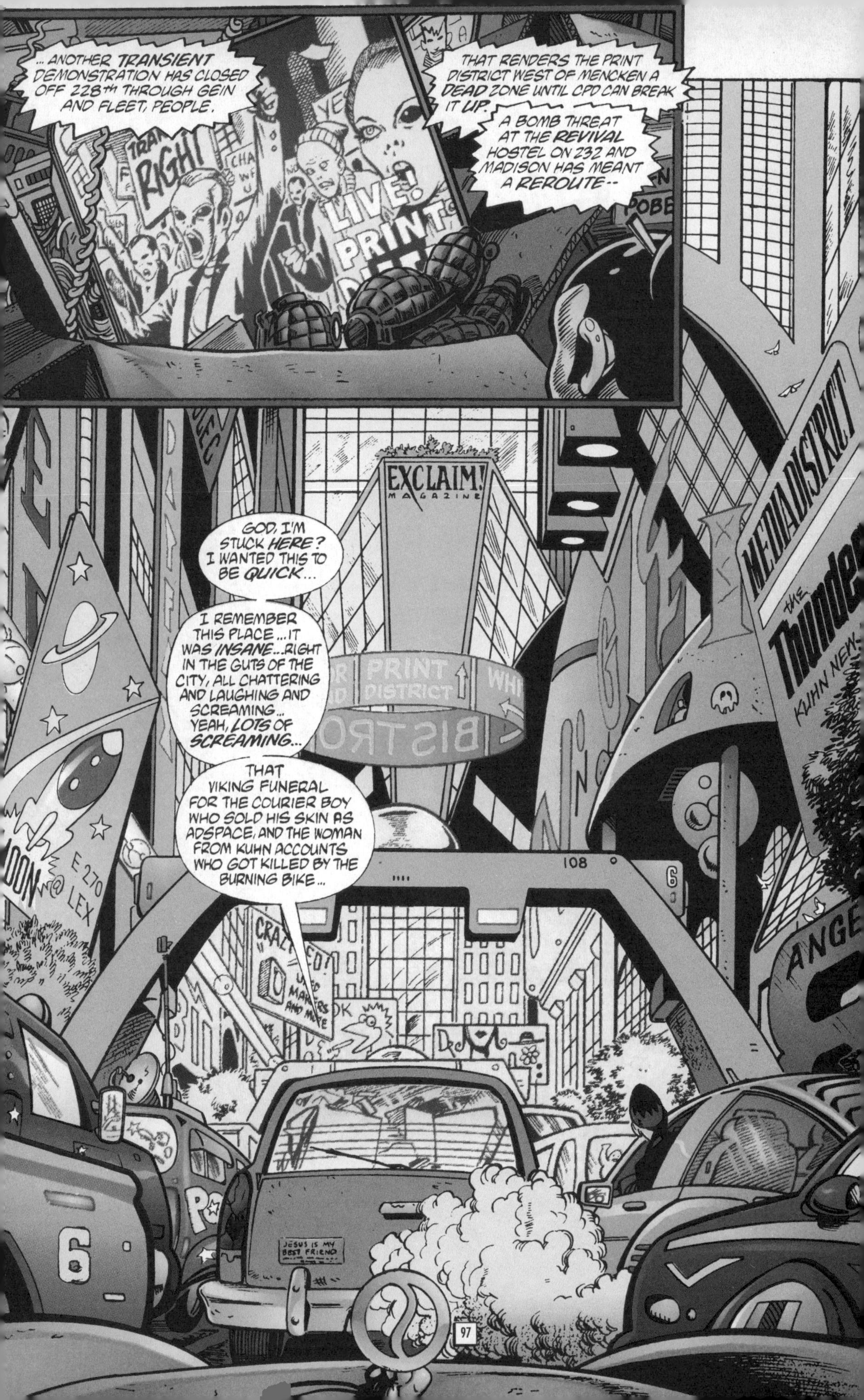
... ANOTHER TRANSIENT DEMONSTRATION HAS CLOSED OFF 228TH THROUGH GEIN AND FLEET, PEOPLE.
THAT RENDERS THE PRINT DISTRICT WEST OF MENCKEN A DEAD ZONE UNTIL CPD CAN BREAK IT UP.
A BOMB THREAT AT THE REVIVAL HOSTEL ON 232 AND MADISON HAS MEANT A REROUTE--
LIVE! PRINT
EXCLAIM! MAGAZINE
MEDIA DISTRICT
GOD, I'M STUCK HERE? I WANTED THIS TO BE QUICK...
I REMEMBER THIS PLACE... IT WAS INSANE... RIGHT IN THE GUTS OF THE CITY, ALL CHATTERING AND LAUGHING AND SCREAMING... YEAH, LOTS OF SCREAMING...
PRINT DISTRICT
BISTRO
THAT VIKING FUNERAL FOR THE COURIER BOY WHO SOLD HIS SKIN AS ADSPACE, AND THE WOMAN FROM KUHN ACCOUNTS WHO GOT KILLED BY THE BURNING BIKE...
E 270 @ LEX
JESUS IS MY BEST FRIEND

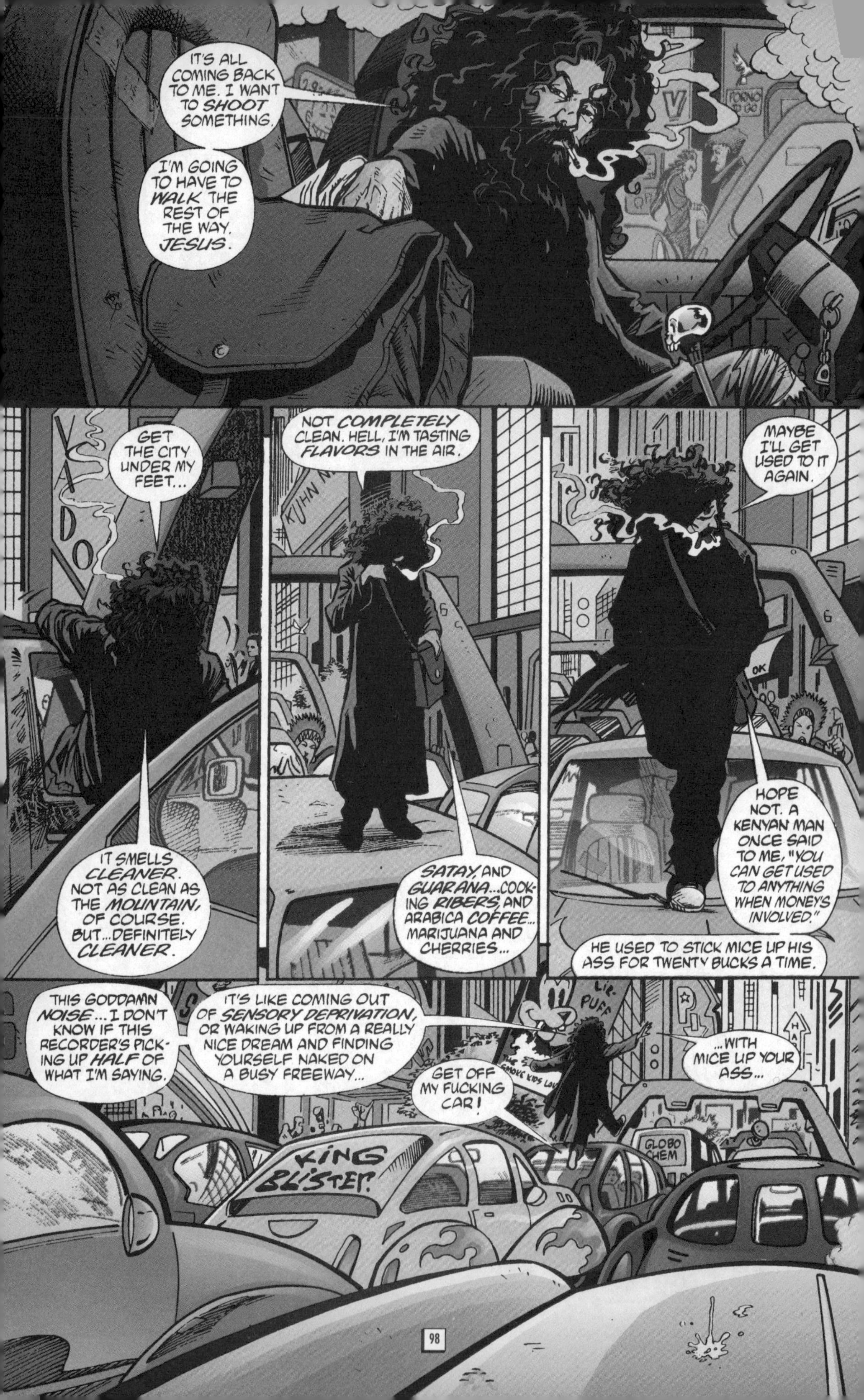
IT'S ALL COMING BACK TO ME. I WANT TO SHOOT SOMETHING.
I'M GOING TO HAVE TO WALK THE REST OF THE WAY. JESUS.
PORNO TO GO
GET THE CITY UNDER MY FEET...
IT SMELLS CLEANER. NOT AS CLEAN AS THE MOUNTAIN, OF COURSE. BUT...DEFINITELY CLEANER.
NOT COMPLETELY CLEAN. HELL, I'M TASTING FLAVORS IN THE AIR.
SATAY, AND GUARANA...COOKING RIBERS, AND ARABICA COFFEE... MARIJUANA AND CHERRIES...
MAYBE I'LL GET USED TO IT AGAIN.
HOPE NOT. A KENYAN MAN ONCE SAID TO ME, "YOU CAN GET USED TO ANYTHING WHEN MONEY'S INVOLVED."
HE USED TO STICK MICE UP HIS ASS FOR TWENTY BUCKS A TIME.
THIS GODDAMN NOISE... I DON'T KNOW IF THIS RECORDER'S PICKING UP HALF OF WHAT I'M SAYING.
IT'S LIKE COMING OUT OF SENSORY DEPRIVATION, OR WAKING UP FROM A REALLY NICE DREAM AND FINDING YOURSELF NAKED ON A BUSY FREEWAY...
GET OFF MY FUCKING CAR!
...WITH MICE UP YOUR ASS...
LIP-PUFF
KING BLISTER
GLOBO CHEM

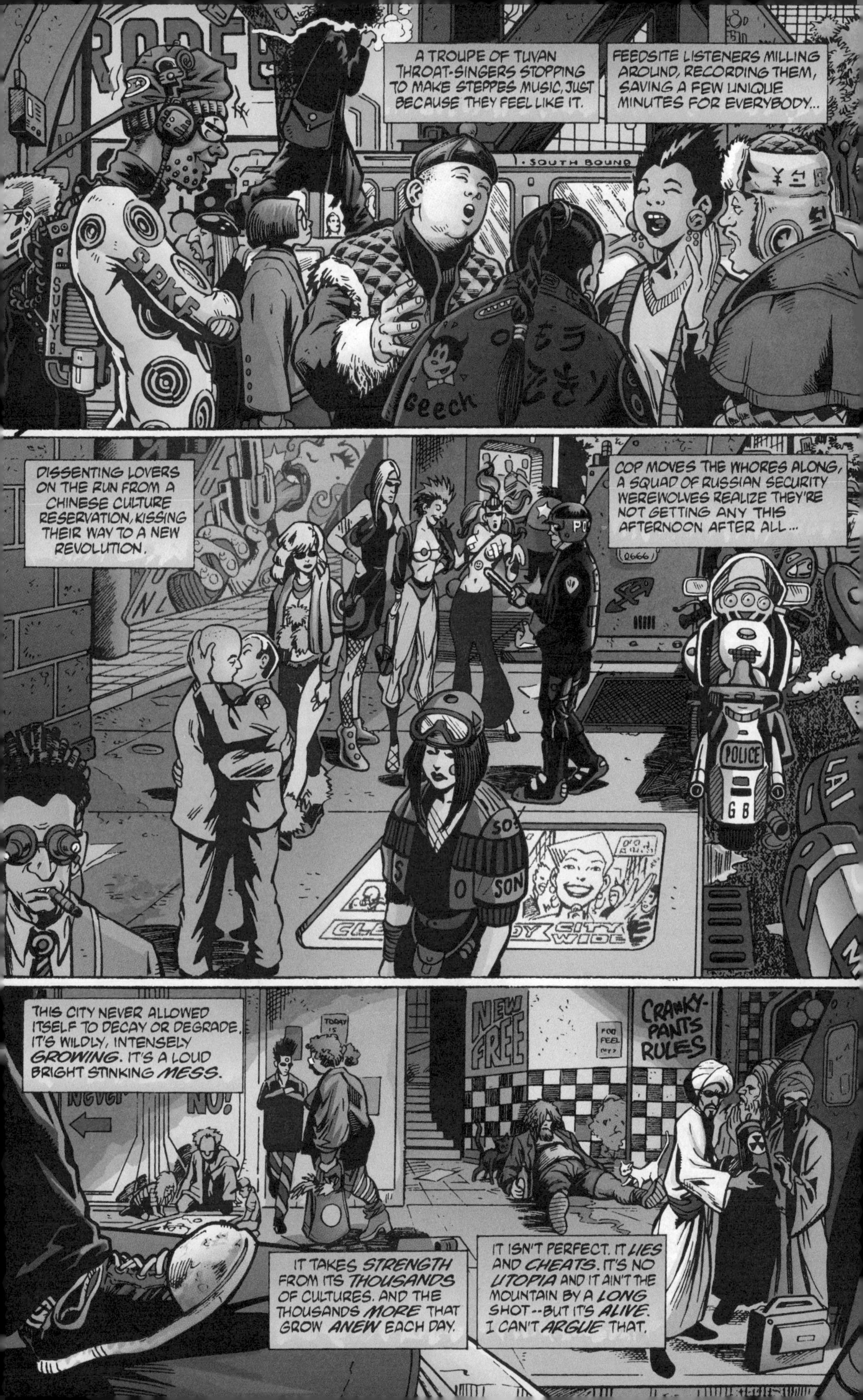
A TROUPE OF TUVAN THROAT-SINGERS STOPPING TO MAKE STEPPES MUSIC, JUST BECAUSE THEY FEEL LIKE IT.
FEEDSITE LISTENERS MILLING AROUND, RECORDING THEM, SAVING A FEW UNIQUE MINUTES FOR EVERYBODY...
SOUTH BOUND
Geech
DISSENTING LOVERS ON THE RUN FROM A CHINESE CULTURE RESERVATION, KISSING THEIR WAY TO A NEW REVOLUTION.
COP MOVES THE WHORES ALONG, A SQUAD OF RUSSIAN SECURITY WEREWOLVES REALIZE THEY'RE NOT GETTING ANY THIS AFTERNOON AFTER ALL...
POLICE
GB
SON
CITY WIDE
THIS CITY NEVER ALLOWED ITSELF TO DECAY OR DEGRADE. IT'S WILDLY, INTENSELY *GROWING*. IT'S A LOUD BRIGHT STINKING *MESS*.
NO!
NEW FREE
CRANKY-PANTS RULES
IT TAKES *STRENGTH* FROM ITS *THOUSANDS* OF CULTURES. AND THE THOUSANDS *MORE* THAT GROW *ANEW* EACH DAY.
IT ISN'T PERFECT. IT *LIES* AND *CHEATS*. IT'S NO *UTOPIA* AND IT AIN'T THE MOUNTAIN BY A *LONG* SHOT--BUT IT'S *ALIVE*. I CAN'T *ARGUE* THAT.

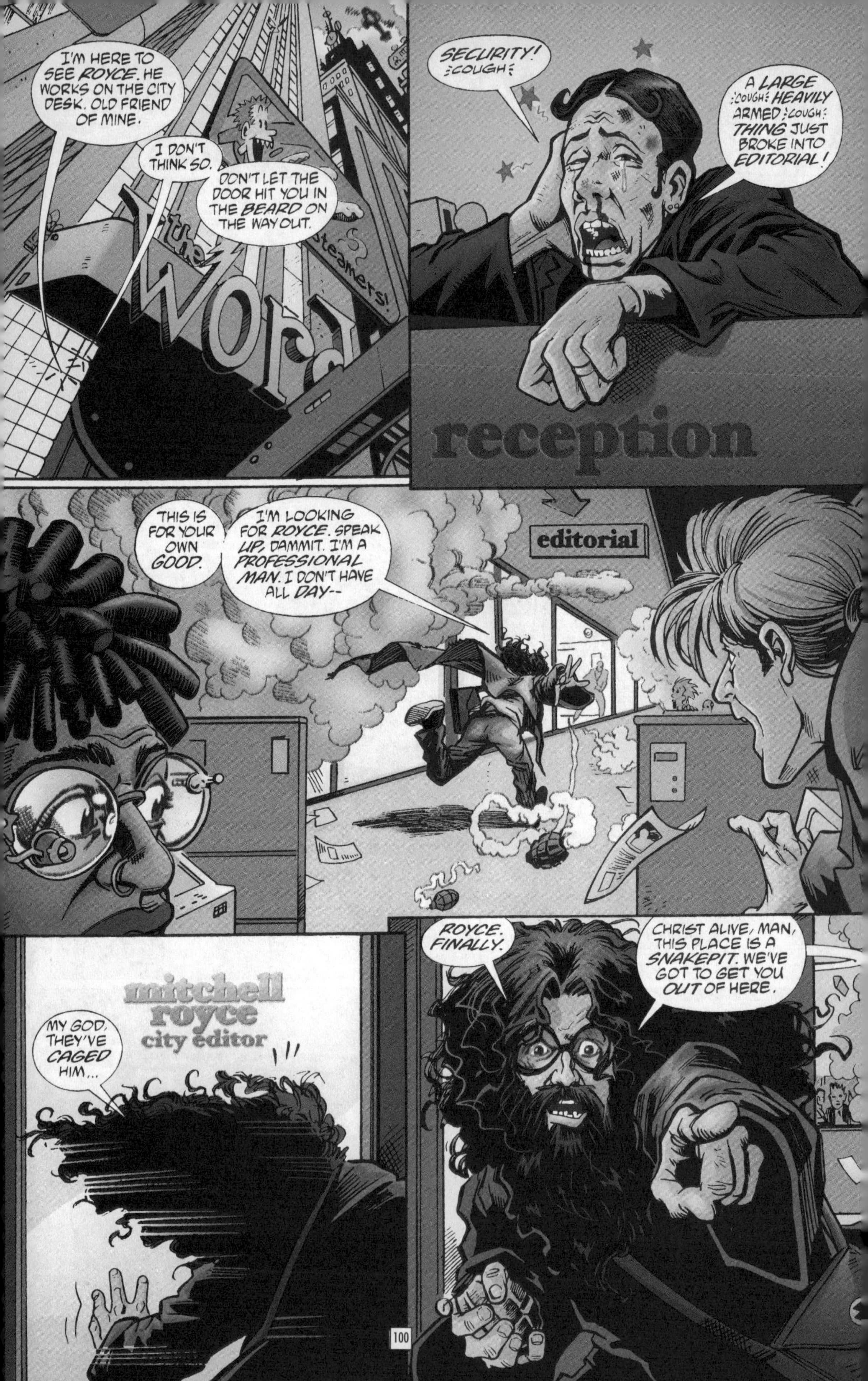
I'M HERE TO SEE *ROYCE*. HE WORKS ON THE CITY DESK. OLD FRIEND OF MINE.
I DON'T THINK SO.
DON'T LET THE DOOR HIT YOU IN THE *BEARD* ON THE WAY OUT.
the Word
steamers!
SECURITY! :COUGH:
A *LARGE* :COUGH: *HEAVILY* ARMED :COUGH: *THING* JUST BROKE INTO *EDITORIAL!*
reception
THIS IS FOR YOUR OWN *GOOD*.
I'M LOOKING FOR *ROYCE*. SPEAK *UP*, DAMMIT. I'M A *PROFESSIONAL MAN*. I DON'T HAVE ALL *DAY*--
editorial
mitchell royce city editor
MY GOD, THEY'VE *CAGED* HIM...
ROYCE. FINALLY.
CHRIST ALIVE, MAN, THIS PLACE IS A *SNAKEPIT*. WE'VE GOT TO GET YOU *OUT* OF HERE.

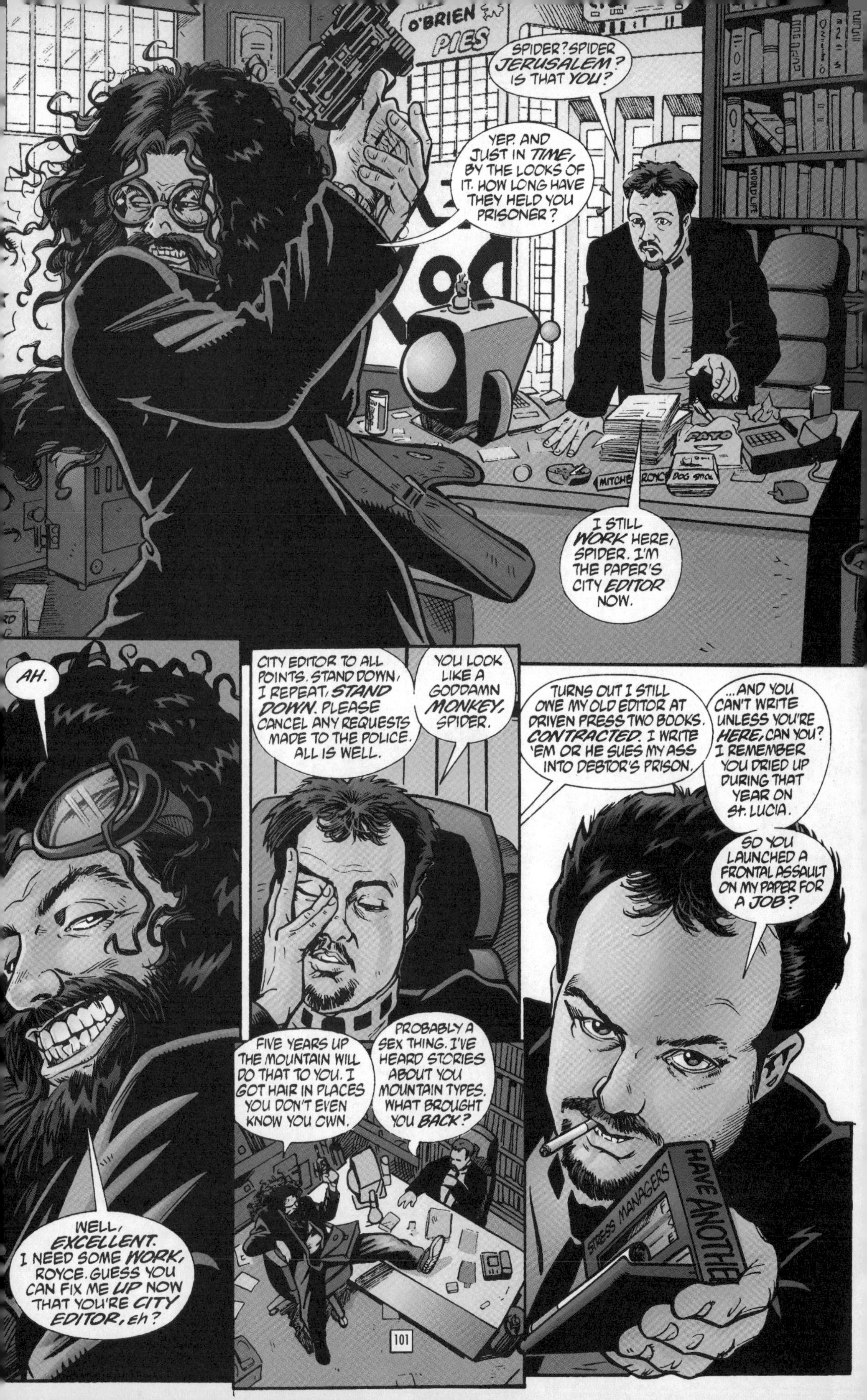
O'BRIEN PIES
SPIDER? SPIDER JERUSALEM? IS THAT YOU?
YEP. AND JUST IN TIME, BY THE LOOKS OF IT. HOW LONG HAVE THEY HELD YOU PRISONER?
MITCHE ROYC
I STILL WORK HERE, SPIDER. I'M THE PAPER'S CITY EDITOR NOW.
AH.
CITY EDITOR TO ALL POINTS. STAND DOWN, I REPEAT, STAND DOWN. PLEASE CANCEL ANY REQUESTS MADE TO THE POLICE. ALL IS WELL.
YOU LOOK LIKE A GODDAMN MONKEY, SPIDER.
TURNS OUT I STILL OWE MY OLD EDITOR AT DRIVEN PRESS TWO BOOKS. CONTRACTED. I WRITE 'EM OR HE SUES MY ASS INTO DEBTOR'S PRISON.
...AND YOU CAN'T WRITE UNLESS YOU'RE HERE, CAN YOU? I REMEMBER YOU DRIED UP DURING THAT YEAR ON St. LUCIA.
SO YOU LAUNCHED A FRONTAL ASSAULT ON MY PAPER FOR A JOB?
FIVE YEARS UP THE MOUNTAIN WILL DO THAT TO YOU. I GOT HAIR IN PLACES YOU DON'T EVEN KNOW YOU OWN.
PROBABLY A SEX THING. I'VE HEARD STORIES ABOUT YOU MOUNTAIN TYPES. WHAT BROUGHT YOU BACK?
WELL, EXCELLENT. I NEED SOME WORK, ROYCE. GUESS YOU CAN FIX ME UP NOW THAT YOU'RE CITY EDITOR, eh?
STRESS MANAGERS

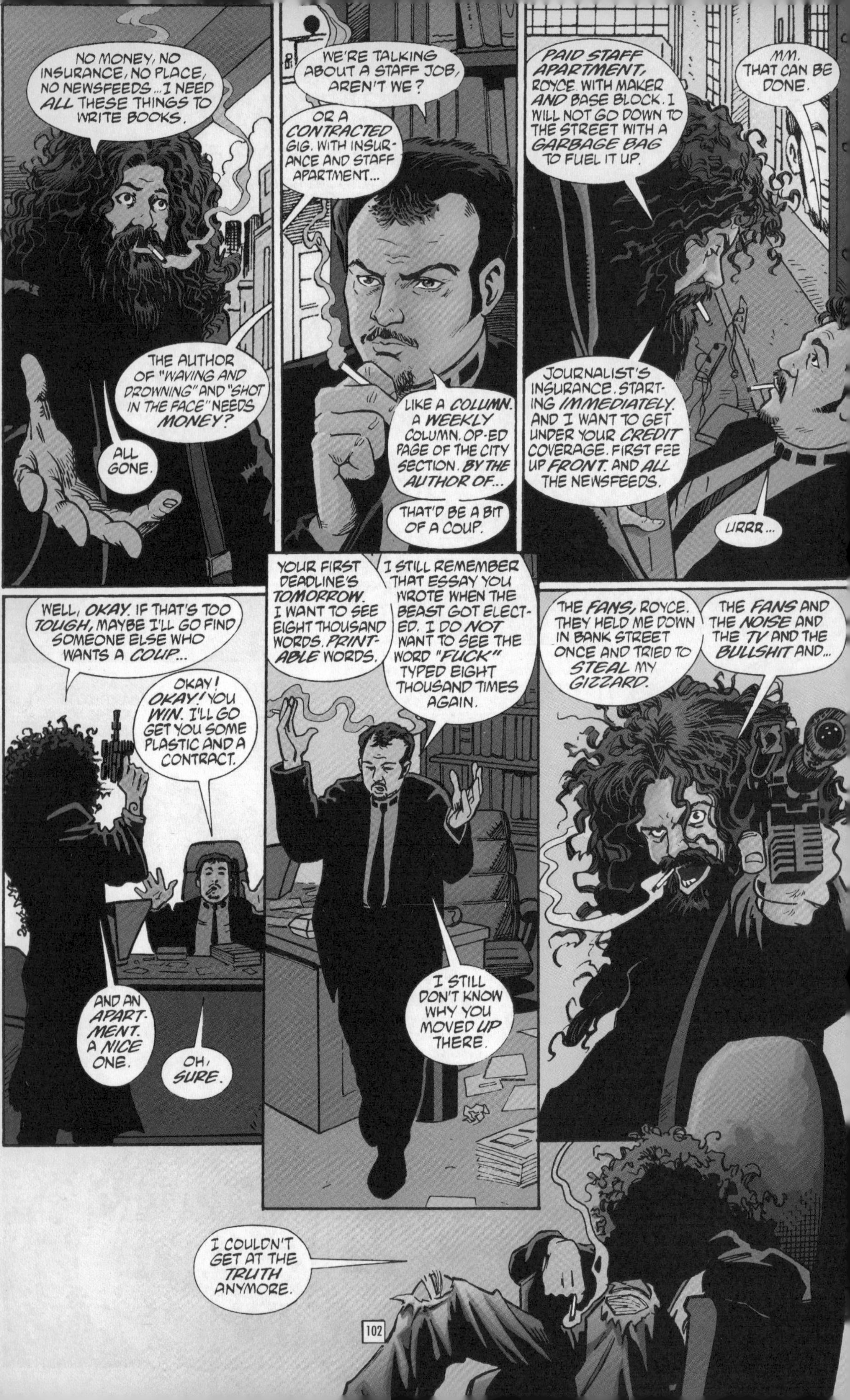
NO MONEY, NO INSURANCE, NO PLACE, NO NEWSFEEDS...I NEED ALL THESE THINGS TO WRITE BOOKS.
THE AUTHOR OF "WAVING AND DROWNING" AND "SHOT IN THE FACE" NEEDS MONEY?
ALL GONE.
WE'RE TALKING ABOUT A STAFF JOB, AREN'T WE?
OR A CONTRACTED GIG. WITH INSURANCE AND STAFF APARTMENT...
LIKE A COLUMN. A WEEKLY COLUMN. OP-ED PAGE OF THE CITY SECTION. BY THE AUTHOR OF...
THAT'D BE A BIT OF A COUP.
PAID STAFF APARTMENT, ROYCE. WITH MAKER AND BASE BLOCK. I WILL NOT GO DOWN TO THE STREET WITH A GARBAGE BAG TO FUEL IT UP.
MM. THAT CAN BE DONE.
JOURNALIST'S INSURANCE. STARTING IMMEDIATELY. AND I WANT TO GET UNDER YOUR CREDIT COVERAGE. FIRST FEE UP FRONT. AND ALL THE NEWSFEEDS.
URRR...
WELL, OKAY. IF THAT'S TOO TOUGH, MAYBE I'LL GO FIND SOMEONE ELSE WHO WANTS A COUP...
OKAY! OKAY! YOU WIN. I'LL GO GET YOU SOME PLASTIC AND A CONTRACT.
AND AN APARTMENT. A NICE ONE.
OH, SURE.
YOUR FIRST DEADLINE'S TOMORROW. I WANT TO SEE EIGHT THOUSAND WORDS. PRINTABLE WORDS.
I STILL REMEMBER THAT ESSAY YOU WROTE WHEN THE BEAST GOT ELECTED. I DO NOT WANT TO SEE THE WORD "FUCK" TYPED EIGHT THOUSAND TIMES AGAIN.
I STILL DON'T KNOW WHY YOU MOVED UP THERE.
THE FANS, ROYCE. THEY HELD ME DOWN IN BANK STREET ONCE AND TRIED TO STEAL MY GIZZARD.
THE FANS AND THE NOISE AND THE TV AND THE BULLSHIT AND...
I COULDN'T GET AT THE TRUTH ANYMORE.

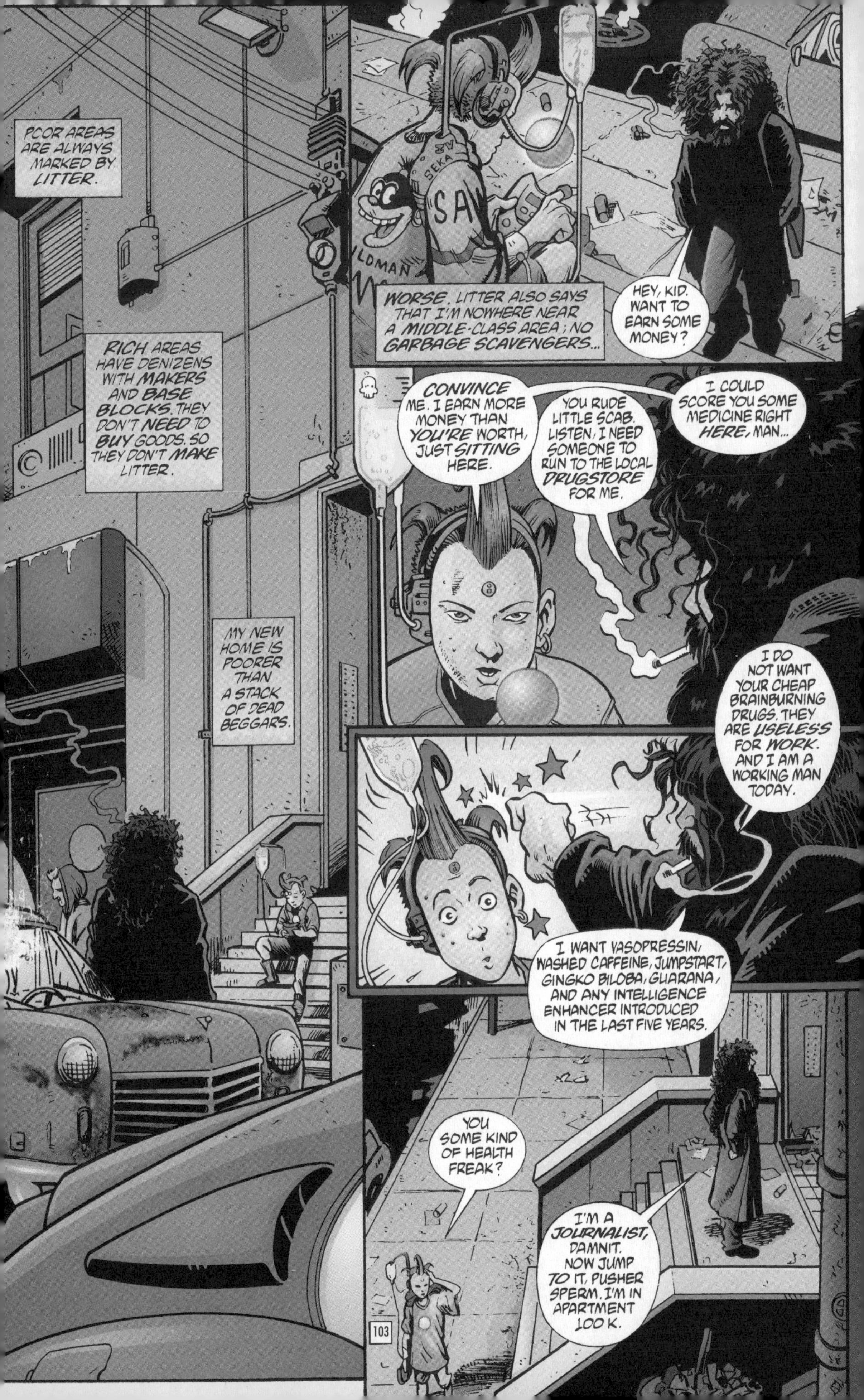

PCOR AREAS ARE ALWAYS MARKED BY LITTER.
RICH AREAS HAVE DENIZENS WITH MAKERS AND BASE BLOCKS. THEY DON'T NEED TO BUY GOODS. SO THEY DON'T MAKE LITTER.
MY NEW HOME IS POORER THAN A STACK OF DEAD BEGGARS.
WORSE. LITTER ALSO SAYS THAT I'M NOWHERE NEAR A MIDDLE-CLASS AREA; NO GARBAGE SCAVENGERS...
HEY, KID. WANT TO EARN SOME MONEY?
I COULD SCORE YOU SOME MEDICINE RIGHT HERE, MAN...
CONVINCE ME. I EARN MORE MONEY THAN YOU'RE WORTH, JUST SITTING HERE.
YOU RUDE LITTLE SCAB. LISTEN, I NEED SOMEONE TO RUN TO THE LOCAL DRUGSTORE FOR ME.
I DO NOT WANT YOUR CHEAP BRAINBURNING DRUGS. THEY ARE USELESS FOR WORK. AND I AM A WORKING MAN TODAY.
I WANT VASOPRESSIN, WASHED CAFFEINE, JUMPSTART, GINGKO BILOBA, GUARANA, AND ANY INTELLIGENCE ENHANCER INTRODUCED IN THE LAST FIVE YEARS.
YOU SOME KIND OF HEALTH FREAK?
I'M A JOURNALIST, DAMNIT. NOW JUMP TO IT, PUSHER SPERM. I'M IN APARTMENT 100 K.

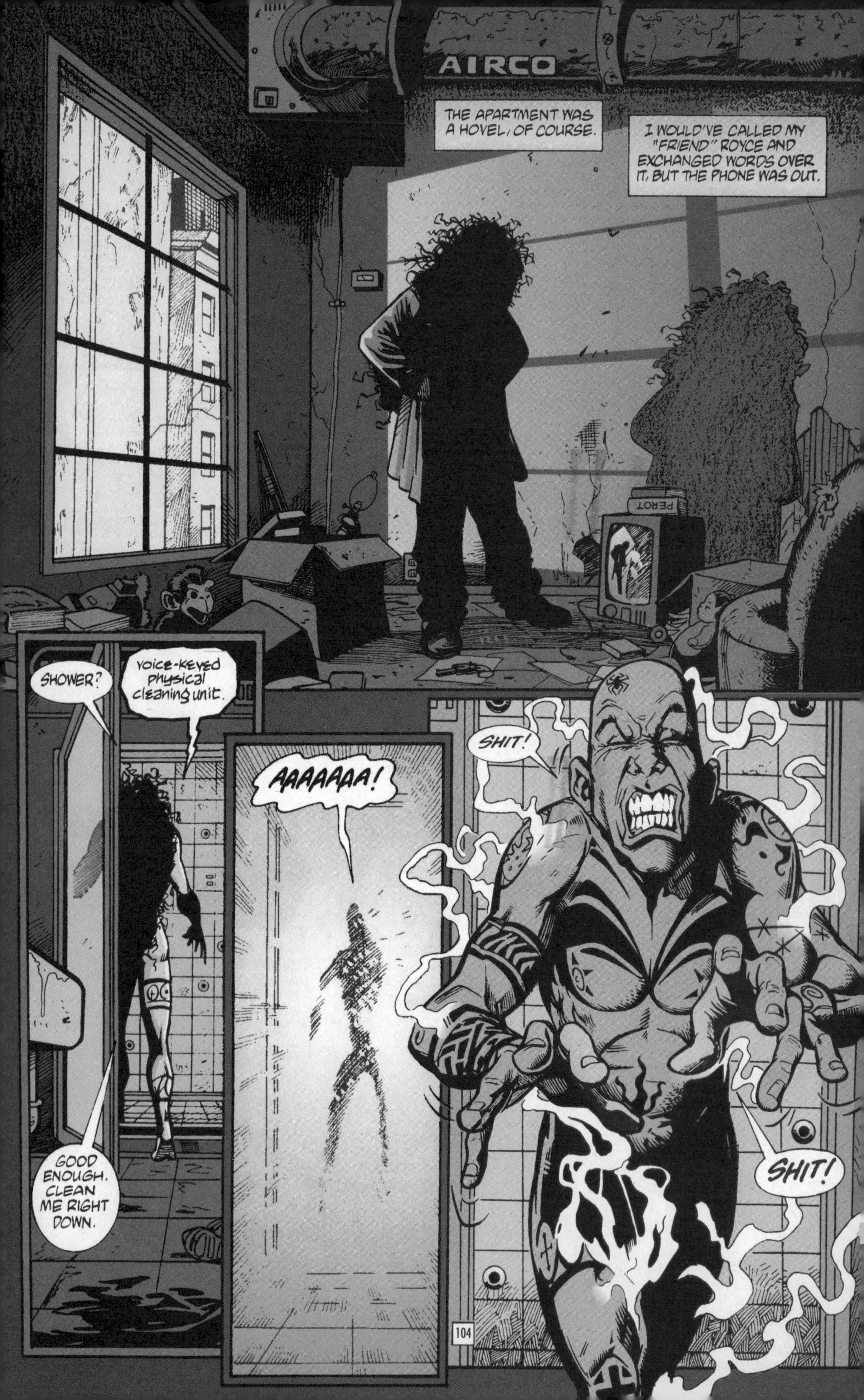
AIRCO
THE APARTMENT WAS A HOVEL, OF COURSE.
I WOULD'VE CALLED MY "FRIEND" ROYCE AND EXCHANGED WORDS OVER IT, BUT THE PHONE WAS OUT.
PEROT
SHOWER?
voice-keyed physical cleaning unit.
GOOD ENOUGH. CLEAN ME RIGHT DOWN.
AAAAAAA!
SHIT!
SHIT!

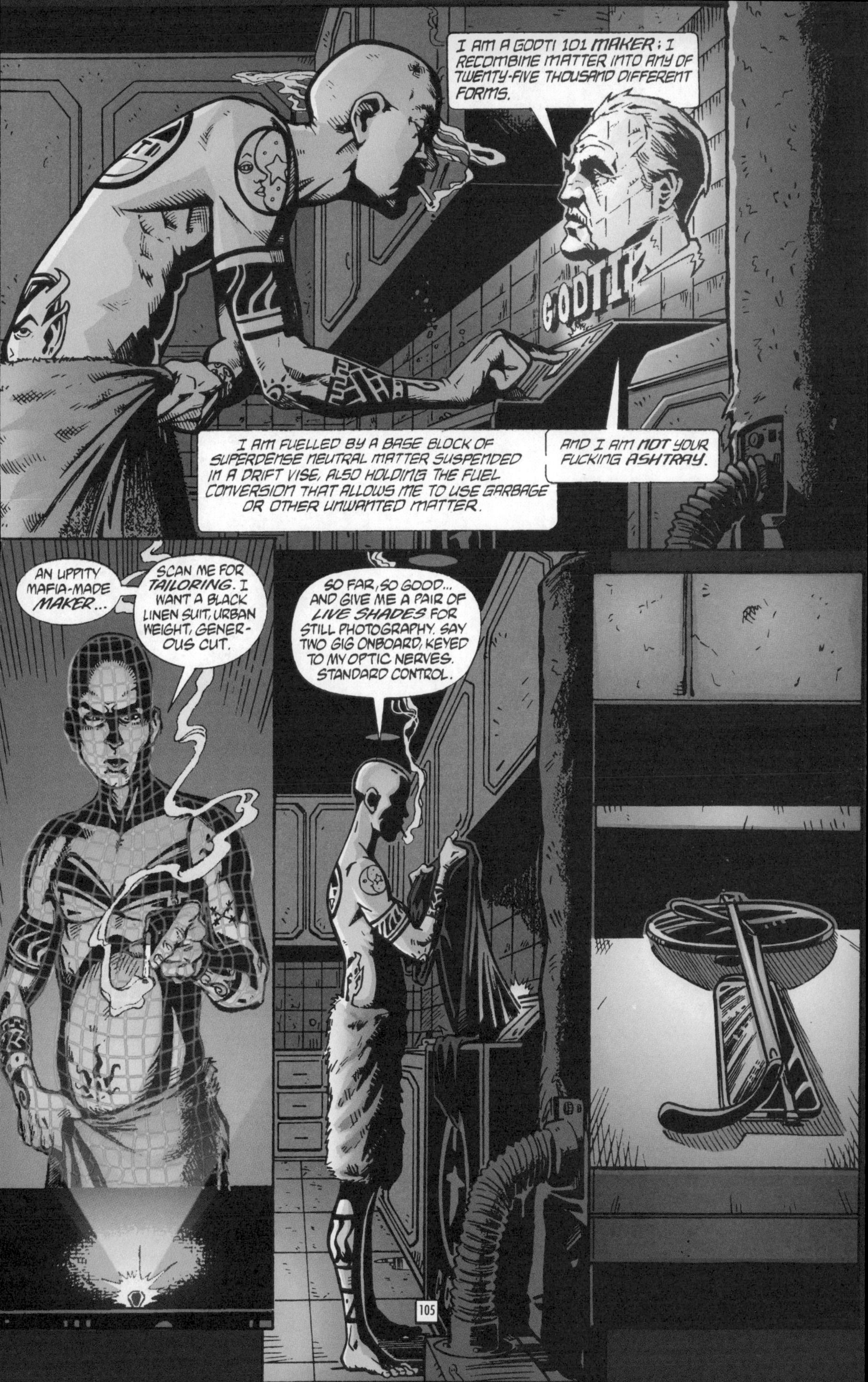
I AM A GODTI 101 MAKER; I RECOMBINE MATTER INTO ANY OF TWENTY-FIVE THOUSAND DIFFERENT FORMS.
GODTI
I AM FUELLED BY A BASE BLOCK OF SUPERDENSE NEUTRAL MATTER SUSPENDED IN A DRIFT VISE, ALSO HOLDING THE FUEL CONVERSION THAT ALLOWS ME TO USE GARBAGE OR OTHER UNWANTED MATTER.
AND I AM NOT YOUR FUCKING ASHTRAY.
AN UPPITY MAFIA-MADE MAKER...
SCAN ME FOR TAILORING. I WANT A BLACK LINEN SUIT, URBAN WEIGHT, GENEROUS CUT.
SO FAR, SO GOOD... AND GIVE ME A PAIR OF LIVE SHADES FOR STILL PHOTOGRAPHY. SAY TWO GIG ONBOARD, KEYED TO MY OPTIC NERVES. STANDARD CONTROL.

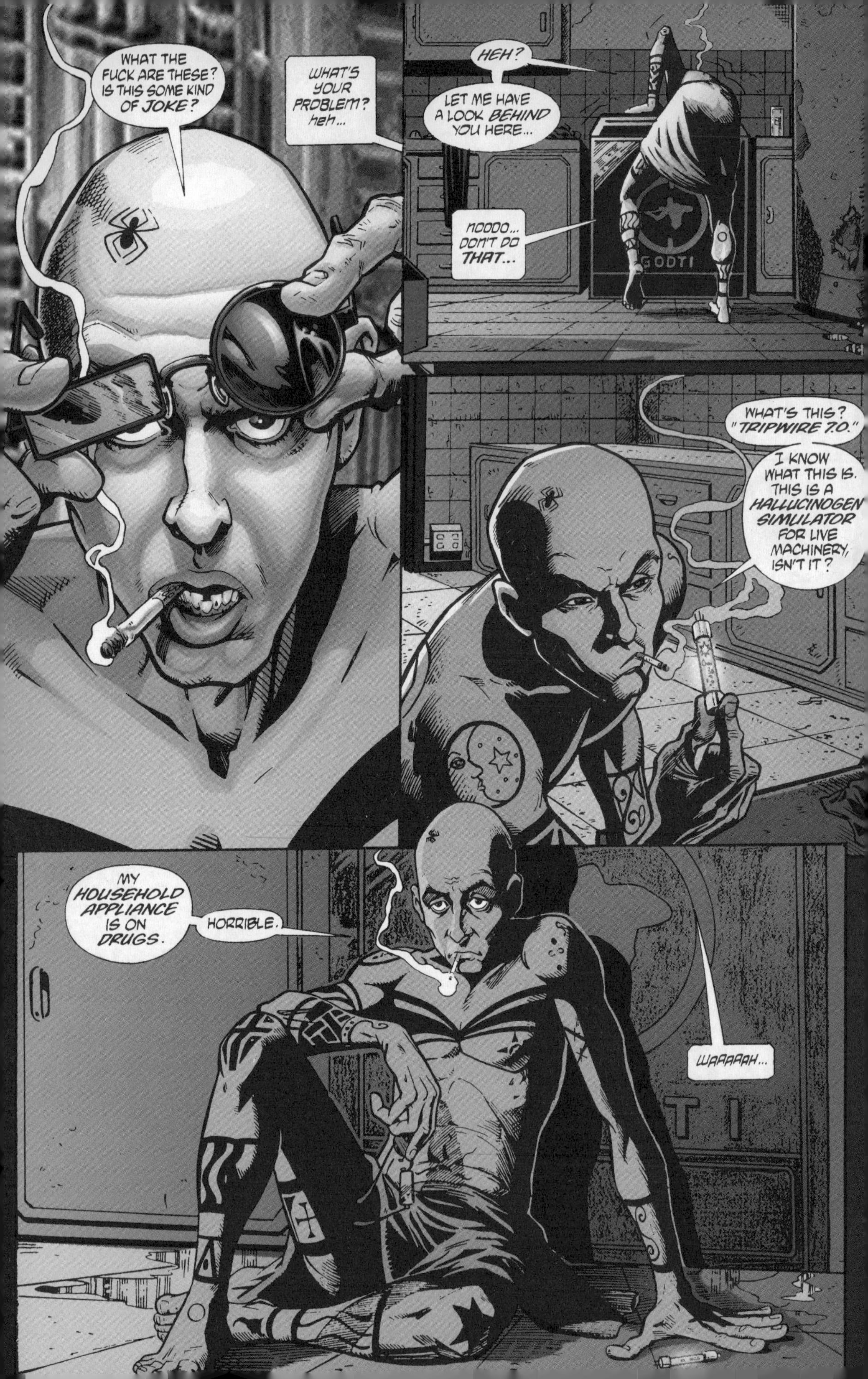
WHAT THE FUCK ARE THESE? IS THIS SOME KIND OF JOKE?
WHAT'S YOUR PROBLEM? heh...
HEH?
LET ME HAVE A LOOK BEHIND YOU HERE...
NOOOO... DON'T DO THAT...
GODTI
WHAT'S THIS? "TRIPWIRE 7.0."
I KNOW WHAT THIS IS. THIS IS A HALLUCINOGEN SIMULATOR FOR LIVE MACHINERY, ISN'T IT?
MY HOUSEHOLD APPLIANCE IS ON DRUGS.
HORRIBLE.
WAAAAAH...

TV: RANDOM CHANNEL CHANGE EVERY TWENTY SECONDS. COMPUTER: RANDOM FEED SWITCH EVERY TWENTY-FIVE.

TONIGHT ON LONELY CITY: THE CONTINUING PLIGHT OF THE REVIVALS, OUR CITY'S SLOW TIME TRAVELLERS, BROUGHT BY CRYONICS TO A FUTURE THEY CANNOT UNDERSTAND.

HOW CAN WE HELP THEM, WHEN THEIR FIRST MERE GLANCE THROUGH A WINDOW LEADS INEXORABLY TO MENTAL ILLNESS? SHOULD WE HELP THEM?

FOG!
The Non-technological Human Community Artifeed

SECURITY WARNING— Feedsite launching Fog 2 App

CANCEL

SECURITY WARNING Feedsite

HAL 9000

HOLO

SKILL 8

NERD

--DEBATE STILL RAGES OVER THE DAY-FAX RELIGIOUS CENSUS, SHOWING THAT A NEW CHURCH IS INVESTED EVERY SIX HOURS IN THE CITY--

"WE ARE THE DOWNLOADED; WE CHOSE TO HAVE OUR HUMAN CONSCIOUSNESS TRANSLATED INTO CLOUDS OF ATOM-SIZED MACHINERY..."

...AFTER THE UGLY CONCLUSION TO THE TRANSIENT RIGHTS DEMONSTRATION ON GEIN STREET THIS AFTERNOON--

IT SEEMS THAT MOST, IF NOT ALL, OF THE CITY'S TRANSIENTS HAVE RETURNED TO THE ANGELS 8 DISTRICT, WHERE THE UNREST BEGAN.

MOVEMENT LEADER FRED CHRIST MADE HIMSELF AVAILABLE FOR INTERVIEW, JUST A FEW MINUTES AGO.

OH, YEAH?

EVENT-CYCLE HOTMENU--JUST RELEASED, THE DATES FOR THE OPENING STAGE OF THE PRESIDENT'S REELECTION CAMPAIGN--

FRED... TV! HOLD CHANNEL!

--CPD HAD ONLY THIS TO SAY: "WANTING A NEW BODY DOESN'T GIVE YOU THE RIGHT TO BE A PUBLIC NUISANCE."

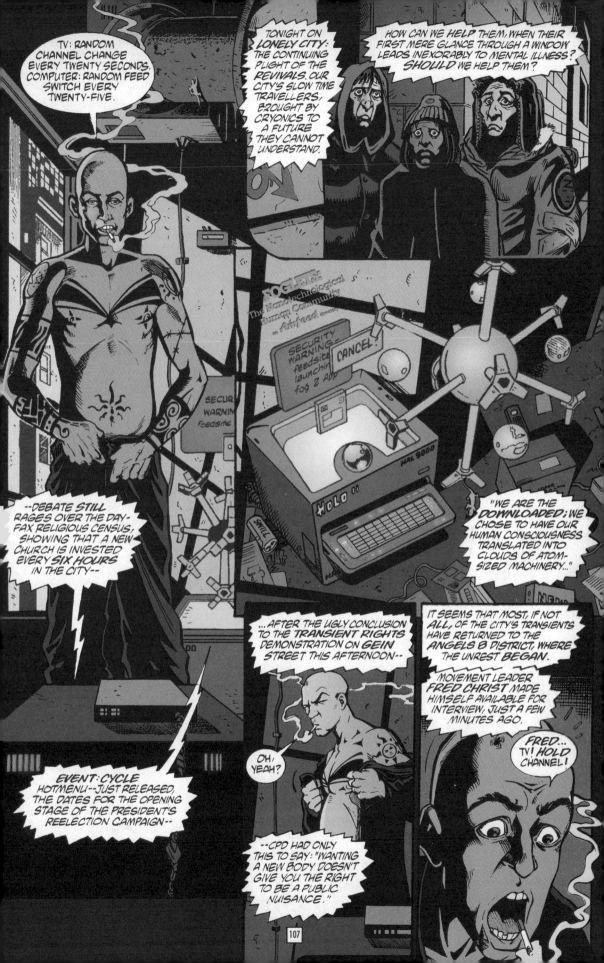

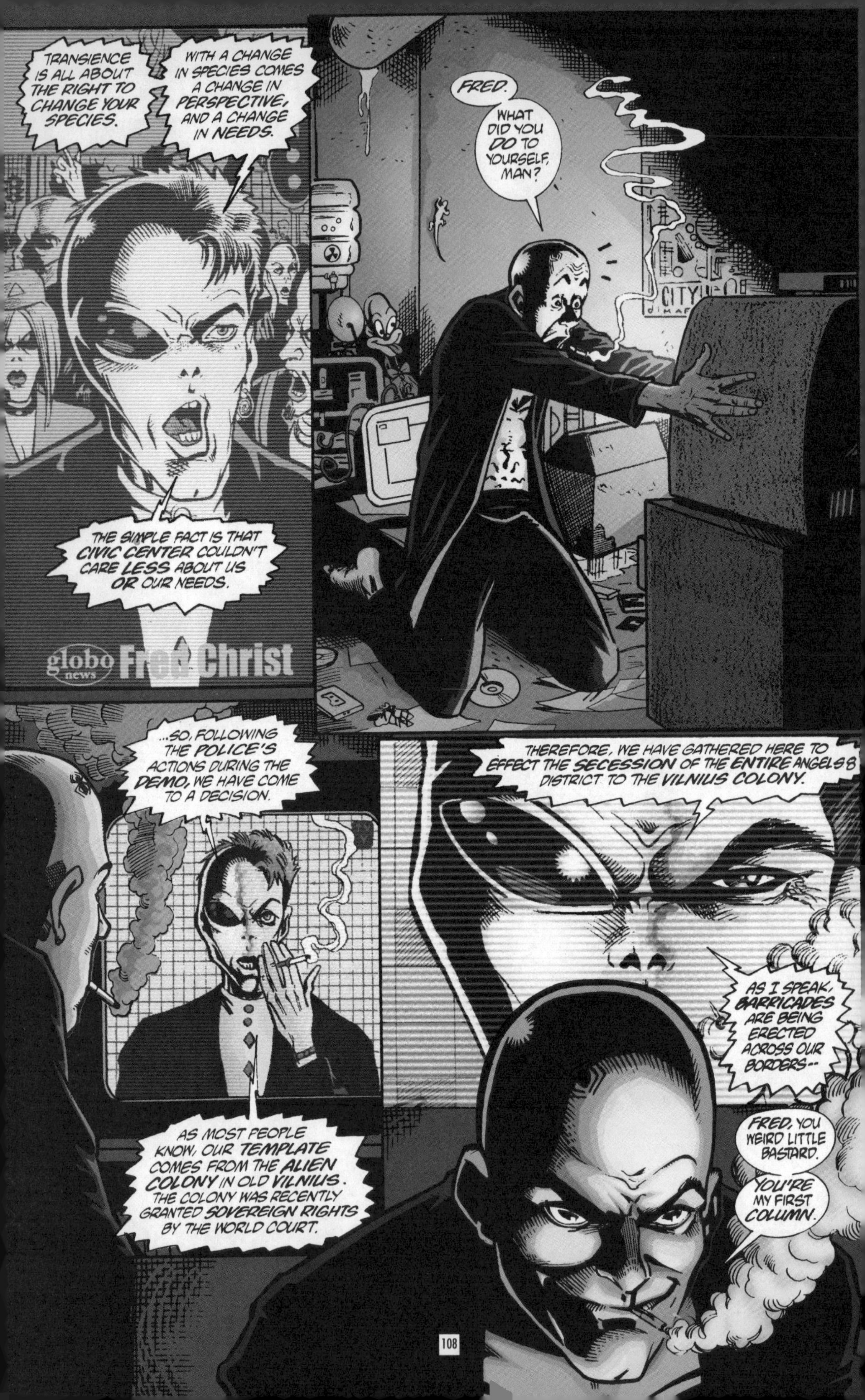
TRANSIENCE IS ALL ABOUT THE RIGHT TO CHANGE YOUR SPECIES.
WITH A CHANGE IN SPECIES COMES A CHANGE IN PERSPECTIVE, AND A CHANGE IN NEEDS.
THE SIMPLE FACT IS THAT CIVIC CENTER COULDN'T CARE LESS ABOUT US OR OUR NEEDS.
globo news Fred Christ
FRED.
WHAT DID YOU DO TO YOURSELF, MAN?
...SO, FOLLOWING THE POLICE'S ACTIONS DURING THE DEMO, WE HAVE COME TO A DECISION.
AS MOST PEOPLE KNOW, OUR TEMPLATE COMES FROM THE ALIEN COLONY IN OLD VILNIUS. THE COLONY WAS RECENTLY GRANTED SOVEREIGN RIGHTS BY THE WORLD COURT.
THEREFORE, WE HAVE GATHERED HERE TO EFFECT THE SECESSION OF THE ENTIRE ANGELS 8 DISTRICT TO THE VILNIUS COLONY.
AS I SPEAK, BARRICADES ARE BEING ERECTED ACROSS OUR BORDERS--
FRED, YOU WEIRD LITTLE BASTARD.
YOU'RE MY FIRST COLUMN.

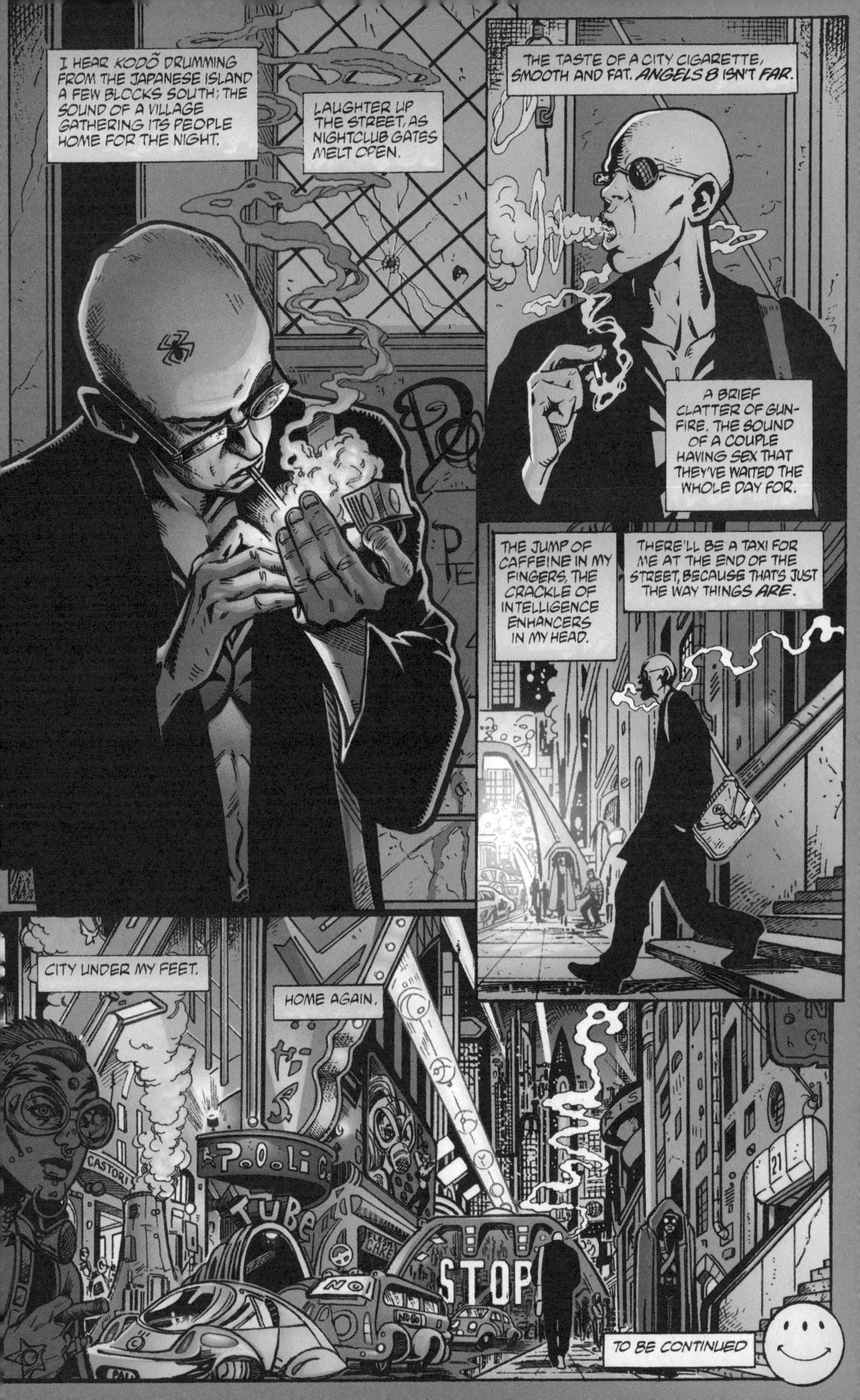
I HEAR KODÕ DRUMMING FROM THE JAPANESE ISLAND A FEW BLOCKS SOUTH; THE SOUND OF A VILLAGE GATHERING ITS PEOPLE HOME FOR THE NIGHT.
LAUGHTER UP THE STREET, AS NIGHTCLUB GATES MELT OPEN.
THE TASTE OF A CITY CIGARETTE, SMOOTH AND FAT. ANGELS 8 ISN'T FAR.
A BRIEF CLATTER OF GUN-FIRE. THE SOUND OF A COUPLE HAVING SEX THAT THEY'VE WAITED THE WHOLE DAY FOR.
THE JUMP OF CAFFEINE IN MY FINGERS, THE CRACKLE OF INTELLIGENCE ENHANCERS IN MY HEAD.
THERE'LL BE A TAXI FOR ME AT THE END OF THE STREET, BECAUSE THAT'S JUST THE WAY THINGS ARE.
CITY UNDER MY FEET.
HOME AGAIN.
CASTORI
P.O.LiC.
TUBE
FLESH CAKE
STOP
21
TO BE CONTINUED

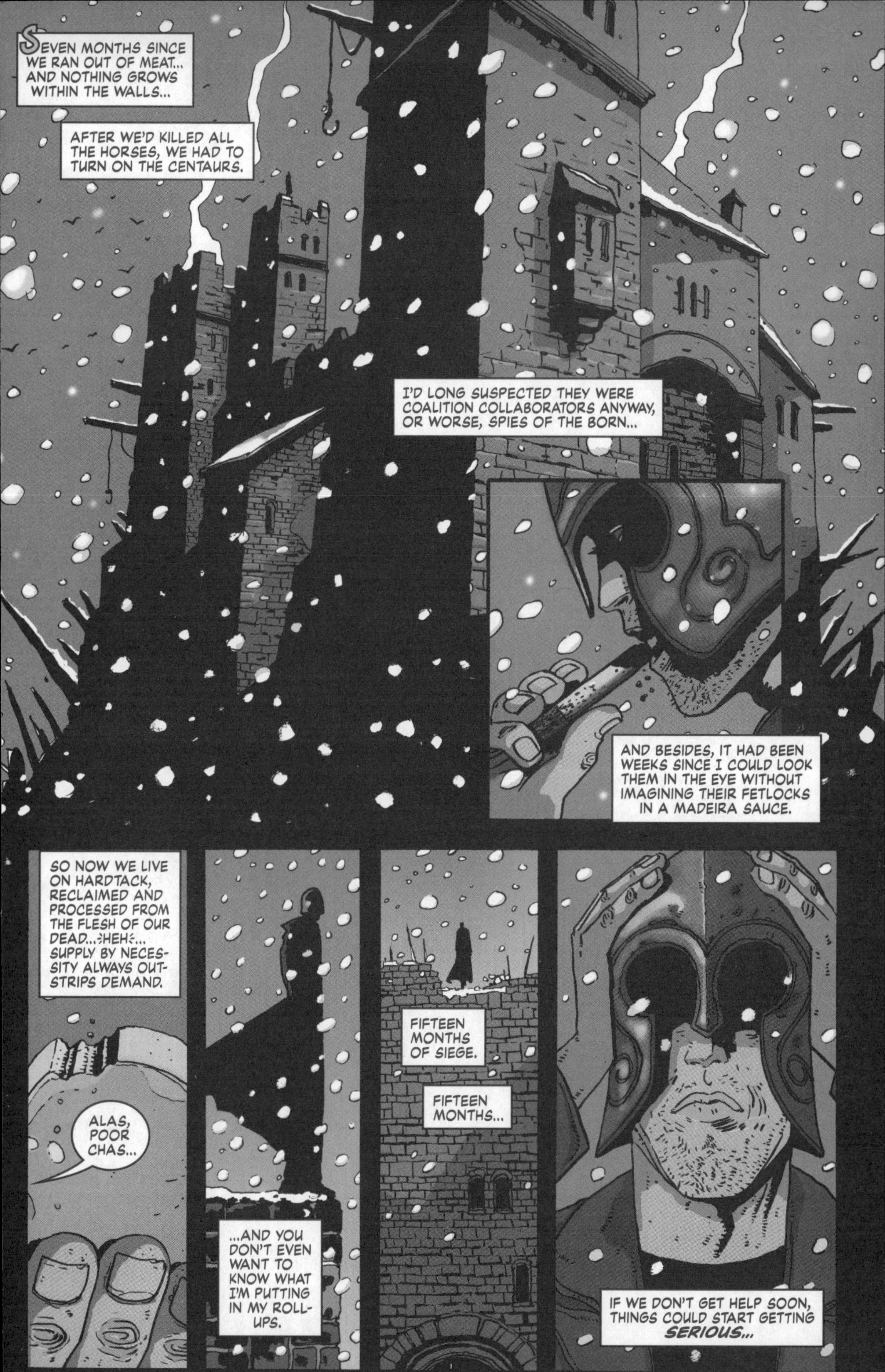
SEVEN MONTHS SINCE WE RAN OUT OF MEAT... AND NOTHING GROWS WITHIN THE WALLS...
AFTER WE'D KILLED ALL THE HORSES, WE HAD TO TURN ON THE CENTAURS.
I'D LONG SUSPECTED THEY WERE COALITION COLLABORATORS ANYWAY, OR WORSE, SPIES OF THE BORN...
AND BESIDES, IT HAD BEEN WEEKS SINCE I COULD LOOK THEM IN THE EYE WITHOUT IMAGINING THEIR FETLOCKS IN A MADEIRA SAUCE.
SO NOW WE LIVE ON HARDTACK, RECLAIMED AND PROCESSED FROM THE FLESH OF OUR DEAD... HEH... SUPPLY BY NECESSITY ALWAYS OUTSTRIPS DEMAND.
ALAS, POOR CHAS...
...AND YOU DON'T EVEN WANT TO KNOW WHAT I'M PUTTING IN MY ROLL-UPS.
FIFTEEN MONTHS OF SIEGE.
FIFTEEN MONTHS...
IF WE DON'T GET HELP SOON, THINGS COULD START GETTING SERIOUS...

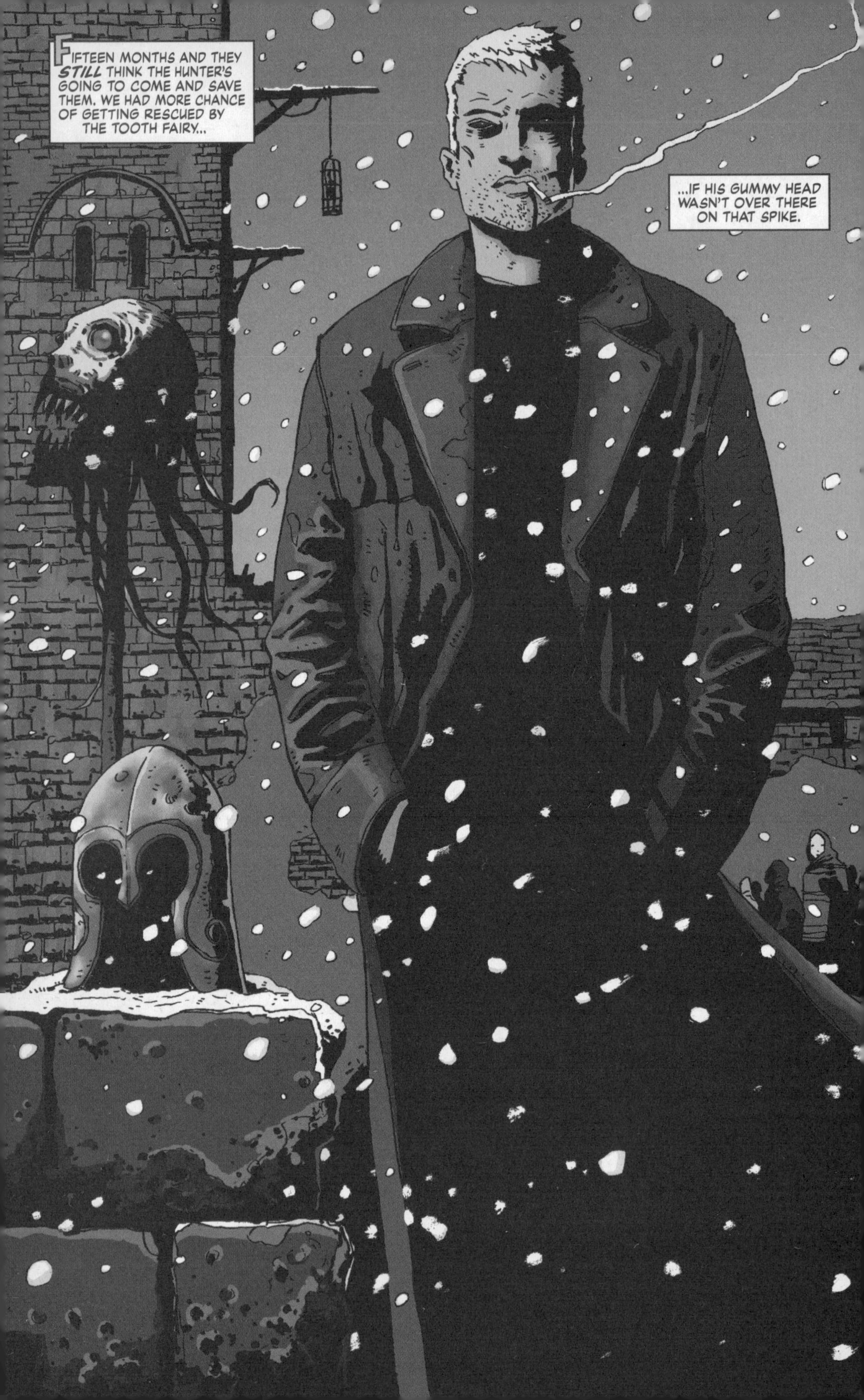
FIFTEEN MONTHS AND THEY STILL THINK THE HUNTER'S GOING TO COME AND SAVE THEM. WE HAD MORE CHANCE OF GETTING RESCUED BY THE TOOTH FAIRY...
...IF HIS GUMMY HEAD WASN'T OVER THERE ON THAT SPIKE.

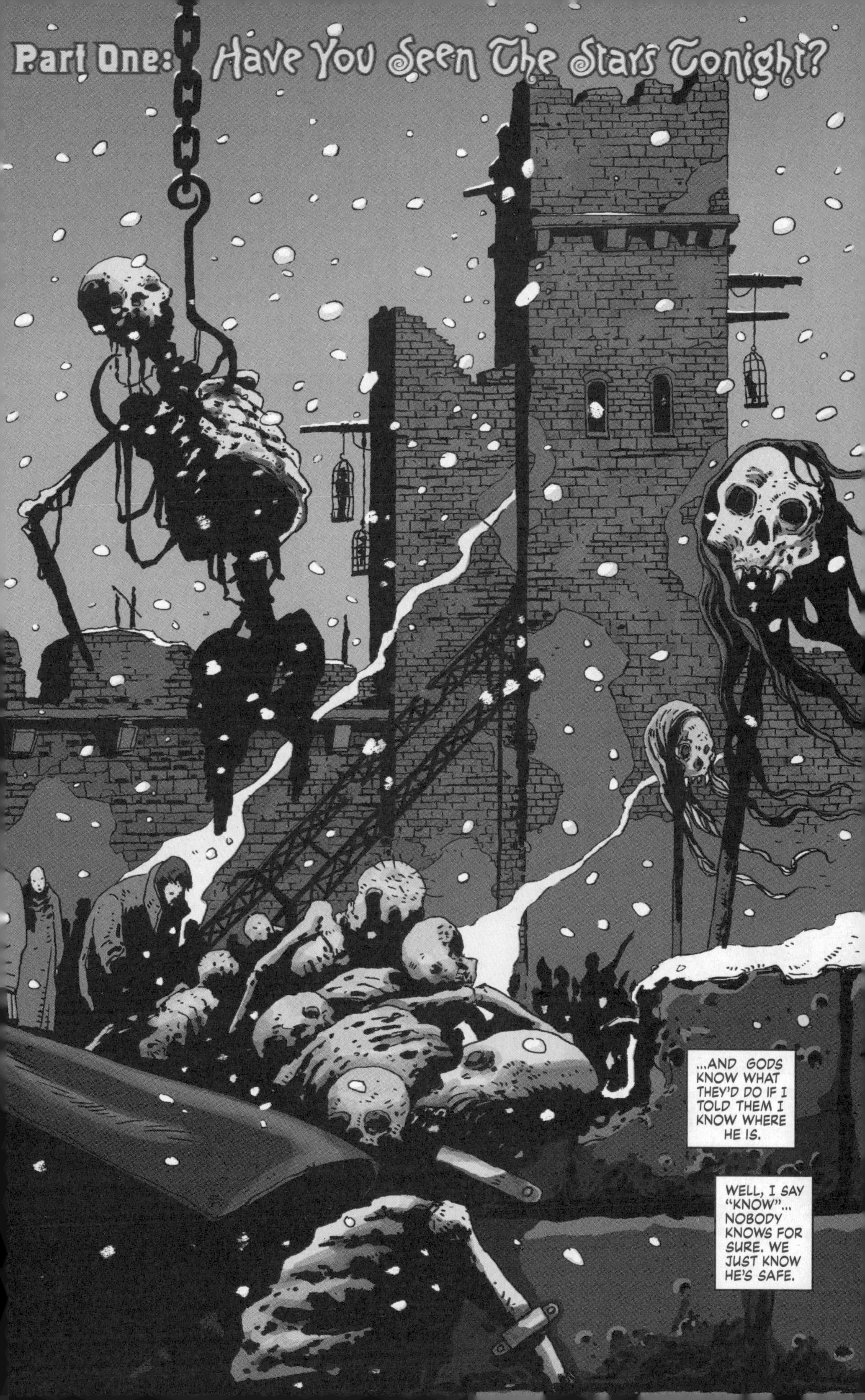
Part One: Have You Seen The Stars Tonight?
...AND GODS KNOW WHAT THEY'D DO IF I TOLD THEM I KNOW WHERE HE IS.
WELL, I SAY "KNOW"... NOBODY KNOWS FOR SURE. WE JUST KNOW HE'S SAFE.

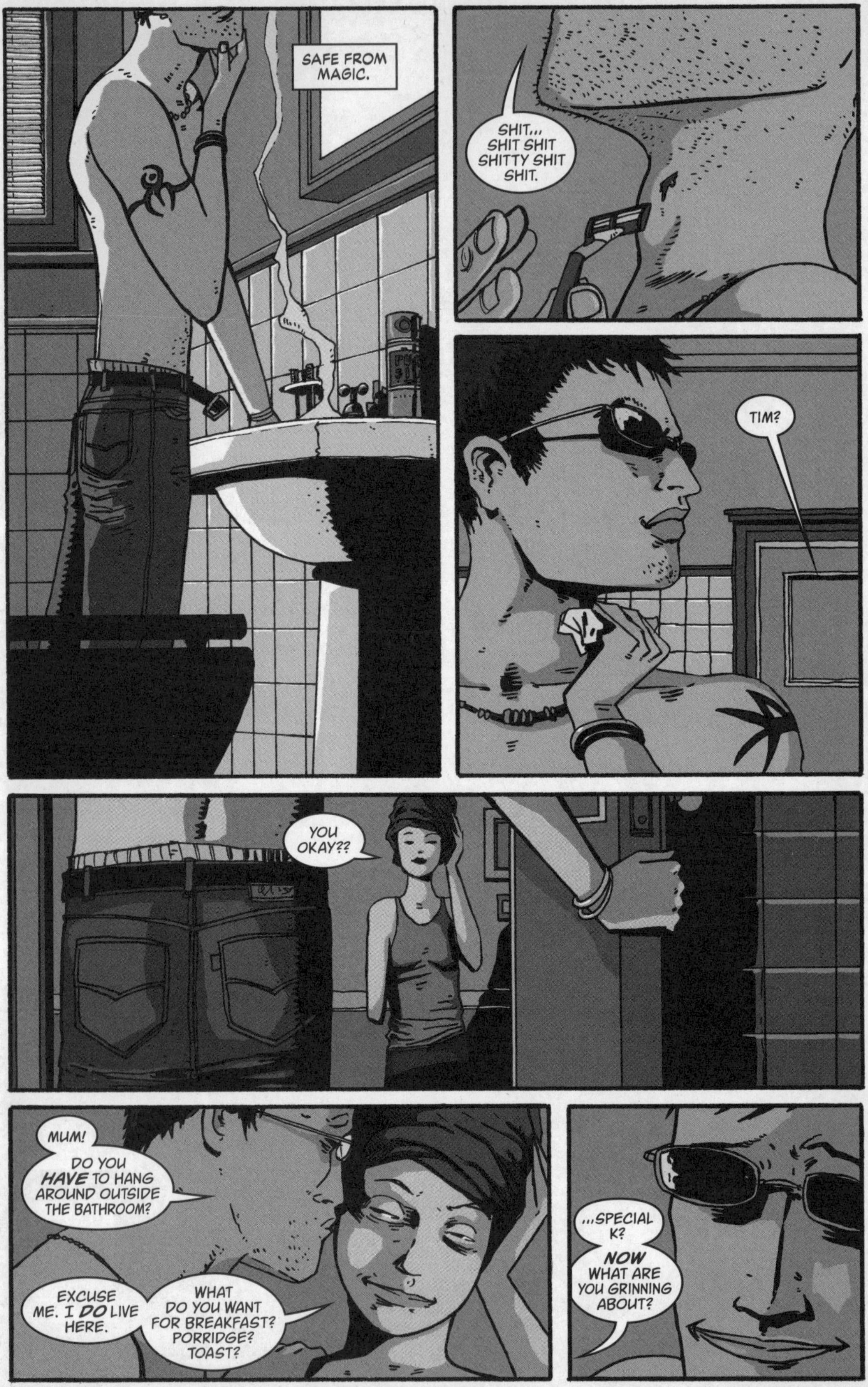
SAFE FROM MAGIC.
SHIT... SHIT SHIT SHITTY SHIT SHIT.
TIM?
YOU OKAY??
MUM!
DO YOU HAVE TO HANG AROUND OUTSIDE THE BATHROOM?
EXCUSE ME. I DO LIVE HERE.
WHAT DO YOU WANT FOR BREAKFAST? PORRIDGE? TOAST?
...SPECIAL K?
NOW WHAT ARE YOU GRINNING ABOUT?

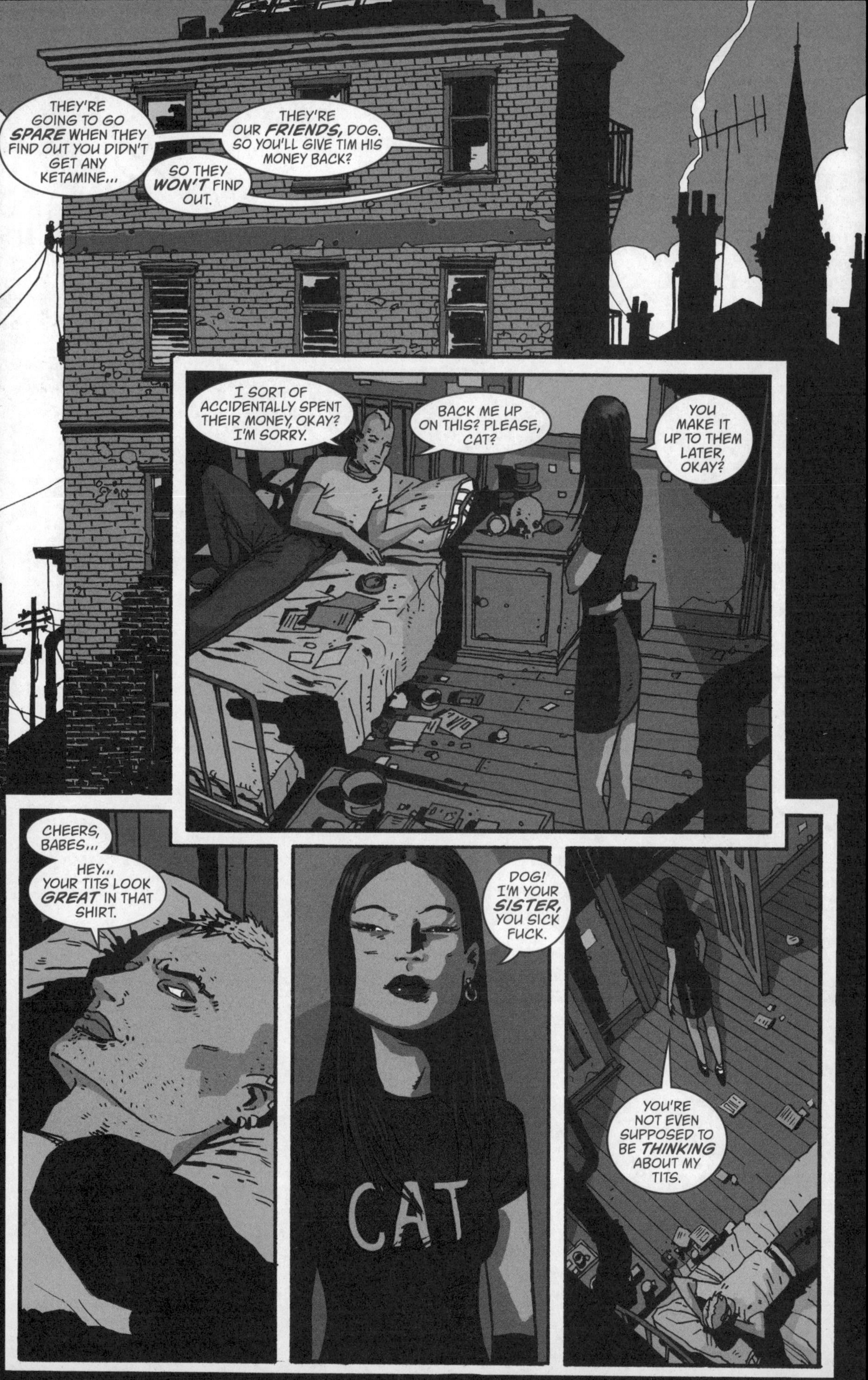
THEY'RE GOING TO GO SPARE WHEN THEY FIND OUT YOU DIDN'T GET ANY KETAMINE...
THEY'RE OUR FRIENDS, DOG. SO YOU'LL GIVE TIM HIS MONEY BACK?
SO THEY WON'T FIND OUT.
I SORT OF ACCIDENTALLY SPENT THEIR MONEY, OKAY? I'M SORRY.
BACK ME UP ON THIS? PLEASE, CAT?
YOU MAKE IT UP TO THEM LATER, OKAY?
CHEERS, BABES...
HEY... YOUR TITS LOOK GREAT IN THAT SHIRT.
DOG! I'M YOUR SISTER, YOU SICK FUCK.
CAT
YOU'RE NOT EVEN SUPPOSED TO BE THINKING ABOUT MY TITS.

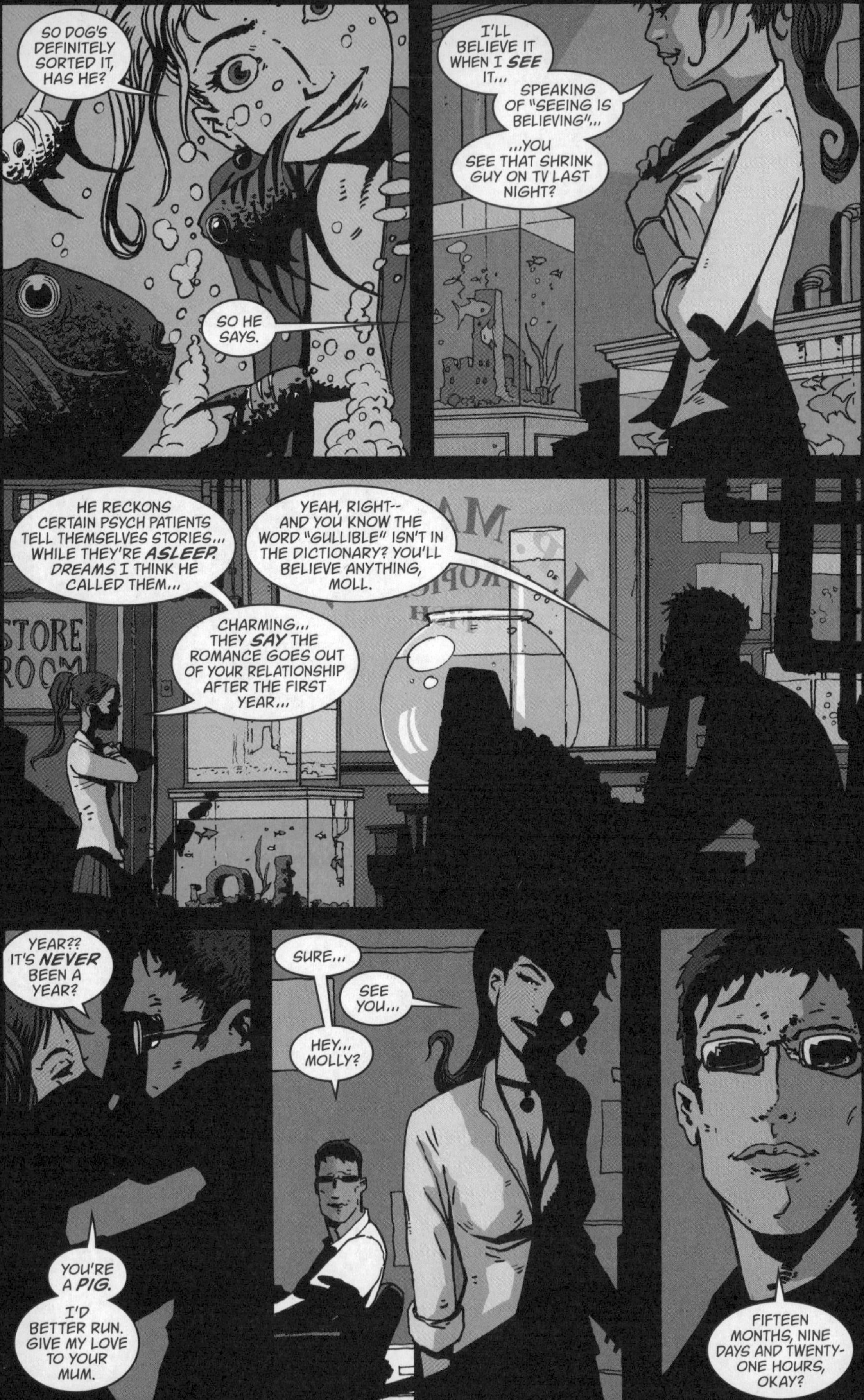
SO DOG'S DEFINITELY SORTED IT, HAS HE?
SO HE SAYS.
I'LL BELIEVE IT WHEN I SEE IT...
SPEAKING OF "SEEING IS BELIEVING"...
...YOU SEE THAT SHRINK GUY ON TV LAST NIGHT?
HE RECKONS CERTAIN PSYCH PATIENTS TELL THEMSELVES STORIES... WHILE THEY'RE ASLEEP. DREAMS I THINK HE CALLED THEM...
YEAH, RIGHT-- AND YOU KNOW THE WORD "GULLIBLE" ISN'T IN THE DICTIONARY? YOU'LL BELIEVE ANYTHING, MOLL.
CHARMING... THEY SAY THE ROMANCE GOES OUT OF YOUR RELATIONSHIP AFTER THE FIRST YEAR...
STORE ROOM
YEAR?? IT'S NEVER BEEN A YEAR?
YOU'RE A PIG.
I'D BETTER RUN. GIVE MY LOVE TO YOUR MUM.
SURE...
SEE YOU...
HEY... MOLLY?
FIFTEEN MONTHS, NINE DAYS AND TWENTY-ONE HOURS, OKAY?

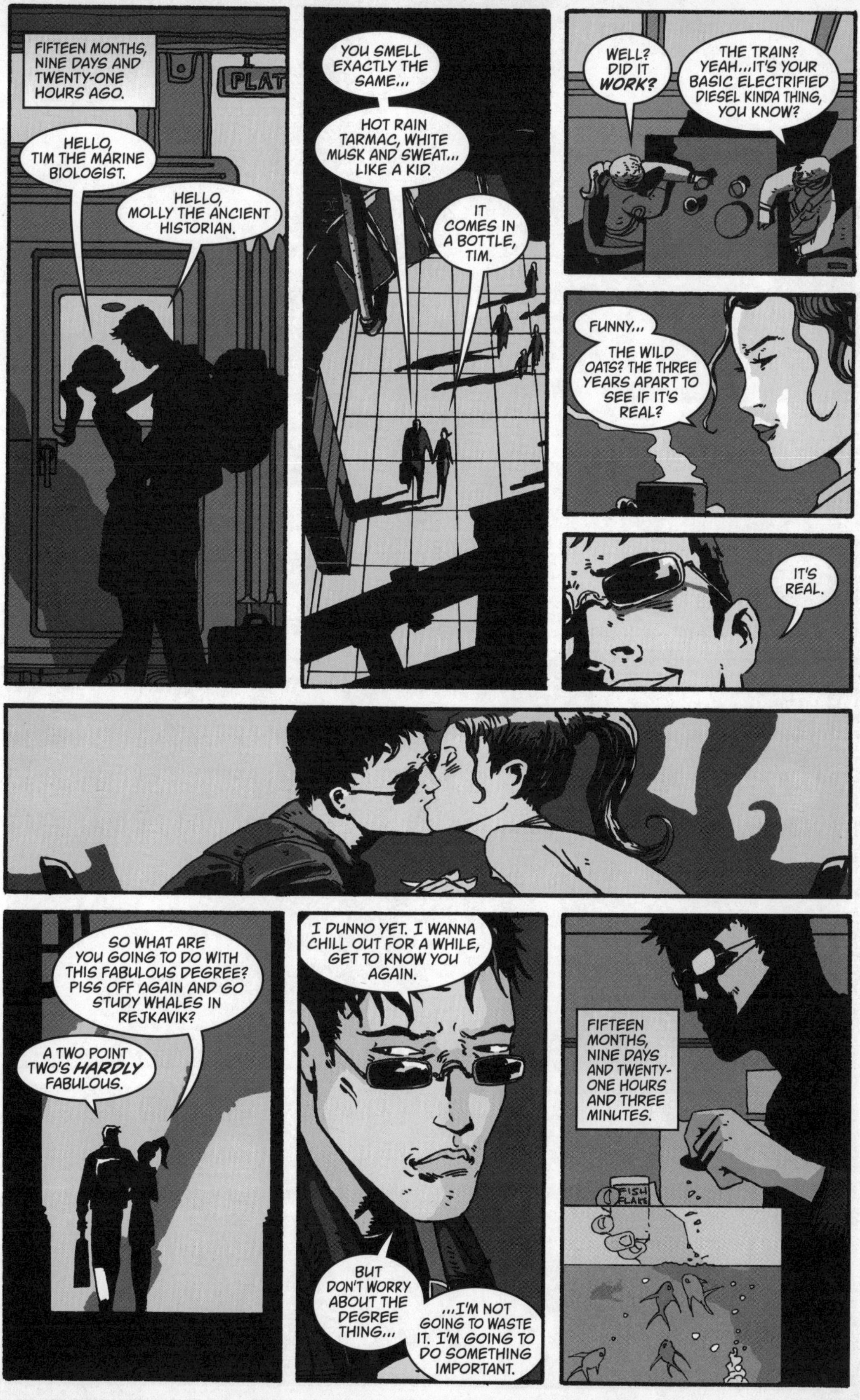
FIFTEEN MONTHS, NINE DAYS AND TWENTY-ONE HOURS AGO.
PLAT
HELLO, TIM THE MARINE BIOLOGIST.
HELLO, MOLLY THE ANCIENT HISTORIAN.
YOU SMELL EXACTLY THE SAME...
HOT RAIN TARMAC, WHITE MUSK AND SWEAT... LIKE A KID.
IT COMES IN A BOTTLE, TIM.
WELL? DID IT WORK?
THE TRAIN? YEAH...IT'S YOUR BASIC ELECTRIFIED DIESEL KINDA THING, YOU KNOW?
FUNNY...
THE WILD OATS? THE THREE YEARS APART TO SEE IF IT'S REAL?
IT'S REAL.
SO WHAT ARE YOU GOING TO DO WITH THIS FABULOUS DEGREE? PISS OFF AGAIN AND GO STUDY WHALES IN REJKAVIK?
A TWO POINT TWO'S HARDLY FABULOUS.
I DUNNO YET. I WANNA CHILL OUT FOR A WHILE, GET TO KNOW YOU AGAIN.
BUT DON'T WORRY ABOUT THE DEGREE THING...
...I'M NOT GOING TO WASTE IT. I'M GOING TO DO SOMETHING IMPORTANT.
FIFTEEN MONTHS, NINE DAYS AND TWENTY-ONE HOURS AND THREE MINUTES.
FISH FLAKE

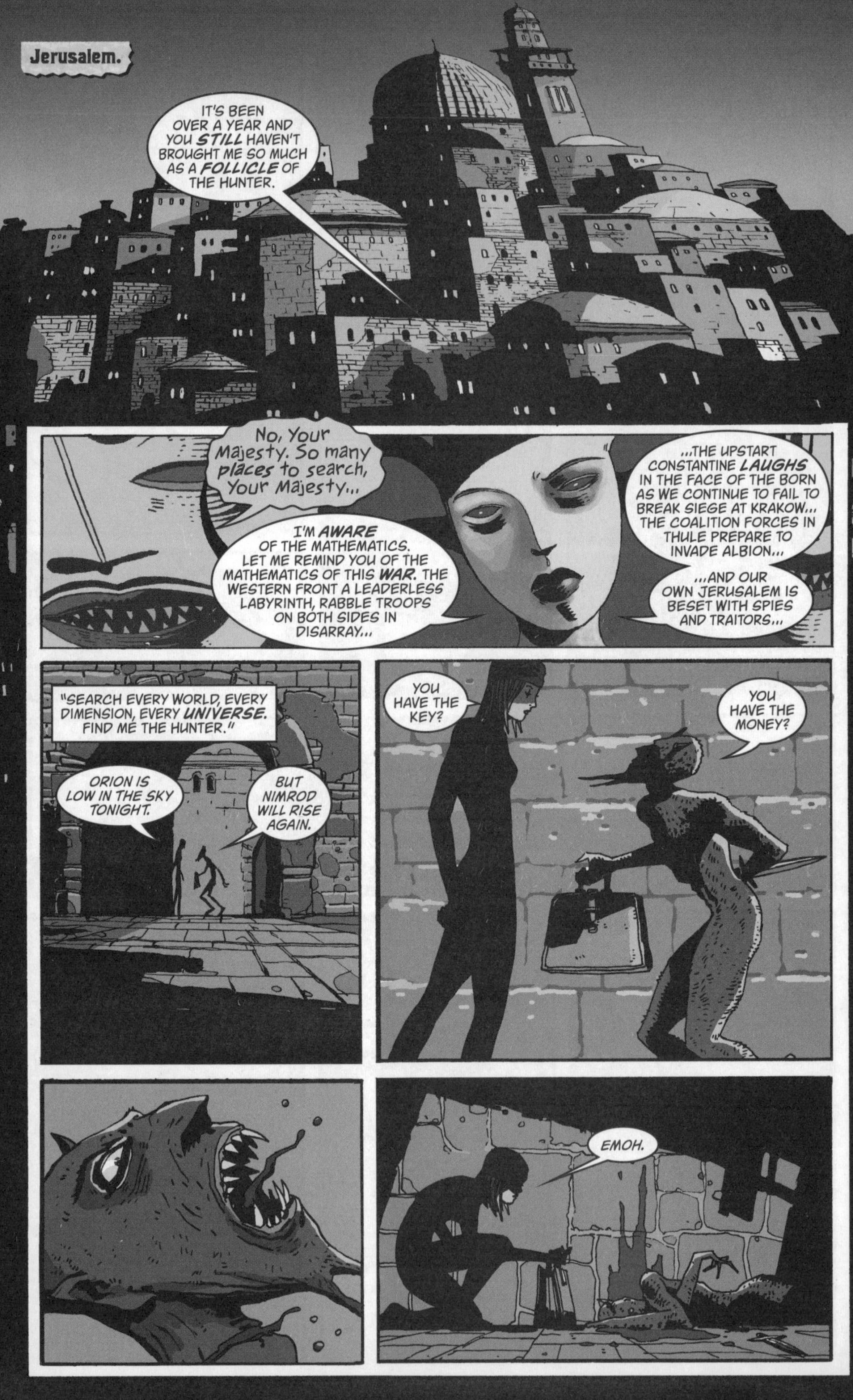
Jerusalem.
IT'S BEEN OVER A YEAR AND YOU STILL HAVEN'T BROUGHT ME SO MUCH AS A FOLLICLE OF THE HUNTER.
No, Your Majesty. So many places to search, Your Majesty...
I'M AWARE OF THE MATHEMATICS. LET ME REMIND YOU OF THE MATHEMATICS OF THIS WAR. THE WESTERN FRONT A LEADERLESS LABYRINTH, RABBLE TROOPS ON BOTH SIDES IN DISARRAY...
...THE UPSTART CONSTANTINE LAUGHS IN THE FACE OF THE BORN AS WE CONTINUE TO FAIL TO BREAK SIEGE AT KRAKOW... THE COALITION FORCES IN THULE PREPARE TO INVADE ALBION...
...AND OUR OWN JERUSALEM IS BESET WITH SPIES AND TRAITORS...
"SEARCH EVERY WORLD, EVERY DIMENSION, EVERY UNIVERSE. FIND ME THE HUNTER."
ORION IS LOW IN THE SKY TONIGHT.
BUT NIMROD WILL RISE AGAIN.
YOU HAVE THE KEY?
YOU HAVE THE MONEY?
EMOH.

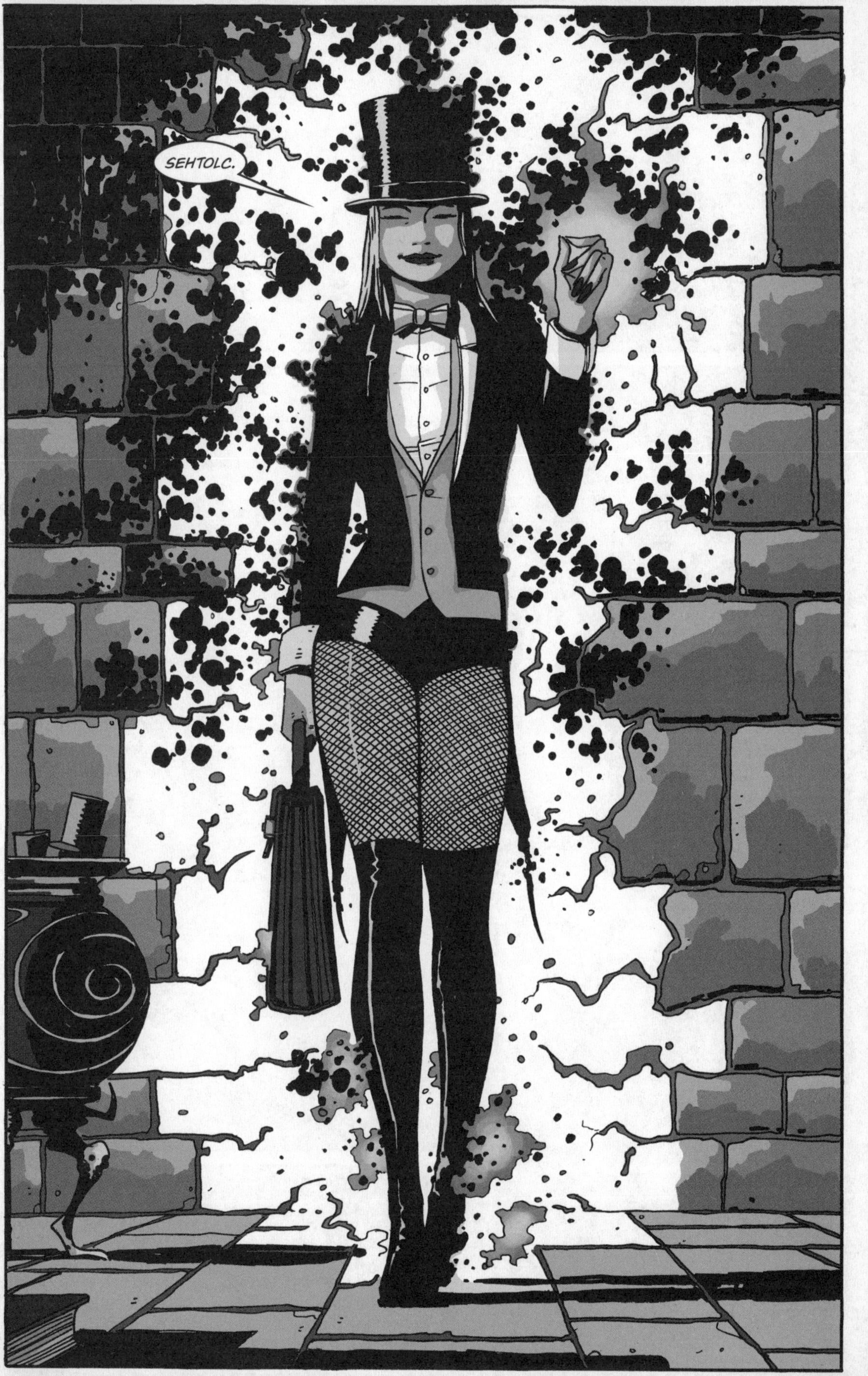
SEHTOLC.

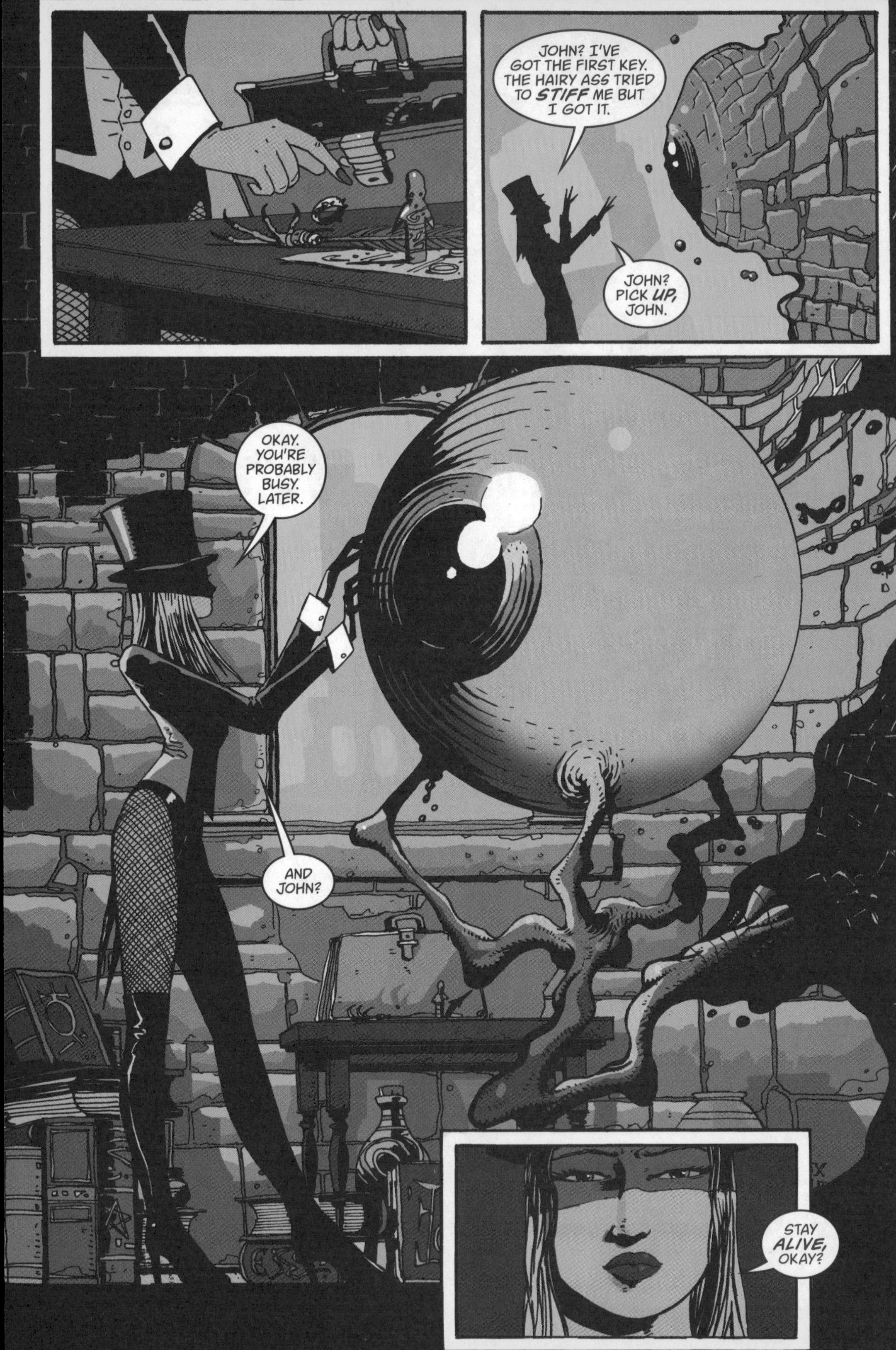
JOHN? I'VE GOT THE FIRST KEY. THE HAIRY ASS TRIED TO *STIFF* ME BUT I GOT IT.
JOHN? PICK *UP*, JOHN.
OKAY. YOU'RE PROBABLY BUSY. LATER.
AND JOHN?
STAY *ALIVE*, OKAY?

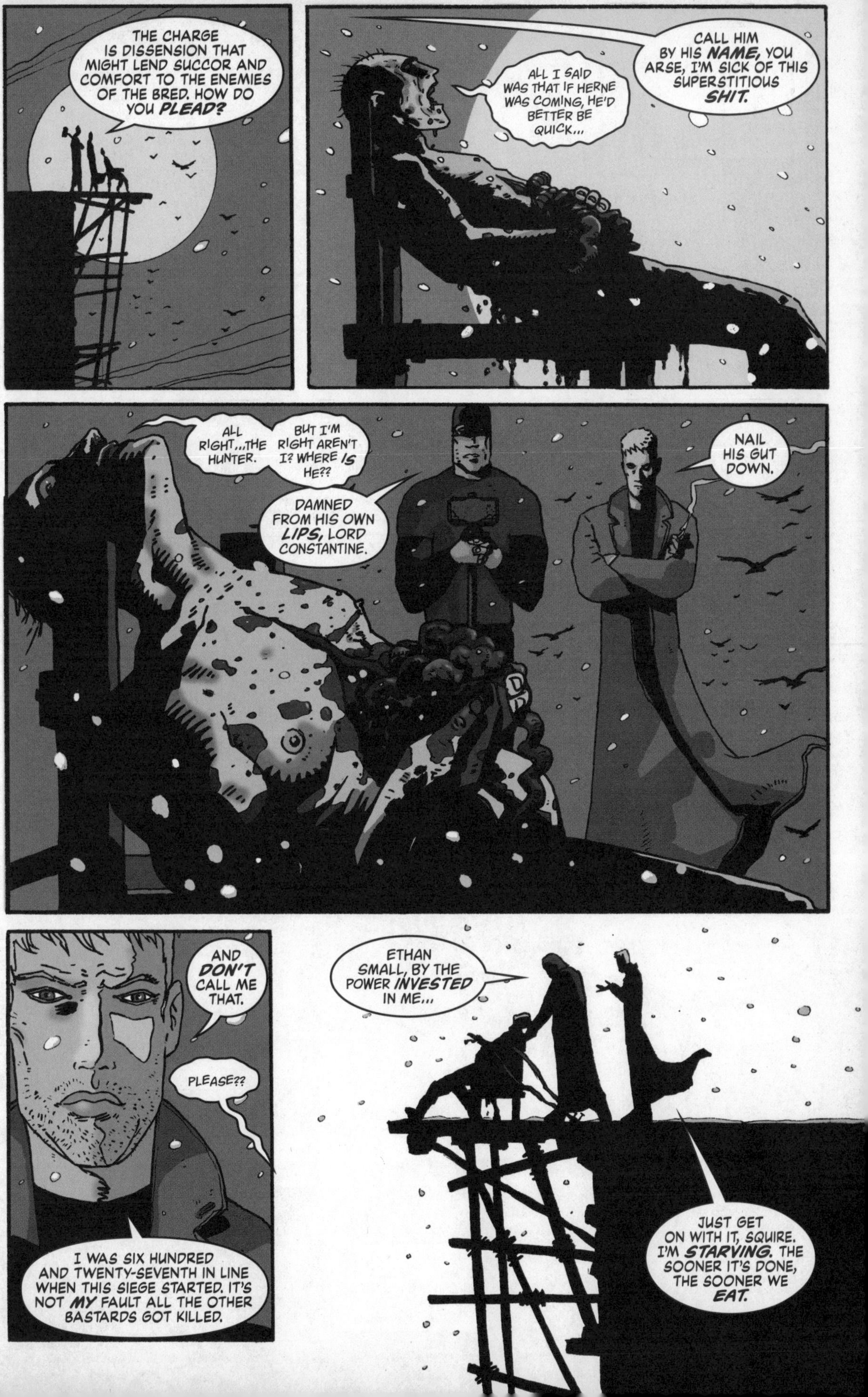
THE CHARGE IS DISSENSION THAT MIGHT LEND SUCCOR AND COMFORT TO THE ENEMIES OF THE BRED. HOW DO YOU PLEAD?
ALL I SAID WAS THAT IF HERNE WAS COMING, HE'D BETTER BE QUICK...
CALL HIM BY HIS NAME, YOU ARSE, I'M SICK OF THIS SUPERSTITIOUS SHIT.
ALL RIGHT...THE HUNTER.
BUT I'M RIGHT AREN'T I? WHERE IS HE??
DAMNED FROM HIS OWN LIPS, LORD CONSTANTINE.
NAIL HIS GUT DOWN.
AND DON'T CALL ME THAT.
PLEASE??
I WAS SIX HUNDRED AND TWENTY-SEVENTH IN LINE WHEN THIS SIEGE STARTED. IT'S NOT MY FAULT ALL THE OTHER BASTARDS GOT KILLED.
ETHAN SMALL, BY THE POWER INVESTED IN ME...
JUST GET ON WITH IT, SQUIRE. I'M STARVING. THE SOONER IT'S DONE, THE SOONER WE EAT.

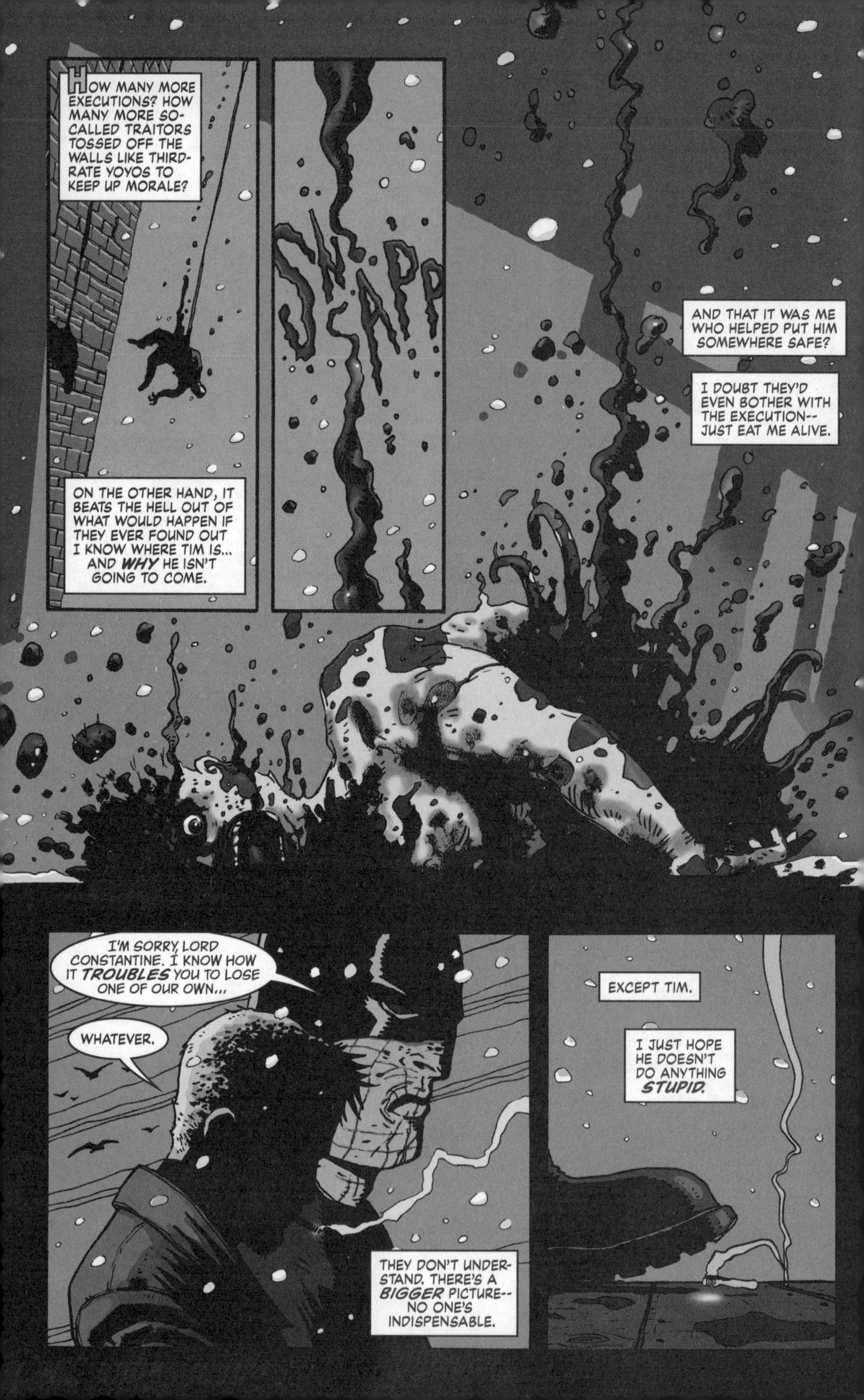
HOW MANY MORE EXECUTIONS? HOW MANY MORE SO-CALLED TRAITORS TOSSED OFF THE WALLS LIKE THIRD-RATE YOYOS TO KEEP UP MORALE?
ON THE OTHER HAND, IT BEATS THE HELL OUT OF WHAT WOULD HAPPEN IF THEY EVER FOUND OUT I KNOW WHERE TIM IS... AND *WHY* HE ISN'T GOING TO COME.
SHLAPP
AND THAT IT WAS ME WHO HELPED PUT HIM SOMEWHERE SAFE?
I DOUBT THEY'D EVEN BOTHER WITH THE EXECUTION-- JUST EAT ME ALIVE.
I'M SORRY, LORD CONSTANTINE. I KNOW HOW IT *TROUBLES* YOU TO LOSE ONE OF OUR OWN...
WHATEVER.
THEY DON'T UNDERSTAND. THERE'S A *BIGGER* PICTURE-- NO ONE'S INDISPENSABLE.
EXCEPT TIM.
I JUST HOPE HE DOESN'T DO ANYTHING *STUPID*.

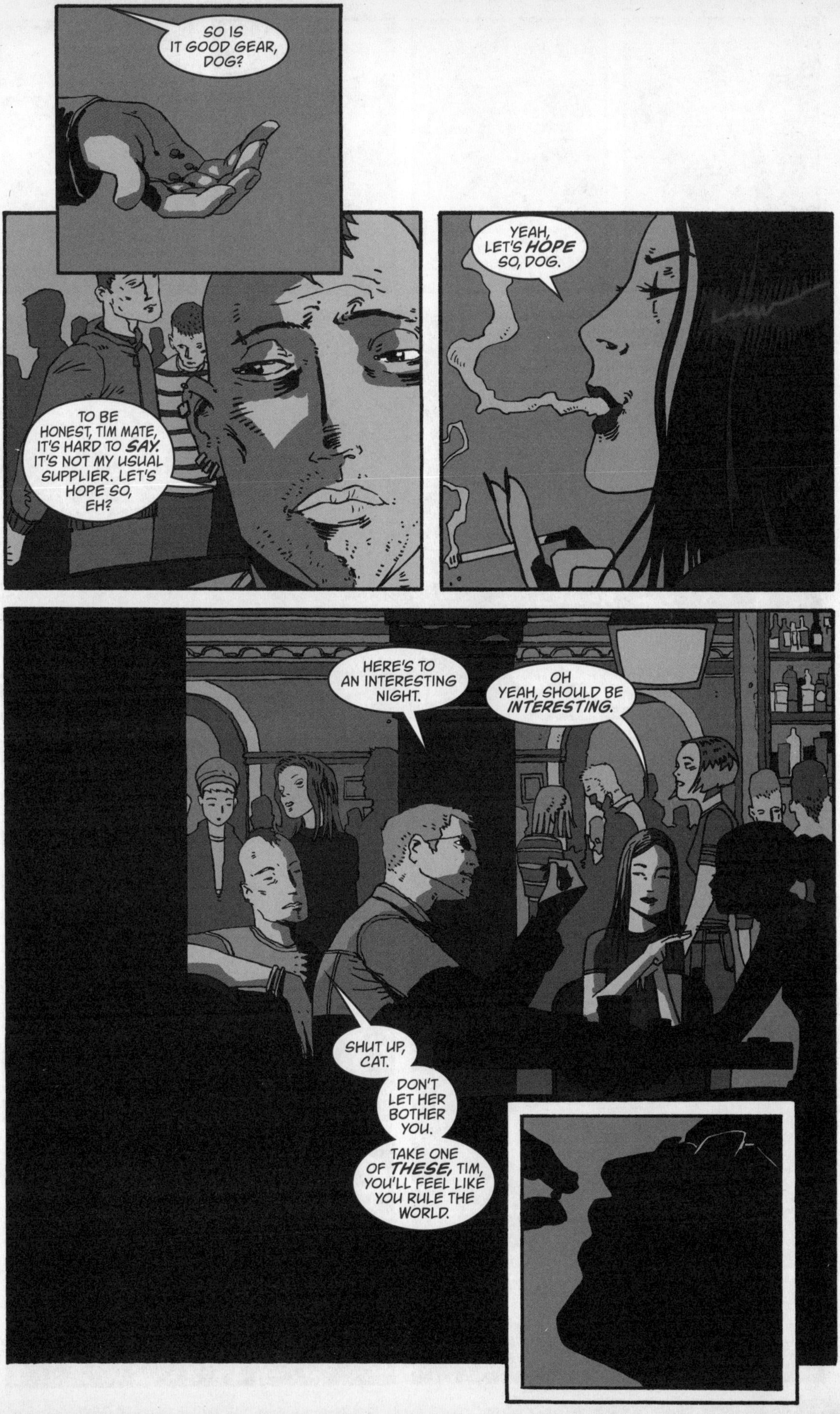
SO IS IT GOOD GEAR, DOG?
TO BE HONEST, TIM MATE, IT'S HARD TO SAY. IT'S NOT MY USUAL SUPPLIER. LET'S HOPE SO, EH?
YEAH, LET'S HOPE SO, DOG.
HERE'S TO AN INTERESTING NIGHT.
OH YEAH, SHOULD BE INTERESTING.
SHUT UP, CAT.
DON'T LET HER BOTHER YOU.
TAKE ONE OF THESE, TIM, YOU'LL FEEL LIKE YOU RULE THE WORLD.

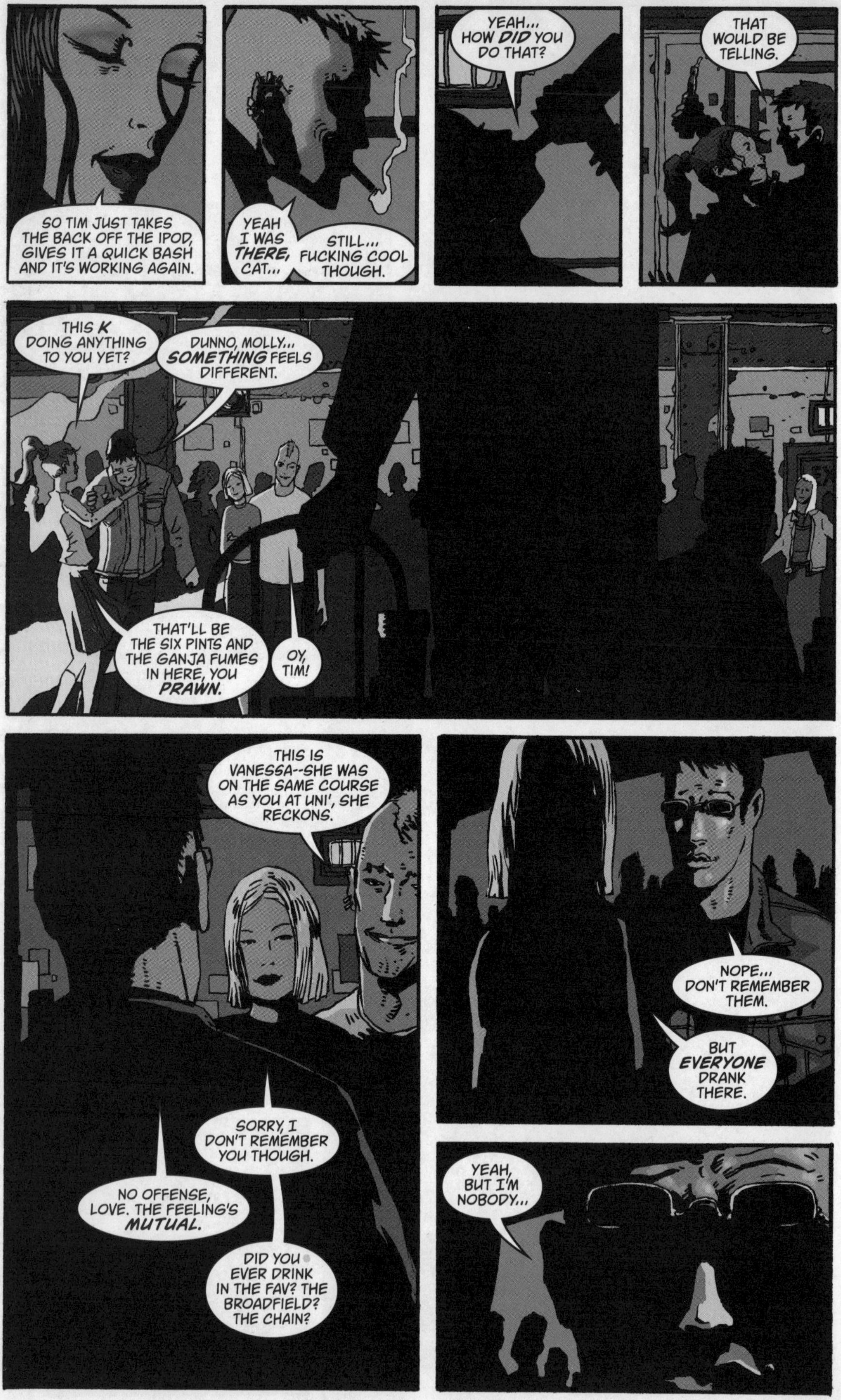

SO TIM JUST TAKES THE BACK OFF THE IPOD, GIVES IT A QUICK BASH AND IT'S WORKING AGAIN.
YEAH I WAS *THERE,* CAT...
STILL... FUCKING COOL THOUGH.
YEAH... HOW *DID* YOU DO THAT?
THAT WOULD BE TELLING.
THIS *K* DOING ANYTHING TO YOU YET?
DUNNO, MOLLY... *SOMETHING* FEELS DIFFERENT.
THAT'LL BE THE SIX PINTS AND THE GANJA FUMES IN HERE, YOU *PRAWN.*
OY, TIM!
THIS IS VANESSA--SHE WAS ON THE SAME COURSE AS YOU AT UNI', SHE RECKONS.
SORRY, I DON'T REMEMBER YOU THOUGH.
NO OFFENSE, LOVE. THE FEELING'S *MUTUAL.*
DID YOU EVER DRINK IN THE FAV? THE BROADFIELD? THE CHAIN?
NOPE... DON'T REMEMBER THEM.
BUT *EVERYONE* DRANK THERE.
YEAH, BUT I'M NOBODY...

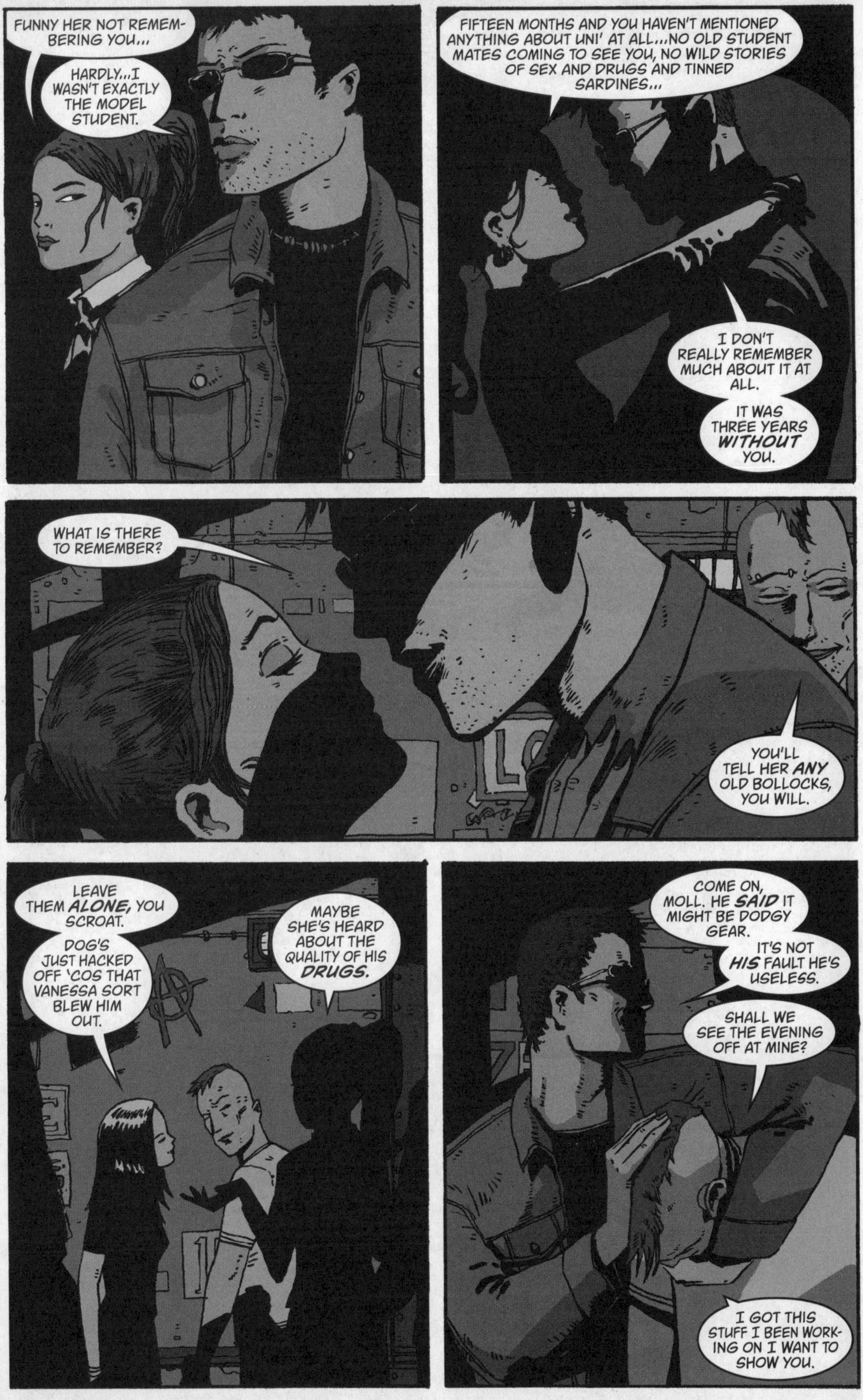
FUNNY HER NOT REMEMBERING YOU...
HARDLY...I WASN'T EXACTLY THE MODEL STUDENT.
FIFTEEN MONTHS AND YOU HAVEN'T MENTIONED ANYTHING ABOUT UNI' AT ALL...NO OLD STUDENT MATES COMING TO SEE YOU, NO WILD STORIES OF SEX AND DRUGS AND TINNED SARDINES...
I DON'T REALLY REMEMBER MUCH ABOUT IT AT ALL.
IT WAS THREE YEARS ***WITHOUT*** YOU.
WHAT IS THERE TO REMEMBER?
YOU'LL TELL HER ***ANY*** OLD BOLLOCKS, YOU WILL.
LEAVE THEM ***ALONE,*** YOU SCROAT.
DOG'S JUST HACKED OFF 'COS THAT VANESSA SORT BLEW HIM OUT.
MAYBE SHE'S HEARD ABOUT THE QUALITY OF HIS ***DRUGS.***
COME ON, MOLL. HE ***SAID*** IT MIGHT BE DODGY GEAR.
IT'S NOT ***HIS*** FAULT HE'S USELESS.
SHALL WE SEE THE EVENING OFF AT MINE?
I GOT THIS STUFF I BEEN WORKING ON I WANT TO SHOW YOU.

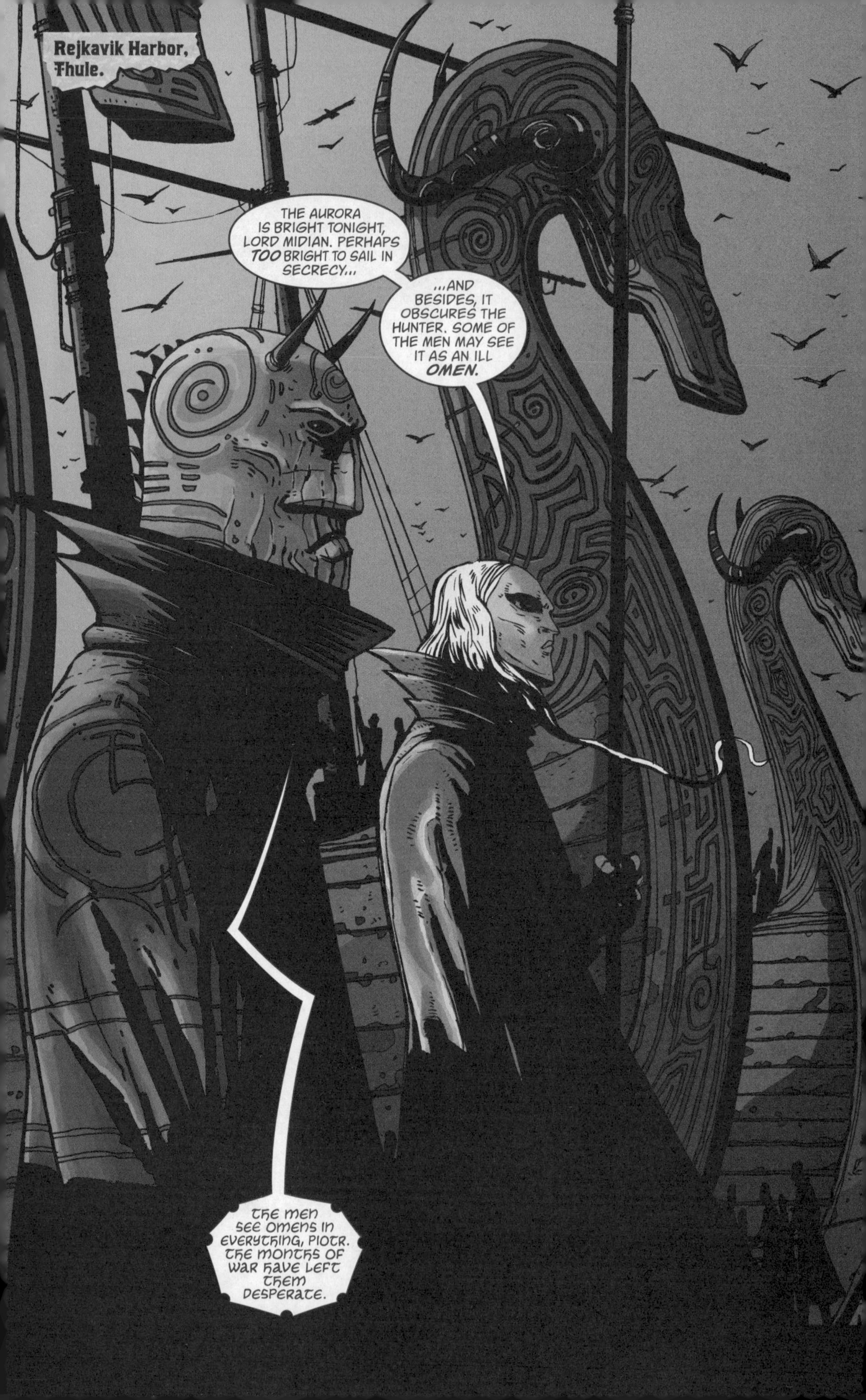
Rejkavik Harbor, Thule.
THE AURORA IS BRIGHT TONIGHT, LORD MIDIAN. PERHAPS TOO BRIGHT TO SAIL IN SECRECY...
...AND BESIDES, IT OBSCURES THE HUNTER. SOME OF THE MEN MAY SEE IT AS AN ILL OMEN.
THE MEN SEE OMENS IN EVERYTHING, PIOTR. THE MONTHS OF WAR HAVE LEFT THEM DESPERATE.

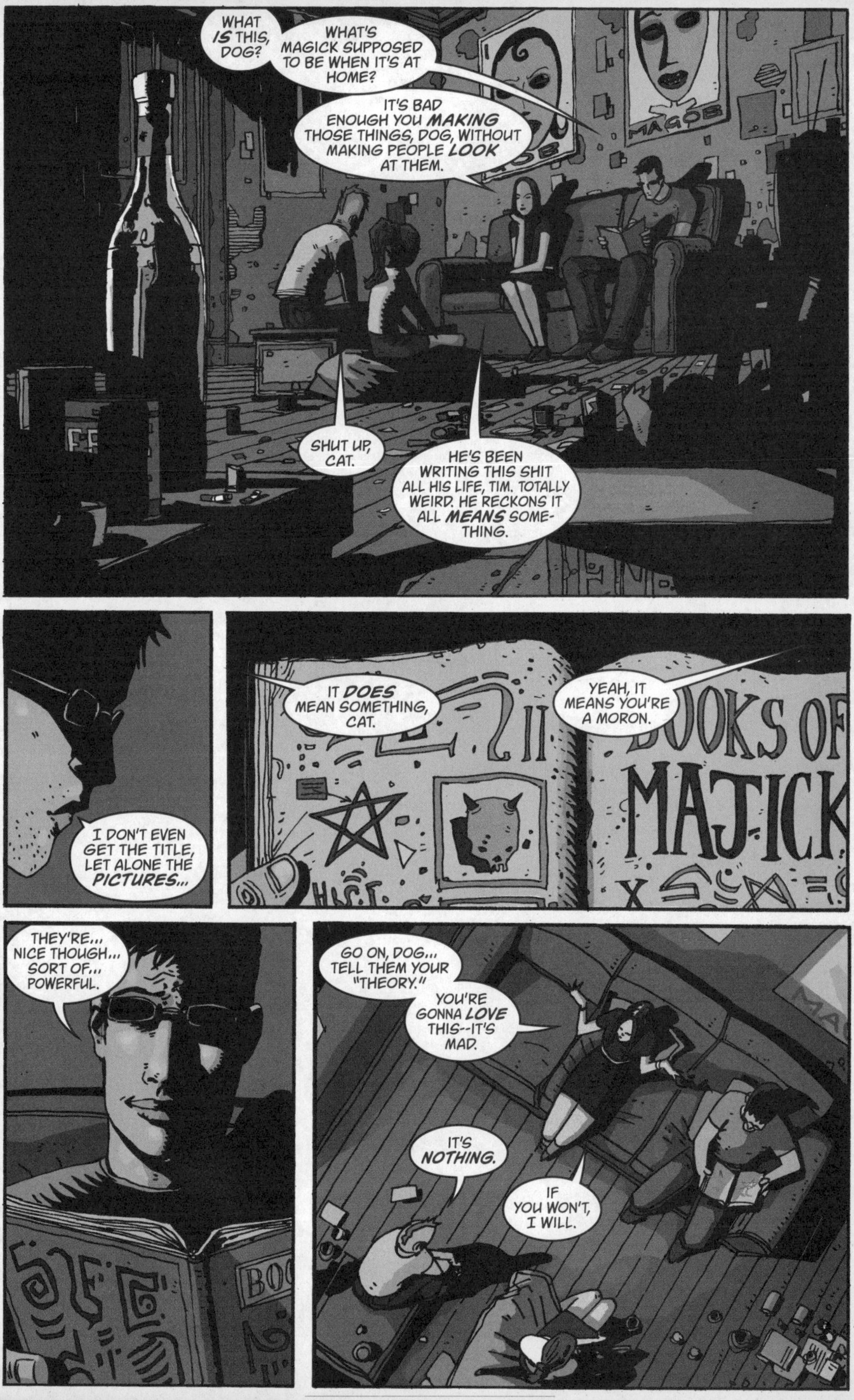
WHAT *IS* THIS, DOG?
WHAT'S MAGICK SUPPOSED TO BE WHEN IT'S AT HOME?
IT'S BAD ENOUGH YOU *MAKING* THOSE THINGS, DOG, WITHOUT MAKING PEOPLE *LOOK* AT THEM.
MAGOB
SHUT UP, CAT.
HE'S BEEN WRITING THIS SHIT ALL HIS LIFE, TIM. TOTALLY WEIRD. HE RECKONS IT ALL *MEANS* SOMETHING.
I DON'T EVEN GET THE TITLE, LET ALONE THE *PICTURES*...
IT *DOES* MEAN SOMETHING, CAT.
YEAH, IT MEANS YOU'RE A MORON.
MAJICK
THEY'RE... NICE THOUGH... SORT OF... POWERFUL.
GO ON, DOG... TELL THEM YOUR "THEORY."
YOU'RE GONNA *LOVE* THIS--IT'S MAD.
IT'S *NOTHING.*
IF YOU WON'T, I WILL.

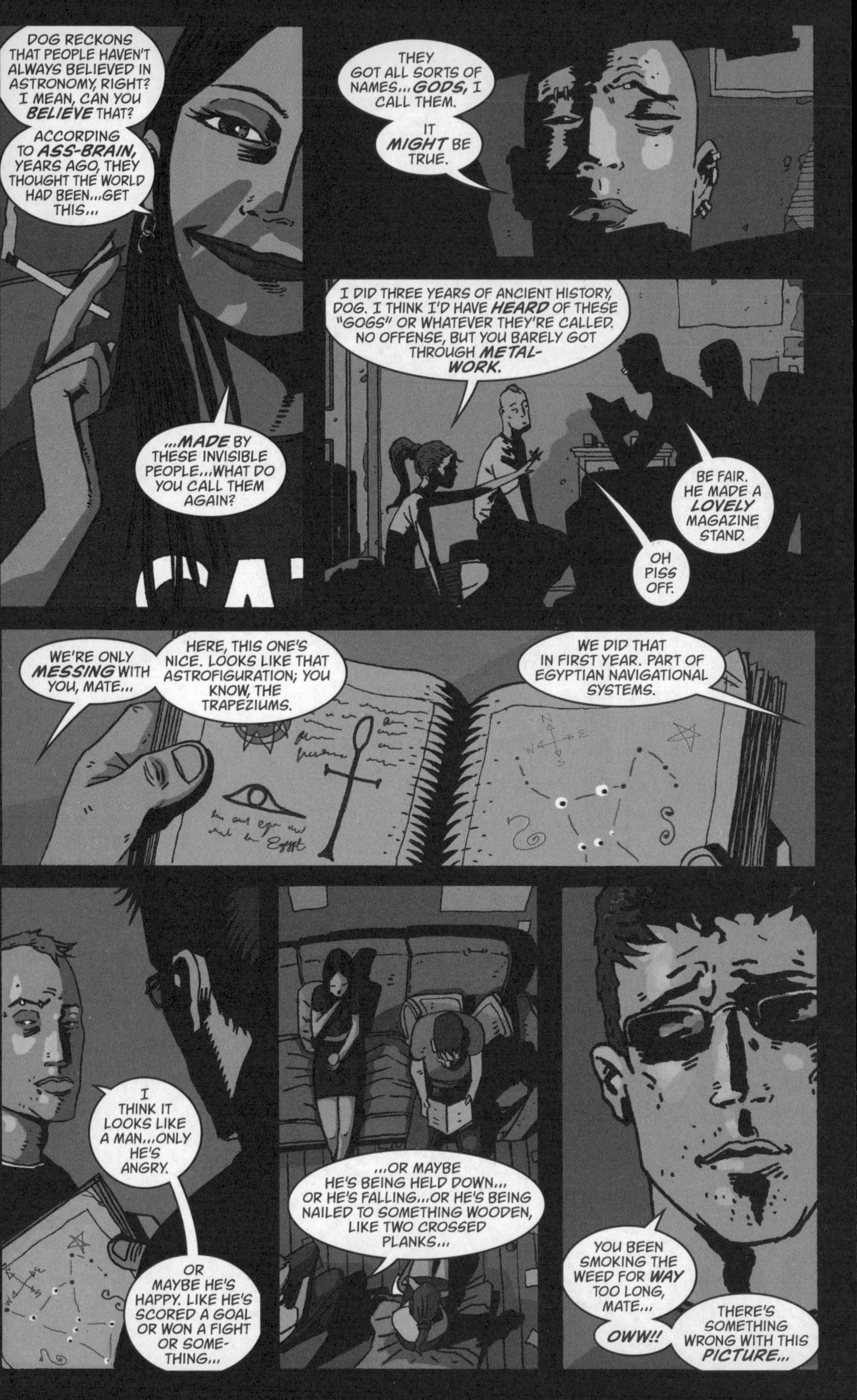
DOG RECKONS THAT PEOPLE HAVEN'T ALWAYS BELIEVED IN ASTRONOMY, RIGHT? I MEAN, CAN YOU BELIEVE THAT?
ACCORDING TO ASS-BRAIN, YEARS AGO, THEY THOUGHT THE WORLD HAD BEEN...GET THIS...
...MADE BY THESE INVISIBLE PEOPLE...WHAT DO YOU CALL THEM AGAIN?
THEY GOT ALL SORTS OF NAMES...GODS, I CALL THEM.
IT MIGHT BE TRUE.
I DID THREE YEARS OF ANCIENT HISTORY, DOG. I THINK I'D HAVE HEARD OF THESE "GOGS" OR WHATEVER THEY'RE CALLED. NO OFFENSE, BUT YOU BARELY GOT THROUGH METAL-WORK.
BE FAIR. HE MADE A LOVELY MAGAZINE STAND.
OH PISS OFF.
WE'RE ONLY MESSING WITH YOU, MATE...
HERE, THIS ONE'S NICE. LOOKS LIKE THAT ASTROFIGURATION; YOU KNOW, THE TRAPEZIUMS.
WE DID THAT IN FIRST YEAR. PART OF EGYPTIAN NAVIGATIONAL SYSTEMS.
I THINK IT LOOKS LIKE A MAN...ONLY HE'S ANGRY.
OR MAYBE HE'S HAPPY. LIKE HE'S SCORED A GOAL OR WON A FIGHT OR SOME-THING...
...OR MAYBE HE'S BEING HELD DOWN... OR HE'S FALLING...OR HE'S BEING NAILED TO SOMETHING WOODEN, LIKE TWO CROSSED PLANKS...
YOU BEEN SMOKING THE WEED FOR WAY TOO LONG, MATE...
OWW!!
THERE'S SOMETHING WRONG WITH THIS PICTURE...

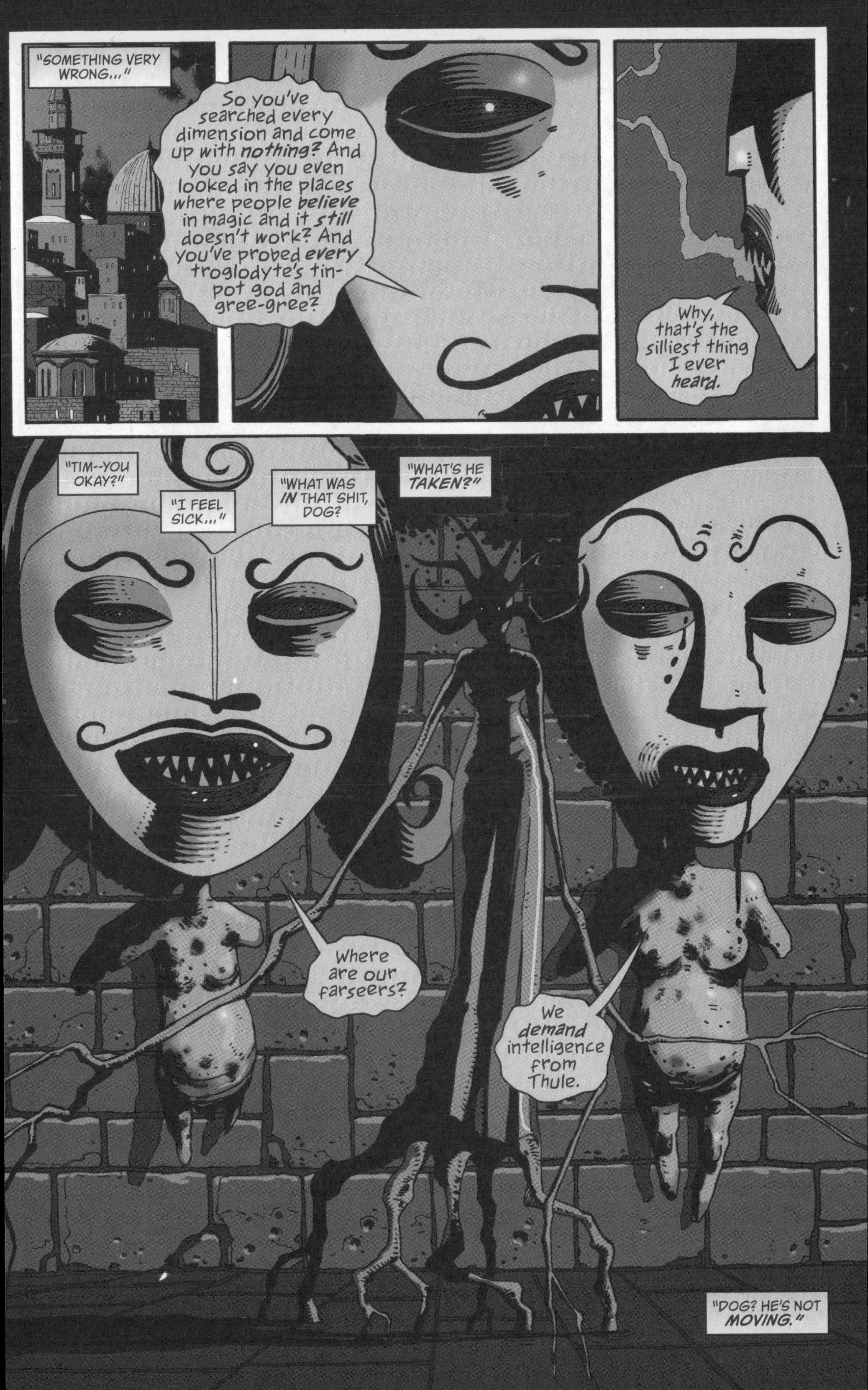
"SOMETHING VERY WRONG..."
So you've searched every dimension and come up with *nothing?* And you say you even looked in the places where people *believe* in magic and it *still* doesn't work? And you've probed *every* troglodyte's tin-pot god and gree-gree?
Why, that's the silliest thing I ever *heard.*
"TIM--YOU OKAY?"
"I FEEL SICK..."
"WHAT WAS *IN* THAT SHIT, DOG?
"WHAT'S HE *TAKEN?*"
Where are our farseers?
We *demand* intelligence from Thule.
"DOG? HE'S NOT *MOVING.*"

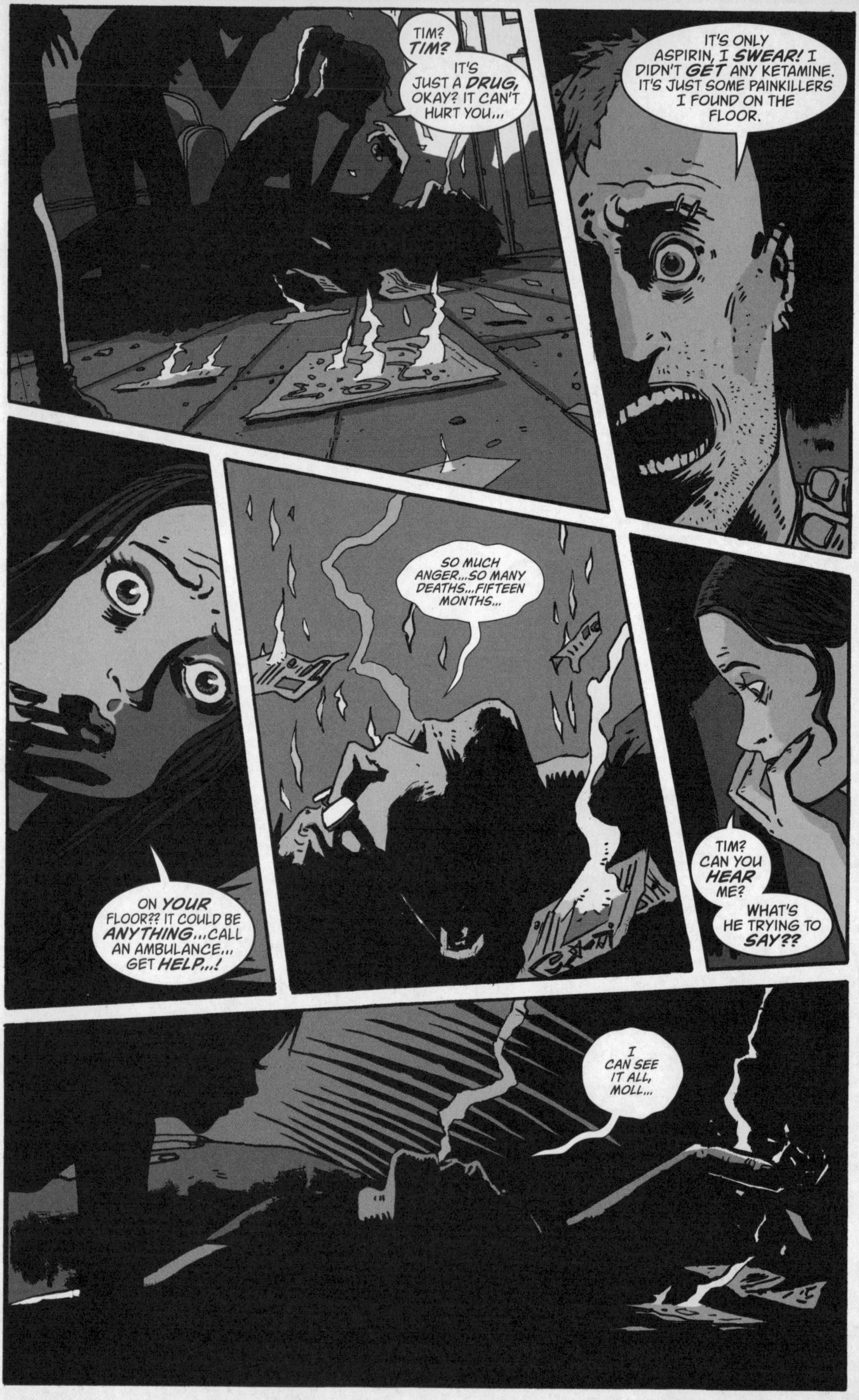
TIM? TIM?
IT'S JUST A DRUG, OKAY? IT CAN'T HURT YOU...
IT'S ONLY ASPIRIN, I SWEAR! I DIDN'T GET ANY KETAMINE. IT'S JUST SOME PAINKILLERS I FOUND ON THE FLOOR.
ON YOUR FLOOR?? IT COULD BE ANYTHING...CALL AN AMBULANCE... GET HELP...!
SO MUCH ANGER...SO MANY DEATHS...FIFTEEN MONTHS...
TIM? CAN YOU HEAR ME?
WHAT'S HE TRYING TO SAY??
I CAN SEE IT ALL, MOLL...

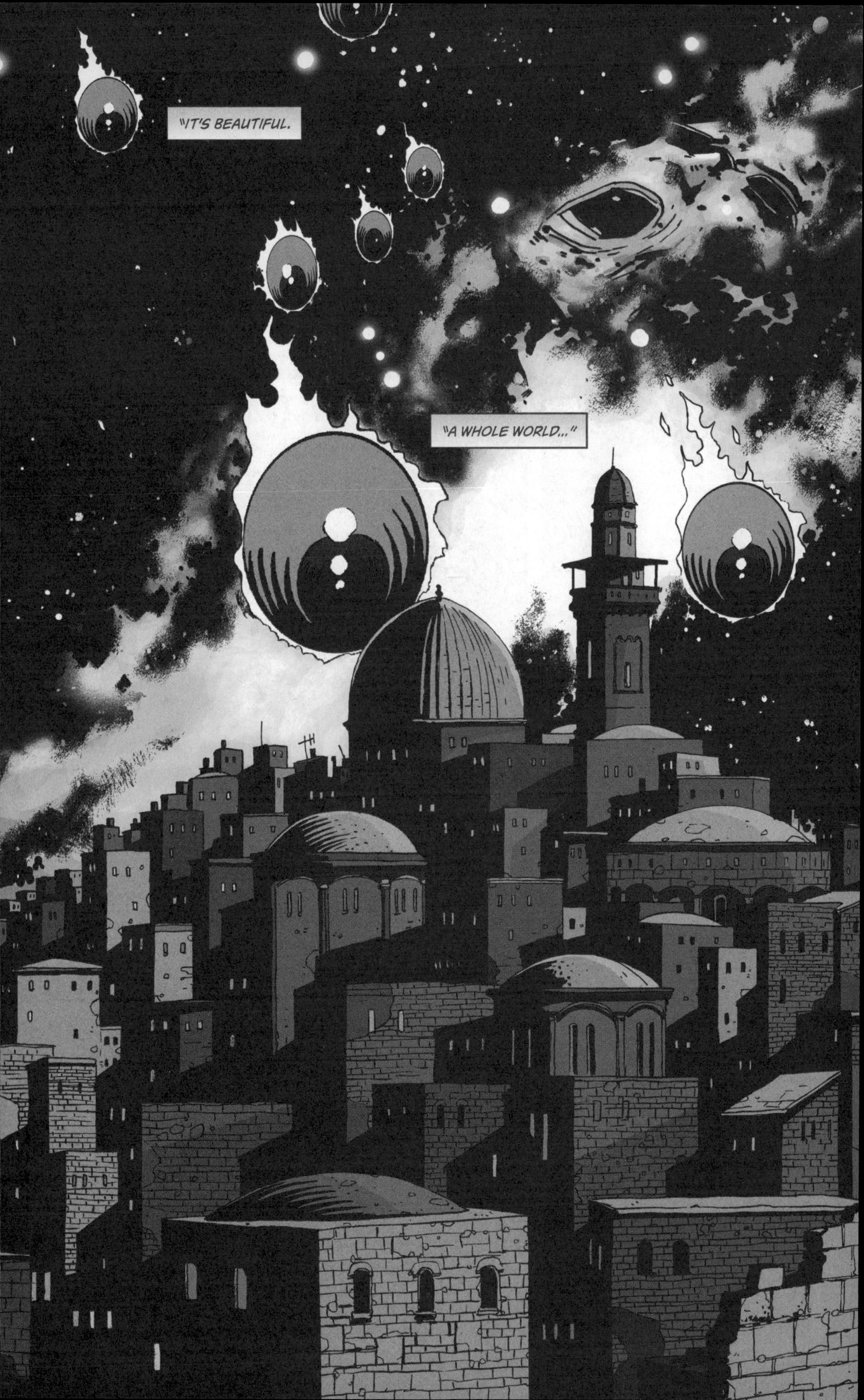
"IT'S BEAUTIFUL.
"A WHOLE WORLD..."

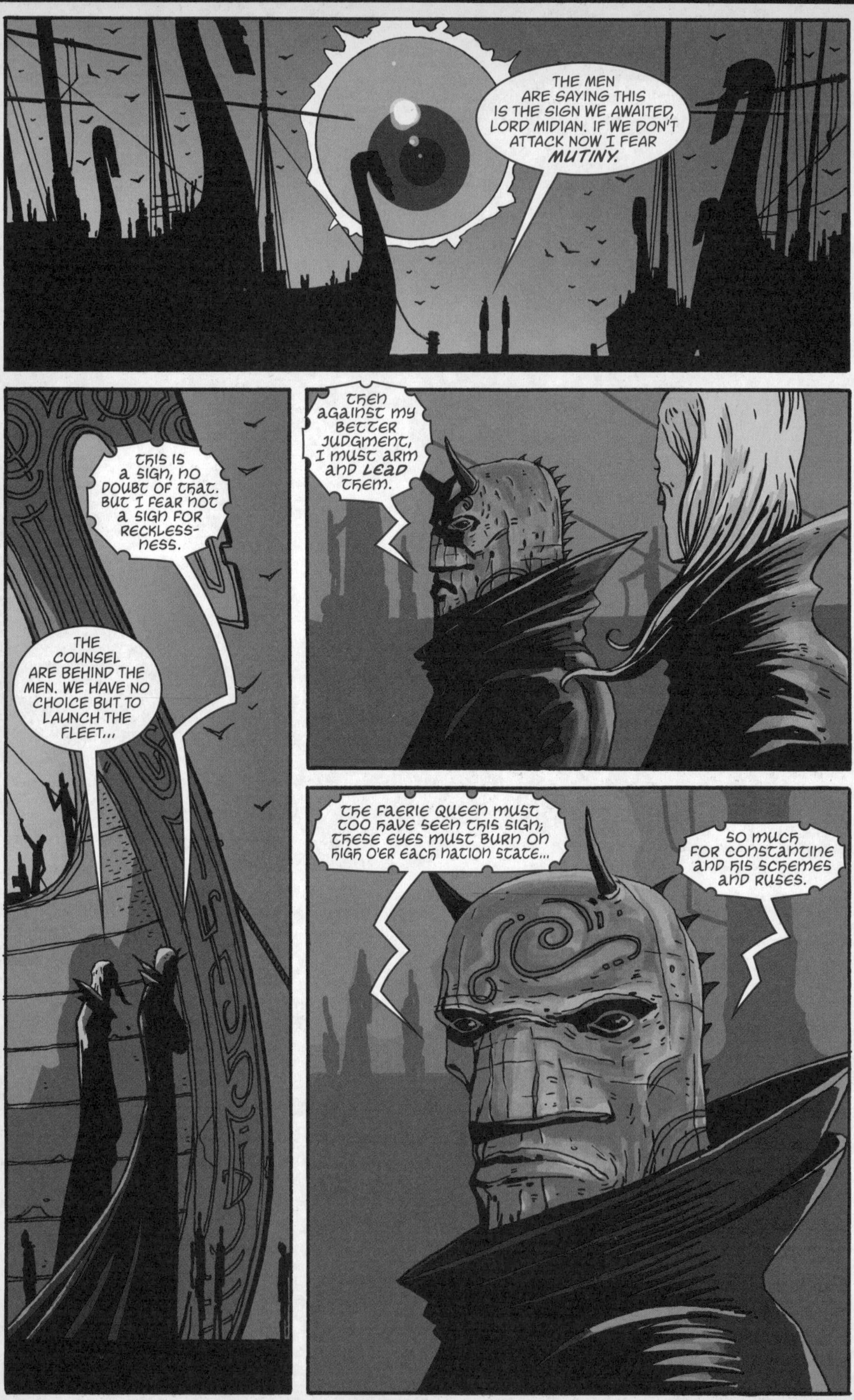
THE MEN ARE SAYING THIS IS THE SIGN WE AWAITED, LORD MIDIAN. IF WE DON'T ATTACK NOW I FEAR MUTINY.
THIS IS A SIGN, NO DOUBT OF THAT. BUT I FEAR NOT A SIGN FOR RECKLESS-NESS.
THE COUNSEL ARE BEHIND THE MEN. WE HAVE NO CHOICE BUT TO LAUNCH THE FLEET...
THEN AGAINST MY BETTER JUDGMENT, I MUST ARM AND LEAD THEM.
THE FAERIE QUEEN MUST TOO HAVE SEEN THIS SIGN; THESE EYES MUST BURN ON HIGH O'ER EACH NATION STATE...
SO MUCH FOR CONSTANTINE AND HIS SCHEMES AND RUSES.

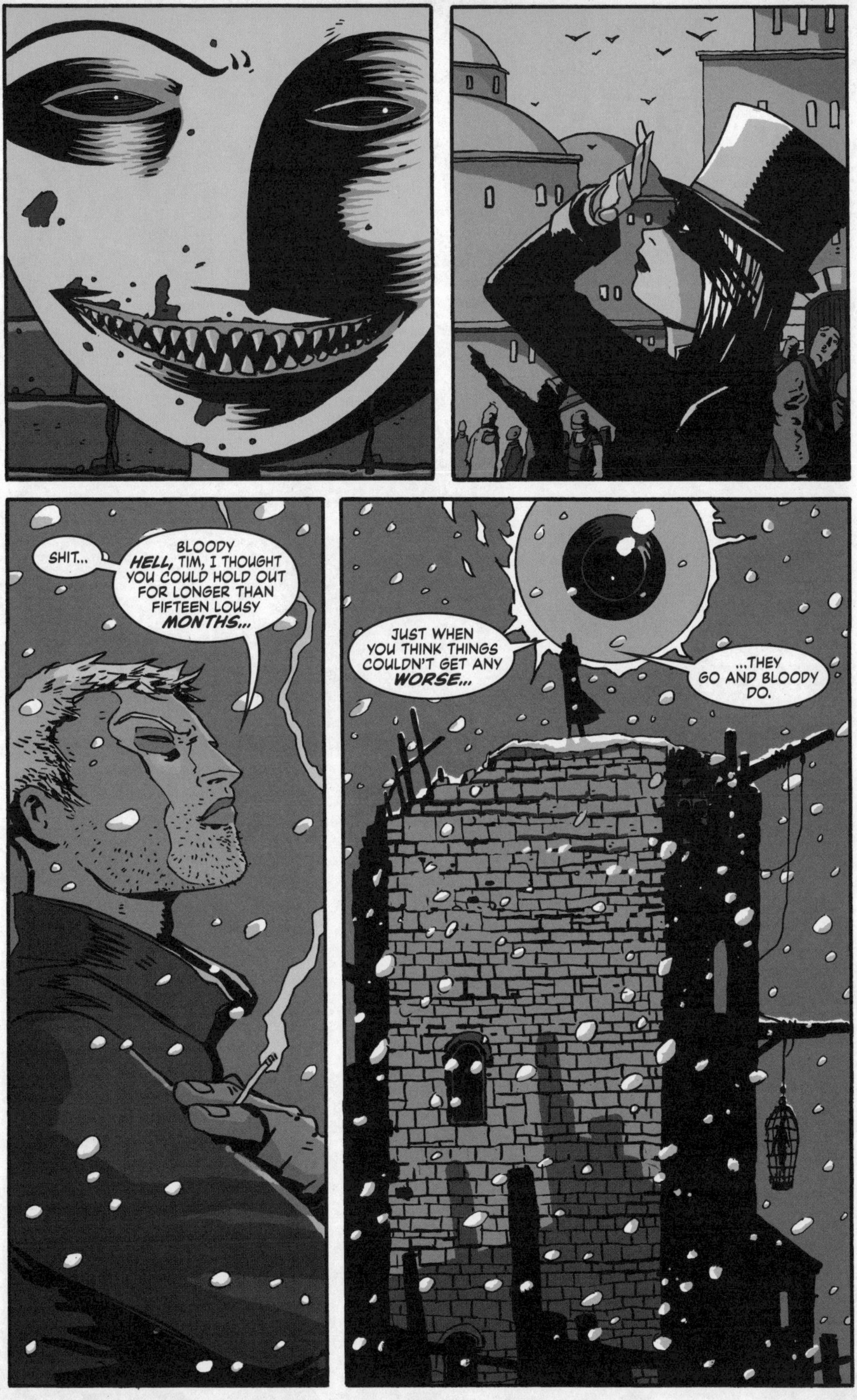
SHIT...
BLOODY HELL, TIM, I THOUGHT YOU COULD HOLD OUT FOR LONGER THAN FIFTEEN LOUSY MONTHS...
JUST WHEN YOU THINK THINGS COULDN'T GET ANY WORSE...
...THEY GO AND BLOODY DO.

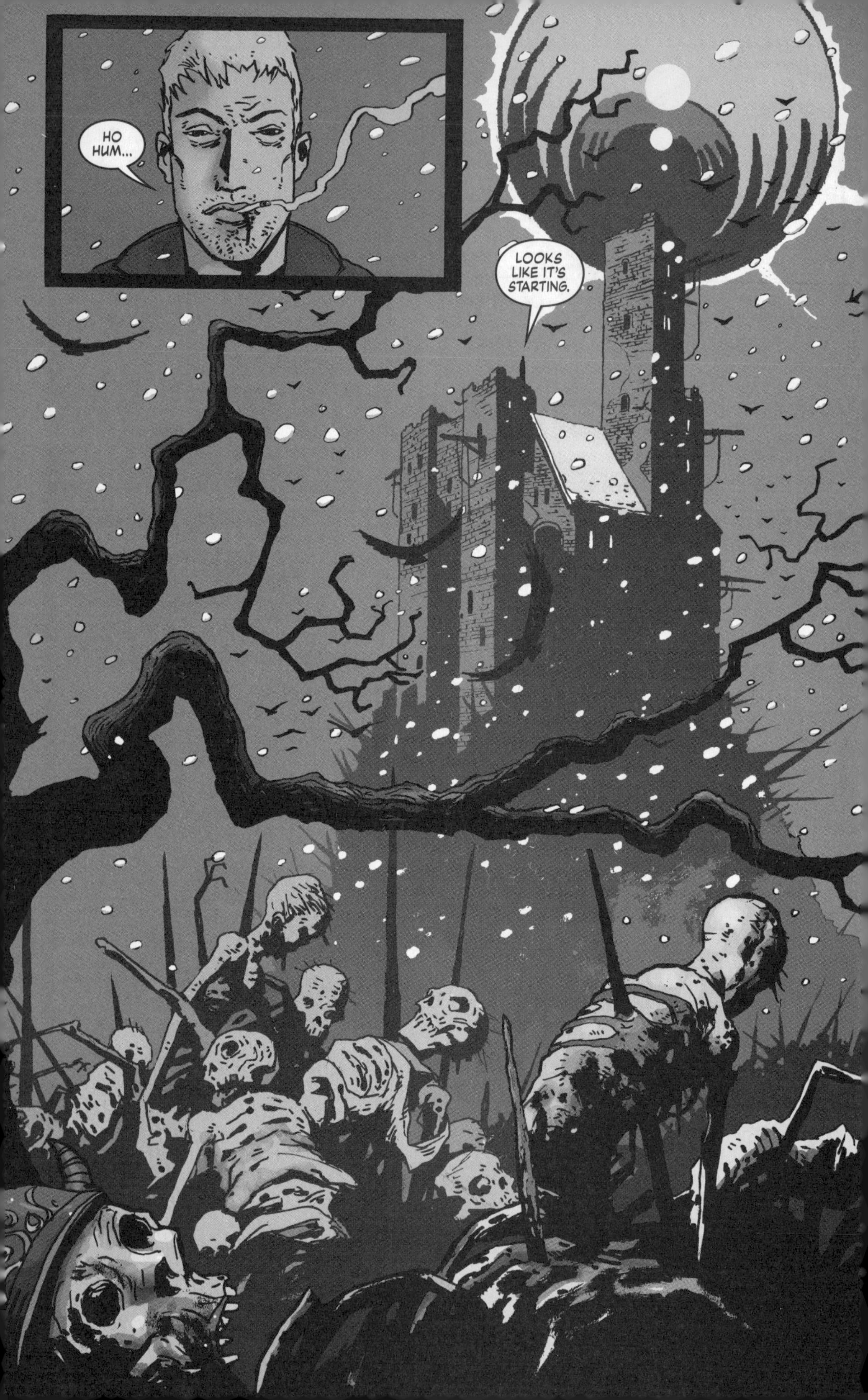
HO HUM...
LOOKS LIKE IT'S STARTING.

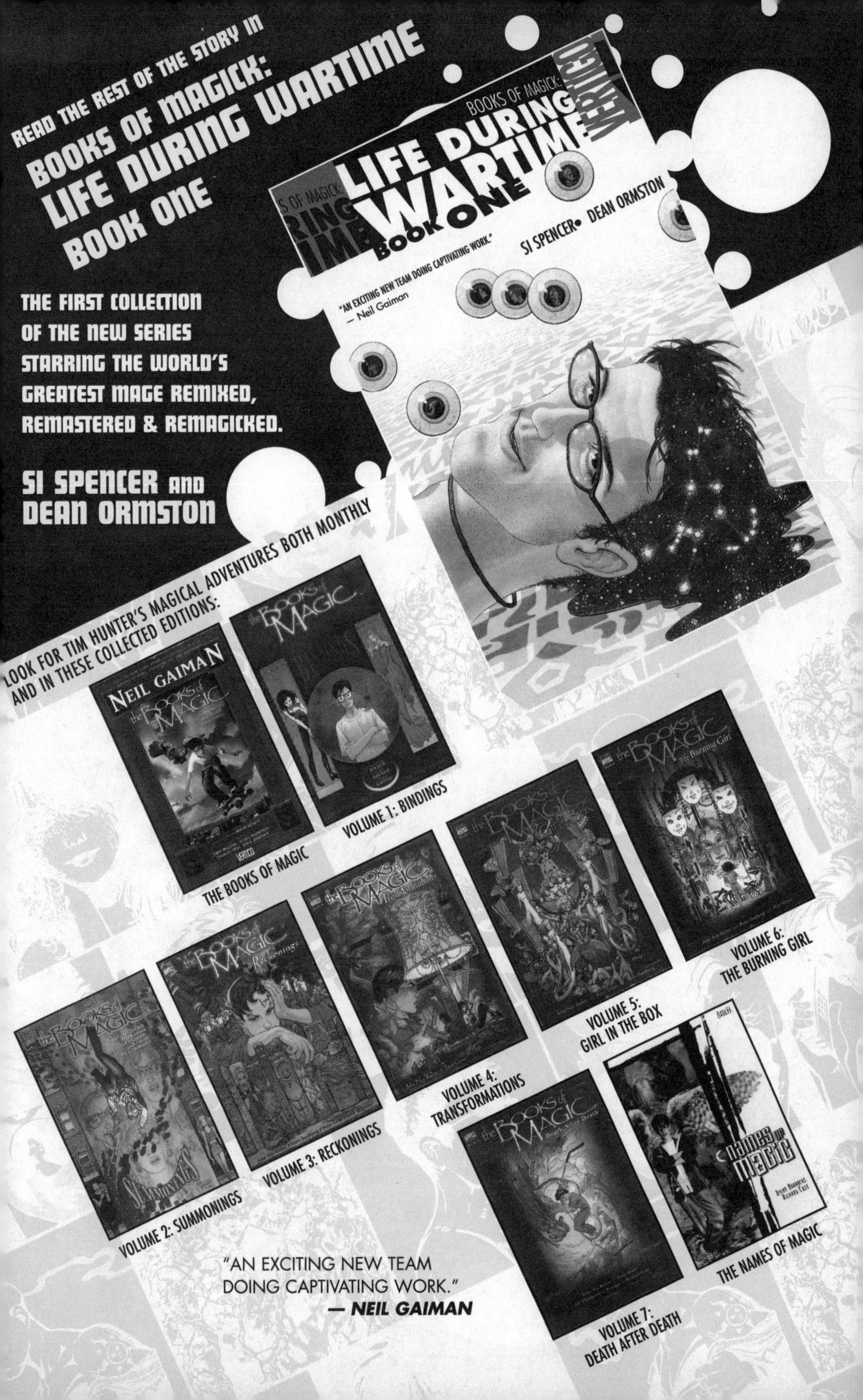
READ THE REST OF THE STORY IN
BOOKS OF MAGICK:
LIFE DURING WARTIME
BOOK ONE
BOOKS OF MAGICK:
LIFE DURING WARTIME
BOOK ONE
VERTIGO
SI SPENCER• DEAN ORMSTON
"AN EXCITING NEW TEAM DOING CAPTIVATING WORK."
— Neil Gaiman
THE FIRST COLLECTION
OF THE NEW SERIES
STARRING THE WORLD'S
GREATEST MAGE REMIXED,
REMASTERED & REMAGICKED.
SI SPENCER AND
DEAN ORMSTON
LOOK FOR TIM HUNTER'S MAGICAL ADVENTURES BOTH MONTHLY
AND IN THESE COLLECTED EDITIONS:
NEIL GAIMAN
the BOOKS of MAGIC
THE BOOKS OF MAGIC
the BOOKS of MAGIC
VOLUME 1: BINDINGS
VOLUME 2: SUMMONINGS
Reckonings
VOLUME 3: RECKONINGS
Transformations
VOLUME 4:
TRANSFORMATIONS
Girl in the Box
VOLUME 5:
GIRL IN THE BOX
The Burning Girl
VOLUME 6:
THE BURNING GIRL
Death After Death
VOLUME 7:
DEATH AFTER DEATH
the names of magic
THE NAMES OF MAGIC
"AN EXCITING NEW TEAM
DOING CAPTIVATING WORK."
— NEIL GAIMAN

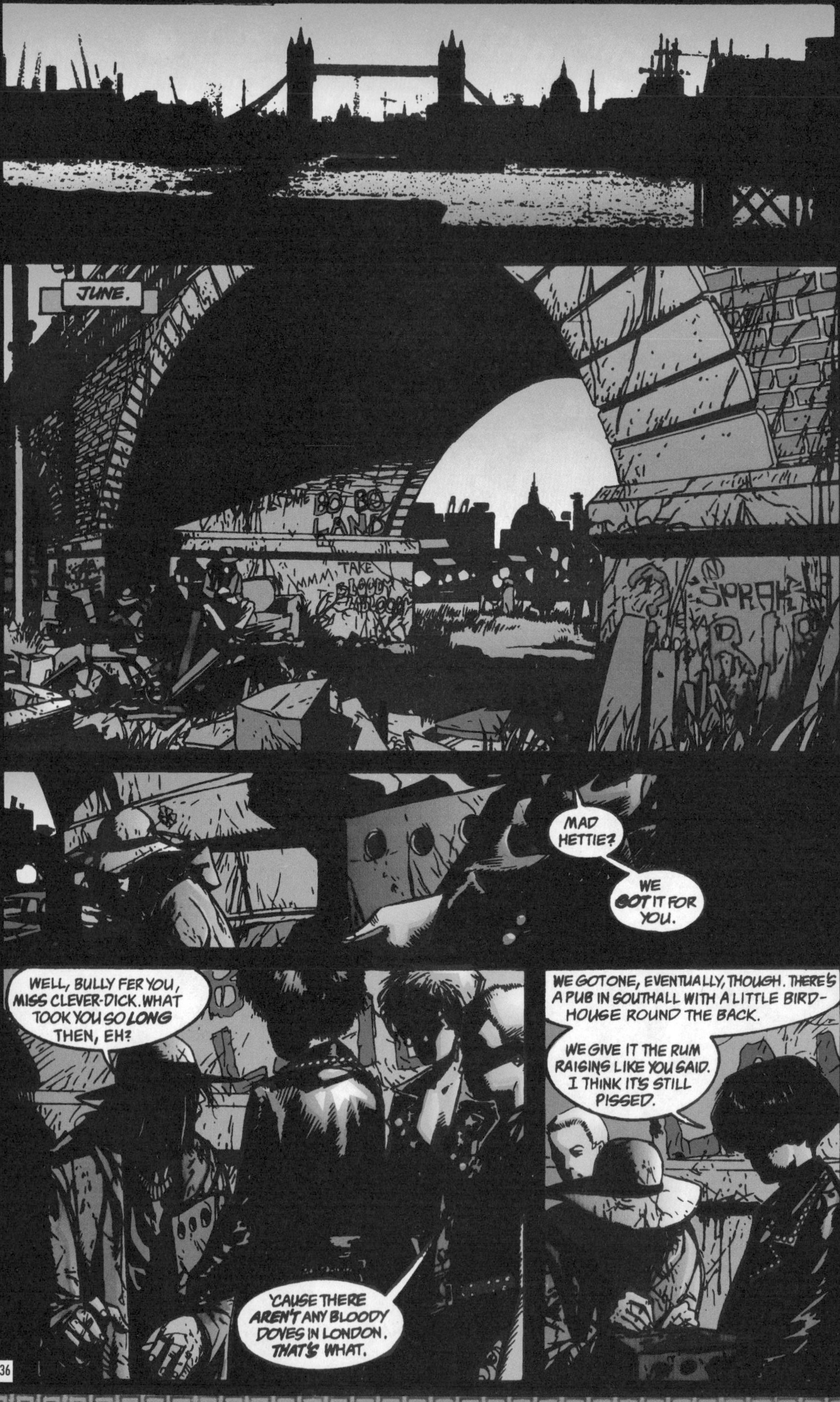
JUNE.
MAD HETTIE?
WE GOT IT FOR YOU.
WELL, BULLY FER YOU, MISS CLEVER-DICK. WHAT TOOK YOU SO LONG THEN, EH?
'CAUSE THERE AREN'T ANY BLOODY DOVES IN LONDON. THAT'S WHAT.
WE GOT ONE, EVENTUALLY, THOUGH. THERE'S A PUB IN SOUTHALL WITH A LITTLE BIRD-HOUSE ROUND THE BACK.
WE GIVE IT THE RUM RAISINS LIKE YOU SAID. I THINK IT'S STILL PISSED.

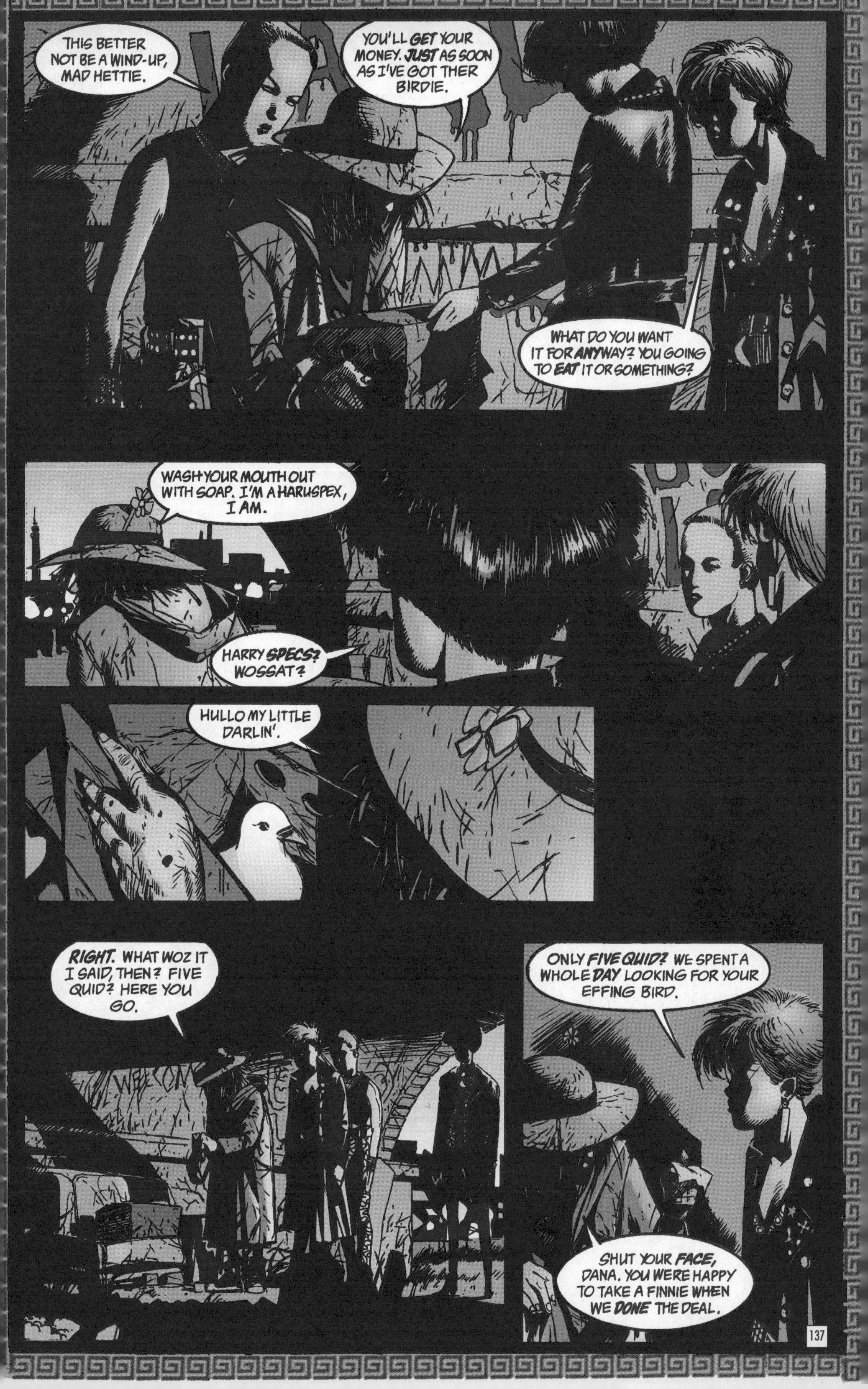

THIS BETTER NOT BE A WIND-UP, MAD HETTIE.
YOU'LL GET YOUR MONEY. JUST AS SOON AS I'VE GOT THER BIRDIE.
WHAT DO YOU WANT IT FOR ANYWAY? YOU GOING TO EAT IT OR SOMETHING?
WASH YOUR MOUTH OUT WITH SOAP. I'M A HARUSPEX, I AM.
HARRY SPECS? WOSSAT?
HULLO MY LITTLE DARLIN'.
RIGHT. WHAT WOZ IT I SAID, THEN? FIVE QUID? HERE YOU GO.
ONLY FIVE QUID? WE SPENT A WHOLE DAY LOOKING FOR YOUR EFFING BIRD.
SHUT YOUR FACE, DANA. YOU WERE HAPPY TO TAKE A FINNIE WHEN WE DONE THE DEAL.

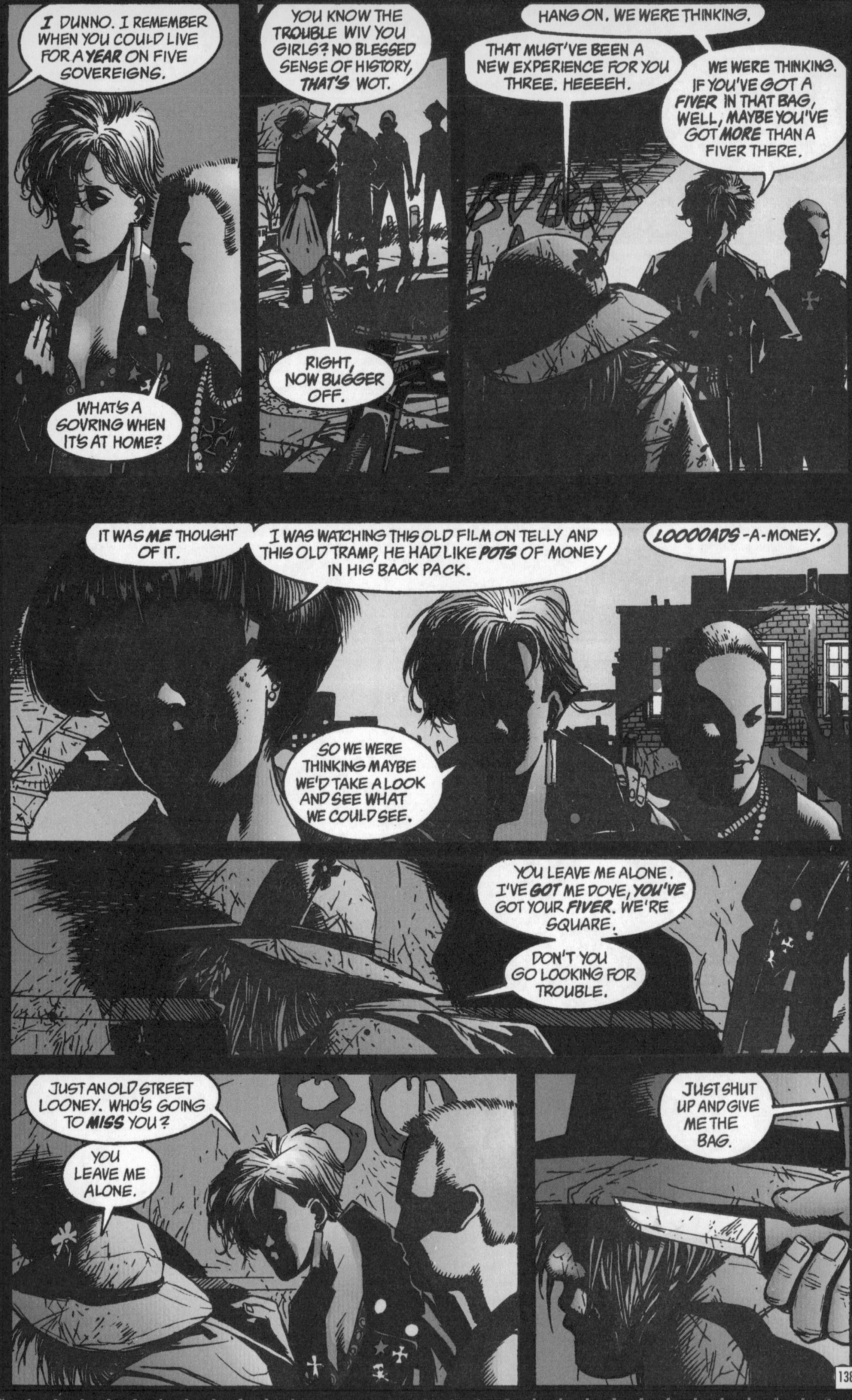

I DUNNO. I REMEMBER WHEN YOU COULD LIVE FOR A YEAR ON FIVE SOVEREIGNS.
WHAT'S A SOVRING WHEN IT'S AT HOME?
YOU KNOW THE TROUBLE WIV YOU GIRLS? NO BLESSED SENSE OF HISTORY, THAT'S WOT.
RIGHT, NOW BUGGER OFF.
HANG ON. WE WERE THINKING.
THAT MUST'VE BEEN A NEW EXPERIENCE FOR YOU THREE. HEEEEH.
WE WERE THINKING. IF YOU'VE GOT A FIVER IN THAT BAG, WELL, MAYBE YOU'VE GOT MORE THAN A FIVER THERE.
IT WAS ME THOUGHT OF IT.
I WAS WATCHING THIS OLD FILM ON TELLY AND THIS OLD TRAMP, HE HAD LIKE POTS OF MONEY IN HIS BACK PACK.
LOOOOADS-A-MONEY.
SO WE WERE THINKING MAYBE WE'D TAKE A LOOK AND SEE WHAT WE COULD SEE.
YOU LEAVE ME ALONE. I'VE GOT ME DOVE, YOU'VE GOT YOUR FIVER. WE'RE SQUARE.
DON'T YOU GO LOOKING FOR TROUBLE.
JUST AN OLD STREET LOONEY. WHO'S GOING TO MISS YOU?
YOU LEAVE ME ALONE.
JUST SHUT UP AND GIVE ME THE BAG.

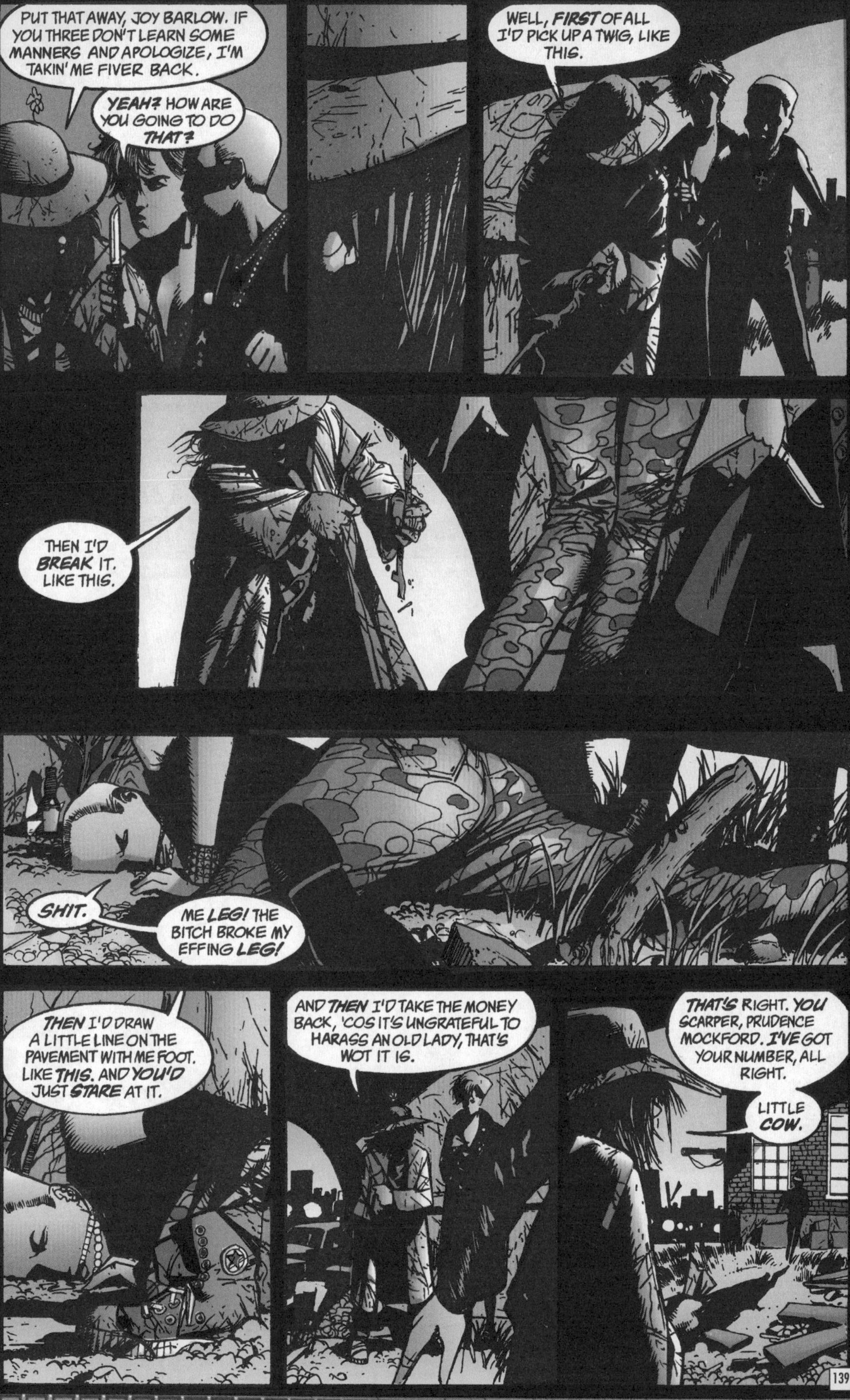
PUT THAT AWAY, JOY BARLOW. IF YOU THREE DON'T LEARN SOME MANNERS AND APOLOGIZE, I'M TAKIN' ME FIVER BACK.
YEAH? HOW ARE YOU GOING TO DO THAT?
WELL, FIRST OF ALL I'D PICK UP A TWIG, LIKE THIS.
THEN I'D BREAK IT. LIKE THIS.
SHIT.
ME LEG! THE BITCH BROKE MY EFFING LEG!
THEN I'D DRAW A LITTLE LINE ON THE PAVEMENT WITH ME FOOT. LIKE THIS. AND YOU'D JUST STARE AT IT.
AND THEN I'D TAKE THE MONEY BACK, 'COS IT'S UNGRATEFUL TO HARASS AN OLD LADY, THAT'S WOT IT IS.
THAT'S RIGHT. YOU SCARPER, PRUDENCE MOCKFORD. I'VE GOT YOUR NUMBER, ALL RIGHT.
LITTLE COW.

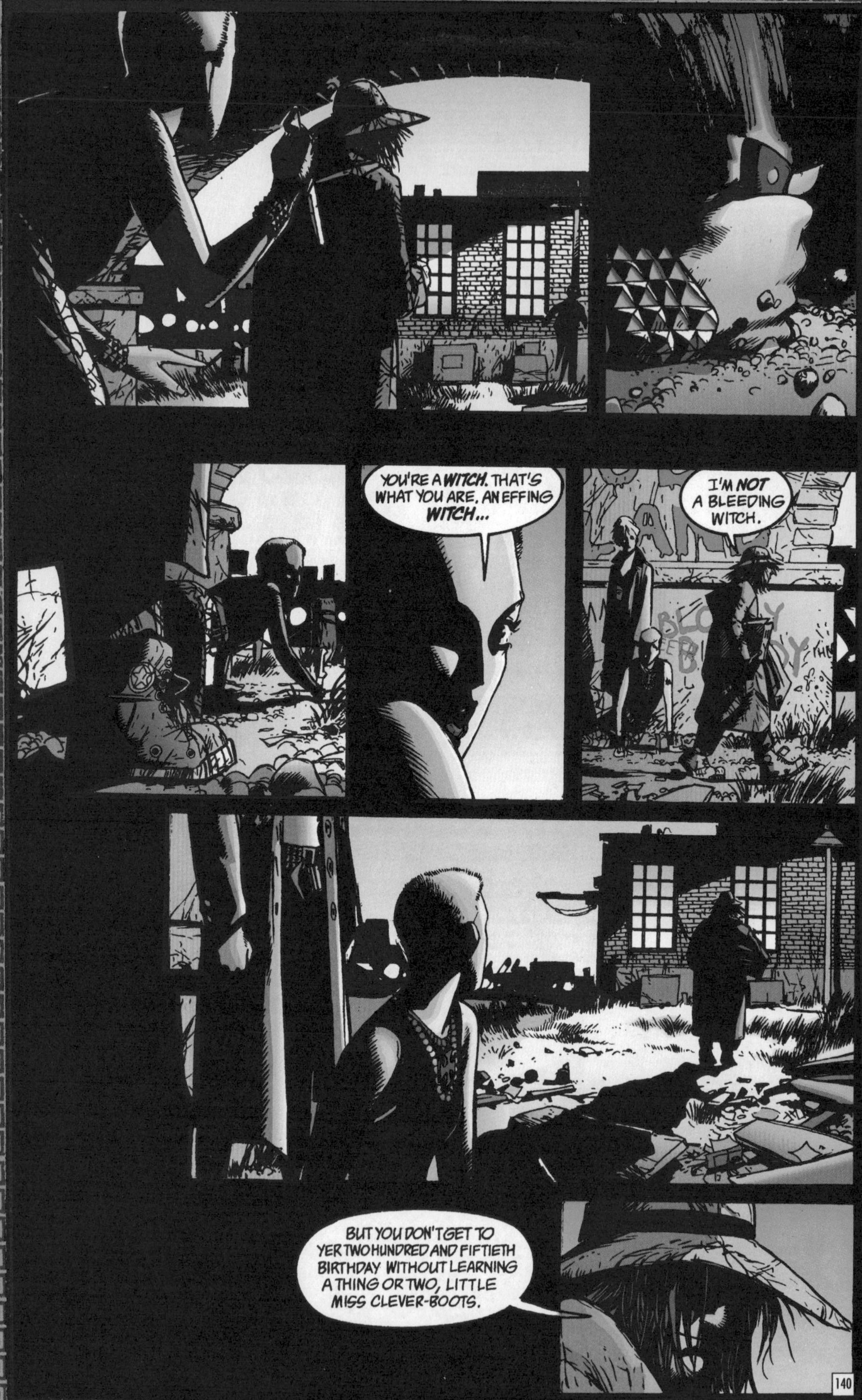

YOU'RE A WITCH. THAT'S WHAT YOU ARE. AN EFFING WITCH...
I'M NOT A BLEEDING WITCH.
BUT YOU DON'T GET TO YER TWO HUNDRED AND FIFTIETH BIRTHDAY WITHOUT LEARNING A THING OR TWO, LITTLE MISS CLEVER-BOOTS.

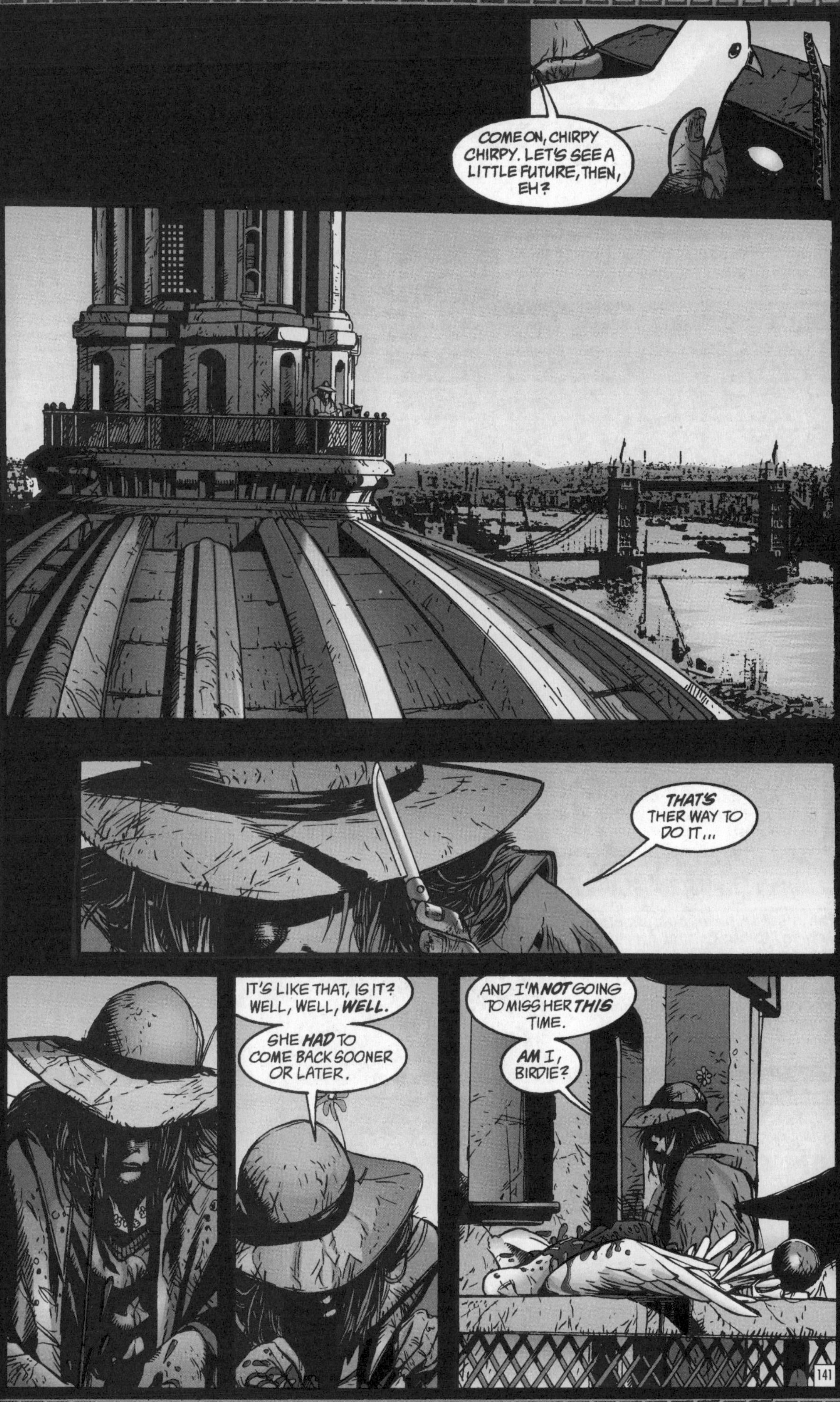
COME ON, CHIRPY CHIRPY. LET'S SEE A LITTLE FUTURE, THEN, EH?
THAT'S THER WAY TO DO IT...
IT'S LIKE THAT, IS IT? WELL, WELL, WELL.
SHE HAD TO COME BACK SOONER OR LATER.
AND I'M NOT GOING TO MISS HER THIS TIME.
AM I, BIRDIE?

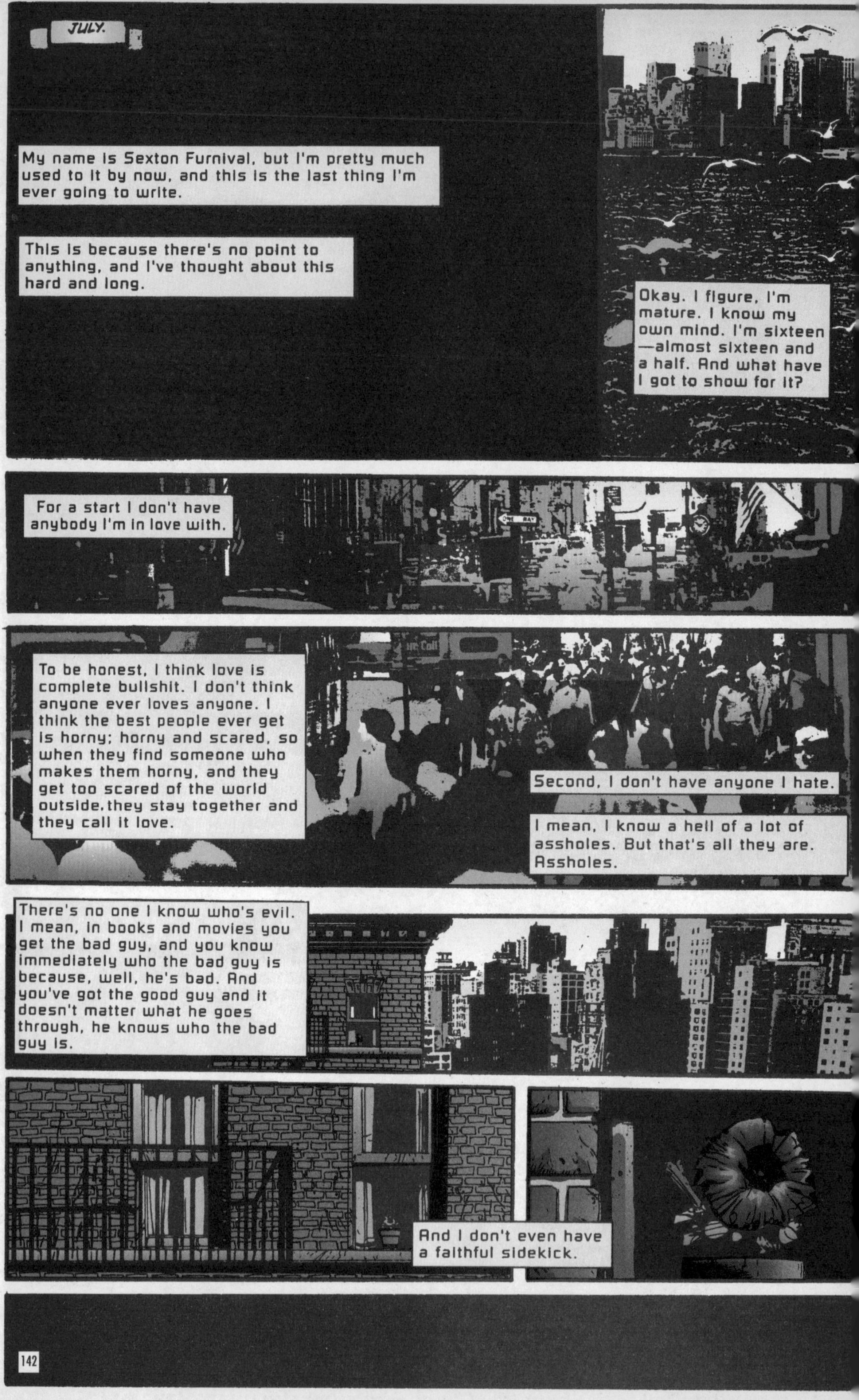

My name is Sexton Furnival, but I'm pretty much used to it by now, and this is the last thing I'm ever going to write.

This is because there's no point to anything, and I've thought about this hard and long.

Okay. I figure, I'm mature. I know my own mind. I'm sixteen —almost sixteen and a half. And what have I got to show for it?

For a start I don't have anybody I'm in love with.

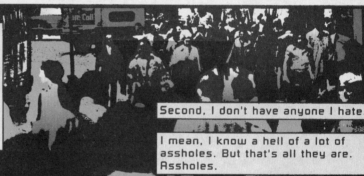

To be honest, I think love is complete bullshit. I don't think anyone ever loves anyone. I think the best people ever get is horny; horny and scared, so when they find someone who makes them horny, and they get too scared of the world outside, they stay together and they call it love.

Second, I don't have anyone I hate.

I mean, I know a hell of a lot of assholes. But that's all they are. Assholes.

There's no one I know who's evil. I mean, in books and movies you get the bad guy, and you know immediately who the bad guy is because, well, he's bad. And you've got the good guy and it doesn't matter what he goes through, he knows who the bad guy is.

And I don't even have a faithful sidekick.

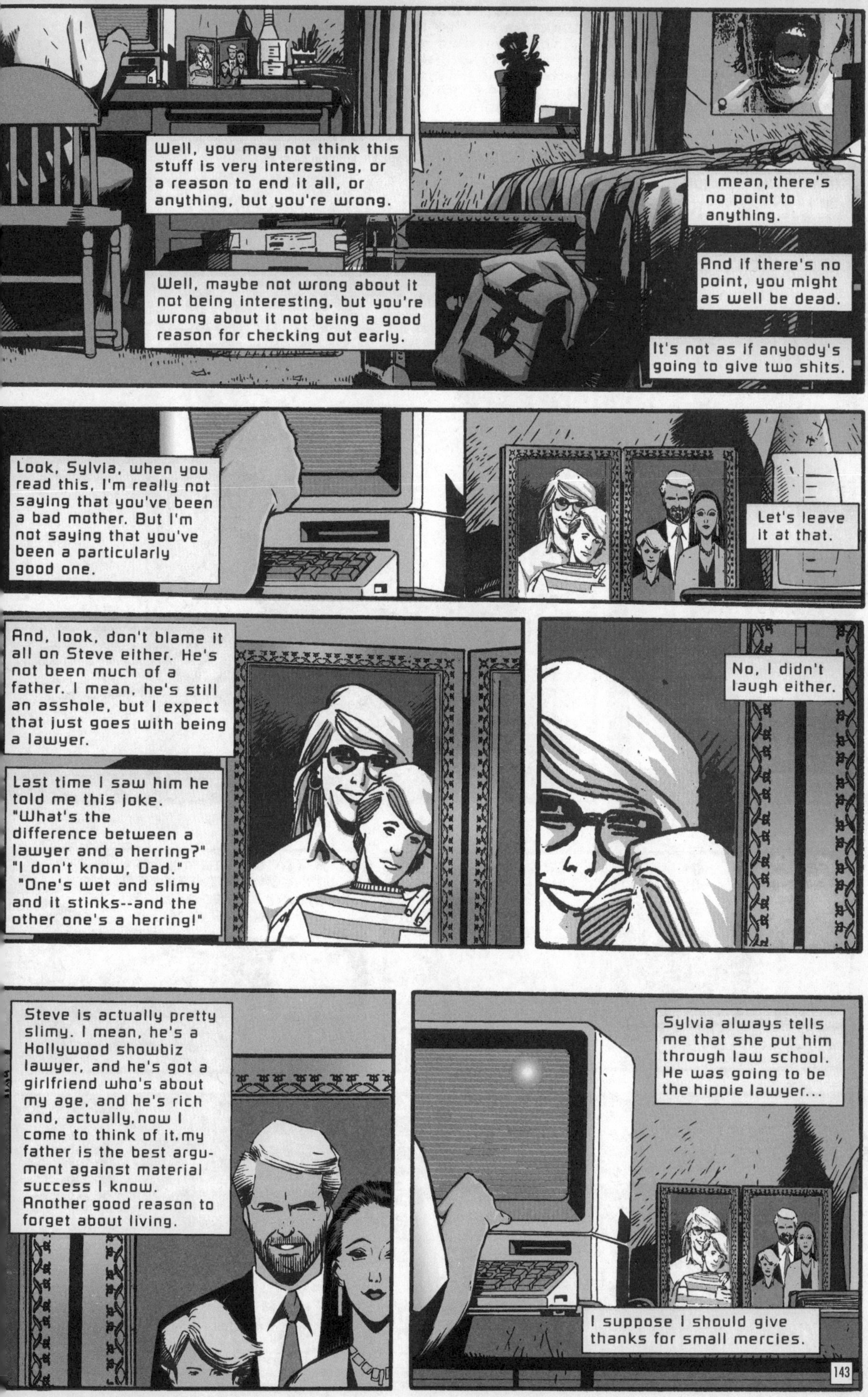

Well, you may not think this stuff is very interesting, or a reason to end it all, or anything, but you're wrong.
Well, maybe not wrong about it not being interesting, but you're wrong about it not being a good reason for checking out early.
I mean, there's no point to anything.
And if there's no point, you might as well be dead.
It's not as if anybody's going to give two shits.
Look, Sylvia, when you read this, I'm really not saying that you've been a bad mother. But I'm not saying that you've been a particularly good one.
Let's leave it at that.
And, look, don't blame it all on Steve either. He's not been much of a father. I mean, he's still an asshole, but I expect that just goes with being a lawyer.
Last time I saw him he told me this joke. "What's the difference between a lawyer and a herring?" "I don't know, Dad." "One's wet and slimy and it stinks--and the other one's a herring!"
No, I didn't laugh either.
Steve is actually pretty slimy. I mean, he's a Hollywood showbiz lawyer, and he's got a girlfriend who's about my age, and he's rich and, actually, now I come to think of it, my father is the best argument against material success I know. Another good reason to forget about living.
Sylvia always tells me that she put him through law school. He was going to be the hippie lawyer...
I suppose I should give thanks for small mercies.

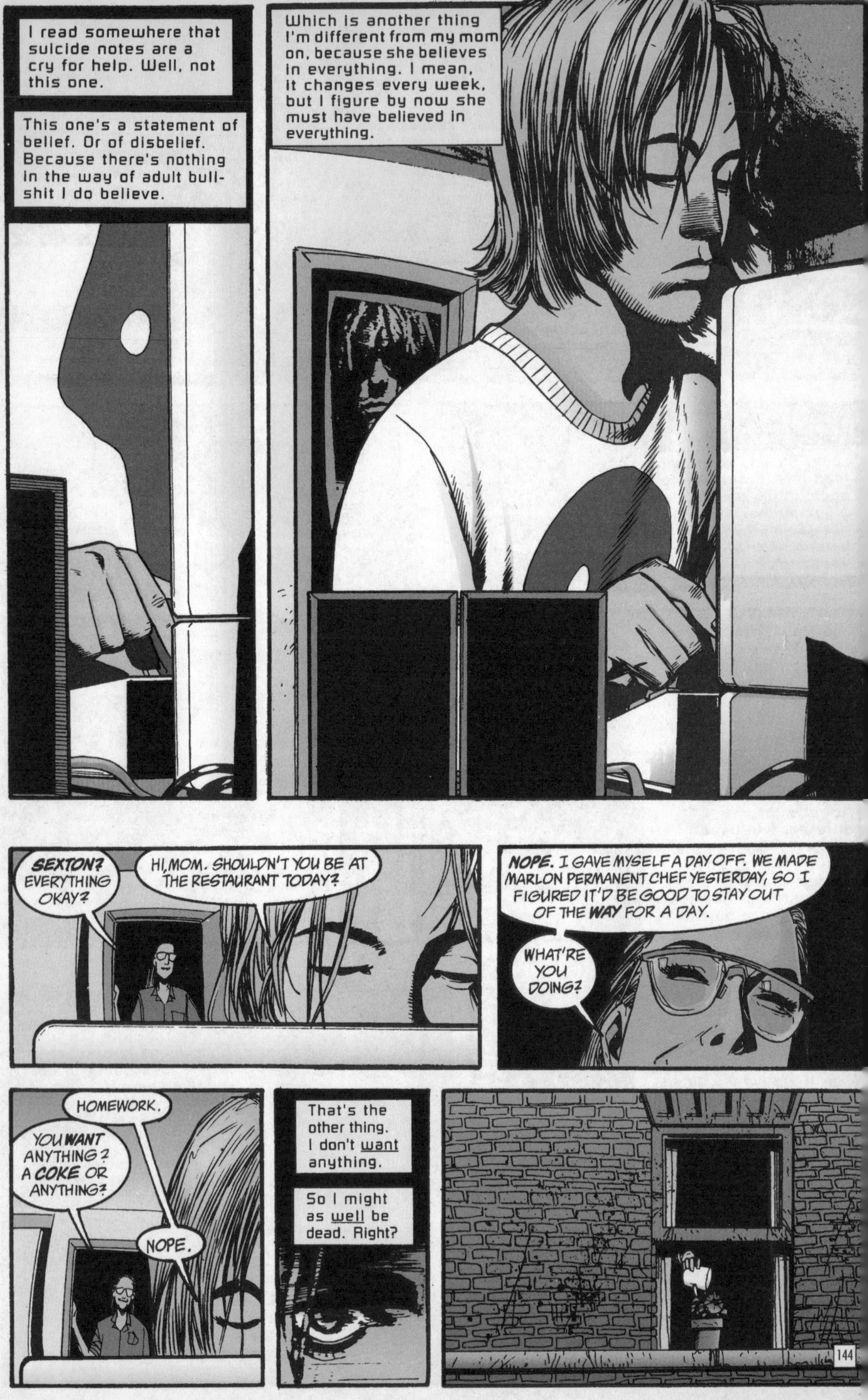
I read somewhere that suicide notes are a cry for help. Well, not this one.
This one's a statement of belief. Or of disbelief. Because there's nothing in the way of adult bull-shit I do believe.
Which is another thing I'm different from my mom on, because she believes in everything. I mean, it changes every week, but I figure by now she must have believed in everything.
SEXTON? EVERYTHING OKAY?
HI, MOM. SHOULDN'T YOU BE AT THE RESTAURANT TODAY?
NOPE. I GAVE MYSELF A DAY OFF. WE MADE MARLON PERMANENT CHEF YESTERDAY, SO I FIGURED IT'D BE GOOD TO STAY OUT OF THE WAY FOR A DAY.
WHAT'RE YOU DOING?
HOMEWORK.
YOU WANT ANYTHING? A COKE OR ANYTHING?
NOPE.
That's the other thing. I don't want anything.
So I might as well be dead. Right?
144

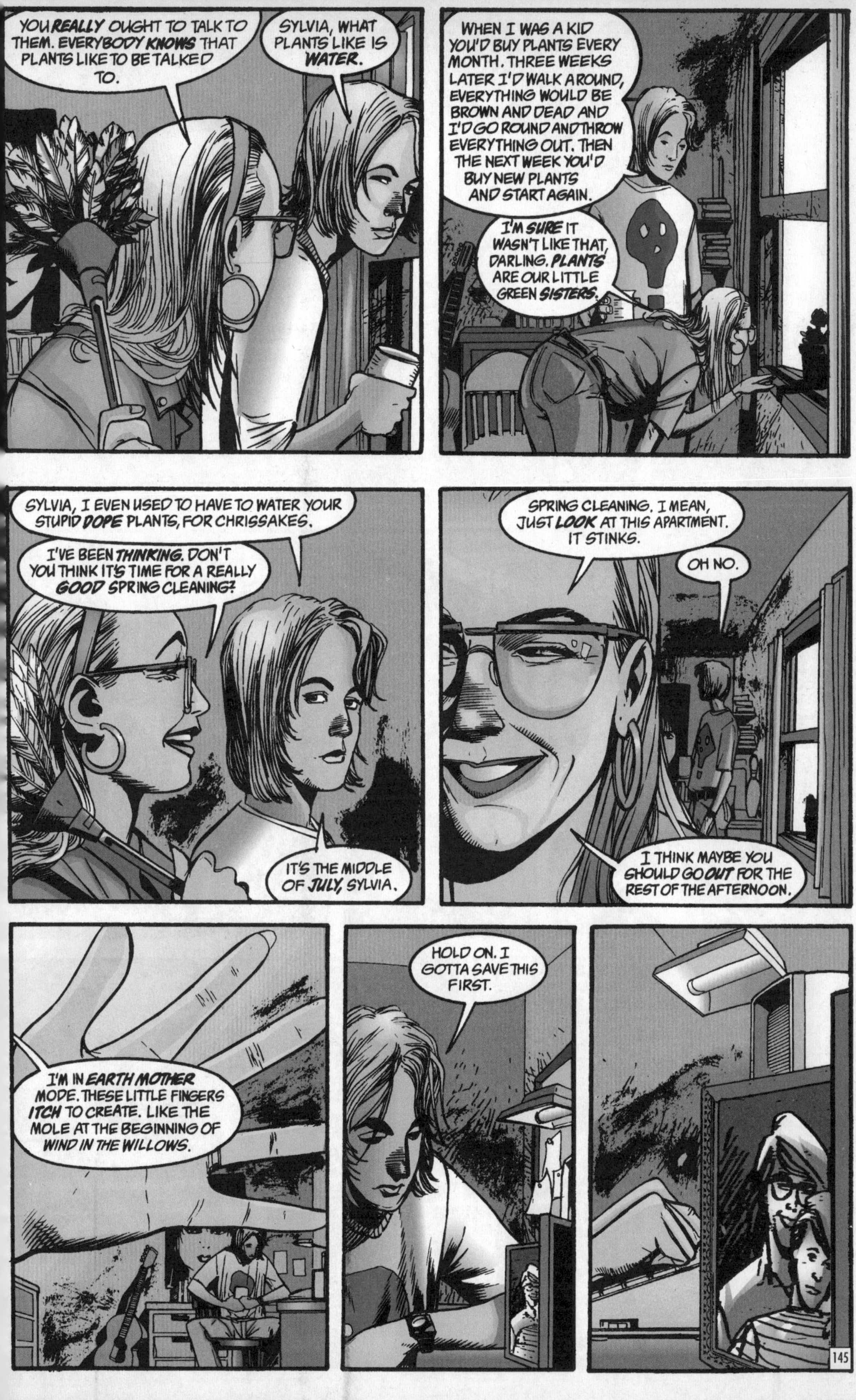
YOU REALLY OUGHT TO TALK TO THEM. EVERYBODY KNOWS THAT PLANTS LIKE TO BE TALKED TO.
SYLVIA, WHAT PLANTS LIKE IS WATER.
WHEN I WAS A KID YOU'D BUY PLANTS EVERY MONTH. THREE WEEKS LATER I'D WALK AROUND, EVERYTHING WOULD BE BROWN AND DEAD AND I'D GO ROUND AND THROW EVERYTHING OUT. THEN THE NEXT WEEK YOU'D BUY NEW PLANTS AND START AGAIN.
I'M SURE IT WASN'T LIKE THAT, DARLING. PLANTS ARE OUR LITTLE GREEN SISTERS.
SYLVIA, I EVEN USED TO HAVE TO WATER YOUR STUPID DOPE PLANTS, FOR CHRISSAKES.
I'VE BEEN THINKING. DON'T YOU THINK IT'S TIME FOR A REALLY GOOD SPRING CLEANING?
IT'S THE MIDDLE OF JULY, SYLVIA.
SPRING CLEANING. I MEAN, JUST LOOK AT THIS APARTMENT. IT STINKS.
OH NO.
I THINK MAYBE YOU SHOULD GO OUT FOR THE REST OF THE AFTERNOON.
I'M IN EARTH MOTHER MODE. THESE LITTLE FINGERS ITCH TO CREATE. LIKE THE MOLE AT THE BEGINNING OF WIND IN THE WILLOWS.
HOLD ON. I GOTTA SAVE THIS FIRST.

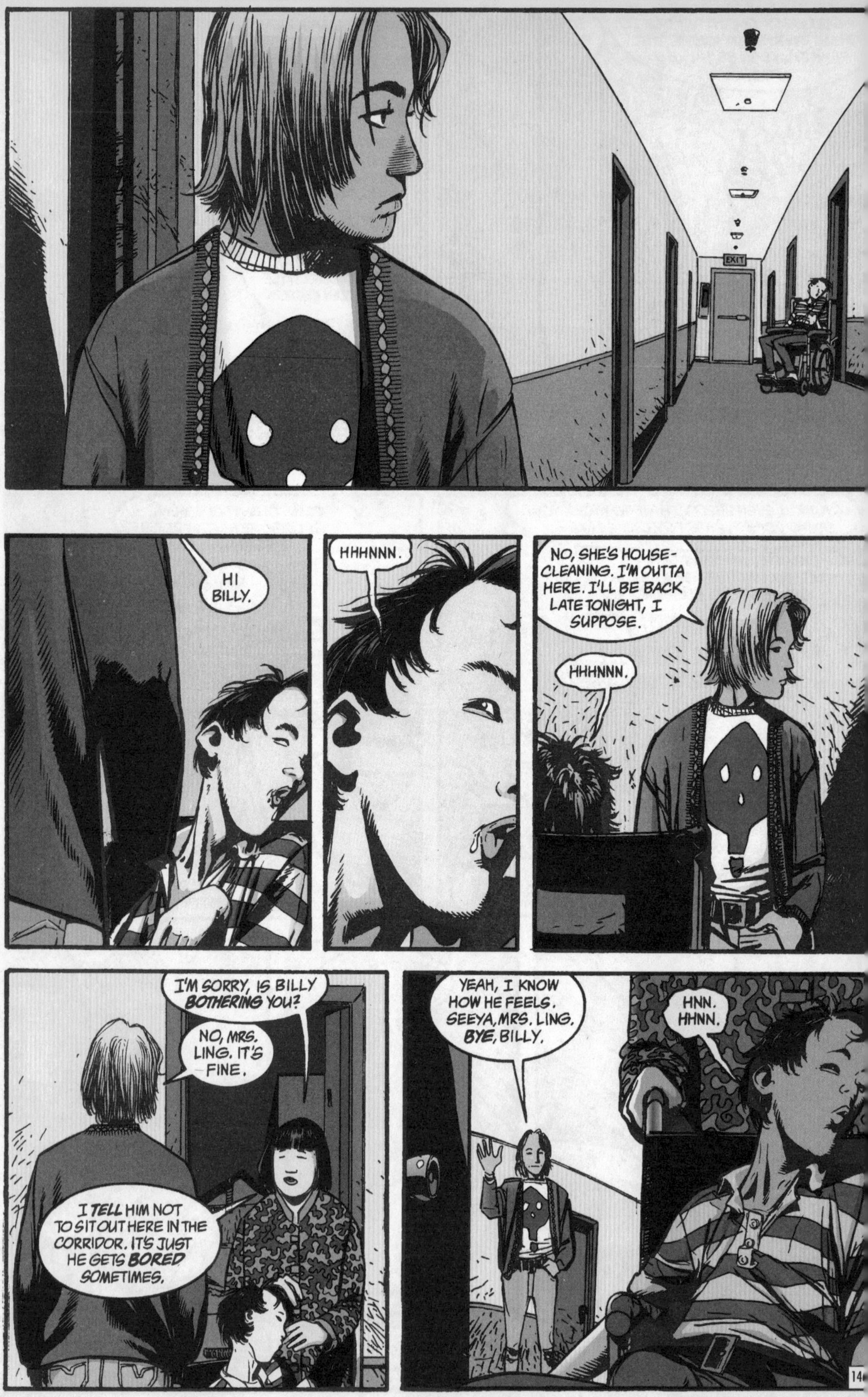
HI BILLY.
HHHNNN.
NO, SHE'S HOUSE-CLEANING. I'M OUTTA HERE. I'LL BE BACK LATE TONIGHT, I SUPPOSE.
HHHNNN.
I'M SORRY, IS BILLY BOTHERING YOU?
NO, MRS. LING. IT'S FINE.
I TELL HIM NOT TO SIT OUT HERE IN THE CORRIDOR. IT'S JUST HE GETS BORED SOMETIMES.
YEAH, I KNOW HOW HE FEELS. SEEYA, MRS. LING. BYE, BILLY.
HNN. HHNN.

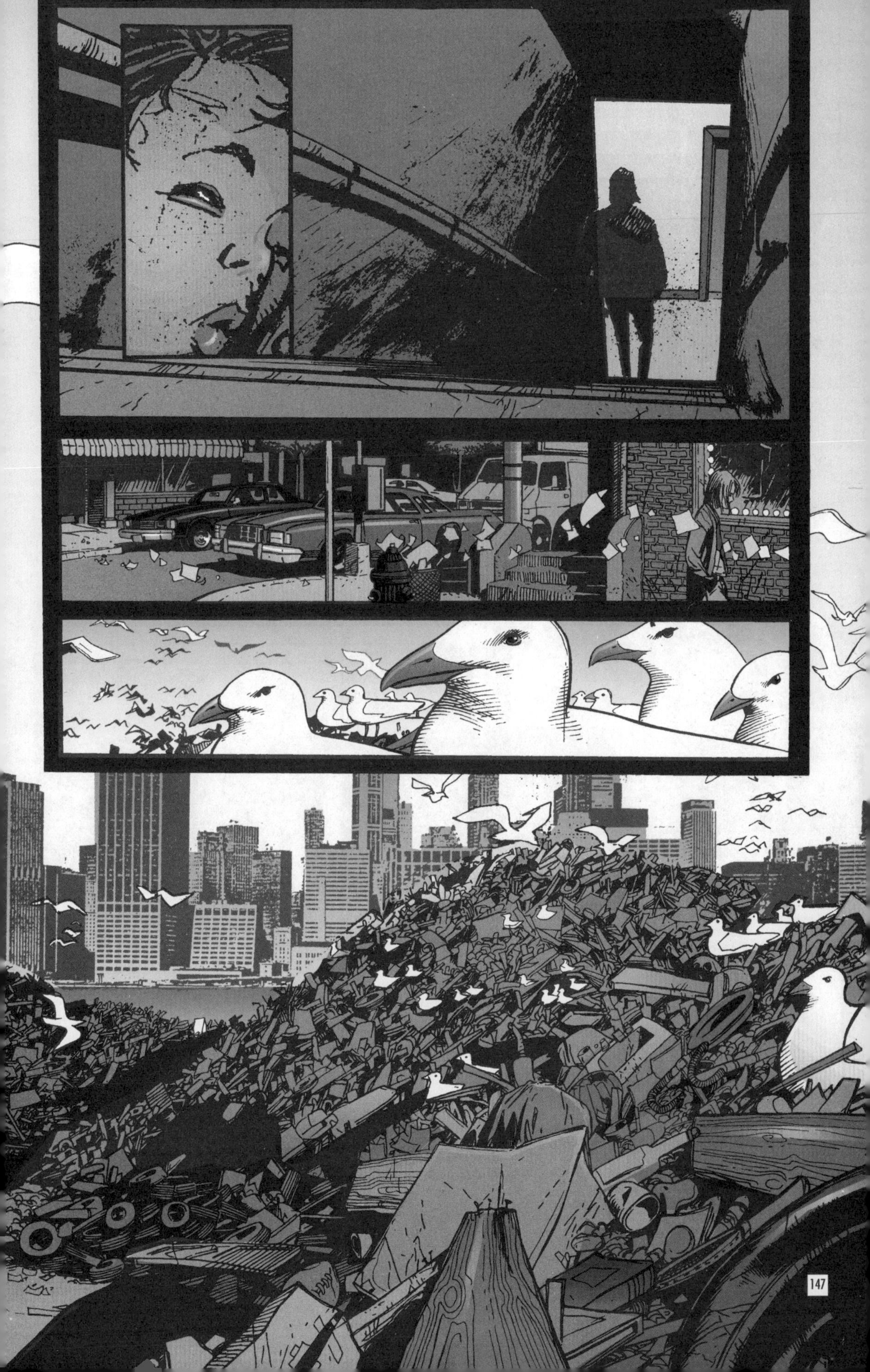

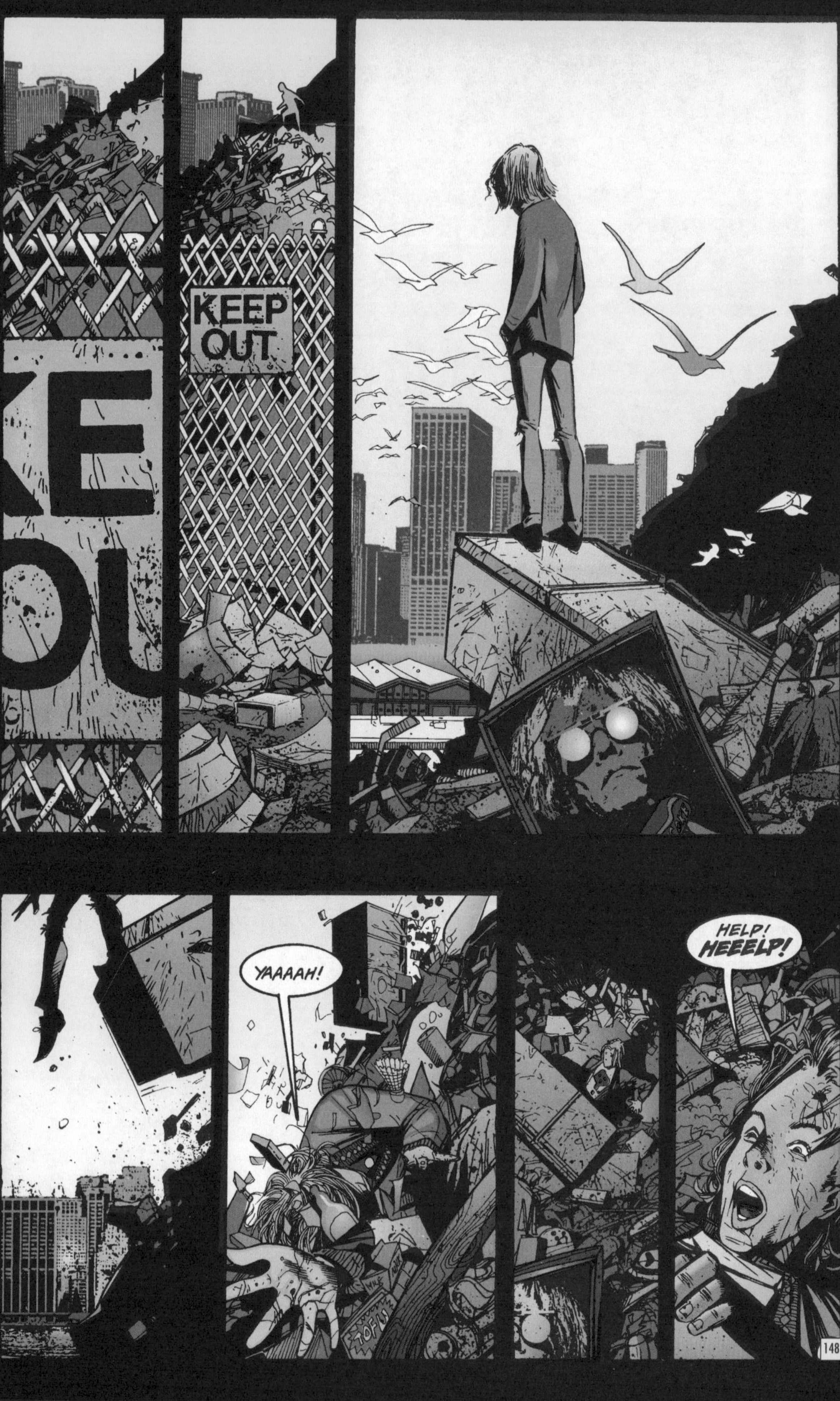
KEEP OUT
YAAAAH!
HELP! HEEELP!

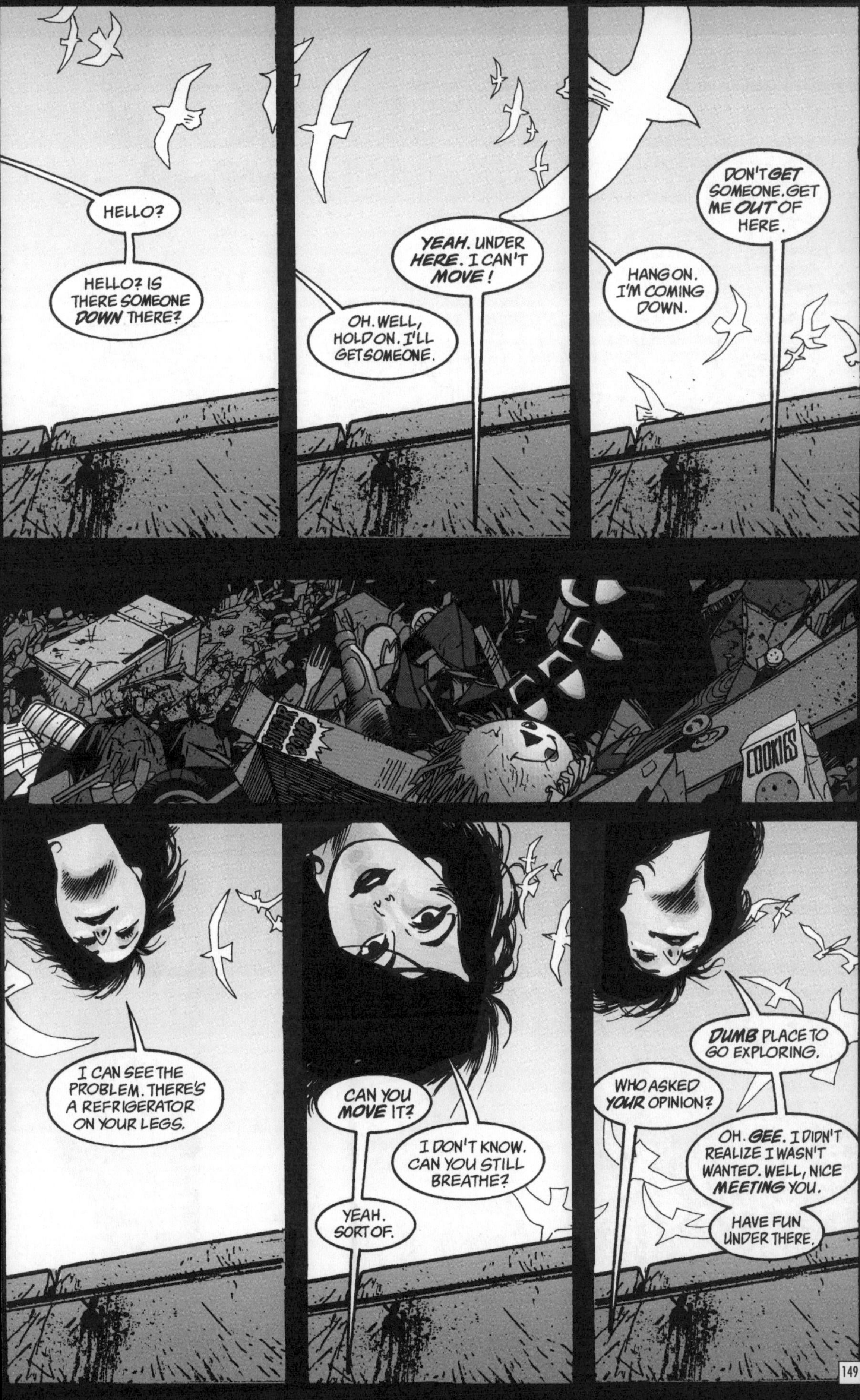
HELLO?
HELLO? IS THERE SOMEONE DOWN THERE?
YEAH. UNDER HERE. I CAN'T MOVE!
OH. WELL, HOLD ON. I'LL GET SOMEONE.
DON'T GET SOMEONE. GET ME OUT OF HERE.
HANG ON. I'M COMING DOWN.
COOKIES
I CAN SEE THE PROBLEM. THERE'S A REFRIGERATOR ON YOUR LEGS.
CAN YOU MOVE IT?
I DON'T KNOW. CAN YOU STILL BREATHE?
YEAH. SORT OF.
DUMB PLACE TO GO EXPLORING.
WHO ASKED YOUR OPINION?
OH. GEE. I DIDN'T REALIZE I WASN'T WANTED. WELL, NICE MEETING YOU.
HAVE FUN UNDER THERE.

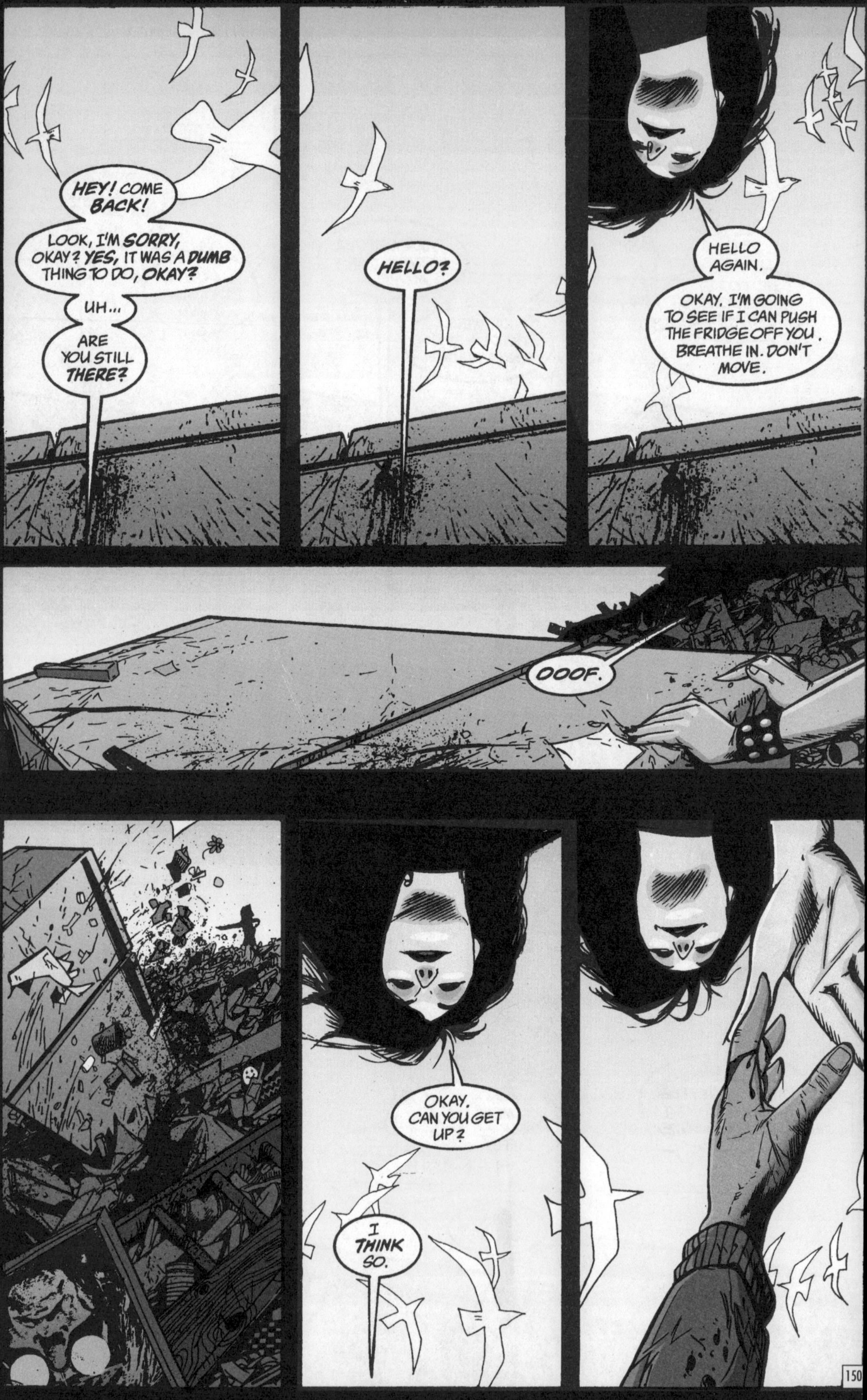
HEY! COME BACK!
LOOK, I'M SORRY, OKAY? YES, IT WAS A DUMB THING TO DO, OKAY?
UH...
ARE YOU STILL THERE?
HELLO?
HELLO AGAIN.
OKAY, I'M GOING TO SEE IF I CAN PUSH THE FRIDGE OFF YOU. BREATHE IN. DON'T MOVE.
OOOF.
OKAY. CAN YOU GET UP?
I THINK SO.

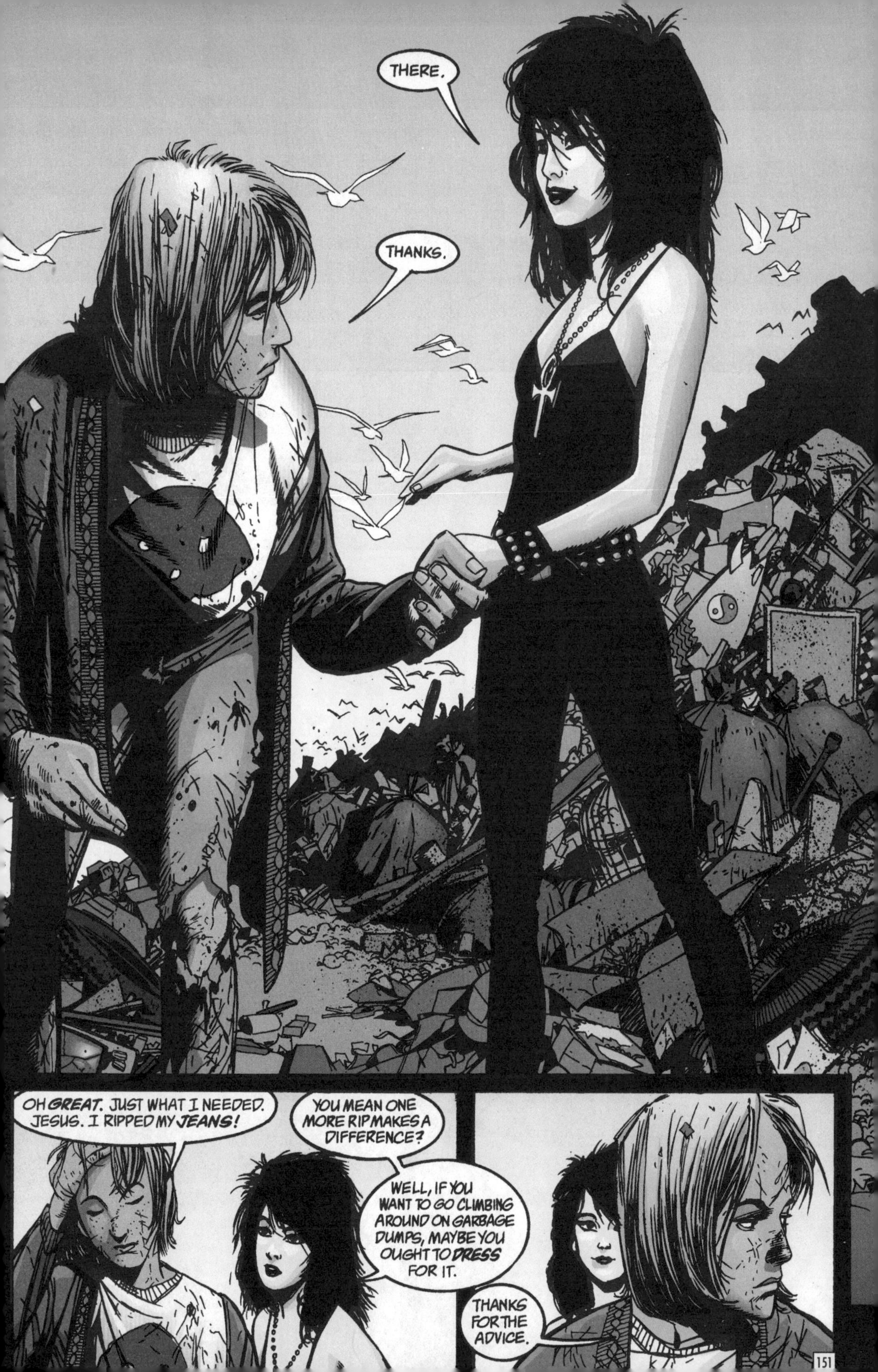

THERE.
THANKS.
OH GREAT. JUST WHAT I NEEDED. JESUS. I RIPPED MY JEANS!
YOU MEAN ONE MORE RIP MAKES A DIFFERENCE?
WELL, IF YOU WANT TO GO CLIMBING AROUND ON GARBAGE DUMPS, MAYBE YOU OUGHT TO DRESS FOR IT.
THANKS FOR THE ADVICE.

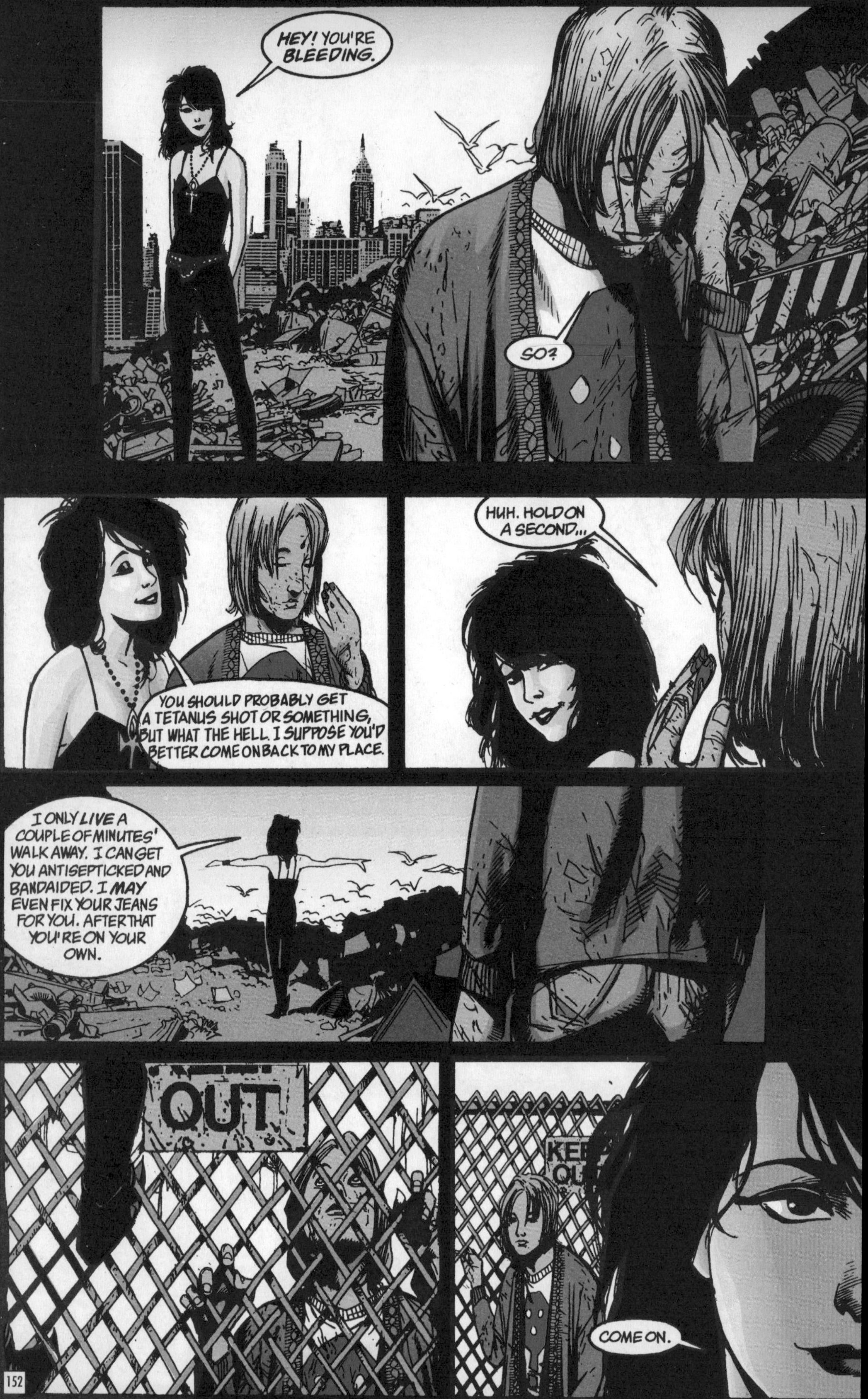
HEY! YOU'RE BLEEDING.
SO?
YOU SHOULD PROBABLY GET A TETANUS SHOT OR SOMETHING, BUT WHAT THE HELL. I SUPPOSE YOU'D BETTER COME ON BACK TO MY PLACE.
HUH. HOLD ON A SECOND...
I ONLY LIVE A COUPLE OF MINUTES' WALK AWAY. I CAN GET YOU ANTISEPTICKED AND BANDAIDED. I MAY EVEN FIX YOUR JEANS FOR YOU. AFTER THAT YOU'RE ON YOUR OWN.
OUT
COME ON.

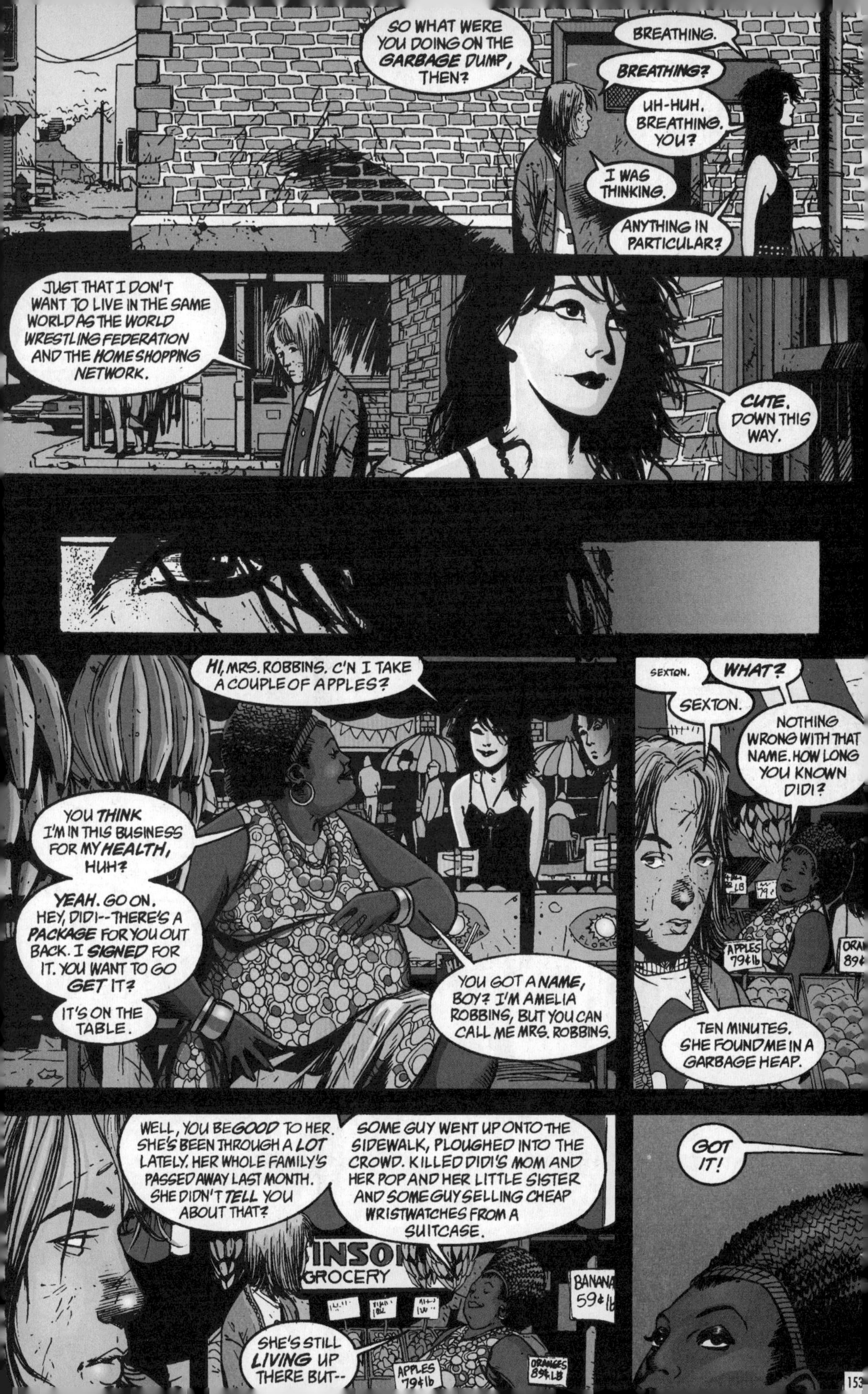

SO WHAT WERE YOU DOING ON THE GARBAGE DUMP, THEN?
BREATHING.
BREATHING?
UH-HUH. BREATHING. YOU?
I WAS THINKING.
ANYTHING IN PARTICULAR?
JUST THAT I DON'T WANT TO LIVE IN THE SAME WORLD AS THE WORLD WRESTLING FEDERATION AND THE HOME SHOPPING NETWORK.
CUTE. DOWN THIS WAY.
HI, MRS. ROBBINS. C'N I TAKE A COUPLE OF APPLES?
YOU THINK I'M IN THIS BUSINESS FOR MY HEALTH, HUH?
YEAH. GO ON. HEY, DIDI--THERE'S A PACKAGE FOR YOU OUT BACK. I SIGNED FOR IT. YOU WANT TO GO GET IT?
IT'S ON THE TABLE.
YOU GOT A NAME, BOY? I'M AMELIA ROBBINS, BUT YOU CAN CALL ME MRS. ROBBINS.
SEXTON.
WHAT?
SEXTON.
NOTHING WRONG WITH THAT NAME. HOW LONG YOU KNOWN DIDI?
APPLES 79¢ lb
TEN MINUTES. SHE FOUND ME IN A GARBAGE HEAP.
WELL, YOU BE GOOD TO HER. SHE'S BEEN THROUGH A LOT LATELY. HER WHOLE FAMILY'S PASSED AWAY LAST MONTH. SHE DIDN'T TELL YOU ABOUT THAT?
SOME GUY WENT UP ONTO THE SIDEWALK, PLOUGHED INTO THE CROWD. KILLED DIDI'S MOM AND HER POP AND HER LITTLE SISTER AND SOME GUY SELLING CHEAP WRISTWATCHES FROM A SUITCASE.
GROCERY
BANANA 59¢ lb
SHE'S STILL LIVING UP THERE BUT--
APPLES 79¢ lb
ORANGES 89¢ LB
GOT IT!

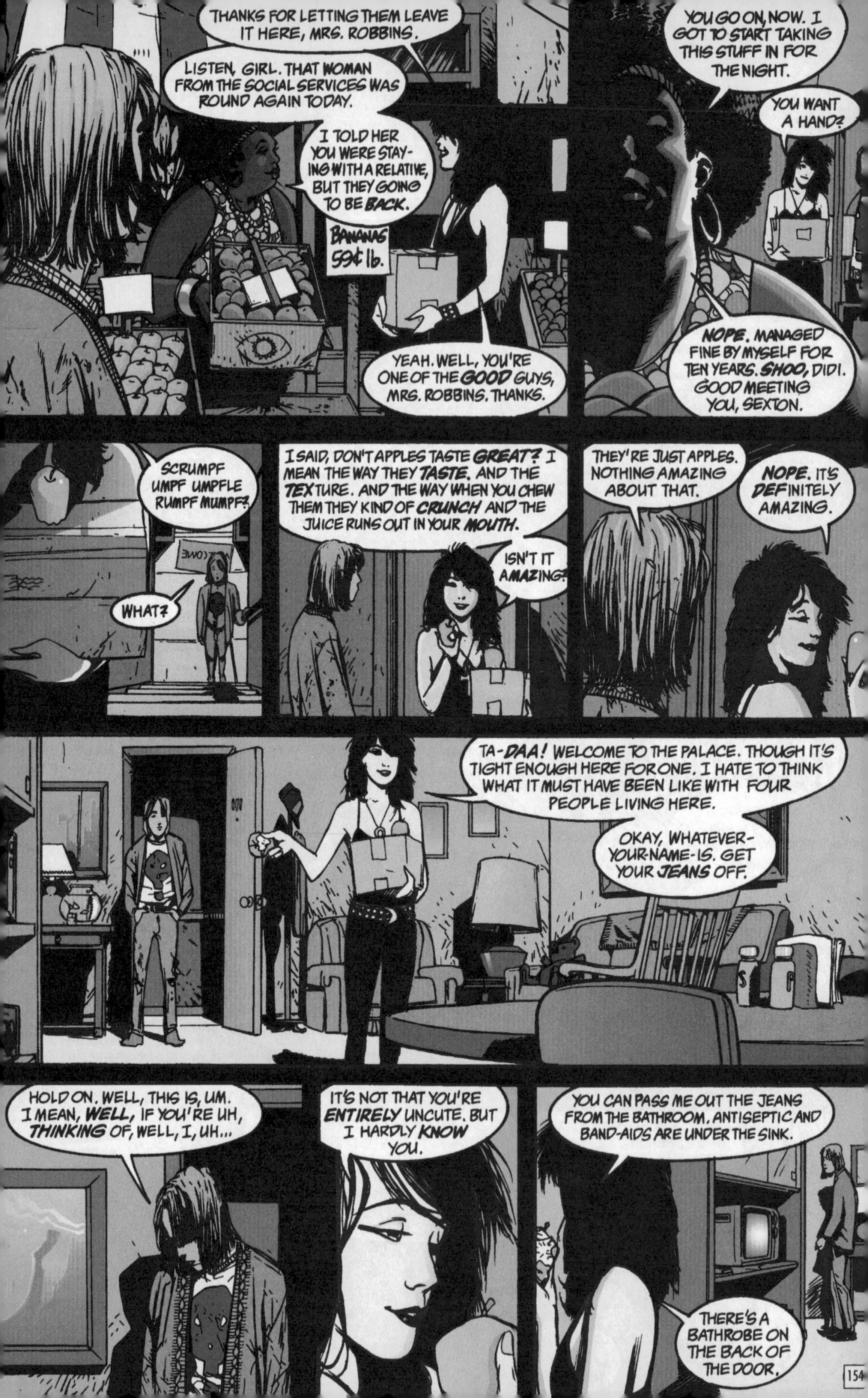

THANKS FOR LETTING THEM LEAVE IT HERE, MRS. ROBBINS.
LISTEN, GIRL. THAT WOMAN FROM THE SOCIAL SERVICES WAS ROUND AGAIN TODAY.
I TOLD HER YOU WERE STAYING WITH A RELATIVE, BUT THEY GOING TO BE BACK.
BANANAS 59¢ lb.
YEAH. WELL, YOU'RE ONE OF THE GOOD GUYS, MRS. ROBBINS. THANKS.
YOU GO ON, NOW. I GOT TO START TAKING THIS STUFF IN FOR THE NIGHT.
YOU WANT A HAND?
NOPE. MANAGED FINE BY MYSELF FOR TEN YEARS. SHOO, DIDI. GOOD MEETING YOU, SEXTON.
SCRUMPF UMPF UMPFLE RUMPF MUMPF?
WHAT?
I SAID, DON'T APPLES TASTE GREAT? I MEAN THE WAY THEY TASTE. AND THE TEXTURE. AND THE WAY WHEN YOU CHEW THEM THEY KIND OF CRUNCH AND THE JUICE RUNS OUT IN YOUR MOUTH.
ISN'T IT AMAZING?
THEY'RE JUST APPLES. NOTHING AMAZING ABOUT THAT.
NOPE. IT'S DEFINITELY AMAZING.
TA-DAA! WELCOME TO THE PALACE. THOUGH IT'S TIGHT ENOUGH HERE FOR ONE. I HATE TO THINK WHAT IT MUST HAVE BEEN LIKE WITH FOUR PEOPLE LIVING HERE.
OKAY, WHATEVER-YOUR-NAME-IS. GET YOUR JEANS OFF.
HOLD ON. WELL, THIS IS, UM. I MEAN, WELL, IF YOU'RE UH, THINKING OF, WELL, I, UH...
IT'S NOT THAT YOU'RE ENTIRELY UNCUTE. BUT I HARDLY KNOW YOU.
YOU CAN PASS ME OUT THE JEANS FROM THE BATHROOM. ANTISEPTIC AND BAND-AIDS ARE UNDER THE SINK.
THERE'S A BATHROBE ON THE BACK OF THE DOOR.

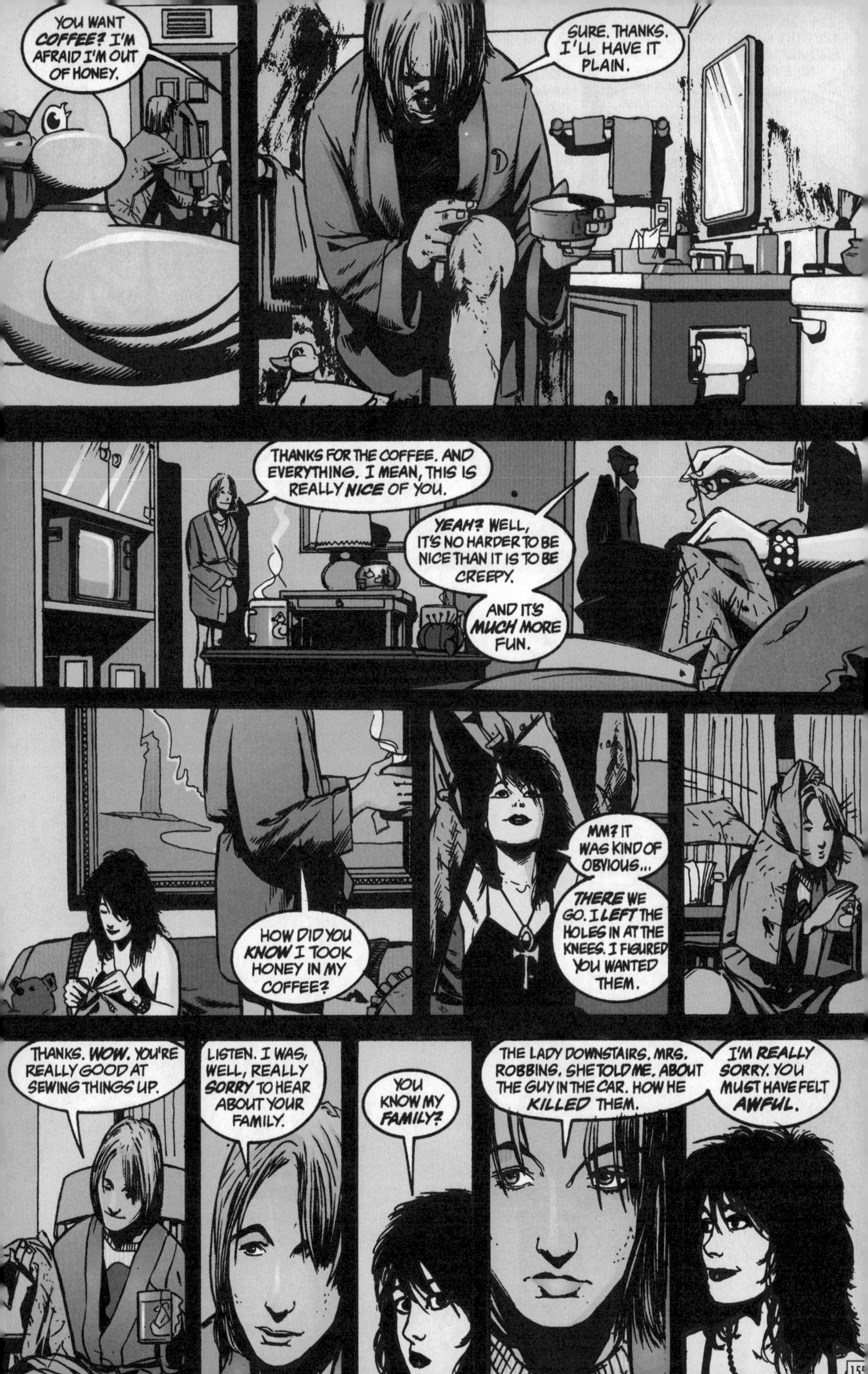
YOU WANT COFFEE? I'M AFRAID I'M OUT OF HONEY.
SURE. THANKS. I'LL HAVE IT PLAIN.
THANKS FOR THE COFFEE. AND EVERYTHING. I MEAN, THIS IS REALLY NICE OF YOU.
YEAH? WELL, IT'S NO HARDER TO BE NICE THAN IT IS TO BE CREEPY.
AND IT'S MUCH MORE FUN.
HOW DID YOU KNOW I TOOK HONEY IN MY COFFEE?
MM? IT WAS KIND OF OBVIOUS...
THERE WE GO. I LEFT THE HOLES IN AT THE KNEES. I FIGURED YOU WANTED THEM.
THANKS. WOW. YOU'RE REALLY GOOD AT SEWING THINGS UP.
LISTEN. I WAS, WELL, REALLY SORRY TO HEAR ABOUT YOUR FAMILY.
YOU KNOW MY FAMILY?
THE LADY DOWNSTAIRS. MRS. ROBBINS. SHE TOLD ME. ABOUT THE GUY IN THE CAR. HOW HE KILLED THEM.
I'M REALLY SORRY. YOU MUST HAVE FELT AWFUL.

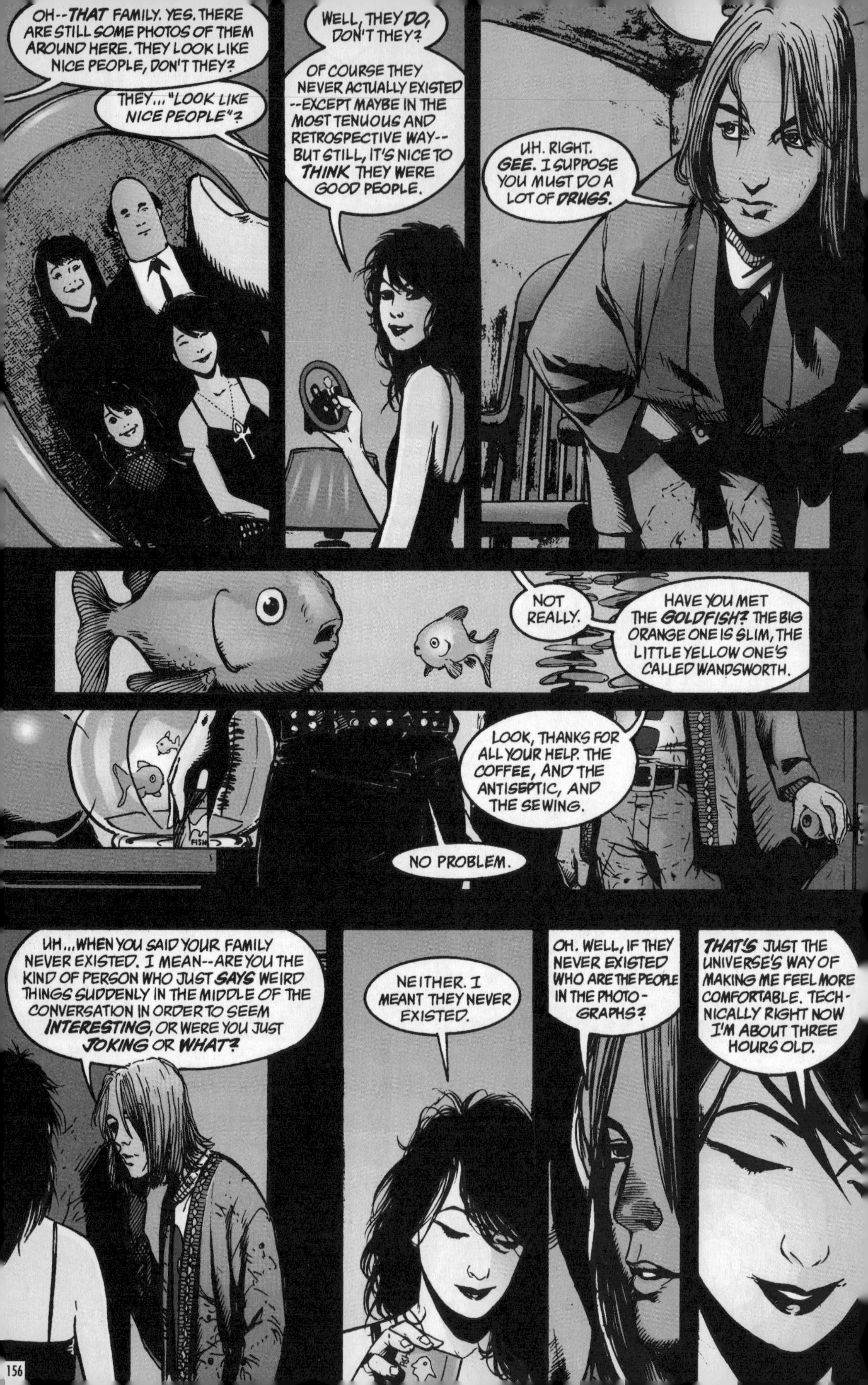
OH--THAT FAMILY. YES. THERE ARE STILL SOME PHOTOS OF THEM AROUND HERE. THEY LOOK LIKE NICE PEOPLE, DON'T THEY?
THEY... "LOOK LIKE NICE PEOPLE"?
WELL, THEY DO, DON'T THEY?
OF COURSE THEY NEVER ACTUALLY EXISTED --EXCEPT MAYBE IN THE MOST TENUOUS AND RETROSPECTIVE WAY-- BUT STILL, IT'S NICE TO THINK THEY WERE GOOD PEOPLE.
UH. RIGHT. GEE. I SUPPOSE YOU MUST DO A LOT OF DRUGS.
NOT REALLY.
HAVE YOU MET THE GOLDFISH? THE BIG ORANGE ONE IS SLIM, THE LITTLE YELLOW ONE'S CALLED WANDSWORTH.
LOOK, THANKS FOR ALL YOUR HELP. THE COFFEE, AND THE ANTISEPTIC, AND THE SEWING.
NO PROBLEM.
UH...WHEN YOU SAID YOUR FAMILY NEVER EXISTED. I MEAN--ARE YOU THE KIND OF PERSON WHO JUST SAYS WEIRD THINGS SUDDENLY IN THE MIDDLE OF THE CONVERSATION IN ORDER TO SEEM INTERESTING, OR WERE YOU JUST JOKING OR WHAT?
NEITHER. I MEANT THEY NEVER EXISTED.
OH. WELL, IF THEY NEVER EXISTED WHO ARE THE PEOPLE IN THE PHOTOGRAPHS?
THAT'S JUST THE UNIVERSE'S WAY OF MAKING ME FEEL MORE COMFORTABLE. TECHNICALLY RIGHT NOW I'M ABOUT THREE HOURS OLD.

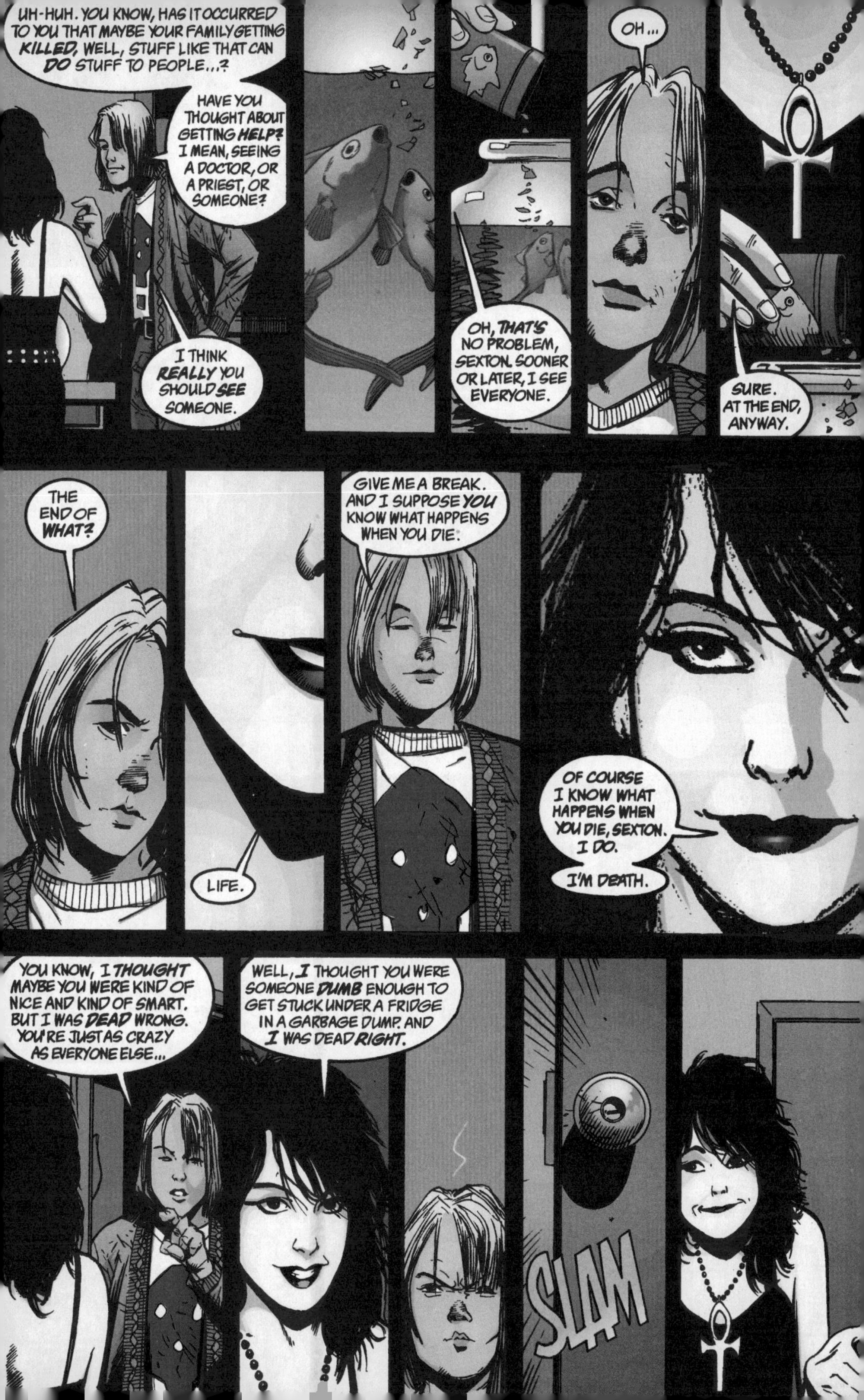
UH-HUH. YOU KNOW, HAS IT OCCURRED TO YOU THAT MAYBE YOUR FAMILY GETTING KILLED, WELL, STUFF LIKE THAT CAN DO STUFF TO PEOPLE...?
HAVE YOU THOUGHT ABOUT GETTING HELP? I MEAN, SEEING A DOCTOR, OR A PRIEST, OR SOMEONE?
I THINK REALLY YOU SHOULD SEE SOMEONE.
OH, THAT'S NO PROBLEM, SEXTON. SOONER OR LATER, I SEE EVERYONE.
OH...
SURE. AT THE END, ANYWAY.
THE END OF WHAT?
LIFE.
GIVE ME A BREAK. AND I SUPPOSE YOU KNOW WHAT HAPPENS WHEN YOU DIE.
OF COURSE I KNOW WHAT HAPPENS WHEN YOU DIE, SEXTON. I DO.
I'M DEATH.
YOU KNOW, I THOUGHT MAYBE YOU WERE KIND OF NICE AND KIND OF SMART. BUT I WAS DEAD WRONG. YOU'RE JUST AS CRAZY AS EVERYONE ELSE...
WELL, I THOUGHT YOU WERE SOMEONE DUMB ENOUGH TO GET STUCK UNDER A FRIDGE IN A GARBAGE DUMP. AND I WAS DEAD RIGHT.
SLAM

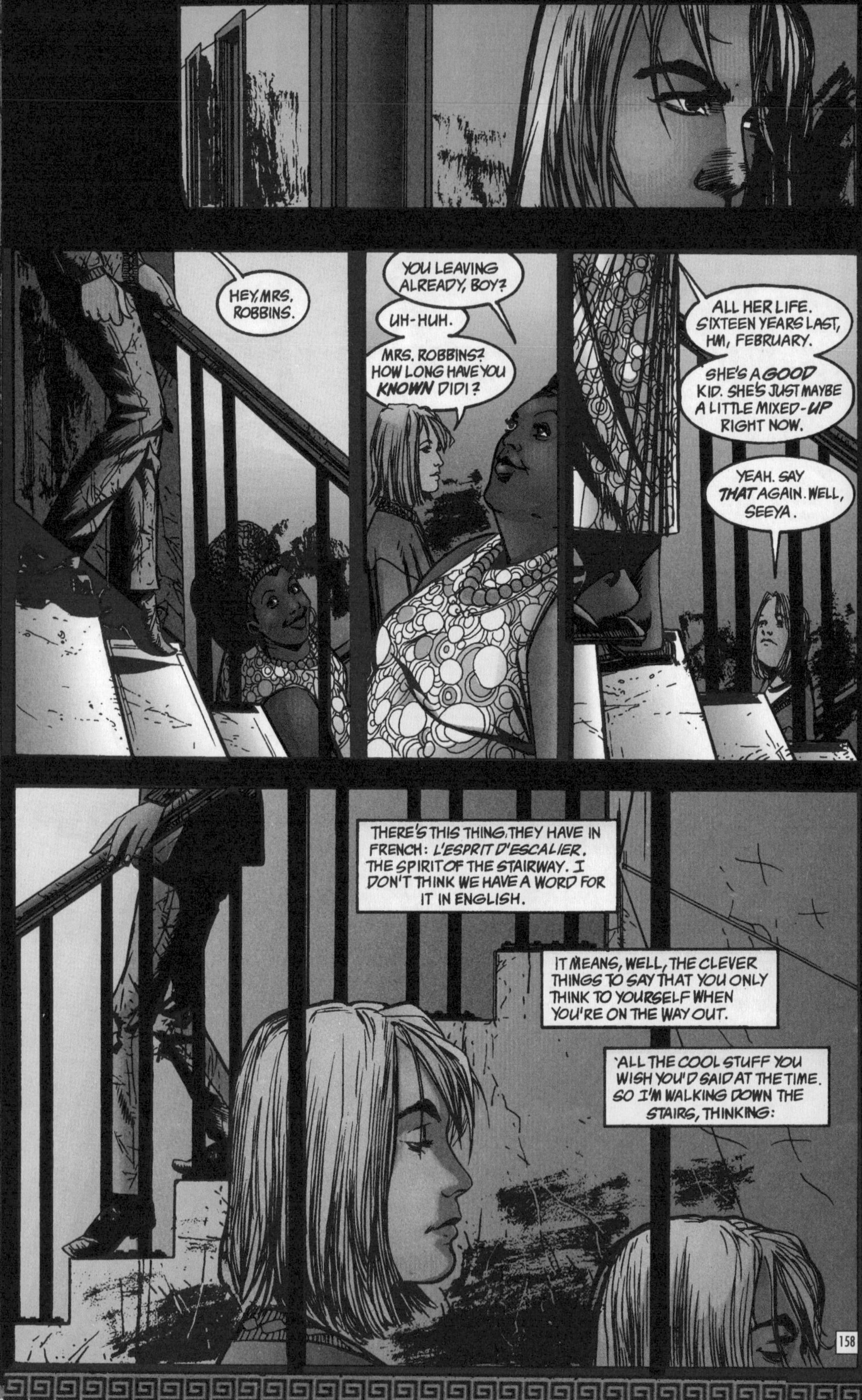
HEY, MRS. ROBBINS.
YOU LEAVING ALREADY, BOY?
UH-HUH.
MRS. ROBBINS? HOW LONG HAVE YOU KNOWN DIDI?
ALL HER LIFE. SIXTEEN YEARS LAST, HM, FEBRUARY.
SHE'S A GOOD KID. SHE'S JUST MAYBE A LITTLE MIXED-UP RIGHT NOW.
YEAH. SAY THAT AGAIN. WELL, SEEYA.
THERE'S THIS THING THEY HAVE IN FRENCH: L'ESPRIT D'ESCALIER. THE SPIRIT OF THE STAIRWAY. I DON'T THINK WE HAVE A WORD FOR IT IN ENGLISH.
IT MEANS, WELL, THE CLEVER THINGS TO SAY THAT YOU ONLY THINK TO YOURSELF WHEN YOU'RE ON THE WAY OUT.
ALL THE COOL STUFF YOU WISH YOU'D SAID AT THE TIME. SO I'M WALKING DOWN THE STAIRS, THINKING:

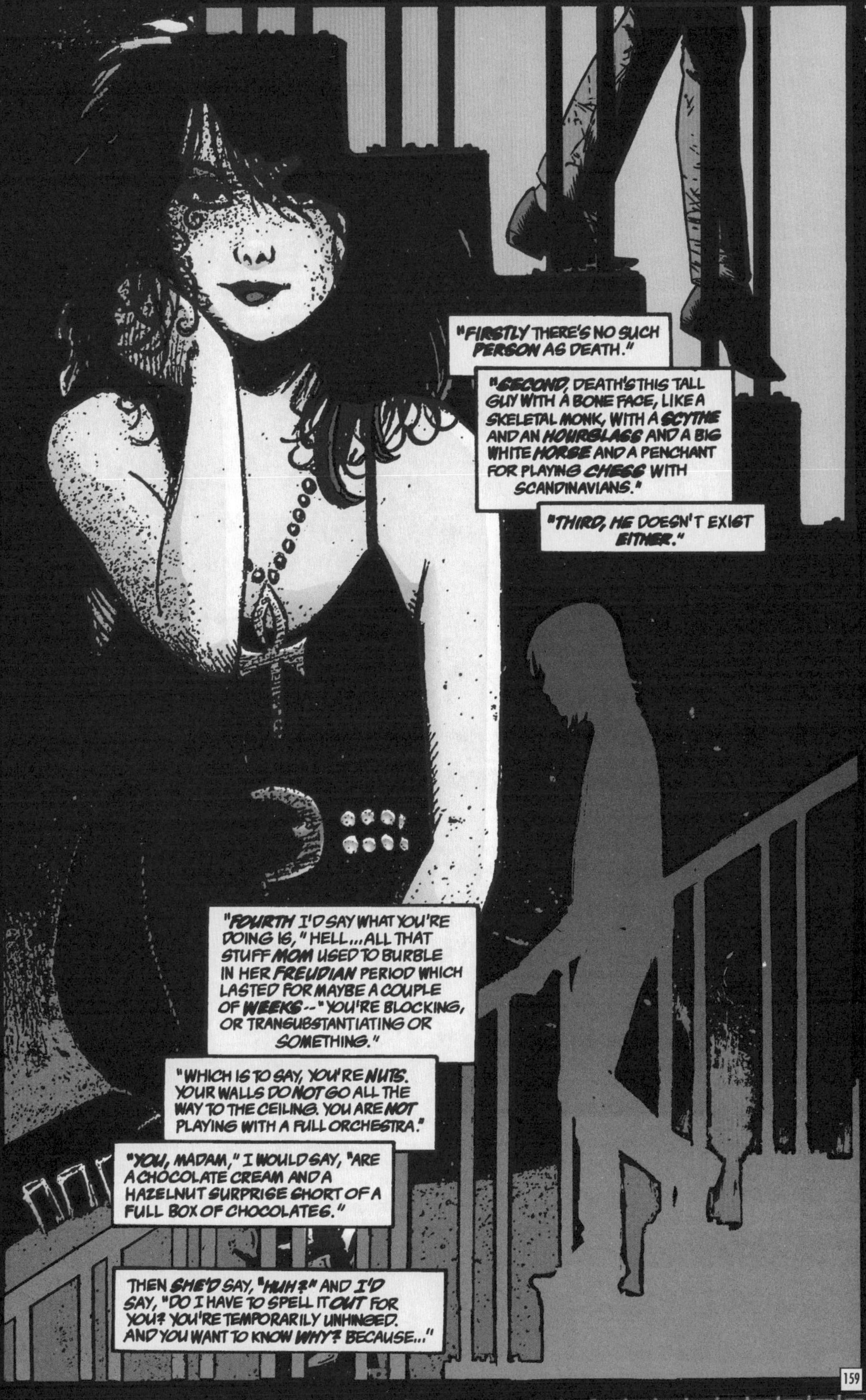
"FIRSTLY THERE'S NO SUCH PERSON AS DEATH."
"SECOND, DEATH'S THIS TALL GUY WITH A BONE FACE, LIKE A SKELETAL MONK, WITH A SCYTHE AND AN HOURGLASS AND A BIG WHITE HORSE AND A PENCHANT FOR PLAYING CHESS WITH SCANDINAVIANS."
"THIRD, HE DOESN'T EXIST EITHER."
"FOURTH I'D SAY WHAT YOU'RE DOING IS," HELL... ALL THAT STUFF MOM USED TO BURBLE IN HER FREUDIAN PERIOD WHICH LASTED FOR MAYBE A COUPLE OF WEEKS--" YOU'RE BLOCKING, OR TRANSUBSTANTIATING OR SOMETHING."
"WHICH IS TO SAY, YOU'RE NUTS. YOUR WALLS DO NOT GO ALL THE WAY TO THE CEILING. YOU ARE NOT PLAYING WITH A FULL ORCHESTRA."
"YOU, MADAM," I WOULD SAY, "ARE A CHOCOLATE CREAM AND A HAZELNUT SURPRISE SHORT OF A FULL BOX OF CHOCOLATES."
THEN SHE'D SAY, "HUH?" AND I'D SAY, "DO I HAVE TO SPELL IT OUT FOR YOU? YOU'RE TEMPORARILY UNHINGED. AND YOU WANT TO KNOW WHY? BECAUSE..."

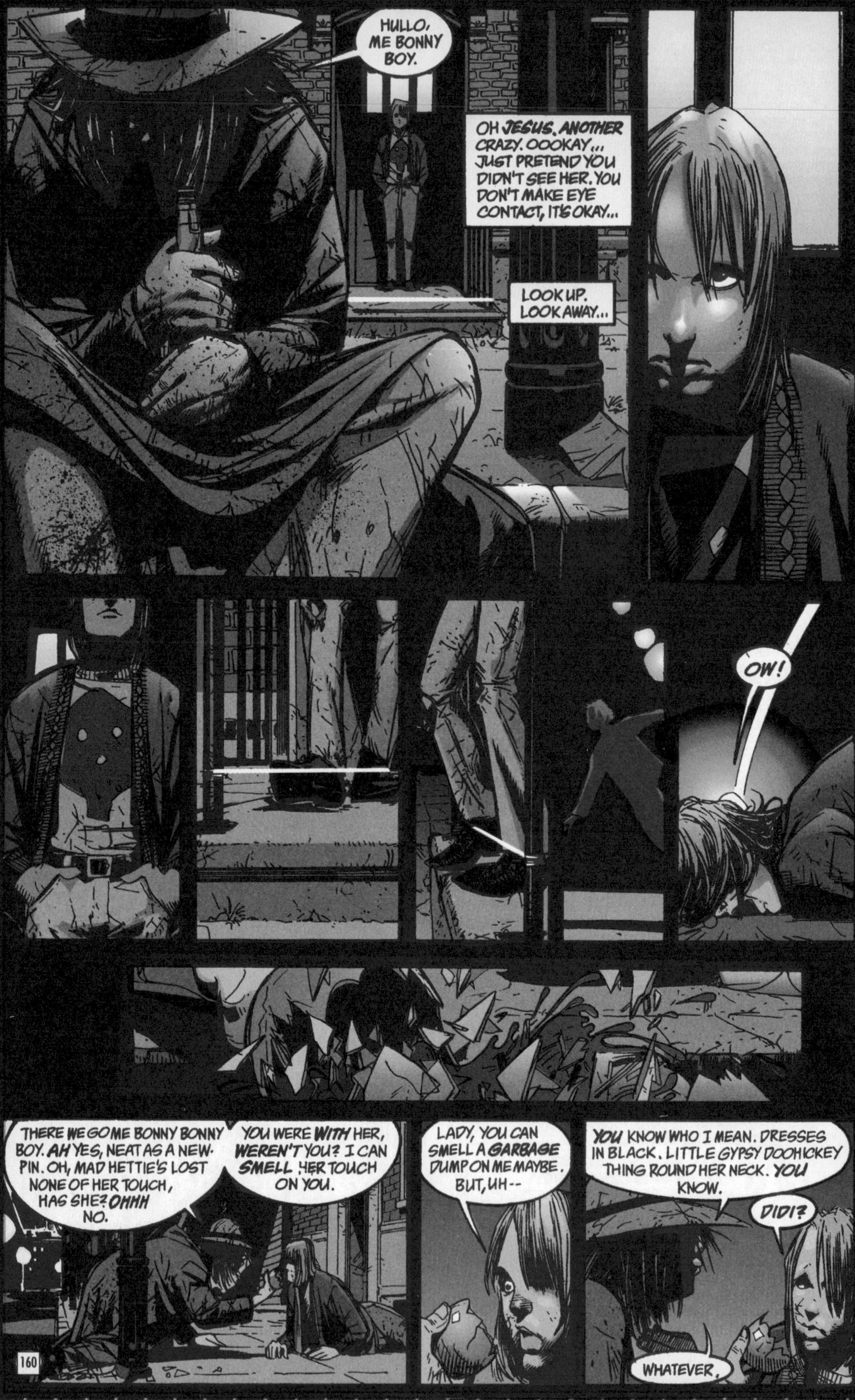
HULLO, ME BONNY BOY.
OH JESUS. ANOTHER CRAZY. OOOKAY... JUST PRETEND YOU DIDN'T SEE HER. YOU DON'T MAKE EYE CONTACT, IT'S OKAY...
LOOK UP. LOOK AWAY...
OW!
THERE WE GO ME BONNY BONNY BOY. AH YES, NEAT AS A NEW PIN. OH, MAD HETTIE'S LOST NONE OF HER TOUCH, HAS SHE? OHHH NO.
YOU WERE WITH HER, WEREN'T YOU? I CAN SMELL HER TOUCH ON YOU.
LADY, YOU CAN SMELL A GARBAGE DUMP ON ME MAYBE. BUT, UH --
YOU KNOW WHO I MEAN. DRESSES IN BLACK. LITTLE GYPSY DOOHICKEY THING ROUND HER NECK. YOU KNOW.
DIDI?
WHATEVER.

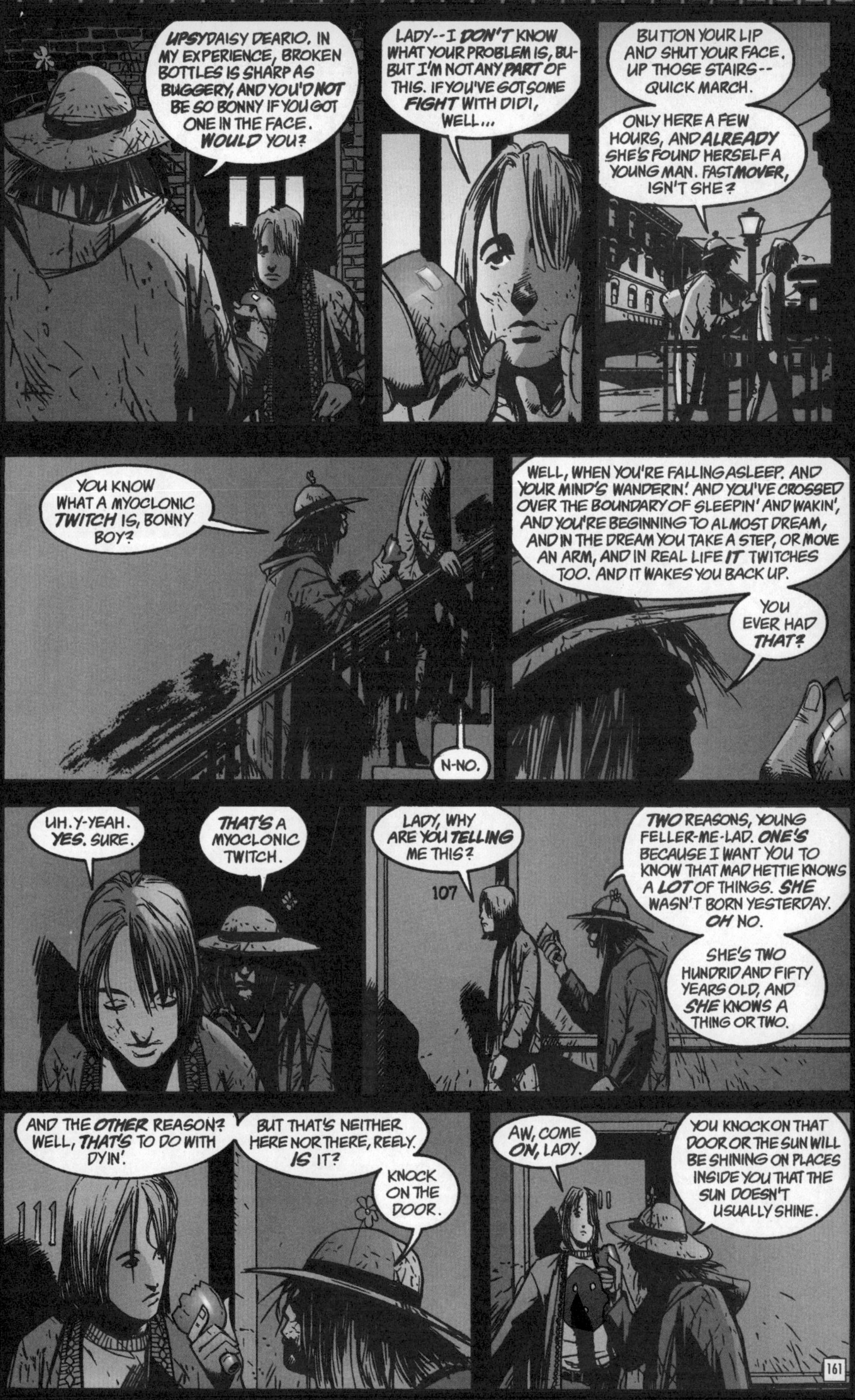
UPSYDAISY DEARIO. IN MY EXPERIENCE, BROKEN BOTTLES IS SHARP AS BUGGERY, AND YOU'D NOT BE SO BONNY IF YOU GOT ONE IN THE FACE. WOULD YOU?
LADY--I DON'T KNOW WHAT YOUR PROBLEM IS, BU-BUT I'M NOT ANY PART OF THIS. IF YOU'VE GOT SOME FIGHT WITH DIDI, WELL...
BUTTON YOUR LIP AND SHUT YOUR FACE. UP THOSE STAIRS--QUICK MARCH.
ONLY HERE A FEW HOURS, AND ALREADY SHE'S FOUND HERSELF A YOUNG MAN. FAST MOVER, ISN'T SHE?
YOU KNOW WHAT A MYOCLONIC TWITCH IS, BONNY BOY?
N-NO.
WELL, WHEN YOU'RE FALLING ASLEEP. AND YOUR MIND'S WANDERIN'. AND YOU'VE CROSSED OVER THE BOUNDARY OF SLEEPIN' AND WAKIN', AND YOU'RE BEGINNING TO ALMOST DREAM, AND IN THE DREAM YOU TAKE A STEP, OR MOVE AN ARM, AND IN REAL LIFE IT TWITCHES TOO. AND IT WAKES YOU BACK UP.
YOU EVER HAD THAT?
UH. Y-YEAH. YES. SURE.
THAT'S A MYOCLONIC TWITCH.
LADY, WHY ARE YOU TELLING ME THIS?
107
TWO REASONS, YOUNG FELLER-ME-LAD. ONE'S BECAUSE I WANT YOU TO KNOW THAT MAD HETTIE KNOWS A LOT OF THINGS. SHE WASN'T BORN YESTERDAY. OH NO.
SHE'S TWO HUNDRID AND FIFTY YEARS OLD, AND SHE KNOWS A THING OR TWO.
AND THE OTHER REASON? WELL, THAT'S TO DO WITH DYIN'.
111
BUT THAT'S NEITHER HERE NOR THERE, REELY. IS IT?
KNOCK ON THE DOOR.
AW, COME ON, LADY.
YOU KNOCK ON THAT DOOR OR THE SUN WILL BE SHINING ON PLACES INSIDE YOU THAT THE SUN DOESN'T USUALLY SHINE.

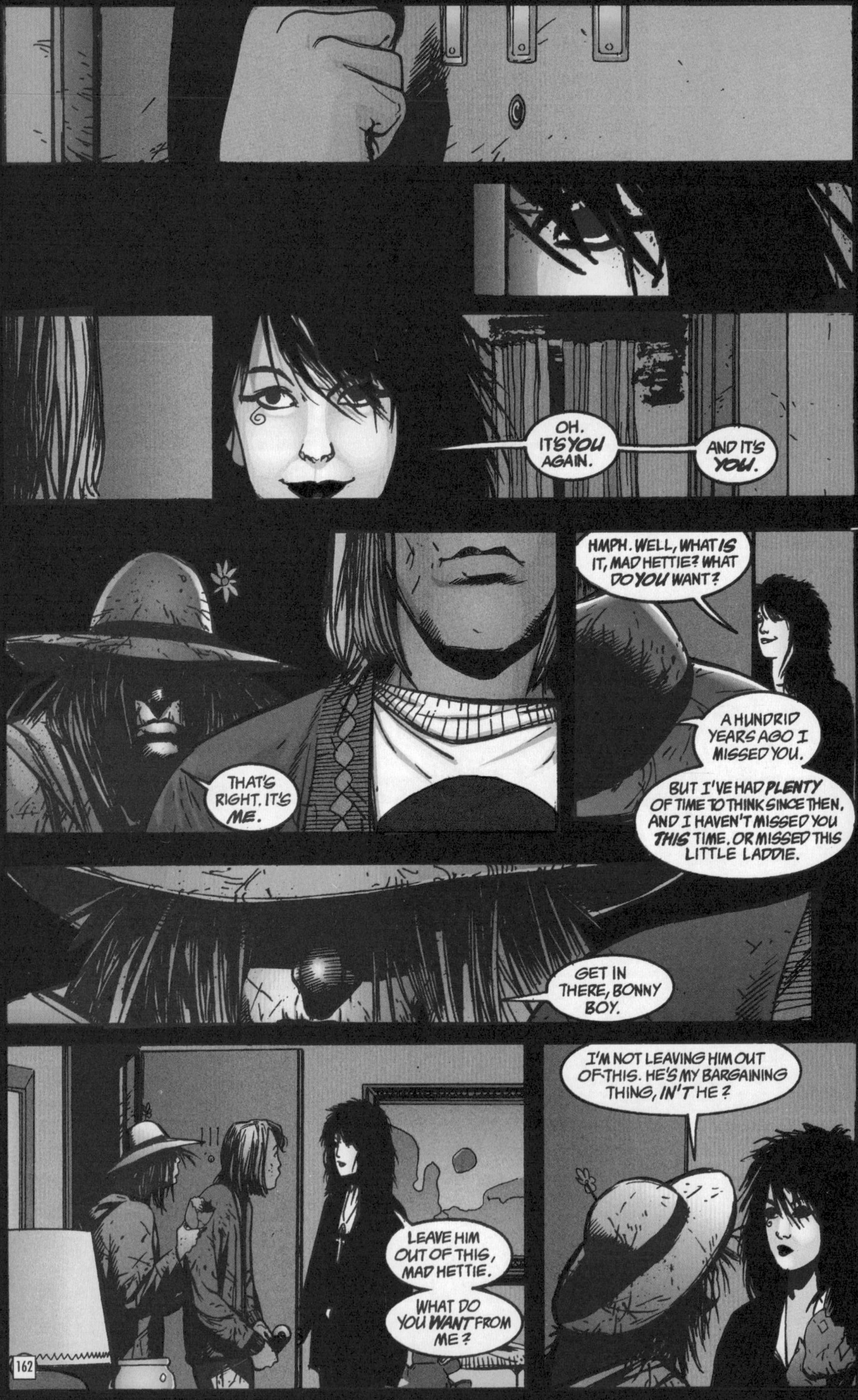
OH. IT'S YOU AGAIN.
AND IT'S YOU.
HMPH. WELL, WHAT IS IT, MAD HETTIE? WHAT DO YOU WANT?
THAT'S RIGHT. IT'S ME.
A HUNDRID YEARS AGO I MISSED YOU.
BUT I'VE HAD PLENTY OF TIME TO THINK SINCE THEN. AND I HAVEN'T MISSED YOU THIS TIME. OR MISSED THIS LITTLE LADDIE.
GET IN THERE, BONNY BOY.
LEAVE HIM OUT OF THIS, MAD HETTIE.
WHAT DO YOU WANT FROM ME?
I'M NOT LEAVING HIM OUT OF THIS. HE'S MY BARGAINING THING, IN'T HE?

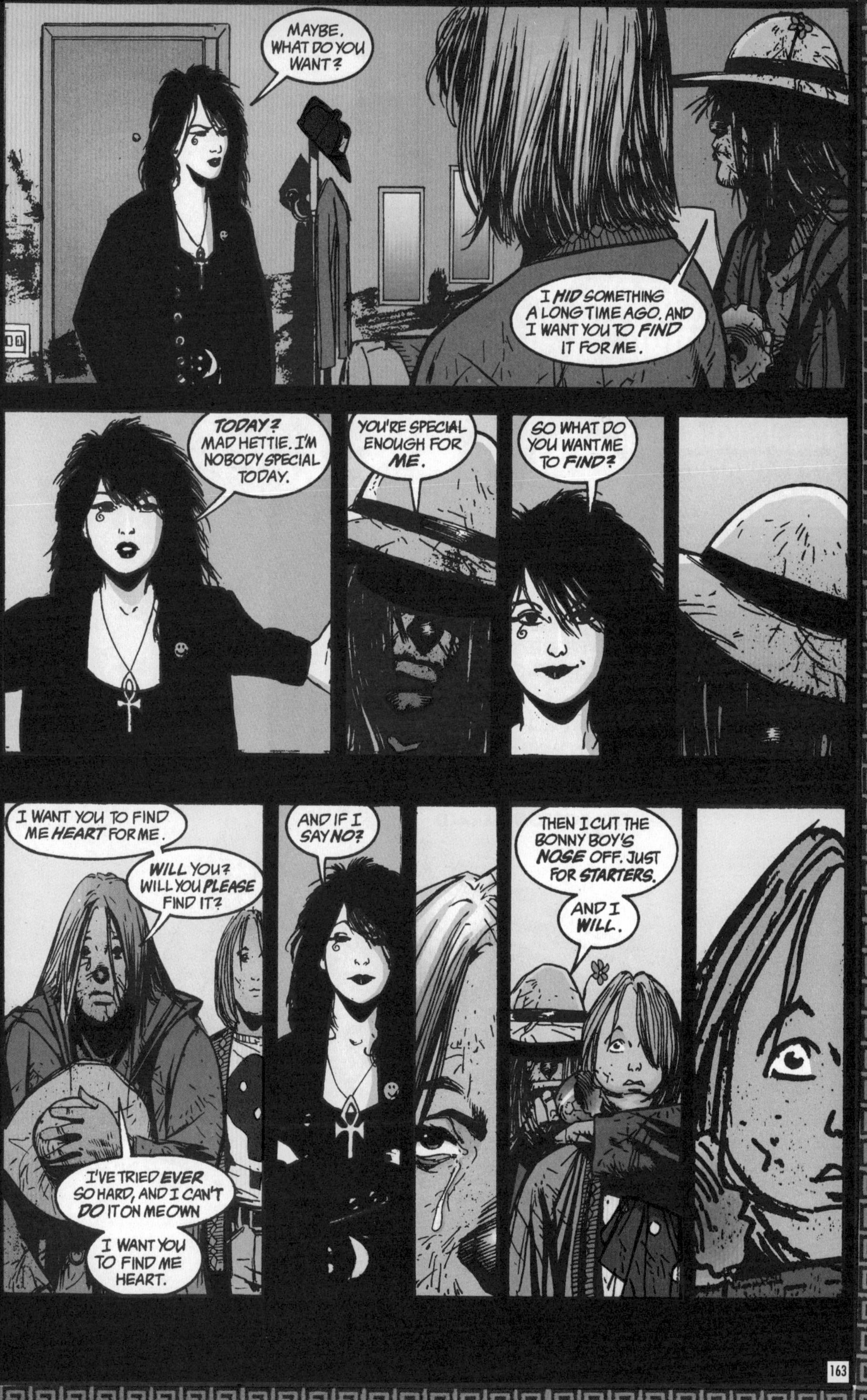
MAYBE. WHAT DO YOU WANT?
I HID SOMETHING A LONG TIME AGO. AND I WANT YOU TO FIND IT FOR ME.
TODAY? MAD HETTIE. I'M NOBODY SPECIAL TODAY.
YOU'RE SPECIAL ENOUGH FOR ME.
SO WHAT DO YOU WANT ME TO FIND?
I WANT YOU TO FIND ME HEART FOR ME.
WILL YOU? WILL YOU PLEASE FIND IT?
I'VE TRIED EVER SO HARD, AND I CAN'T DO IT ON ME OWN
I WANT YOU TO FIND ME HEART.
AND IF I SAY NO?
THEN I CUT THE BONNY BOY'S NOSE OFF. JUST FOR STARTERS.
AND I WILL.

ALSO AVAILABLE FROM

VERTIGO

THE SANDMAN LIBRARY

BY NEW YORK TIMES BEST-SELLING AUTHOR NEIL GAIMAN

One of the most acclaimed and celebrated comics titles ever published — a rich blend of modern myth and dark fantasy in which contemporary fiction, historical drama, and legend are seamlessly interwoven.

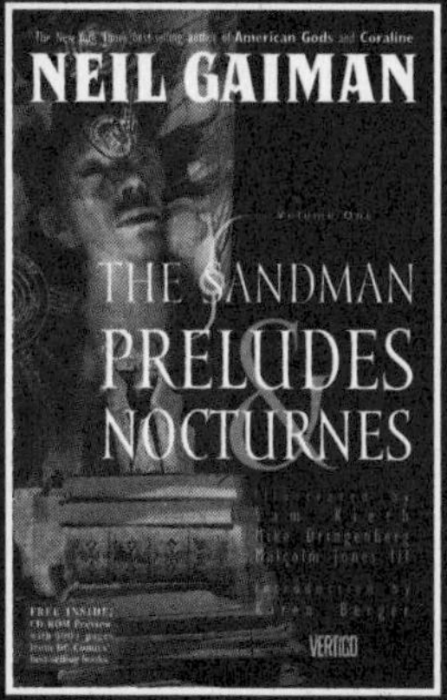
The New York Times best-selling author of American Gods and Coraline
NEIL GAIMAN
THE SANDMAN
PRELUDES & NOCTURNES

Volume 1: PRELUDES & NOCTURNES

Neil Gaiman/Sam Kieth/Mike Dringenberg/Malcolm Jones III

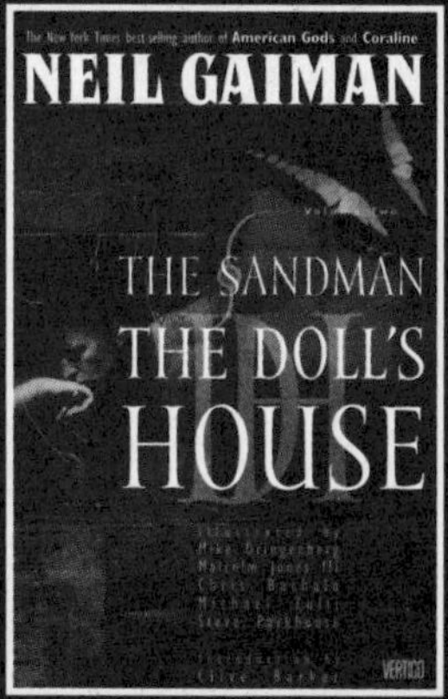
NEIL GAIMAN
THE SANDMAN
THE DOLL'S HOUSE

Volume 2: THE DOLL'S HOUSE

Neil Gaiman/Mike Dringenberg/Chris Bachalo/various

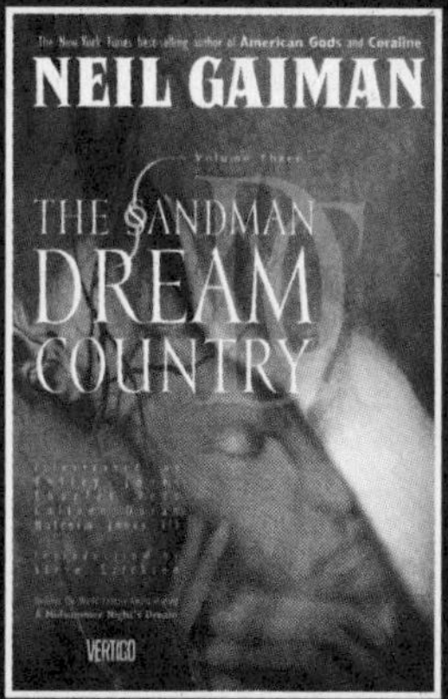
NEIL GAIMAN
THE SANDMAN
DREAM COUNTRY

Volume 3: DREAM COUNTRY

Neil Gaiman/Kelley Jones/Charles Vess/various

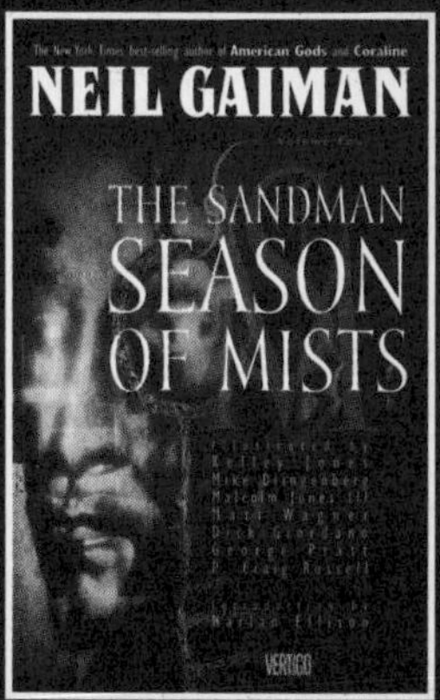
NEIL GAIMAN
THE SANDMAN
SEASON OF MISTS

Volume 4: SEASON OF MISTS

Neil Gaiman/Kelley Jones/Mike Dringenberg/various

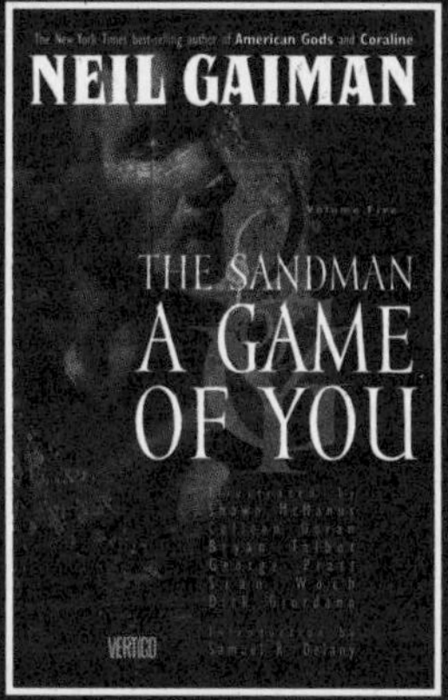
NEIL GAIMAN
THE SANDMAN
A GAME OF YOU

Volume 5: A GAME OF YOU

Neil Gaiman/Shawn McManus/various

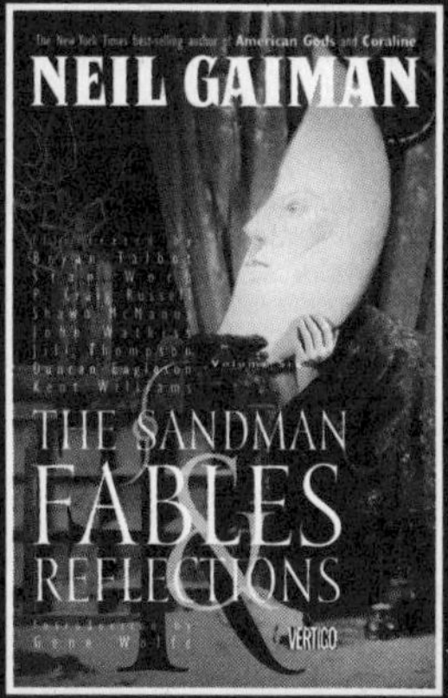
NEIL GAIMAN
THE SANDMAN
FABLES & REFLECTIONS

Volume 6: FABLES & REFLECTIONS

Neil Gaiman/various

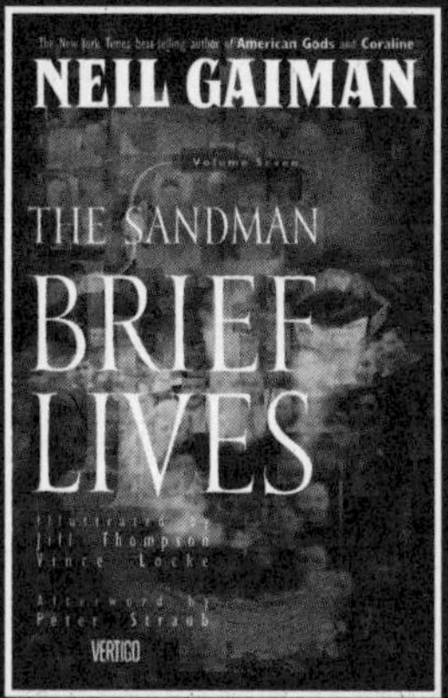
NEIL GAIMAN
THE SANDMAN
BRIEF LIVES

Volume 7: BRIEF LIVES

Neil Gaiman/Jill Thompson/Vince Locke

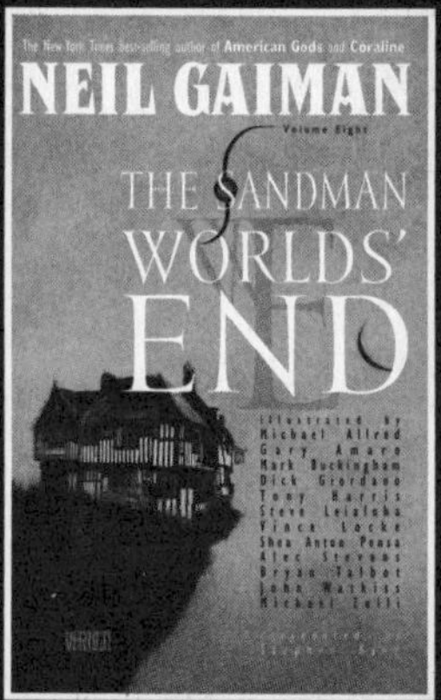
NEIL GAIMAN
THE SANDMAN
WORLDS' END

Volume 8: WORLDS' END

Neil Gaiman/various

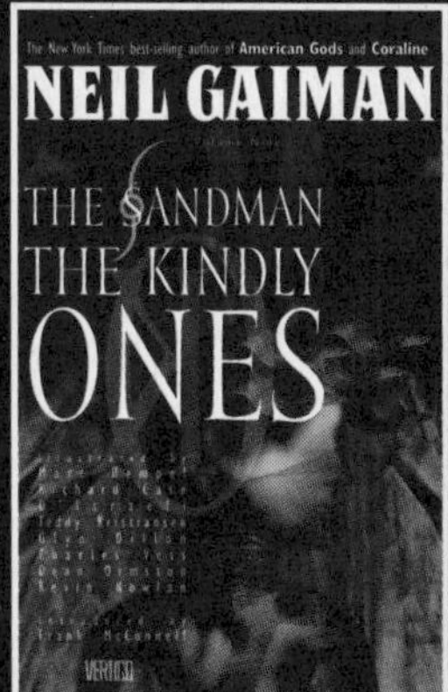
NEIL GAIMAN
THE SANDMAN
THE KINDLY ONES

Volume 9: THE KINDLY ONES

Neil Gaiman/Marc Hempel/Richard Case/various

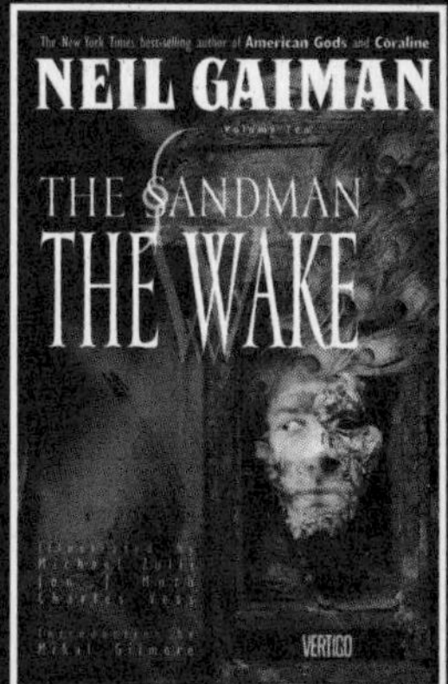
NEIL GAIMAN
THE SANDMAN
THE WAKE

Volume 10: THE WAKE

Neil Gaiman/Michael Zulli/Jon J Muth/Charles Vess

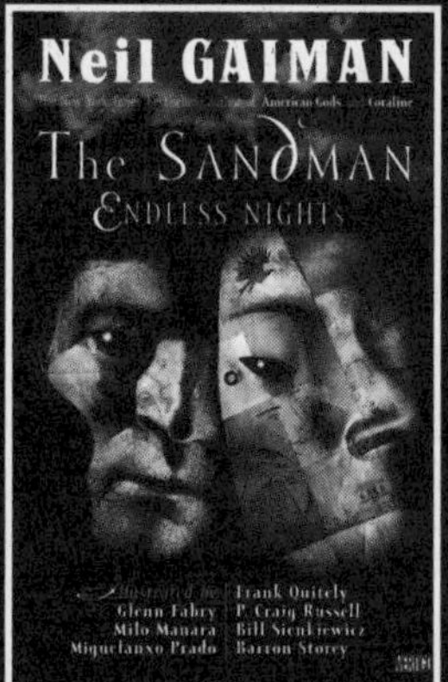
Neil GAIMAN
The Sandman
Endless Nights

Volume 11: ENDLESS NIGHTS

Neil Gaiman/Frank Quitely/P. Craig Russell/Milo Manara/various

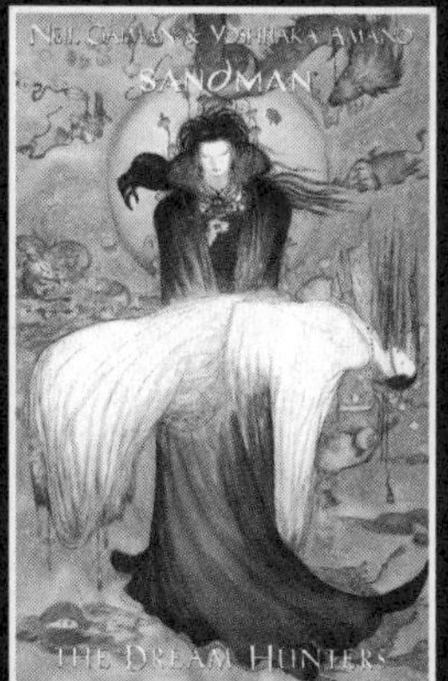
SANDMAN
THE DREAM HUNTERS

THE SANDMAN: THE DREAM HUNTERS

Neil Gaiman/Yoshitaka Amano

ALL VERTIGO TITLES ARE SUGGESTED FOR MATURE READERS

ALSO AVAILABLE FROM

VERTIGO

THE HELLBLAZER LIBRARY

14 definitive collections chronicling the legendary anti-hero John Constantine and his journeys through Hell and back. Where horror, dark magic and bad luck meet, John Constantine is never far away.

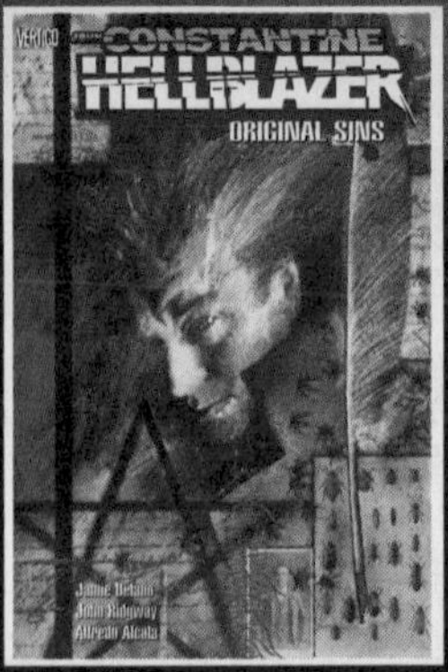
HELLBLAZER
ORIGINAL SINS

ORIGINAL SINS
Jamie Delano/John Ridgway/ Alfredo Alcala

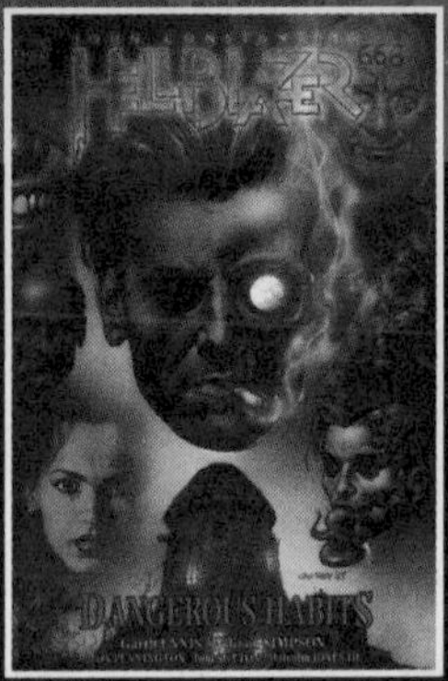
HELLBLAZER
DANGEROUS HABITS

DANGEROUS HABITS
Garth Ennis/William Simpson

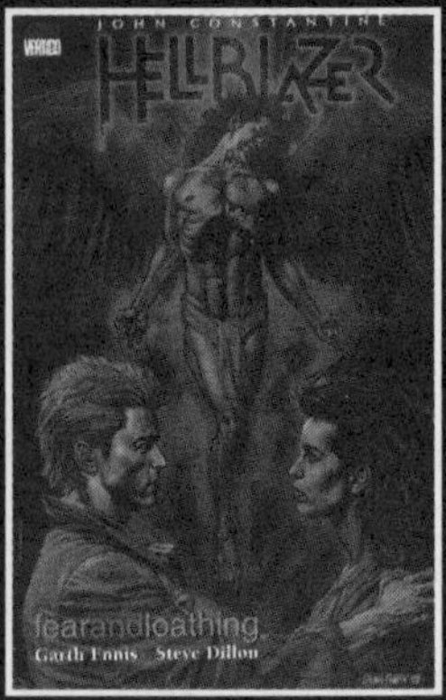
JOHN CONSTANTINE
HELLBLAZER
fearandloathing
Garth Ennis Steve Dillon

FEAR AND LOATHING
Garth Ennis/Steve Dillon

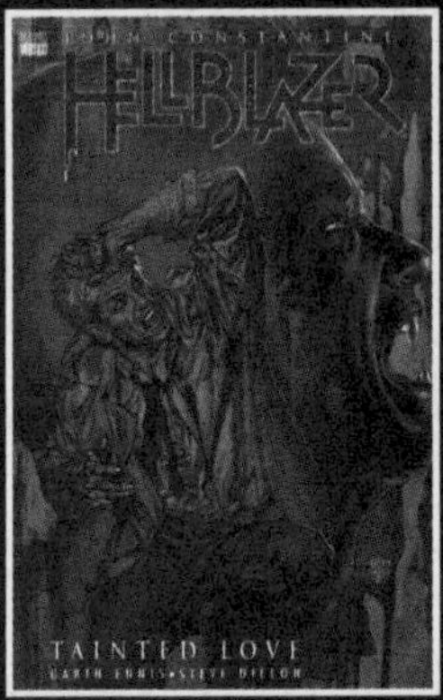
HELLBLAZER
TAINTED LOVE

TAINTED LOVE
Garth Ennis/Steve Dillon

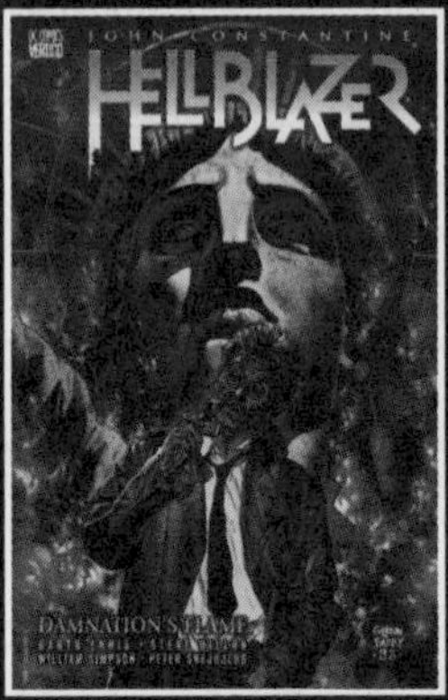
JOHN CONSTANTINE
HELLBLAZER

DAMNATION'S FLAME
Garth Ennis/Steve Dillon/ William Simpson/Peter Snejbjerg

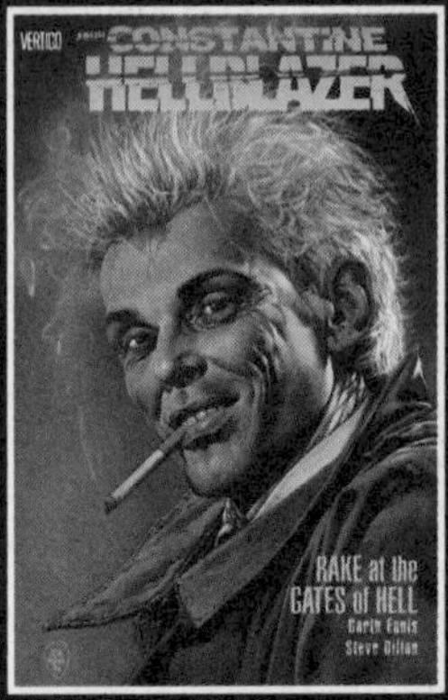
CONSTANTINE
HELLBLAZER
RAKE at the GATES of HELL
Garth Ennis
Steve Dillon

RAKE AT THE GATES OF HELL
Garth Ennis/Steve Dillon

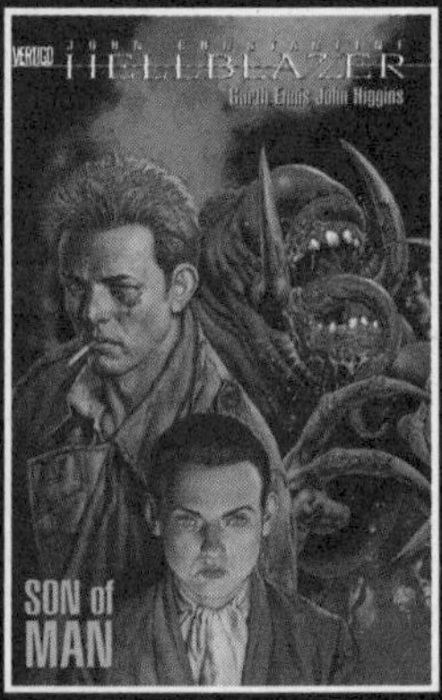
HELLBLAZER
SON of MAN

SON OF MAN
Garth Ennis/John Higgins

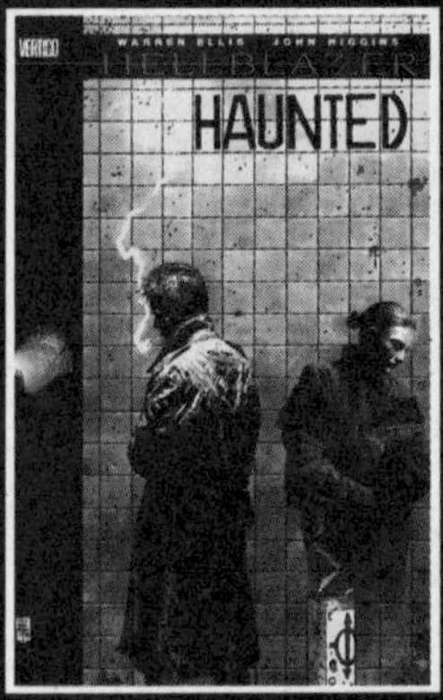
HAUNTED

HAUNTED
Warren Ellis/John Higgins

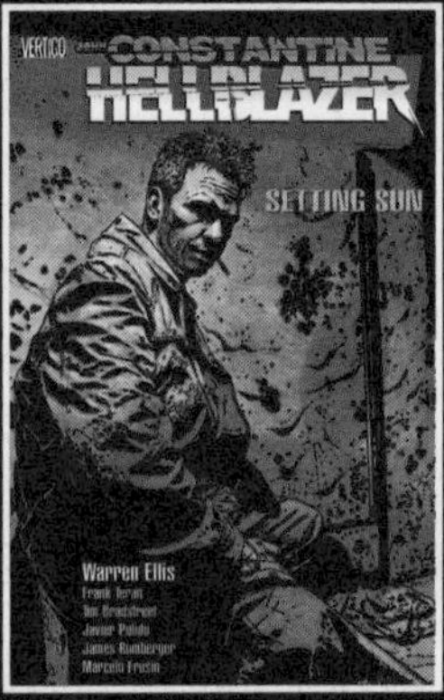
CONSTANTINE
HELLBLAZER
SETTING SUN
Warren Ellis

SETTING SUN
Warren Ellis/various

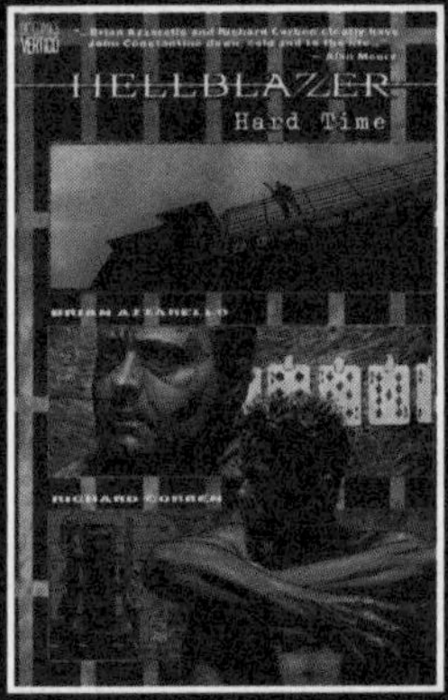
HELLBLAZER
Hard Time

HARD TIME
Brian Azzarello/Richard Corben

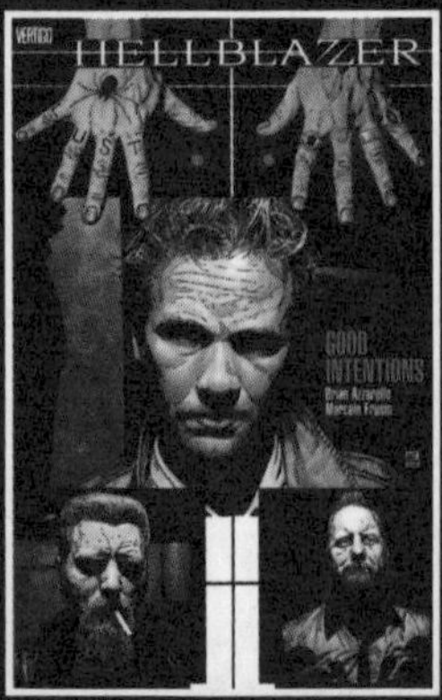
HELLBLAZER
GOOD INTENTIONS

GOOD INTENTIONS
Brian Azzarello/Marcelo Frusin

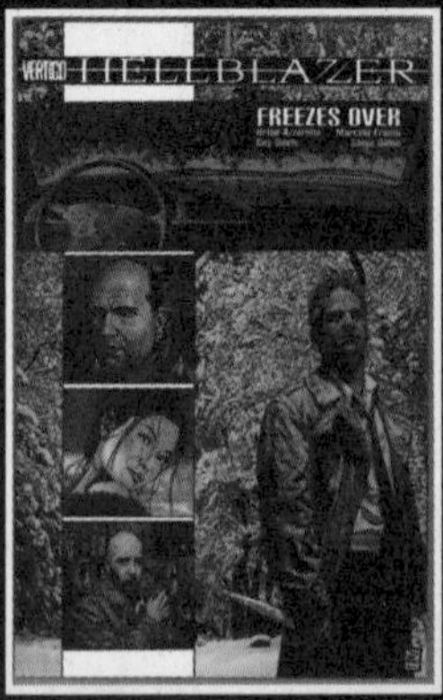
HELLBLAZER
FREEZES OVER

FREEZES OVER
Brian Azzarello/various

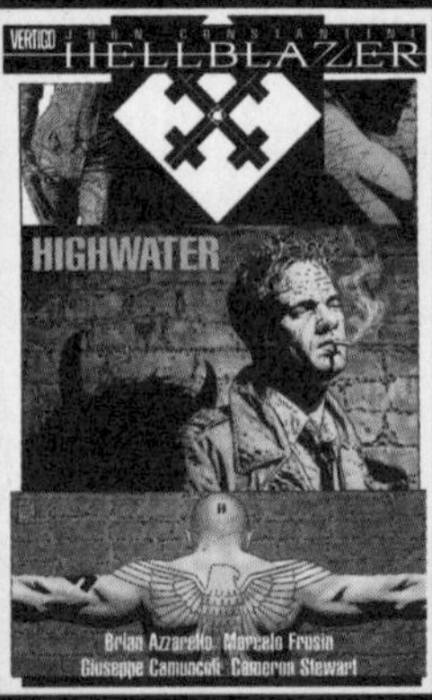
HELLBLAZER
HIGHWATER

HIGHWATER
Brian Azzarello/various

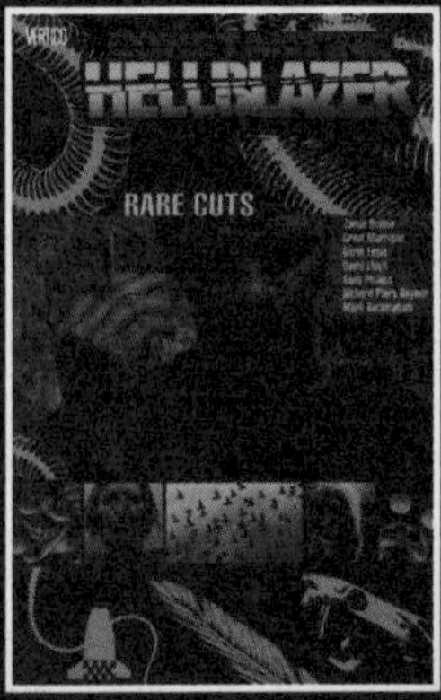
HELLBLAZER
RARE CUTS

RARE CUTS
Grant Morrison/Jamie Delano/ Garth Ennis/David Lloyd/various

ALL VERTIGO TITLES ARE SUGGESTED FOR MATURE READERS

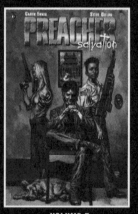